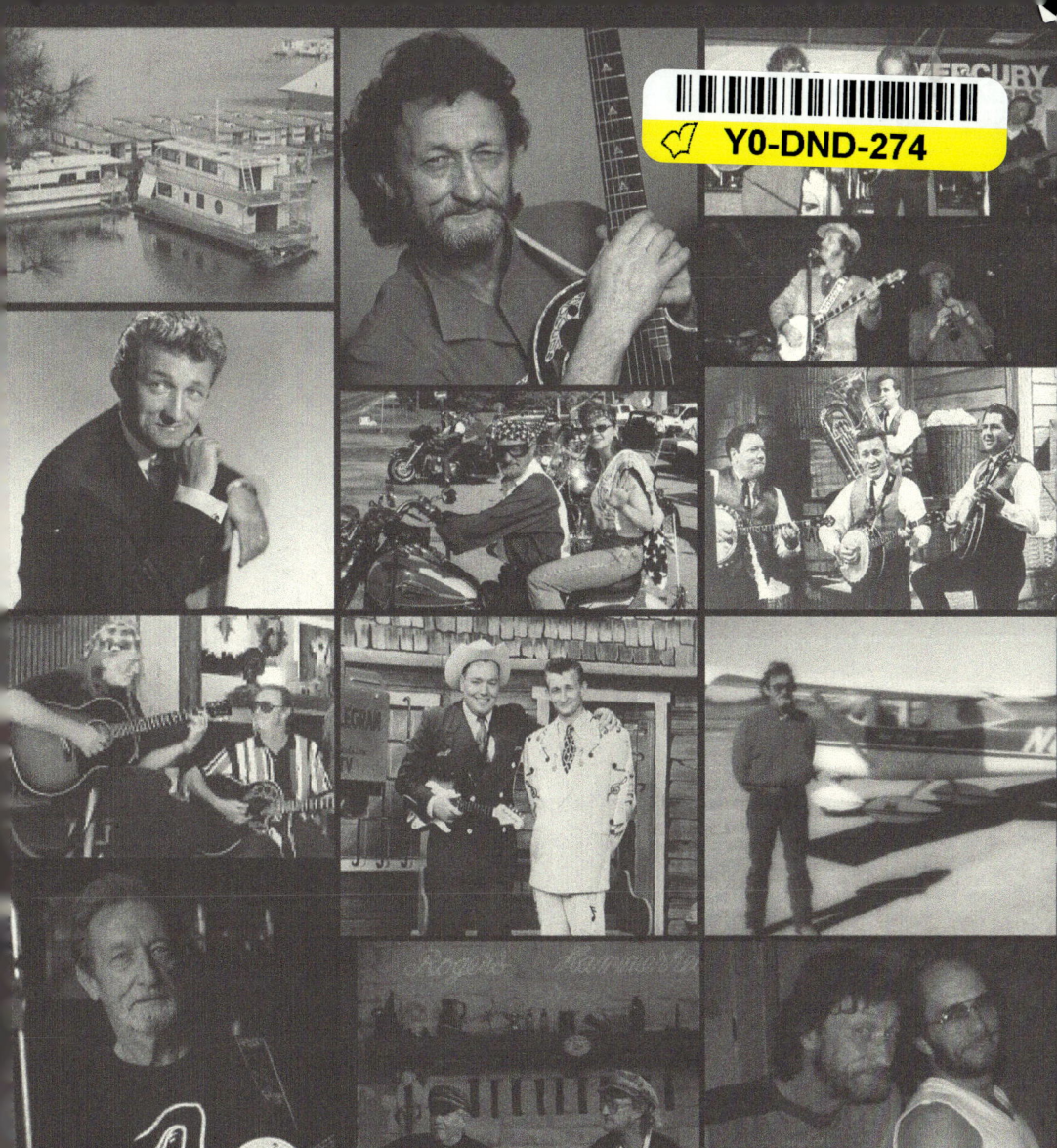

The Spree of '83

THE LIFE AND TIMES OF FREDDY POWERS
WITH EXCLUSIVE COMMENTARY FROM WILLIE NELSON AND MERLE HAGGARD
Written by Freddy & Catherine Powers with Jake Brown
Co-Starring: Tanya Tucker, Big & Rich, Sonny Throckmorton, and many more!

LISTEN WHILE YOU READ ALONG TO BRAND NEW FREDDY POWERS MUSIC!!!

(Portrait by Robert Hurst)

Over 30 Never-Before-Heard Performances Spanning Freddy Powers' 5-Decade Career!!

Listen for the first time to Freddy Powers & The Powerhouse IV LIVE IN VEGAS & LIVE IN RENO!!

STREAM ON SPOTIFY, DOWNLOAD ON iTUNES, LISTEN ON YOUTUBE, AND MANY OTHER DIGITAL MUSICAL PLATFORMS!!

THE LIFE AND TIMES OF FREDDY POWERS

By Freddy and Catherine Powers
with Jake Brown

© 2021 Natural High Books / Freddy Powers, Catherine Powers and Jake Brown

THE SPREE OF '83: THE LIFE AND TIMES OF FREDDY POWERS

All rights reserved. No part of this publication may be reproduced, stored in a retrieval system or transmitted in any form or by any means, electronic, mechanical, photocopying, recording or otherwise without the prior permission of the publisher or in accordance with the provisions of the Copyright, Designs and Patents Act 1988 or under the terms of any license permitting limited copying issued by the Copyright Licensing Agency.

Published by: Natural High Books/Baker & Taylor

www.naturalhighbooks.com

Layout by: Cesar A Torres
Photo Chapter Layout by: Baris Celik and Cesar A. Torres

Cover Design by: Cesar A Torres, Catherine Powers & Jake Brown; www.jakebrownbooks.com

Http://Twitter/com/Naturalhighbks
www.naturalhighbooks.com

Photo Credits: We Appreciate All the Friends, Fans, Family and Peers who submitted photographs across the 8 decades of Freddy Powers' life for inclusion in this book. All Implied Permissions Have Been Granted With Submissions.

Associate Editor: Debra Richardson

A CIP record for this book is available from the Library of Congress Cataloging-in-Publication Data

ISBN-10: 1733025170
ISBN-13: 978-1733025171

THANK YOU(S)

Freddy Powers Thank You(s): Over the years I have many people to thank. I wish I could list them all. So many that worked with me. That opened many doors and taught me so much and gave of their time and support. I must start with my parents who without them I would have probably never had a music career. Their support was truly beyond what any child could have grown up with. My upbringing was in a musical home with a family of musical background. My brother Wallace who introduced me to the guitar. My sister Mary Lou who introduced me to songwriting. To my brother Don for being my best friend and one of my biggest fans and supporters. To my sister Norma who was there for me when I needed her the most. To my brother and sister Jerry and Susie for their love and support. To Paul Buskirk who recognized my talents and mentored me to become the musician I became. To Willie Nelson for the many years of friendship and support. To my best friend and brother in music The Mighty Merle Haggard. I love you dearly. I could never thank you enough for all the time, energy, love and support you've given me over all these years. You taught me about songwriting and I will forever be indebted to you. So many thanks to all the cast and characters that shared your time and stories for this book. And finally to my wife Catherine who was my rock and always there for me. You are the love of my life and my best friend. Thank you for loving me so much. Your love was a Pillar of Strength for me. You held my hand and stuck by me through all the ups and downs and all the struggles. Without your love and your strength I would not have been able to continue my life through my Parkinson. I love you forever and thank God for the blessing of having you.

Catherine Allen-Powers Thank You(s): My first Thank You is to my wonderful husband for choosing me to spend the rest of his life blessing me. What a wonderful romantic adventurous life full of many experiences, fulfilling dreams that all girls only dream of. You are the love of my life and I will love you only for the rest of my life. Like Freddy, there are so many people that we would both like to thank. So many that have stood beside us and supported us and been the best friends that we could have ever have. Unbelievably huge, thank you to Freddy's younger sister Norma Marlowe for helping us get the bus that Freddy's spent his final years in. Living the way he loved and most accustomed to. Without her, no telling what would have happened and how long he would have fought the Parkinson's so he could live and enjoy his life. We are Forever indebted to you and your beautiful heart that you shared with your brother. Many abundant Thanks for all those that gave at times without Freddy's knowledge because they felt there was no need for him to worry. They helped me keep him on the road and active. Without your help and support, I wouldn't have been able to keep his life QUALITY as well as quantity. Willie

Nelson, Thank you for all your generosity and paying off our car and credit cards. Giving us a fresh start when I felt it was more important to put fuel in the bus and keep Freddy active. Getting his needed medical supplies first rather than keeping up with our car payments and credit cards. I will forever be indebted to you and all your family for all the love and support you all have shown. Freddy and I are sincerely thankful. Thank You to Merle and Theresa Haggard, Marc and Greg Oswald, John Rich and Big Kenny Alphin, Gretchen Wilson, Tanya Tucker, Mary Sarah, Todd and Patty Gross, Joe Gilchrist, CW Colt, Susie Cochran - who more than once, twice, even three times when this bus broke down paid for the repairs. They sent me numerous gas cards to keep fuel in the bus so Freddy could still come out and see your shows. This kept Freddy out touring and performing while he still could.

A huge thank you to my road warrior girls; my sister Debbie Langham, Cass Hunter, our granddaughter Kasie Finkie, Tanya Tucker, Joi Davis and past (or ex I just like past or better yet just daughter) but always our daughter in law Carrie Powers. Our boy roadie and grandson Freddy Powers the 3rd. They all took turns going out to assist me in taking care of Freddy so I could drive the bus and keep the wheels rolling. If they weren't already a nurse like Joi Davis, they pretty much learned to be one from doing simple things like sitting on the side of the bed and feeding Freddy tiny bites of food for an hour or so so he had less chances of choking and mixing his water with thickeners. To learning to give him his medication and feed him through a feeding tube. Thank you Joi Davis for all the days you spent at the hospitals with us, leaving your job at your hospital in Muscle Shoals and your responsibilities to be with us. And all the many hours you sit with him at his bedside giving me a break for rest and food. And for helping me understand the doctors when I didn't. Several times that made the difference in his life and death, and once again to John Rich for having flown Joi all over the country when or wherever needed.

Thank you to Freddy's niece Vickie, our daughter Karen Finkie for coming wherever we were and staying nights in the hospital. Washing my clothes, feeding me and all the large and small things you did. Thank you Debra Richardson for being my best friend 56 yrs of my life to date, being my rock and shoulder every time I needed one and all the things you did helping with Freddy every time we were near you. Thank you to Terry Booth and all the Coondicks of Austin Texas for seeing to it that we had a hospital bed installed in the bus. Freddy could not only ride safely but in comfort. Not to mention making it easier on my back cuz it's at the front door not all the way to the back of the bus where his original bed was that I carried him to on my back. A thousand billion thanks to Joe Gilchrist who saw the need for Freddy to have a good healthy place to spend his last days. Also affording Freddy to stay within the realm of the music scene he loved so much. With a view we all wish for and blessed with. Being able to lay in his hospital bed and look out his front windshield and watch the Dolphins swimming by. Seeing the boats and fisherman but also able to see the Blue Angels fly over on their practice days, and always making sure I had what you call walking around money. I also have to include in that thank you for our beautiful location for living, along with Joe Gilchrist, other owners of the Flora-Bama, John McInnis, Pat McClellan, Cameron Price and the Tamary family. Even at a time of going against county codes for us to live in the Flora-Bama parking lot. With hookups they especially had set up.

I owe the world to the Flora-Bama family, all the owners and their families. To all the customer service that helped me get Freddy in and out of the bus, and helped get him to and from the Flora-Bama for Freddy to be able to listen to his favorite musicians and songwriters always paying tribute to Freddy by singing one of his songs and introducing him to the audience and boasting about his career. You could always see the twinkle in his beautiful blues eyes when they did. I also Salute with many thanks to the United States Marines. Who many times showed up at shows and also here at the Flora-Bama to get Freddy from one location to another, and for providing him with a beautiful Marine Military service with full honors and doing your homework. For knowing his status and rank in his military career and also his music career and fame. Huge gratitude of thanks to Diane Strict and Tina with Covenant Hospice Care for all that you did helping me take care of Freddy and seeing that all his medical needs were met and he was comfortable and clean.

Last but not least to all our friends and family, each and every one of you. So many to list, that if I listed you all it would take all 356 pages, leaving no room for this story. To all that came and set with Freddy so I could go to the store or run to the doctor or do whatever I needed to do. And all you that just came to visit with him and spent time with him and let him know that he was loved and respected by you and many more. Thank you all sincerely, you have all been a very special blessing in both of our lives. We want you to know we couldn't have done it without you and we love you deeply and sincerely, thank God for you. Never to be forgotten so many wonderful thanks to our sweet Lord who without him nothing would be possible. Blessings of my Church "Worship On The Water" at the Flora-Bama that has become the most important thing in my life. Without my congregation and friends from the church my survival would never have been possible. Helping me with small bills, keeping food on my table, all those that cooked for me, thank you so much. I'd be even skinnier without you. To Donna and John Mason Smith for taking me under your wings and teaching me about God and the love he has for me. Thank you to Pastor Jeremy Mount. I miss you so much. Thank you to Pastor Joe Brantley for being a wonderful Bible school teacher and a wonderful friend. To my loving and caring Pastor Dan Stone and Robin Harpster thank you for being with me during his final hours holding my hand and praying with us, you both were such strong rocks for me. Robin your friendship means the world to me thank you for sharing your love and your family with me. A million thanks to all the people that contributed with helping me with some of Freddy's medical bills and raising the money to put me in the Playa Del Rio RV Park and covering one whole year's rent in advance. That took so much worry off my shoulders. I will forever be indebted to each and every one of you. And finally to Jake Brown who saw that this book needed to be published and needed to be read by all Freddy Powers fans. With you this book went from a dream to reality. Please know if I have left anyone out please know in my heart I thank you and I treasure you all.

Jake Brown Thank You(s): Over 50 published books in the past 20 years, this has by far been one of the two or three most personal to me. From how we all grew up with just a little bit of Freddy Powers (whether we knew at the time he'd written the hit or not ☺, and especially in the 1980s with the Merle Haggard All in the Game album for me personally.) To meet Freddy at the hospital in Nashville in 2012 when the doctors all thought he wasn't coming out. And to then have the opportunity to work with him and Catherine week after week on the bus while he could still talk and tell and sing me his story. These were some of the most prized times I've spent with anyone working on a memoir in many. As I met and interviewed his extended family of friends, peers and fans, it wasn't always relaxed, but as they were in the midst of action helping Freddy's devoted wife/manager/nurse Catherine taking care of him. And keeping his name out there bigger and brighter lights than ever for a new generation of millennial fans was more motivating than ever. This kept us all in the common cause of working with Freddy to keep his career moving even as this vicious disease tried to take more and more from him. Hearing his words out loud and then writing them later on paper was a full-circle experience that I think few writers get the chance to see given he was fighting to say every one of them physically, and even when he couldn't talk past a whisper toward the very end. He could still communicate clearly and brilliantly with a tight squeeze of your hand or through his bright blue eyes. The people I have to thank therein are the same you'll come to meet throughout this truly moving story and we hope will be as entertained, inspired and moved by as they were Freddy's music, personality and star presence in the first place. First thank you Catherine Powers for being my co-pilot on this project the past 8 years, especially through the bonding experience after Freddy had left us of adapting he and your story to film together; the star-power that lined up behind this project to celebrate Freddy, especially Merle Haggard, Willie Nelson, John Rich and Big Kenny Alphin of Big & Rich, Tanya Tucker, Larry Gatlin, Sonny Throckmorton, J. Gary Smith, Cass Hunter, Tracey and Whitey Shafer, Frank Liddell, and all of the other amazingly colorful cast of supporting characters I've met in the course of us all telling Freddy's story together, he'd be proud. Thank you Stephen Betts of Rolling Stone Country for the awesome back-of-book review and Rolling Stone coverage for the book. Our amazing attorney Rachel Simes Guttmann, Esq. of Stephanie Taylor Law PLLC; Baker & Taylor; Ryan and Jason at Bookmasters; Cesar A. Torres for the amazing layout work as always. Personally my wife Carrie, our dogs, the late legend Little Hannie and Little Molly our feisty Westie. My parents James and Christina Brown; my brother Ret. Sgt. Joshua T. Brown; the old-school crew: Alex Schuchard, Andrew McDermott, Cris Ellauri, Sean Fillinich, Richard Kendrick, Bob O'Brien; Paul and Helen Watts; the extended Brown, Thieme and Brock families; my engineers Ray Riddle and Aaron Harmon; and anyone else in my sphere who helps keep the wheels turning book after book, and especially on this one, THANK YOU!

TABLE OF CONTENTS:

FOREWORD BY TANYA TUCKER

CHAPTER 1: SIR FREDERICK

CHAPTER 2: THE 50s — FREDDY ENLISTS, MEETS BUSKIRK, WILLIE NELSON & THE WORLD

CHAPTER 3: THE 60s — THE TONIGHT SHOW & RULING RENO

CHAPTER 4: DIAMOND GEM'S

CHAPTER 5: THE CASINO DAYS

CHAPTER 6: OVER THE RAINBOW

CHAPTER 7: THE SPREE OF '83 BEGINS!

CHAPTER 8: NATURAL HIGH

CHAPTER 9: THE BREAD & BUTTER BAND & LIFE ON THE ROAD WITH THE STRANGERS

CHAPTER 10: AIR CRAFT CARRIER ON A LAKE

CHAPTER 11: THE AIR FRED BAND

CHAPTER 12: LOOKING FOR A PLACE TO FALL APART

CHAPTER 13: THE COUNTRY JAZZ SINGER

CHAPTER 14: LAST DAYS ON THE LAKE

CHAPTER 15: THE BALLAD OF FREDDY AND CATHERINE

CHAPTER 16: ROAD TO MY HEART

CHAPTER 17: WILLIE'S HILL & COACH ROYAL'S PICKIN' PARTIES

CHAPTER 18: ROGERS & HAMMERHEAD

CHAPTER 19: THE ROMANCE CONTINUES

CHAPTER 20: FREDDY POWERS' 70TH BIRTHDAY ROAST

CHAPTER 21: THE ROYAL KNIGHTS OF THE RACCOON

CHAPTER 22: PARKINSON' DISEASE

CHAPTER 23: FREDDY'S 2ND ACT

CHAPTER 24: THE STOP THE TRUCK BAND

CHAPTER 25: FREDDY POWERS LEGENDARY PICKIN' PARTIES

CHAPTER 26: MENTORING A NEW GENERATION OF STARS

CHAPTER 27: THE FLORA-BAMA

CONCLUSION: GUITAR ON THE WALL

EPILOGUE: JUNE 21ST, 2016

CAST OF CHARACTERS:

Freddy & Catherine Powers: Co-Authors

Norma Powers-Marlowe: Freddy's sister

Don Powers Jr: Freddy Powers' nephew

Troy Powers: Freddy Powers' nephew and band member

Willie Nelson: Freddy's longtime friend, Prankster and fellow picker

Paul Buskirk: Represented in Spirit, Texas music legend / Mentor to Freddy and Willie

Merle Haggard: Freddy's best friend and songwriting sidekick, band mate, and pickin' partner

Coach Darrell Royal: Represented in Spirit, Legendary Texas Longhorns Football Coach / Longtime friend of Freddy and Willie's, Supporter of Songwriters

Edith Royal: Widow of the late Coach Darrell Royal

Tanya Tucker: Multi-platinum Country Music legend and close friend

Rattlesnake Annie: Internationally-Famous Country Artist/Friend & Collaborator of Freddy's

J. Gary Smith: Veteran Texas/Nashville Performer/Producer/Club Owner

Ralph Sanford: Freddy's 1st Banjo Player/Member of the Powerhouse IV

Ray Rogers: Freddy's 2nd Banjo Player/Member of the Powerhouse IV

Milton Quackenbush: Keyboard Player, The Powerhouse V

Augie Savage: Freddy's Keyboard Player, The Air Fred Band

Anne Reynolds: Widow of the late Deanie Bird Reynolds, Freddy's longtime bass player

Bev Dunbar: Waitress, Diamond Gem's

Mike Kelleher: Bartender, Diamond Gem's

Ralph Emery: Legendary Country Television TV Host

Linda Mitchell: Manager, Silverthorne Resort, Merle Haggard's Former Assistant

Damon Garner: Freddy's Flight Instructor

Norm Hamlet: The Strangers' Band Leader/Pedal Steel Player

Scotty Joss: Silverthorne House Band Fiddle Player, Mid-1980s / The Strangers Fiddle Player

Marc Oswald: Longtime Merle Haggard Tour Manager/Freddy Friend

Biff Adams: Longtime Drummer for Merle Haggard's The Strangers

Sherrill Rogers: Co-writer, "Let's Chase Each Other Around the Room"

Ray Baker: Merle Haggard/Freddy Powers' Record Producer

Janine Fricke: Country Music Star

Larry Gatlin: Lead Singer, The Gatlin Brothers

Bill McDavid: Freddy's Best Friend, Co-Host, Rogers & Hammerhead TV Show

Sonny Throckmorton: Legendary Texas Country Music Songwriter, Friend of Freddy's

Terry Booth: Co-Founder, The Royal Knights of the Raccoon / Texas Heritage Songwriters' Association

Wayne Ahart: Fellow Member, The Royal Knights of the Raccoon

Floyd Tillman: Legendary Texas Singer/Songwriter

John Rich & Big Kenny Alphin: Lead Singers/Songwriters of Big & Rich

Ray Wiley Hubbard: Famed Texas Country Singer-Songwriter

Spud Goodall: Legendary Texas Country Singer-Songwriter

Moe Monsarrat: Bassist, The Air Fred Band, 2000s

Steve Carter: Guitar Player, The Air Fred Band, 2000s

B.B. Morse: Freddy's Stand-Up Bass Player, The Air Fred Band, 1990s

Pauline Reese: Freddy Protégé and Texas Country Music Star

Theresa Figg: Co-Curator, Freddy Powers Pickin' Parties

Lucas Souza: Lead Singer/Guitarist, The Lucas Souza Band

Cass Hunter: Catherine's Road Warrior/Close Family Friend

Joi Vinson Davis: Freddy's Personal Nurse & Daughter by Another Mother and Father

Mary Sarah: Freddy Powers Protégé / The Voice TV Show Finalist

Molly McKnight: Talent Scout, Daughter of Texas Senator Peyton McKnight

Joe Gilchrist: Founder of Frank Brown Songwriter Festival, Co-owner of the Flora-Bama

John McGinnis: Co-Owner of the World Famous Flora-Bama

FOREWORD BY TANYA TUCKER

I remember one time with Freddy, he sang the whole chorus of *"Delta Dawn"* to me! That was incredible, I was so freaked out over that. He wasn't talking much at all at that point. So when he sang that whole chorus to me, I was just elated and Catherine was sitting back with her mouth open, she couldn't believe it and I was like "O.M.G!" I felt so honored that he would sing that for me, like I was the only one he would do that for. Freddy is a great singer; I love to hear him sing. I love his voice, and I could listen to a whole album of Freddy singing because his voice is so easy and so calming to the ears.

I loved to watch him play guitar too. I remember I used to watch him on Austin City Limits, and do different things with Merle, and he's not just a great songwriter, but he has great melodies, which I think comes from being a great guitar player. He really has that Jazz kind of sound in his songs, and his music is so palpable to the ear. It's so easy on the ear, and just floats, and is a beautiful experience to listen to some of his melodies. Of course his words are great, but he just creates these melodies that are unforgettable.

He's just as great a writer too, and I think he's one of the least-recognized of the great country songwriters, and doesn't really get his credit due. He's not just a writer of country music either, I love songs of his like *"Little Hotel Room,"* and a lot of the older stuff he's written years ago I have in my head to record later on. He's got so many songs that I think would be good records to this day, just certain songs that stand the tests of time. His music will be great in any era, no matter what year it is, you'll still want to hear a Freddy Powers song!

"Freddy was a Troubadour..." – Catherine Powers

Freddy and brother Don Powers Growing Up
in the early 1940s in Seminole, Texas

CHAPTER 1: SIR FREDERICK

Catherine Powers: Freddy was born in Duncan, Oklahoma, the middle child of seven. His father was a cotton farmer and worked on oil rigs, and when he was seven years old, the family moved to a farm outside Seminole, Texas.

Norma Powers-Marlowe: We moved down to Seminole, Texas from Oklahoma. We came through Andrews, Texas into Seminole, and oh my God, the sand storms!!! I remember the sand was blowing and the tumbleweeds were crossing the highway, and we got to the city limits, and Daddy said "We're home," and my mother started crying! She's got seven kids in the car packed like sardines, and she says "How could you move your family to this God forsaken place?" (laughs)

Back in Oklahoma, there were trees and creeks and all kinds of stuff to do, you know. My little sister Suzie was just a baby and my brother Jerry was really small too, and I wasn't much older but I remember it well: there wasn't nobody saying a word in that car, and that's how we started out in Seminole. Later on, we ended up buying the Mayor's house, and it was a nice house, and behind it, there was car lot.

When we moved out in the country, we had more company than we did when we lived right there in town. When they would come out there, it was like anything goes because we had all this space so you could be outside with no neighbors telling you to be quiet or anything like that. We lived a life that was a lot more interesting than the Walton's, or any of those other families you'd see on T.V., because we did things together. They liked to hunt, and were really good at catching rabbits, and would kill birds with their slingshots and whittle and all kinds of stuff. We used to go the pasture, and we would find a hole and pour water down it and drown out these little ground squirrels. They would run on that little wheel and it was really cute.

Catherine Powers: At night, the whole family gathered in the living room and made music together. His whole family was musical, and in fact. His mother had grown up on stage performing in Vaudeville-type shows with her sisters, traveling around with their father who was a fiddle player. As kids, on the weekends, Freddy's parents would throw parties where all their family and friends would come out to the house. They would move the furniture out, so the house could become a stage and a dance floor.

Freddy and his older sister Mary Lou were singers, and they both entered and won school talent contests. After Freddy's older brother Wallace came home from the Service, he had learned to play a little guitar, and Freddy picked that up from him and started learning how to play guitar while he sang. Freddy's sister was a writer, and she'd had a couple songs she'd written and had been recorded already by a Texas country music star Hank Thompson. That intrigued Freddy that his sister was writing songs and getting paid for it. So his sister helped him get into songwriting after that. They had a family band they all sang and played.

> **Norma Powers-Marlowe:** My mother could sing and grew up in a very musical family as well. My grandmother would play the drums and my grandfather – we called them "Big Mama" and "Big Daddy" – and Big Daddy would play the trombone, and some other instruments. They lived in Ft. Worth, Texas when she was growing up, and they had a garage that they made into a little theater. My Aunt Thelma played the piano very well as a matter of fact and all the other girls – there were five sisters – I'm telling you, they could put the McGuire Sisters to shame! They sang until they started dying off, and they had beautiful voices. So it was kind of in our family through my mother's side that the music came from I'm sure.

At night, just about the time everybody was supposed to go to bed, everybody got wound up and nobody wanted to go to sleep. Freddy would start making up songs and every night all the kids would put on these little music shows! We did all kinds of stuff. Wallace and Freddy would play guitar and Don, Freddy and Wallace – all of 'em – would sing. Freddy always stood out because he was the most vocal and it was just in him to be a performer, it was in his blood.

My father participated in our antics and stuff like that. He would do a jig and would move his head funny. Daddy would just have a big time, a fine time, and Mama would usually sing right along with the kids! She could really sing those Rhythm and Blues numbers like "A Good Man is Hard to Find," and we all participated in all of that. It was like a family band, and we sang sometimes all night long! We would be playing music and doing all kinds of funny stuff! Back then when we were living out in the country, Hank Williams was really big, and Don used to sing that "*Love Sick Blues,*" and he could really sing. Our older sister Mary Lou played "*Boogie Woogie*" and other popular songs of the day on the piano. In our household growing up, we had a lot of the Rhythm and Blues, Country Western. Buddy Killen came to see us one time and raved over my mother's biscuits! (laughs)

Freddy also would do some slapstick and tell jokes, and sing. Freddy had a high voice when he were growing up. I always used to joke that we had our very own Alfalfa! (laughs) He had a high voice, and he loved to dance, Freddy was really good. He would tap dance and enter talent shows, he'd do acrobatics on the stage. The whole family would always come watch him perform. We used to joke that Freddy was our little crooner, and there was always some little girl involved he was singing too.... (laughs)

Ft. Worth Star Telegram: "Seminole, Texas (was)...where 12-year-old Freddy Powers taught himself to play the guitar so he could join his two brothers in country dance bands playing the area."

Texas Music Magazine: "With the guiding apron strings and euphonious vocals of their mother Mary, who had already dabbled with her own success as a singer. They formed a family band and toured the VFW halls and honky-tonks from West Texas to Hobbs, NM."

Freddy Powers: "I started out when I was real young, just a kid in family bands, you know, with my brothers. Everybody in my family either played something or tried to. Out in West Texas, in Seminole, if you didn't play guitar or do something, you'd go out of your mind. There wasn't anything else to do and as my dad used to say, 'Everything that crawls, bites, everything that flies, stings and every bush that grows out there, has a thorn on it.' That's just about telling the whole story...My musical indoctrination occurred – at the ole' country dance. Each week, it would be at one ranch or the other, all of them good people, church people, but on Saturday they would loosen up. That was my training ground and the training ground for all great country musicians."

Catherine Powers: Freddy grew up poor, but he didn't know it. In fact, when they were young boys, their mother made Freddy and his brothers' shirts out of potato sacks. At Christmas, to get a whistle or a little toy gun was huge for them. The way kids celebrate Christmas today did not compare to anything like they got. They got homemade gifts and maybe one bought gift. It was an extremely humble existence materially but the house was always full of life and love. Freddy came from such a big family. Freddy and his older brother Don were the two middle children and they were very close in age. Just like the two oldest children, Mary Lou and Wallace, were close in age, and then there was Norma, Jerry and Suzie. Freddy and Don were extremely close and mischievous.

Norma Powers-Marlowe: Freddy growing up was never, ever without friends. Freddy was always upbeat and looking back, of course, he was bound to be in show business of some kind. Every time they would have something at school, Freddy would be in anything. If they had any kind of play or talent show around the house he was there. He was like our little "*Song and Dance*" man. He liked to sing, and Don did too, he had a really nice voice as well. You'd never see Don without Freddy, they were close as any twins or just like best friends, I've never known them to fight, disagree or fuss. They went along together just like they were joined at the hip. Freddy and Don liked to crack jokes, and they would work together. They kept us laughing all the time.

Freddy Powers: My brother Don and I were always outside playing army or getting into all kinds of mischief as kids on the farm! One of our favorite shenanigans was my brother Don and I stealing chickens from our Dad. After he went to work, they would run down to a neighbor's and sell the chickens for a quarter. Then we'd have our movie, popcorn and soda money for that Saturday afternoon movie matinee. Unfortunately, Daddy caught wind before too long when that neighbor came asking for more chickens, and wound up busting us! He actually came up with a pretty original punishment of making us both sleep out in the chicken coop to protect those chickens from any other thieving. (Laughs)

Norma Powers-Marlowe: They were good boys. I can truthfully say that Freddy was always a gentleman. He never was disrespectful or anything to any of us kids, and they didn't get into too much mischief. I remember one time there was this filling station, and I mean it was a little bitty thing. They crawled in the bathroom window one time and took a couple of packages of cigarettes and climbed back out the window. Well, Daddy found out about it and took them downtown where the jail is and scared the daylights out of them. They thought they were going to have to go to prison! (laughs) Another time, we had a haystack, and they would bundle it and stack it where if it rains, it won't leak. Back then, we didn't have a garbage service, so you had to have a garbage barrel and burnt your garbage and they'd pick it up. Well, they had gone to get the last load of trash and there was an old tire they'd been burning. Freddy or Don was poking at it with a stick to put it out and a piece of flaming tire flew back up onto that haystack. And boy, you talk about a fire!! Oh my God, this looked like the end of the world, and the fire department was there at our house. So they were like normal boys, they got into mischief but never did anything to harm anybody.

He and Don didn't like me to mess with their pet snakes. It was a big old blue Texas Indigo snake. I'd sit on the porch and wait till they got out of sight. Then I could really get out there and get that snake, and scare everybody in the neighborhood! I'd terrorize the neighborhood, then I'd put it back like nothing happened. It's hard to zero in on just Freddy because we were a family. We were together a lot, so it was like all kinds of mischief! (laughs) One day, a bunch of us kids were out there in that pasture way off from our house and everything. We came up on an old cellar where there's been a house there long before, and found a bootlegger's stash down there!

Well, we went back across the highway and got our little old wagon that had sides on it. We loaded that wagon up – I never will forget – it was these little, tall bottles of beer, and all kinds of stuff. We made I don't know how many trips, back and forth, back and forth. The neighbor eventually came home and saw us with all that stuff and said, "Where in the world did you get all this stuff?" We told him, "Oh, we found it," and then he asked more pointedly. "Where did you find it?" So we told him, "Over there in the pasture," and his response was funny because then he asked, "Is there any more of it?" (laughs) We told him "No, we got it all," and he told us not to go over there anymore. The funny part is: all of us kids over there were barefooted and had tracked sand all down in the bottom of that cellar. So you could see these little old bitty feet prints everywhere! It was fun growing up, we did have a good childhood.

Catherine Powers: Freddy's whole family were the wittiest bunch I've ever seen in my life, every one of them is funny, it totally amazes me. They all could have been comedians – his son, his grandson – so it's like it was born in Freddy and instilled in him to be comical. Freddy used that in his music, combining comedy into his performing persona. That's when he got into the banjo and that's where he started developing his unique style of guitar playing as well, which is rooted through his banjo.

Norma Powers-Marlowe: I have to tell you another really funny, true story. Freddy was home, and we all went out Saturday to the theater to see what was usually a Country and Western show. By this time, we didn't live in town at the Mayor's house anymore. We lived out in the country on the other side of the city limits. When we walked out of the show, we heard Freddy playing that steel guitar out in the yard. He was playing that thing wide open! We heard him from outside the theater all the way out there at our house. He wasn't always Country and Western either, not at all. The times when I really enjoyed Freddy's music the most actually was when he got into Dixieland Jazz. Freddy could really play the banjo, *Oh My God*, he was really good at playing that banjo!

Catherine Powers: As a teenager, Freddy was always a comedian and always up to something. One time when their daddy was out somewhere, Freddy and Don decided to take their father's car for a little joyride. So they're driving around the fields and all of a sudden pull up on the sand embankment. They were bogged down and got their daddy's car stuck! Well, they were trying to dig it out, and before too long, ran the battery down. So now they're really starting to panic. All of a sudden, over the horizon, they could see their daddy riding up on his horse, looking like a Texas Ranger or something, boots, cowboy hat and all. Now they both know they're about to be in real trouble, and their daddy asks. "What's going on here boys?" Well, they had to own up to joyriding. This was one of those old cars that had the crank. So their dad gets the tool out to crank it up, starts to wind it up, and as he did, the crank came off and hit him in the head and knocked him back onto the ground. Well, now Freddy and Don are staring down at him, and their daddy looks up at the two boys and says, "Well, don't just stand there like a monument of shit, help me up!"

Freddy Powers: One night we took a cop car for a joy ride after the officers pulled up outside a donuts shop and left the car running. Don and I and two other buddies left it parked at the city dump! It even made the papers for a couple days because the cop car was missing. Luckily, we never got caught for that one, and years later, our Daddy told us both, "It was a good thing I didn't know back then because I'd have tanned your hides!"

Catherine Powers: Another time, Freddy, Don and some buddies of theirs found this swimming hole. Which was in a tank, because being out there on the plains of West Texas, there weren't any lakes or ponds around where they were. So the kids would go swim in these tanks that they used for the cattle to drink out of. Well, this one old man didn't like them swimming in his tank. He decided he was going to put an end to it, and put some barbed-wire down in that tank. Well, when they showed up to go swimming the next day, they discovered that barbed-wire and went home and told their daddy. So he jumped on a horse, went over, and was gonna jump on this guy, and the guy looked up at him, and said "Roy, for little or nothing, I'd yank you off that horse, and kick your ass!" And Roy looked down at him and said, "Now, what the hell do you think I'm gonna be doing while you're doing all this ass kicking?"

Norma Powers-Marlowe: My father was a hard-working man, but he was fun. Let me tell you something, we had good parents. That's not to say that my daddy would put up with any crap because he wouldn't! It didn't make a difference if you were the girl in the family or who you were, if you got into trouble, you got punished. I remember Don would never cry, he'd lean over and just take it. Once my daddy got a hold of Freddy, oh my God, he would carry on like it was the end of the world, screaming, he'd go crazy... but it was all an act! (laughs)

Catherine Powers: His parents were both always very supportive of Freddy's musical development growing up, and it's kind of sweet. Even though I'm not going to say in any way that his parents loved any one child more than they loved the other, Freddy was "Sir Frederick" to his Mama and Daddy. So much so, that on the last days of his mama's life, she still addressed him as "Sir Frederick." That nickname stuck around the house when Freddy was a kid. One of Freddy's first bands was Sir Frederick and his Little Men. Because his parents came from musical backgrounds themselves, not only were they extremely supportive when he was still living at home, but after he'd gotten out of the service. Freddy was getting his start in the music business touring around Texas. His parents would follow Freddy to watch him play. The family moved to Arlington when Freddy did. When Freddy moved to Houston, the family moved, so even though he was the middle child, wherever Freddy lived, they followed him.

Norma Powers-Marlowe: Daddy would have given us anything, any kind of lesson pertaining to anything musical or any other kind of education that we had the ambition and get-up-and-go to go do it. So my father and mother were absolutely supportive of Freddy, or any of us if we'd wanted to do that.

Catherine Powers: As a matter of fact, with his baby brother Jerry. Freddy was more than a big brother to him, he was his hero. He was his idol, and when you would say Freddy's name to Jerry, he'd get this smile as big as Texas on his face. He was so proud and looked up so much to his older brother. Whenever Freddy would pull back into town when he'd been out on the road, his whole family – mother, father, brothers, sister – would all get the instruments out and they would play music together. His sister would play piano, his daddy would play fiddle, his brothers would play bass and lead guitar, and Freddy would play rhythm on his banjo, so they were a very close family.

"Like Nelson, (Powers) came of age musically in the Texas honky tonks. In Ft. Worth, he got to know guitarist Paul Buskirk, another close collaborator with Nelson. All three men shared an affinity for expanding country's sonic landscape to include swing and jazz."
– MUSIC ROW MAGAZINE

Alameda Naval Base

Freddy Playing the Banjo in the 50s

CHAPTER 2: THE 50s –
Freddy Enlists, Meets Buskirk, Willie Nelson & the World

Catherine Powers: Freddy was a teenager in the later 40s after WWII when all those John Wayne movies made war seem that it was glamorous. His older brother Wallace had been in the service so Freddy looked at the joining the military as being something of a patriotic duty. He was 15 the first time he ran away from home and joined the Air Force. Once he got in there and they realized he was under age, they called his father, who came and got him and took him back home. Well, a year later, at 16, Freddy ran off again, and this time joined the Marines.

He'd gone down to the enlistment office, and when he walked in, the recruiter looked him over and said, "You don't look 18 to me son," and Freddy said "Okay, see you later!" The guy goes, "Oh, no, no, no, now wait a minute, and sat Freddy back down, and he ended up BS-ING his way through the interview and was able once again to join the military. Well, as soon as he got into boot camp, it didn't take long for these experienced drill instructors to realize Freddy wasn't 18. Once again, his father picks up a ringing phone back home telling him déjà vu, your son's done it again. Well, this time, when his father drove down to the base where Freddy was stationed, they all sat down and talked it out. They saw that he was determined to be in the military, and decided to let him stay in under a special set of conditions: 1.) he would finish high school in the service, and 2.) he was restricted to the base until he came of age.

Norma Powers-Marlowe: We were very, very patriotic at our house and we had every reason to be. I remember when the boys were in the service. Back at home, we turned our kitchen into like a candy factory or something. We made fudge, meat loaf and all kinds of stuff and sent packages to the boys. They'd divide everything up between them. We did this with my oldest brother Wallace when he was in World War II. Wallace saw a lot of awful things over there. A lot of people didn't come back, but fortunately, all of my brothers came back alive. Jerry, my youngest brother, was in the Navy, Freddy was in the Marines, Don was in the Army and Wallace was in the Navy too. They were all during different wars, and they all proudly served. When Wallace went into the service he was 18 years old, and Freddy was 16 when he ran off to join the Marines. In fact, Freddy was in a car wreck that kind of hurt his back, and he missed going over there in that first division of the Korean War, and they wiped them out. So that wreck really was kind of a blessing or he probably wouldn't even be here.

Catherine Powers: Freddy was so gung-ho that when the Drill Sergeant would come and get right up on his nose and scream at him. Freddy was one of those that would stand at attention and yell right back, "Yes sir! Yes sir!" He wanted to be in that military so bad that he ended up being a six-year Vet in the Marines. He became C.I.D. during the Korean War, and during that war, not everybody who went to Korea came back. He would tell me stories that every night he would lay in his bed and hear guys in the barracks who knew they were being shipped off the next day to Korea crying and scared to death.

So Freddy wanted to be in the military, but he didn't want to go kill anybody and didn't want to be killed. At the base, he was running the cleaners, and it was a safe gig. He was even able to make money on the side on his off days. He would still go and work the cleaners and wash his buddies' clothes and they'd pay him a couple of bucks. So every time Freddy's number would come up, they couldn't let him go until he trained somebody else to run the cleaners. Naturally, every time they'd send somebody over, after a bit when somebody asked him, "Well, how are they doing?" Freddy would say, 'Eh, I don't think they're gonna get it.' They never could afford to get rid of him. Through that luck, he was able to stay on American soil while still staying in the Marines while running the cleaners.

One time in the service, Freddy was standing post at the guard gate. Everyone in his platoon had to take turns on guard gate duty. So Freddy was leaning up against the building falling asleep standing up. Well, the Sergeant came through and of course, yelled "POWERS!" Freddy jumped and he said, "You know I could put you in the brig for sleeping on the job," and he replied, "Oh no Sir, I wasn't asleep, I was resting my eyes." Next, the Sergeant said, "It looked to me like the rest of your body joined in too!" Another time, Freddy, was in the guard house standing post, and this was down in Ocean Side. He was playing around with his gun and it went off and he shot a hole through the guard shack, which is a big, big no- no. That hole is there to this day, he took me back years later to see it.

After he'd been in the service a while, Freddy came home for a visit. Freddy was driving his very first car, and he was so proud of this car. That night, a few of his buddies got in the car for a ride around the country, and the way he tells the story, they came upon this watermelon field, and pulled Freddy's car up into this patch. They loaded his trunk with watermelons! Well, they saw lights come on at the farmhouse. They all jumped in the car and were getting ready to get the heck out of there. When Freddy tried to crank up his car, it was so weighted down with watermelons that it was bogged and he couldn't get out. So now all his friends leap out of the car and take off running. The farmer who owned the watermelon patch comes running up on Freddy with his shotgun in hand, yelling and cussing!

Initially, Freddy had followed the rest of his buddies running off into the darkness until he remembered, "Hey, wait a minute, that's my car!" Sure enough, when Freddy got back to the car, that farmer took a closer look, lowered the shotgun, and said "You're one of the Powers boys!" (laughs) Freddy and Don were known so well around town for being the mischief-makers while they were growing up that the farmer recognized him right away, and then made Freddy feel bad, "There's no reason for you boys to come over here and steal my watermelons. All you had to do was come and ask me, and I'd have told you to take all the watermelons you want!"

Norma Powers-Marlowe: One time when Freddy had just come home from the Marines, he bought a little Coupe that was solid black. He went off somewhere, and I thought I'd surprise him and clean up that little car. I got out there and used Old English Furniture Polish on it and polished that little old Coupe up. Then here comes a horrible sand storm, what a mess because the sand stuck all over the car! Freddy never growled or snapped at me. He just got out there with soap and water and worked like a Trojan horse trying to get that grease off of there! (laughs)

Freddy Powers: "My first professional gig was in 1953 in Dallas at a place down on Elm Street. On my opening night I got hit in the middle of the face with a salt shaker that they threw at me so hard it damn near knocked me crazy. That was my introduction to Dallas nightclubs and show business."

"I also got my start playing over in Hobbs, New Mexico. They had those old Honky-Tonks that hired bands. Lots of people would come through there, like Bob Wills. That's when I got interested in songwriting. All of those old acts would come through and I'd get to see 'em live – closest thing to 'show biz. That was in the (late 40s)."

Catherine Powers: Once he got out of the Marines, Freddy immediately got married. He'd been brought up to focus on having a family while he was young, that's just the way it was back then. Still, his goal and dream was to be a professional musician and he never lost sight of that. He oldest daughter was born in 1954, and because he still had to be the breadwinner, he worked in the oil industry with his father and opened up his own bar. Knowing it guaranteed him a place to play. Another thing he did to put food on the table was go to barber school. Back then, a lot of musicians went to barber school, because 1.) he could control his schedule, and 2.) make money during the day and still go play music at night. So that's how Freddy kept food on the table and his career going at the same time in the early years.

Freddy Powers: I first met Willie Nelson way back in the early 50s shortly after I'd gotten out of the Marines. I'd come straight back to Texas with my heart set on breaking into the music business. I'd grown up in a musical family that played Dixieland Jazz for local town dances in our hometown of Seminole. When I'd returned back home in my early 20s, I went to Barber school in Dallas to make ends meet while I was getting things going. Johnny Gimble was actually a classmate of mine. While I was playing in Dallas, I began taking banjo lessons from Paul Buskirk – my hero and mentor, and a major influence – Who in turn introduced me to Willie when he was just another young country singer-songwriter.

> **Willie Nelson:** The first time I remember seeing Freddy, he was playing in a Banjo band in Arlington, Texas. It was like a noon-time show at some club; that was many years ago. Then we ran into each other up in Houston when he was down there with Paul Buskirk. Freddy, Paul and I played a lot of music together and had a lot of fun.

Catherine Powers: Freddy pursued Paul Buskirk! (laughs) He was living in Arlington, Texas in an apartment complex. Back then one of his fellow neighbors turned out to be Paul Buskirk. Before he'd ever introduced himself to Paul, every day, he would see this guy dressed in a nice suit walking around with his instrument. Freddy was like, "Wow, this guy looks like somebody I need to meet." So whenever he would see that Paul was pulling into the parking lot, Freddy would open up his window and start singing and playing his guitar as loud as he could to get his attention. That's how he first caught the attention of Paul Buskirk.

Freddy Powers: "We met in Dallas in the 1950s. I had just gotten out of the service and was there to become a barber. Paul drove a big ole' white Buick. I would sing extra loud by the window. Paul heard me one day and came over to talk with me. He hired me and things moved fast from there. We started doing a Noon Day Jones show in 1955. It was a news/weather show. Neil Jones was the emcee and Paul was the sidekick."

> **Willie Nelson:** The first time I heard Paul, he was playing with Johnny and Jack out of Memphis, TN. And then I heard him again when I ran into him down in Houston. He had a music studio, and we began making some records together. I would teach guitar lessons in his studio.
>
> **Paul Buskirk:** There's so many stories about you Freddy, I could sit for hours and reminisce and talk about the good times we've had. What a trip.

Freddy Powers: "Paul was a wonderful friend of mine! My first paying job was with him. He was such a father figure to me. We played Europe and Vegas together, my gosh, son. I knew him so well. He was even the one who introduced me to marijuana, hahaha! Paul was hardnosed when it came to music. He was a serious player, and a serious musician!"

Catherine Powers: Willie would play as a feature act at Freddy's club back then too. So through that their friendship grew, and they started touring around Texas together. The funny thing about that was, back then, though both Willie and Freddy smoked pot. Neither Willie nor Freddy knew yet that the other smoked. So when they'd all be out on the road together – Freddy, Paul, Willie and his wife at the time Shirley and they would stop. Because Freddy and Paul didn't know Willie was a pot smoker, they would take off and go their own way and hide from Willie to get stoned. While Willie and Shirley were going the opposite direction to do the same thing! The laws were so strict back then – especially in the Lone Star state – that getting caught with one joint could land you a stiff prison sentence. So after that, when they were on the road, to make sure they didn't get caught, they would sneak out into the middle of the desert where they could see cars coming for miles, and get high.

> **The Austin Chronicle:** "Nelson even joined Powers' band on bass for a short time, working the infamous honky-tonks along the Jacksboro High-

way. They had to cover the tuba with a mesh screen to keep the crowds from flinging their beer bottles into the bell."

Freddy Powers: "Later Paul and I started doing the Pat Boone Show around 1955/56. We played service clubs and officers clubs in Europe. We had a show with three banjos, three vocalists, and a tuba. Paul had a gypsy wagon built on wheels with a stage and lights in the 1960s. We would pull up on a Saturday afternoon to places like furniture store parking lots and Paul would sweet talk the owners into letting us play. We made good money! Paul was never a honky-tonk player. He was so far advanced and beyond us, he was like a professor of music, and he got better with age!"

"Here's a funny story for ya'. One time a young guy came up to him at the National DJ Convention Festival in Nashville in the 1950s and said, 'Paul Buskirk, the greatest mandolinist in the world.' Paul remarked, 'The only one in the world!' That was Elvis. Elvis had a WSM corncob pipe and was surrounded by girls, by the way. Willie was a standup DJ when they met. With all absolute due respect, Paul could eat Bill Monroe alive. Buskirk was from a different mold. If I hadn't met him, there's no telling which direction I'd have gone."

Paul Buskirk: I was thinking about (us) in Europe when we started to come home from Germany on that little Military tour we did over there. I thought about you sitting at the airport saying: "They've got this one seat on another plane, why don't I catch this plane and come on in on my own? I can bring the car around in New York!" (laughs)

J. Gary Smith: I opened my first club in downtown Houston on Milo Street back in the 50s when I first met Freddy and Paul Buskirk. It was a banjo sing-along club that was a second location owned by Edward Ed, who ran The Levy in Dallas, which was a world-famous banjo sing-along club with Ronnie Dawson, and all these guys. So they hired me to run the one in Houston. The next thing you know, I open the doors and am meeting all these banjo players and amazing musicians, and that's how I first wound up working with Paul Buskirk – and through him I met Freddy. Paul was a mentor to all of us.

By then, Paul and Freddy had already been working together for a few years, they'd toured all over the country together. My first impressions of Freddy when I met him was that he was a crazy son of a bitch, I loved him! He was a great entertainer, the funniest sob in the world, non-stop jokes, and a good person. Everybody loved Freddy, he just had that kind of personality. Freddy played the pizza parlors down there in Houston. Don Payne's Pizza Parlor was one I remember, which was a banjo place, and they did well over there. Paul and he played Shakey's too, they had a lot of music in those places back then, a whole touring circuit. After a while, Paul Buskirk was funny because he didn't want to leave town, he didn't want to travel anymore, he'd worked with everybody by then. After work, he and Freddy would smoke their asses off! It was so funny, they'd get shit-faced blind, and I'd go with them. See, I can't smoke and inhale a cigarette or joint, but I'd still get stoned from just being in the hotel room with them! (laughs)

Rattlesnake Annie: You remember years ago when pizza parlors had those guys who played in them? Freddy did that back in the 50s starting out, and those players came more from the Dixieland, and then he played Western Swing. It is akin to Jazz, and my love of Jazz and ability to sing those chords and hear it, I think that's what really connected me to Freddy was Jazz, with those great lyrics. One thing I learned from Freddy were these chord progressions that I'd call Western Swing, which are often Jazz progressions. That's one of the things that I find fascinating about those songs. The patterns that he used, there's a consistency to them where the chords are more disciplined Jazz. Freddy was able to combine Jazz with just about everything he played within the country styles. So I look at Freddy's music as being Western Swing sort of, he used to say sometimes I'd take his Western Swing songs and turn them into Bluegrass, because I played them real fast! (laughs)

A very common dominator on my communication with Freddy was Spud Goodall. Freddy introduced me to Spud, and Spud was a great guitar player and a great teacher and had a lot to share. The things Spud was teaching me were closely related to Freddy, and he adored Freddy! So I was never quite able to separate the two in my thinking, even though I was only with the two of them together a couple of times at Willie's studio. They were definitely soul mates in music, I know that.

Freddy Powers: We all had some great times together traveling around the country. I'm sure Willie misses Paul as much as I do, God rest his soul. In 1955, I actually wound up being one of the first country artists to ever record one of Willie's tunes, *'Heartaches of a Fool.'*

Catherine Powers: That made Freddy actually the first artist to record a Willie Nelson song, and to get radio play for a song written by Willie.

Freddy Powers: "My sister wrote a song for Hank Thompson, she wasn't a performer or anything, but she played the piano and wrote great songs. I think that's where the idea came from, when she cut that tune, I started thinking, 'Hey… maybe I could to that?' "

Catherine Powers: Freddy's songwriting career got its start in the 1950s too. Freddy was a writer on *"There She Goes"* by Carl Smith. Freddy's father had been so impressed with his talent for writing that he'd paid for Carl to go in the studio and demo the song and record it. Freddy had run home and excitedly told his wife at the time, "We've broken into the business, we have a song coming out on the radio," the whole nine yards, but when it came out, Freddy's name was nowhere to be found on the songwriting credits. He'd been cut out, and all the money his father had invested had been lost, and in those days, if you didn't have a name as a writer to go and try and fight somebody that was already reputable in the business, you didn't have a chance. Then Freddy had a song recorded by The Wilburn Brothers where his name was on the record as a writer, *"Nothing at All,"* but that's exactly what he received in the way of songwriting royalties. It was another one of those rip-offs, and that discouraged Freddy and he gave up on writing for a while to focus on being a performer and just writing songs for his band.

Freddy Powers: "The Wilburn Brothers had some kind of hits out there on the Grand Old Opry, and I wrote a song with them. I soon found out that I was signed up with a publisher that was really unscrupulous. I never saw any money from that. I don't know what happened back in the days. I didn't have an idea on how to collect any money, and I sort of got disenchanted on selling songs."

"Nothing At All"

If you only care for things money can buy
You're a man who's found fortune and fame
Just remember before life has wilted away
Without true love you don't have a thing

Nothing at all nothing at all
Without love you've got nothing at all
Nothing at all nothing at all
Without love you've got nothing at all

When you find a love that will never grow old
Then you'll know dreams are free and not bought
You'll have your cup full without treasures of gold
And be richer than you ever thought

Nothing at all nothing at all
Without love you've got nothing at all
Nothing at all nothing at all
Without love you've got nothing at all

"Powers took up a musical residency at the Riviera Casino in Las Vegas, mixing comic elements with his Dixieland jazz-country music. His band, the Powerhouse Four…was a popular Sin City attraction through the early seventies." – ROLLING STONE MAGAZINE

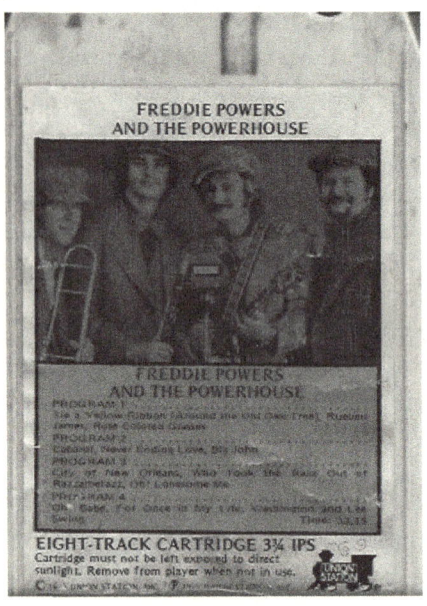

Freddy 60s 8-Track

CHAPTER 3: THE 60s —
The Tonight Show & Ruling Reno

Ralph Sanford: I met Freddy after I got out of the Army in September of 1961, and he wanted to open a club in Ft. Worth with the banjos, which was kind of popular back then. Freddy was funny and a character, and I liked him right off!

Freddy Powers: "I was doin' stand-up comedy and Dixieland. We had these costumes of old-time knickers with argyle socks and little snap caps. That wasn't in the country vein. It was three banjos and a tuba. It was 'hell raisin' Dixieland like Bill Bailey and stuff like that. I kinda got lost from country music there during that folk period."

Ralph Sanford: We opened the Crestview Club in a warehouse building, and we were only using part of it. It had a small bar in it, and there was a private room area inside, and we filled that up almost from when we opened the door. People started coming and Freddy had to tear that partition down. That opened us up to the full bar area, and that was full by the end of the first week. It went really good and people seemed to like us. It was very popular. We played 6 nights a week, Monday through Saturday, we didn't play on Sunday. Our sets would run from 45 minutes to an hour, and we would start at 9 PM, do an hour, take a 15 minute break, and then played to Midnight. There was a $1 cover charge to get in.

J. Gary Smith: Around that time, I opened another club, The Texas Breeze. It was one of the most fun clubs to play in Houston, it was like Cheers with a live band, except nobody danced. When you walked in, there was a long bar that ran all the way to the back, and the stage was on the other end of the building. It only seated around 300, but we would pack that sob where there was a line out the door, and I remember when Freddy performed there and people loved him!

Freddy would bring his mother around and he got her up on stage a bunch of times to sing. She was an old entertainer, his whole damn family was around the business all their lives, and she was a hoot! She'd get up and sing old classic stuff and the audience loved it! Without question, Freddy got a lot of his sense of humor from his mama, the whole Powers family was light and fun. Everybody played and sang, it seemed like.

Ralph Sanford: The original members of The Powerhouse IV were Freddy, myself, Kenneth Cobb who played bass, and Bill Hudson, who played lead guitar and also played banjo. I think the reason we did well is because we were having a ball! We didn't do a lot of rehearsing, he'd just call a song and everybody fell in and we just did it. We did arrangements on a lot of things as we went along, but we'd get up on stage and just have fun, just four guys who loved music. The people enjoyed us I think because we were on our ball. We had fun and I think that's what made the people have fun. I actually met my wife Barbara there, and we've been married 57 years.

Elston Brooks, Ft. Worth Star Telegram: "The real break came when NBC-TV's TODAY show came to Texas. Producer Don Silverman, a ragtime nut, heard about the boys and asked for a special audition. It was at the UN-musician-like hour of 9 A.M. in Powers' empty Arlington nightspot. They made The Tonight Show later. Silverman invited them to New York for more appearances on The Today show. A spot on the TONIGHT SHOW followed. The TODAY and TONIGHT Shows were just logical culminations of day and nice practice for Tuba man Bobby Hollingsworth.

Freddy Powers: 'Bobby had only played the tuba for a short while in the Waco High School Band. I thought it would be an interesting sound to go with the banjos, but the first night it was awful. It was 117 years before he could take that vacant building in Arlington and make it into his Crestview Club. I just named it after the Arlington telephone exchange. If I had known the banjos were going to go so good, I've had called it the River Boat.'"

Ralph Sanford: The Today Show came around very early in our situation, and wanted us to audition for them for Six Flags. They were going to do a live broadcast from Six Flags, and were checking all the talent out in Dallas-Ft. Worth. We got the call that we'd got the job for that. We were all excited. Now, once we did The Today Show, we had to move back to the Warehouse section of Freddy's club where he started renting tables because there were so many people coming. It just floored us because we didn't have anywhere to put the people! One of our jobs after the Today Show came when the man who owned Phillip Petroleum Company hired us to play a show in Oklahoma. We traveled there in a little Plymouth Valiant, and then Freddy bought a 1962 Chevrolet Station Wagon, and we made trips to gigs back and forth in it. We went to New York in it the 2nd time, and also went to Canada. ITA booked us for a month in Canada, and we did that whole trek in Freddy's white Chevrolet station wagon.

> After we made the first trip to New York to play The Today Show, they booked us again after we did the first one in the Arlington area because we got such a mail draw. Hugh Downs told us we had the largest mail draw of anyone in the history of The Today Show, at that time, and they had us back pretty quick because of all of the phone calls and mail. So we drove up to New York in a Cadillac Eldorado our first trip to New York. Five of us packed in there with our instruments and suit cases, and that big Bass Tuba! We played two Tonight Shows, we recorded an album in about a two week period of time. Jimmy Dean actually hosted the Tonight Shows when we played, and I remember one of the nights, the show ran too long and we were cut short, but we played both nights. Freddy would get uptight and start to bounce around backstage before the shows, but then we just went on stage and did our thing.

Freddy Powers: "By the 60s, I was doin' The Today and Tonight Shows with a little banjo band I had for a while. I did two albums as '*Freddy Powers and the Powerhouse IV*' for Warner Bros. Records."

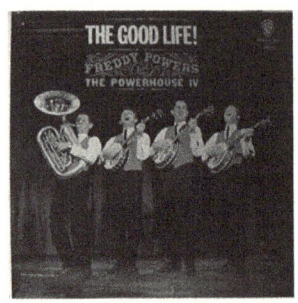

Ralph Sanford: The Powerhouse IV even made a record! Joe Finger Carr, he was a pianist who was on RCA Victor and they hired him to arrange the album. We worked on it while we were in New York in Warner Bros. Studio. We were in there rehearsing, putting songs together. Peter and Paul of Peter, Paul and Mary were standing in an announcer's booth that was connected to this little studio we rehearsed in, listening and giving us peace signs and applause in the booth. They were the biggest thing in the nation at that time with *"Puff the Magic Dragon,"* and why we didn't stop and go meet them is beyond me. So we rehearsed in this little, smaller studio where they did voiceovers, and then we recorded it.

One night, the show producer Don Silverman and the head of IPA, our booking agency, they went out with Freddy to the Copa Cabana, along with Freddy's cousin Cotton Powers. Freddy was smart enough to have a photographer come along and take photos of us, which cost a lot of money at that point, maybe $100 something dollars for the photos. Well, Freddy didn't have all the money, I think he thought it was going to cost way less! (laughs) Cotton bailed him out and wound up paying for the photos.

Catherine Powers: Based off the strength of the Today and Tonight Show appearances, Freddy along with headlining at the bar he owned in Arlington was frequenting the Dallas area clubs with his band. Through playing that circuit, he got to know another bar owner by the name of Jack Ruby, who became a good friend of Freddy's, and as a matter of fact, Jack even gave Freddy a puppy. Jack Ruby would of course go on to live forever in infamy after he shot and killed Lee Harvey Oswald following Oswald assassination of President John F. Kennedy, who was Jack's hero. Jack was friends with all the police because of all the protection money that club owners paid to the cops back in those days, and Freddy in fact was still in touch with Jack in the early 60s when he shot Oswald. Freddy always thought they really took it too far, the whole conspiracy angle, because Jack Ruby, like Freddy, was just an extremely patriotic American.

Ralph Sanford: I only met him one time. He wanted us to do some entertaining in his club, so Freddy had asked me to go over with him. So we went to Jack's club in downtown Dallas, and visited with him in a booth at the Carousel. Freddy had more visitations with him than I did.

Don Powers Jr: Freddy was supposed to play for President Kennedy and Lyndon Johnson and Governor John Connolly the next day after JFK was killed! The reason Freddy had that honor is because he'd campaigned for Governor Connolly during his re-election campaign. But sadly, the Governor also got shot sitting in the front seat in the same car with Kennedy.

Don and Freddy both knew Jack Ruby, who had a bar in Dallas and Ruby would come over to Arlington, Texas to the Crestview Club, which Freddy and Dad used to own together. They would swap entertainment so they'd have different bands, a variety of groups, and so my dad and Freddy both knew Jack Ruby.

Freddy Powers: "West Texas couldn't hold me, nothing ever could. I've known that for as long as I can remember. I've always followed my heart and my songs wherever they take me."

Austin City Limits: "During the early '60s, he appeared on the 'Hootenanny' television show, and the next thing he knew he had jumped from the honky-tonk to the coffee house circuit."

Elston Brooks, Ft. Worth Star Telegram: "State Rep. Don Kennard, who wanted to be State Senator Don Kennard, asked us to suggest a musical group for his campaigning. We mentioned the little group at Arlington Crestview Club that had been setting the customers on fire, and Kennard engaged their services. The fact that Kennard now signs his letters State Senator, and Doyle Willis is running for the Fort Worth City Council, may be traced to the musical attraction of the Powerhouse IV. In any event, it allowed them to play the Governor's inauguration party on the same bill with Joey Bishop, Vic Damone and the Ames Brothers."

Freddy Powers: "In the sixties I was traveling – I had a territorial band out of Minnesota. Minnesota was a good training ground, because they had casinos of Elks Clubs. They had illegal gambling and they let them get away with it. It wasn't legal, but everyone in town did it, and we often got paid under the table."

Nevada Appeal, Star Talk: "Powers has been entertaining since he was 15 and he began appearing in Las Vegas early in the 1960s..."

Freddy Powers: We had to be! We'd do anything to raise publicity back then, now that we were on a roll following the success we had on both The Today Show and The Tonight Show, I was riding my first wave of fame all the way from Texas to Nevada. For the next couple years, I played every casino lounge, road house, and juke joint you can imagine up and down Highway 80 and 95, from Middlegate Station, the Outdoor Inn, the Santa Fe Saloon, the Paradise Valley Saloon, The Lucky Spur Saloon, and the Gold Point Saloon, Elko Nevada.

Catherine Powers: Once he was playing the Casino circuit, Freddy was always trying to pull publicity stunts, so one night – and this was after the whole

Roswell thing – Freddy decided that he was going to make people think Martians had landed. When they would see cars coming, they would run across the highway, thinking all these cars would stop, hoping that it was gonna make the front page that Martians had landed outside of Reno, then say "Hahaha, it was us!" It was little stunts like that Freddy would do, trying to get publicity.

Freddy Powers: "We went out on the highway and one of the guys in the band and I wrapped ourselves in tin foil, put plastic bags over our heads, stuck antennas on the bags. We had a huge amplifier in the car, and played that warbling whistle you always hear in flying saucer films. Cars pulled over, trucks pulled over, people were shouting. Not one paper printed a word about it!"

Anne Reynolds, Deanie-Bird's Widow: That's one that still stands out! It's crazy, but Dean would always laugh recounting for me the time he and Freddy and the boys in the Powerhouse IV were acting silly and wound aluminum foil around themselves to look like Martins, and would stand in the bend of the road where the big truckers would be swinging their big rigs around the corner. When their headlights would shine on Freddy and Dean all wrapped up in this tin foil, they looked like they were outer-space men! (laughs) That's the kind of stupid stuff they used to pull, and even years later, they'd laugh themselves silly recalling it.

Ralph Sanford: Freddy loved trailers! He'd always have a real nice trailer he'd pull behind his Cadillac, and knew all about them. He was an expert of trailers, they were always real nice because he traveled so much. So that always impressed me that he was a nomad.

Merle Haggard: Freddy and I go way back to the early 1960s when he was doing stand-up comedy playing a banjo. I remember seeing Fred was in Las Vegas, and I think he was playing at the Showboat at the time and I was playing at the Nashville Nevada club. I was playing bass for Wynn Stewart.

Freddy Powers: The first time I ever met Merle Haggard was years before, way back in 1961. He was an unknown side man playing bass for Wynn Stewart. They were working at the Nashville Nevada Club in Las Vegas, and I was working down the street at the Showboat Hotel/Casino. I had a Dixieland band on the bill with Spike Jones and his band The City Slickers. I remember one evening Merle came over either on his break or after their show, and told me he liked our show and our style of music. He told me he was working down the street and so the next night, I made sure to go over and catch his show. That soon became a nightly ritual for us where he'd usually come over and watch my show, then after I'd finished my set, I'd go over to the club he was playing and do the same. I always set up on the left side of the stage, that's the side Merle was on. We liked each other and had respect for each other's style of music so we became fast friends and hung out together during our engagement there, but lost touch as the 60s and our respective careers went on.

Elston Brooks, Ft. Worth Star Telegram: "Joe (Fingers) Carr calls it 'music with lumps in it.' Hugh Downs calls the musical mixture 'the greatest combination since Jimmy Valentine sandpapered his fingers and opened his last safe.' Freddy Powers, the local lad who is the subject of the professional adulation, calls it 'a different ragtime sound.' Powers leaves the more colorful quotes to those better equipped to describe the unlikely sound of three banjos and the tuba. Eight years ago, the 30-year-old Powers was just a barber dreaming of the time when he could be a 30-year-old success in show business. No more does Powers take just a little off the sides, his cut now is strictly off the top. What kind of a Barber was he? 'One of the best,' he says without hesitation. Now, that's what others around the nation are saying about his Powerhouse IV band, the little ragtime group that found its way from Arlington to Manhattan in less than a year."

Ralph Sanford: I don't know how long Freddy had played banjo, but I hadn't played one until we started his club out there. Mine was a tenor banjo, and I tuned it like the first 4 strings of a guitar, and Bill Hudson tuned his the same way, like he was playing the first 4 strings of a guitar.

Ray Rogers: I started working at a place called The Levy in Houston in 1962 or 1963 in a banjo band and that's when I first met Paul Buskirk. Paul was an incredible musician, he could play flute, tenor banjo, which is different from how a lot of people who play banjo tune it like a guitar. Tenor banjo is tuned like a Viola, and I think Freddy played a Plectrum banjo, and Paul taught Freddy a lot as he taught me a lot. He would do it in a subtle way, not to say "Let me show you how to do that…", but more like "Try this." He was great in that way. I think they both had a great respect for each other because they were both professionals. They always dressed right, and they both worked hard at what they did. Paul told me that Freddy Powers was looking for somebody to come on the road with him, so I accepted the gig and Paul loaned me his car, and I drove up to meet Freddy in Hobbs, New Mexico. He was learning to play the trombone, and we were on the 2nd or 3rd floor and there was kind of a u-shaped building with a courtyard in the middle. If there wasn't anybody in the courtyard, he would lean out the window and play "Lassiter's Trombone!"

I played banjo, but in Freddy's band, I also played cocktail drums for the dance sets. Banjo shows were real popular back in those days. We went from there to Atlanta to play the Clintwood Club and from there to Puerto Rico to play the Roosevelt Air Force Base and on and off through the years, I worked for Freddy on the road. We'd play up in the Midwest too, and places like Iowa. Back in the 60s, one of the big things in the Midwest was Supper Clubs. For example, we played a place called Mason, Iowa, which they called the River City, at a place called Coastal Supper Club. The farmers would drive 90 miles in to have dinner and see a show, and especially back in those days, they LOVED the banjo stuff, and we'd do a really good dance set for them too.

Normally we'd play 45 on, 15 off, and we'd do a dance set, a show, a dance set, a show and then maybe another dance set. So he usually filled up 4 hours at least. Freddy always participated in the show too. He wasn't like a lot of guys who would let the band just play the dance sets and then he comes up for the show. He would play all through the night, he was a hard worker, oh my Gosh! Back in the olden days with the banjo band, he would do a lot of patriotic medleys. Then we'd do songs in the set like "*Do You Know What It Means to Listen to Arlene?*" "*Grand Ole Flag*," "*Give Our Regards to Broadway*," "*Yankee Doodle Dandy*," and a lot of old Dixieland stuff like "*Floating Down the River*" and "*Swanee*" by (Bill Bailey). Freddy used to enjoy the parties after the show too!

Don Powers Jr.: They did a 40s/50s show and dressed of that era in Zoot suits, and when they'd head for the stage, they'd come out of the elevator and would play walking all the way through the floor of the Casino – around the Blackjack tables, around the slot machines and then head to the showroom to do their show, and people loved that! They would parade in with Freddy up front playing the banjo, then a guy behind him with the clarinet and so forth, and they did Dixieland Jazz and Comedy.

Freddy Powers: "When I hear an audience exploding with real belly laughs, I get cold chills up and down my spine. I love this business now more than ever, and I intend to stay in it until they carry me on and off – and then I'll play dead! I never felt I was truly successful until I got into comedy. My show was in real demand!"

Freddy Powers Live, 1960s, Nevada Lounge:

*Ladies and Gentleman, I'd like to change
the pace a little bit for you tonight,
with this second song, actually. I'd like
to dedicate this to my wife, who is no longer
with us. She's in Nashville Tennessee
with all my money and my car
and a few other things! (laughs)*

*She had been on this see-food diet for years:
everything she'd see, she'd eat!
I mean, she got so big they finally gave
her own zip code. The other night she got arrested
going home. The policeman arrested her,
and threw her in jail. Woke her up the next morning
and said 'Lady, you got one phone call…'
She ordered a pizza! (laughs)*

*A funny footnote to the future,
years after I wrote that joke with my brother Don.
Pizza Oven used it in one of their most popular
commercials, and funny enough, after they closed up,
it started showing up on Domino's commercials.
And we never got credit or saw a dime for it! (laughs)*

*One other thing I'd like to say about my wife
that used to really get me, I mean, this one
used to really get me. I mean, this used to
really make me mad! Every time we'd start to
make love, she always kept her eyes closed.
She never could stand to see me having fun! (laughs)*

Ray Rogers: They LOVED Freddy, they really loved Freddy, because he was always so funny. Freddy was great at making funny faces, he always had a comical expression on his face. When I first met Freddy, he was always just funny all the time. One of the things he always wanted to do was keep the band laughing and happy. So he was constantly telling jokes and doing funny things. Freddy was always funny, and we all used to call him "Mr. Freddy," and I always loved working for him, that's for sure.

One of the funniest acts Freddy used to do on stage was something he called the Whistling Navel. It was something originally done by Spike Jones in his act. Freddy would wear this HUGE hat, kind of like a top hat, but big enough to put your arms up in and cover your head and your arms. Then he'd draw eyes on his nipples and paint a mouth on his naval, and below that he'd wear a sports coat, so it looked like it was this big head. He'd have one of the guys in the band from backstage whistle "*Anchors Away*" and he would come out and do that during the show at one point and people in the audience would just fall over laughing!

Ralph Sanford: Freddy loved being a host, you never knew what Freddy was going to do next! Freddy did a good job as front-man, he had a good rapport with the audience. Bill did one funny song where he sang, but the lead vocals were mainly Freddy and I, and we all did something. So Freddy would do one, then I would come up and sing one, and if we'd been doing some fast things then I would slow it down, because I did a lot of slow, pretty things. Freddy was really good at the fast ones, he had a good voice for that.

One night, before we started and before Freddy got there, I bought some Limburger cheese and taped it under his music stand where he couldn't see it. And BOY, that room got HOT as it filled with people. So as the night went on, that stuff started stinking. We were playing a real fast banjo thing and being an excellent guitarist, Bill Hudson could play lead on the banjo, and we were cooking! Well, when we got through with that, we were really going fast at the end, and Freddy looks over at me when we finished and said, "Boy, we were playing so fast my pick got to smelling!" He thought his pick got hot and started smelling! (laughs)

Don Powers Jr: Freddy used to play when he had the Dixieland band all over the state of Nevada: Elko, Wendover, Winnemucca, Las Vegas, Reno, pretty much everywhere. He was voted best Showroom Group two years in a row by Guy Richardson, who even bought a Cadillac for Freddy. My dad worked dealing blackjack at the El Dorado and I worked across the street. Freddy played mostly at the El Dorado Casino in Reno, Nevada. They had Freddy redesign the showroom and he put red velvet all over the walls and hung banjos all over to decorate it. He was the house band there and really started to pull that Casino out of the red after that.

Freddy Powers: "One slow night at Harvey's Casino playing opposite the DeCastro Sisters the place was completely empty. I stripped down to my shorts, pulled on the long zoot suit jacket and slunk out into the chairs in front of the stage. Peggy DeCastro about melted into the stage."

Augie Savage: "The best music I ever played was with Freddy. Every real musician wanted to play with Freddy, because he lets them play."

B.B. Morse: I met Freddy in the early 70s, but was aware of him before I met him, and was a part of that audience many times before I became more closely associated with him. The magic and fascination he created, and level of talent of the individual players in the band, and if you were there to see something extraordinary, it never missed. There was a certain amount of the show that was pre-planned, the rest of what happened was serendipity.

Freddy had a strobe light going inside his banjo while he played, and the band was very animated, it was Vaudevillian. Being a bassist, I was always attracted to the character and the melodic presentation of the bass. So I zeroed in on Deanie Bird and Milton Quackenbush, and they were always having fun on stage but it was controlled chaos. The banter and the slapstick comedy, it's like an assignment, so you'd go out there and its everybody's job on the stage to connect with one or two people close to the stage, and that draws an attraction. So you do a little sideshow as you're building it up. These were sold-out shows, it was overflowing into the pit area with people standing around cock-tailing. It would be 2:45 - 3:30 in the morning when he was doing those last shows.

Freddy Powers: I was always meeting new musicians and new people at every engagement. I like most people can't remember ever person's name I meet.

CHAPTER 4: DIAMOND GEM'S

Lilydale, Minnesota, 1968.

Freddy Powers: As an entertainer, you get used to playing lots of crazy clubs and casinos. With dizzying backgrounds between the spinning slot machines, the crowd going 110 miles an hour on the dance floor, cocktail waitresses zig-zagging between the blackjack tables carrying drinks. But NOTHING compared to the circus going on up at a dinner club I played way up in Lilydale, Minnesota called Diamond Gem's every winter in the late 60s.

> **Bev Dunbar**, Waitress, Diamond Gem's: In its day, it was perfect. It was located at one end of what you could call a Frontier town. A strip that had all sorts of little shops, and at either end, there was the Supper Club. It was the white table cloth dining. We had orchestras down at that end. Like Clyde McCoy was down there, and at the other end was called the MAIN club called Diamond Gem's, and that's where the main acts played.
>
> On the inside of the main club, it was all 1900s decor, of a Diamond Gem era. A lot of red velvet, the walls were textured with velvet decor on it. We had great big huge pictures hanging on the walls of very big, heavy set women in very sexy poses in 1900s dresses. We had a lot of those pictures around. The stage was one you'd think you'd see in the 1900s, and on that main stage, you couldn't dance up there, so it was strictly for show. We had two shows a night, a 7 o'clock show and a 9 o'clock show. Sometimes, depending on the popularity of the act, you'd have to put on a 3rd show.

Mike Kelleher, Bartender, Diamond Gem's: There were two shows, and usually a couple hundred people per show, so I'd say 400 – 600 people a night, because some would come to the 6 o'clock show and others to the 9 o'clock show. They had over 100,000 people who had memberships there. You paid $10 a year for their membership card, and $20 in later years, and showed your card and were let in. You paid for your meal and drinks, but right off the bat they had over $100,000 to pay for the entertainment. The owners liked Freddy very much. He was a favorite of the owners, and the manager, he was there quite a bit. He used to have other gigs where he'd go for months and them come back.

Diamond Gem's was originally a character in New York and who it was named after, and there was a club called Diamond Lowell in Minneapolis. Diamond Gems opened around 1966 and I worked there for 14 years. When I first started, the bar was open, and they had two great big nude paintings hanging above the bar! It was like early 1900s kind of era. There was an organ that would come up through the floor and go down through the floor, it was like a garage door that would kind of fold, and this pipe organ would come up through the floor and that would start the night. Then Freddy, if he was playing, would do his show, then another act would do a show after that, and it was quite a night.

Freddy Powers: The snow would be falling, but every night the place was still packed! It was an old-20s saloon-style private dinner club. My band and I would play on the stage while trapeze girls would be swinging from the ceiling down over the heads of diners and the band and then back up again. It was a wild thing to watch, let me tell you, because while the paying guests ate dinner and listened to us play, there was a circus act going on around them through the whole show at the same time. It was hard competition for the crowd who couldn't take their eyes off them while the girls were flying through the air, you could hear their gasps as they sailed two and fro.

Bev Dunbar: The ceilings were very tall, I tell you, if I'd ever gotten up on one of those swings I'd have had a nose bleed, because you were really up high. These girls had to have some athletic ability to do this too, because they would hang by their toes, they didn't just swing back and forth, but did Trapeze acting, which was a lot more acrobatic. They threw garters at the people in the audience as they swung by. They were dressed in the 1900s outfits, and of course the customers loved that!

Mike Kelleher: Usually, where Freddy played, right in front of the stage, there would be one trapeze girl, and there were several swingers. They'd swing before each show. I knew about 10 of them, one was an airline stewardess named Holly, and her stage name was Holly Hudson. So she would swing there every night that she wasn't flying, and she swung twice a night. When they swung, she came down by her knees, head down towards the ground, and her hands out, and then she'd come back down. When she swang back to the bar, the maître d' would grab her waist and help her down a little bit, and I did that once but was afraid I'd drop her. Then she'd take a bow and walk off.

Freddy Powers from the stage:

Aren't they something! Let's give these
talented girls a hand Ladies and Gentleman!
It's time for us to present our big Musical
extravaganza! I'd like to sing a Cowboy
song for you, and before I sing this cowboy
song, I would like to say that the only reason
I sing cowboy songs is because they don't write
good Sheep Boy songs! (audience laughs)

Vs 1

Well I drove a herd of cattle
down from old Nebraska way
that's how I came to be
in the state of Iowa
I met a gal in Iowa
Her eyes were big and blue
I asked her what her name was?
She said "Sioux City Sue,"

Chorus
Sioux City Sue
Oh little lady
with those pretty eyes so blue
And I'd swap my horse
and my dog for you
Sioux City Sue
Oh little lady
there ain't no gal as true
as my sweet Sioux City Sue

(Written by Gene Autry)

Mike Kelleher: I knew Freddy, Freddy was a character. He told me he'd never had a cavity in his head ever, and I said "That can't be true. That water in Texas must have been hard, hard water!" He was kind of a regular group there, Freddy Powers and the Powerhouse IV. He had 4 or 5 guys in the band, and one of them was local, named Dan Steenblock who played the Trumpet. He had a trombone player and drummer too, and Freddy played the guitar and banjo and sang. He had one guy who played the horn, and he would get up above the bar on this narrow ledge – this is before they put a seating area above the bar – and he'd play the tune "*Man With a Horn*" while they had the spotlight on him. Then they'd go back down to the stage for Freddy's next song. He was married to his second wife Melody then, boy was she gorgeous. She would sit at the end of the bar while the show was on and I'd serve her drinks, she was a real nice gal.

Bev Dunbar: I worked at the Main Club most of the time, and at the Supper club. Over at the main club, the crowds were always extremely lively, it was always a very happy crowd. A lot of people of course knew each other **as** this was a Member's club. You couldn't just go to Diamond Gem's, you had to be a member, and back then, to get in, you had to put your card in a slot in the door for it to open. Memberships were $20 at the time, and back in the 60s, that was a lot of money to spend and buy dinner, a lot of people came quite often to the club. There was a buffet at the main club that had real good food, and you ate first and had your cocktails. You'd have to order 2 or 3 cocktails BEFORE the show because there was no serving of cocktails during the shows.

The shows would always be packed, and people enjoyed Freddy, they always came when he was there. People would come down to the Supper Club at 7 o'clock and have dinner and then they'd go up to the main club for the 9 o'clock show. Or vice verse, and sometimes they had an 11 o'clock show. For instance we had Phil Foster once, who was on Laverne and Shirley, and we had so many people they were standing on the rafters trying to see him. Some of the shows were so full at the main club that they'd come down and do a 3rd show at the supper club too. Freddy's band played up at the main club, but in between shows, they'd come down to the supper club and have a cocktail and visit with people he knew down there. It was a very family friendly atmosphere. We'd all been there a long time, you got to know the entertainers, and it was just a great place to work.

Up at the main club, we also had what was called The Banker's Room, which was a big, square room – you could call it the Peanut room – because they threw peanuts on the floor. They had salted peanuts in shells on all the tables and you could eat those and throw the shells on the floor, and that was really an old-time bar-saloon. It had the swinging doors when you walked in and the old-fashioned wooden tables and chairs.

They always had an act in there, either a piano player with a straw hat on that played ragtime or fun songs you could sing to, or they'd have a comedian, or a singer playing in there. I remember once there was one gal I remember they had play in there from Seattle and she was wonderful. She was a riot, she'd put down people when they walked in, just a good comedian and very funny. When the main show was over, people always tried to get into the Banker's Room right away, that was another fun part of Diamond Gem's.

Freddy Powers: Our band used to back whoever came through there as a headliner. Whether it was Jerry Van Dyke, Dick Van Dyke's brother, Buddy Sorrell, Louis Nye, Maureen O'Hara, and Lesley Gore, who was best known for her signature hit *"It's My Party (And I'll Cry If I Want To)"* to name a few. I got to be pretty good friends with many of them. Louie and I hung out together, and I played banjos a lot with Jerry Van Dyke.

Bev Dunbar: Freddy was in what I pretty much called an Okobojo group. They were bands that played in different night clubs from Illinois all the way up to North Dakota, but it started there, and then Madison, Wisconsin, and the Playboy Club in Geneva. It was a circuit of places that Diamond Gem's was part of, so we always knew when Freddy was coming through town, but ALL those groups were *really good*. Sometimes down at the Supper Club, Maury Amsterdam, Bob Hope, Pat O'Brien, the Diamonds, the Suns of the Pioneers, Helen O'Connell, who did *"Green Eyes"* with Bob Everly. We had Charo there, which was kind of fun, and Bobby Rydel, Frank Avalon, and Carmel Quinn would perform. George Goba would come down to the supper club and have lunch every day and sit with the help. We had an act, Lloyd Limrock, who played Jazz harp and had an orchestra, and Clyde McCoy, we'd pack the house when he was there. We had some big name 6 piece orchestras.

Freddy had a real fun show, and he was a really funny emcee of his group, The Powerhouse IV. They had a trumpet player named Danny Steamblock who was just excellent, he'd play different trumpets, and they were all good musicians. They played fun songs and Freddy and they would all sing. Freddy, oh God was he a good banjo player! Everybody loved Freddy and they loved his music. He'd play a Country and Western set that was good and he did some Bluegrass that would just knock your socks off. Then they had a comedy routine they did and they played some of the big band songs of way back and did a lot of Dixieland. They pretty much could play ANYTHING! It was a very electric show, you weren't talking during his show, you watched it. Freddy had such a cute accent, a real Texas accent, that he kind of put on even more during the show. He was one hell of a musician and a funny person off the stage too, just a really nice guy.

Mike Kelleher: Freddy was quite a character. He played a joke on another act one time. A comic named Larry King Cole from Chicago who did a drunk act, guzzling water down pretending it was Gin. Well, Freddy filled it up with Gin one time and he had to do it in front of an audience because what was he going to do. He got back at Freddy soon after that. Sometimes he would go through the audience with his band, play a tune and then go back to the stage. But he had to go back through a hall way to get on the stage through a door. Harry locked the door one night so he couldn't get on the stage! That was to get even with him for putting real Gin in his gin bottle!

Freddy was kind of a house band for a while, because the Swinging Ambassadors were the house band after Freddy. Freddy played both winter and summer seasons over the years, so he was there quite often. He had a part of his show called The Hat Act, where he'd put a big top hat on his head, and he'd be whistling "*Sailor's Away*" with his Belly Button! So you didn't really see his head, his head was his stomach, and his eyes were his nipples, and he did this whistling act.

Freddy Powers from the stage:

Thank You folks! You know, I got in an automobile accident a while back, and had to take a little break from the stage to go see the doctor, you've probably been there yourself. I went to my doctor's office, he gave me six months to live, and when I didn't pay my bill so he gave me six more months...
Boy, while I was there, the doc was checking me out, you know, and asked me once, 'You ever suffer from Hemorrhoids?', and I answered back 'Well hell yes, what the hell else are you supposed to do with them?!'

Bev Dunbar: After the show, Freddy and the boys would always be looking to keep the good times rolling. Some of us waitresses even lived together, and we'd have after work parties. Freddy would go to all of them. Everybody would unwind after a full night of working, and pretty much you'd go to somebody's house. There would be all sorts of people who would come, and there would be food and cocktails and lots of laughs about what happened that night or the night before. Or we'd go out and have breakfast, and Freddy would go. Frank Fontaine was a great one for going to the bathroom when the bill came.

Mike Kelleher: Freddy used to stay across the street at a Motel called Mendota Heights Motel. I went over there and he cut my hair and some of the other fellas a few times. His whole group stayed at that motel.

Freddy Powers: I made pretty good friends with a lot of my fellow acts who passed through. Jerry Van Dyke and I used to set around playing banjos, and Louis Nye picked me out of the crowd when I first met him. He pointed at me and said "You're the one," wanting to get stoned and knowing at first sight I was the usual suspect.

> **Bev Dunbar:** He was a musician, and he was always high and up. He was always funny and I don't ever remember seeing him sad. Maybe mad about his Cadillac, but other than that, that's the most happy he'd have been. Let me tell you that Cadillac story! (laughs) I remember one fall he'd gotten a brand new red Cadillac, and he was so excited about it. He came up to the supper club and got my husband, who'd just driven me to work, and said. "Come take a ride with me in my new Cadillac." It was kind of a hazy day, it wasn't a real nice day, and had been raining the last few days before that. So then we went down towards the Mississippi in Lillydale, and there are roads down there that were pretty bad, well they got stuck down there in the mud in this brand new Cadillac. And they couldn't get it out! He had a show coming up that night, and of course, they didn't have cell phones then. So they had to walk all muddy through Lillydale up to this real exclusive place called the Pool and Yacht Club, and to call somebody to come down and get them. Then Freddy had to pay to have the car towed out of there, this brand new beautiful Cadillac that was full of mud! We laughed that night about that so hard, because that was the first day he got it and he had to have it towed out of there.

Freddy Powers: Whenever we weren't playing, one of my favorite pastimes was when me and the boys would go bar-hopping on snow mobiles! See it was so cold up there and the snow was sometimes so deep from falling almost constantly that you couldn't have gotten up the street in a car. You would have frozen to death trying to walk in what was sometimes 3 to 4 feet of snow. So we'd strap on our goggles and ride 2 or 3 people sometimes on same snow mobile. (Diamond Gem's owned), and off we'd go!

Bev Dunbar: Freddy was one of the gang, when he came he knew everybody, and the main club was closed Monday night so I'm sure they went out on Monday nights. They used to bar hop along what's called Highway 13, and you could go to a little bar called Dandy's, and further down 13 to a place called Parker House, which was a very nice supper club, and next door to that was a bar, and one across the street. All in this little tiny, tiny town called Mendota. So that's what Freddy and the boys would do, go as far as that and then back up 13 to Diamond Gem's. They could have driven down, but thought it was more fun to ride in snow mobiles!

Freddy Powers: I loved playing in the snow for a while, but it wasn't too long before I found myself heading back home to the warm desert air of Nevada to return to my headlining gigs on the Casino circuit.

"Hired to lead the house band at the Stardust, the flagship enterprise of Allen Glick's Chicago Mafia-backed Argent Corp., in the plush red booths at the back of the lounge, Powers spent his evenings drinking with notorious gangsters like Lefty Rosenthal and Tony Spilotro, who were running operations at the Stardust behind titled fronts like 'Entertainment Director'. Rosenthal and Spilotro would later become the inspiration for Robert DeNiro and Joe Pesci's characters in the film Casino.." – THE AUSTIN CHRONICLE

Freddy Powers Casino Comedy Show - Early 1970s

CHAPTER 5: THE CASINO DAYS

Freddy Powers
(live from the El Dorado Stage):

Good Evening Ladies and Gentleman! I tell you what, you have to be careful who you pick a fight with in a Honky Tonk because they do NOT fight fair! For instance, this guy one time said 'I'm gonna whip your ass!', and I threw my hands back there for protection and he hit me right in the nose! He kept saying, 'You're the one who keeps spreading those rumors all over town that my wife has a wart on her breast!', and I said 'Sir, that's the way rumors get started. I didn't say your wife had a wart on her left breast, I said it 'Felt like a wart.'" (loud laughs from crowd)

Milton Quackenbush: I met Freddy in the late 60s when I saw him perform in my hometown of Houston, Texas. He was fantastic, what a great showman, and very professional, and all the Powerhouse V Band was top of the line. Freddy was an entertainer, and that you don't see too many of, they're mostly all singers. Back home in Houston, Freddy used to play a lot at the Village Inn Pizza Parlor, which was fantastic. He's a great banjo player, and his comedy was superb, just all around a great entertainer.

Troy Powers: My dad Wallace was the oldest sibling in the Powers family, and my dad got Freddy started basically, they were all in a band together with Don, Jerry, Freddy, and Wallace, called the Circle W Boys. Back then, there was a phone number on the head of the bass drum to call for bookings. When Freddy would come through town, the family would always get together to make music. In fact, I remember one time when Freddy was playing the Golden Rooster in Odessa. I was just a little kid, probably in the 7th grade, and all our parents' went to see him, but they wouldn't let me go. So one night, I got my buddy Scott to talk his mom into taking us to Odessa – which was a good 60 miles away – to see her mother, Scott's grandmother, who stayed home while we went "to the rodeo." So after the rodeo, we were staying at a hotel that was just around the corner from the Golden Rooster, so Scott and I snuck out to watch the show. Freddy told me later from up on stage, "All I could see were the tops of these two little cowboy hats in the back!" (laughs)

Milton Quackenbush: Freddy was playing up in Minnesota, and I heard he was going to be up there and a lot of the guys in the band were from my hometown. So I went up to check out the show and afterward, Freddy took me aside and said, "Hey, listen, my keyboard player's going to be leaving the group pretty soon, would you be interested in joining?" I immediately said "Yeah, you BET I WOULD!" In the beginning when I joined the Powerhouse IV, it was just four pieces. Bob Minetti on drums and trumpet, Larry Kinsora on Clarinet and Saxophone, myself on organ and trombone, and Freddy on lead with banjo. Freddy was a great producer and entertainer, that's the word I really like to stress, because besides being a great songwriter and player, he was great with the audience and knew what to do, and his comedy was excellent. From there, we headed to Nevada.

The first gig I did with Freddy was in Elko, Nevada at the Commercial Hotel. We had to really watch the volume in those places. We did all the little small towns like Jackpot, Nevada and back then there was nothing there but 3 little casinos, but now, it's a big high-rise place, and we worked Wendover, Nevada, which we used to call Bendover. (Laughs) I remember one time we were in Wendover, and the crowd could care less if you're on stage performing because it was a show bar. One day before our set, Freddy said, "Come on guys, I want to get you all high," and we didn't mess around that much because we were all drinkers. But Freddy insisted, "Oh no, come on, ain't nobody gonna know because nobody's going to notice anyway..." So we all got stoned with Freddy, and did a real fast opener that night called "Avalon," and as the curtains were going up, it was already falling apart. Freddy was standing behind me playing, and I turned to him and said "Brother Fred, Brother Fred, we're losing it! We're losing it!", but we kept on playing. It was terrible really, but after the show, Freddy said "They probably didn't even notice!" (laughs)

When we weren't on stage playing, most the time, we'd hang out, stay up all night and drink and Freddy would get high. After we got off work sometimes, we'd find a place to go where we could sit in and play some more music. Hawthorne, Nevada was another one of those little towns we played, these desert gigs out there, there was nothing to do really, except if you're a heavy drinker or else you gambled. That's about all there was to do. One time we played Hawthorne, and Freddy was carrying around 2 banjos with him, and we just went over to the dressing room before the show and started jamming just the two of us. Another time, when we played Carson City, we got to know the owner down at this little local bar called The Timbers, and he had a piano in there. So a lot of times, when we got done with the show, we'd go down there and stay till the sun came up, drinking and playing. Of course we got free drinks, that's why we did it, and we did that wherever we could. We had certain spots and they'd take care of us.

Freddy Powers: Reno was a top-notch party town, especially if you were living in a penthouse apartment on top of a hot hotel and casino. It was just a great party atmosphere. I was the star of the nightly show, I was one of the most popular entertainers in Reno back then. After the show each night, I had my pick of a WHOLE lot-ta ladies to choose from every night, and I say Ladies because some of them became good friends I even wrote a poem about it:

There are some ladies
that know I did wrong
Because I was weak
When I should have been strong

There are some that I loved
And some that I used
Some that were willing
And some that refused

*We took of the things
That would cloud up our minds
And loosen resistance
For a sexual time*

*The touch of a woman
The world's greatest high
I'm addicted to women
Till the day that I die*

Freddy Powers: I make no apologies for my party days, it was fun and one more source of some good memories. That may sound somewhat corny, but that's just the way that I am, addictions come in all different flavors, and sex is mine (laughs), like it is for millions probably. That's why the music business was a natural setting for guys like me. I know people that spend their life looking for sex but would never admit that they were addicted to it. I'm to this day, still addicted to sex, I'm happily married now and true to my wife Catherine. She doesn't mind that I'm somewhat oversexed (she's a willing participant! ☺). There are some ladies that I know I did wrong, because I was weak when I should have been strong. There's some that I loved and some that I used and some that were willing and some that refused. For a sexual time, the touch of the woman was the world's greatest high. I'm addicted to women till the day I die.

Milton Quackenbush: Whenever we weren't in Reno playing shows and out on the road, we'd visit Brothels quite often. A legendary brothel owner named Mona had a nice piano over there, and the first time Freddy and I went into Mona's – which had a bar attached to the brothel – to get a drink. So Freddy went outside and got his banjo and we started playing and that place was jumping in there. After a few hours, Mona came out and Freddy said, "Look, we're going to have to go, we have to find a room tonight," and she said "No you're not, both you guys are going to stay here." So she gave us a room each, and when we got up the next morning, the gals came in and said "Hey, Mona told me to take care of you before you leave!" I said "Wow." Sometimes, we'd just go in those places just to have a drink.

Freddy Powers: I had worked several years in Las Vegas and Reno before coming to the Eldorado. After years on the road, in the mid-1970s, we'd finally landed a dream-sit down gig at the Eldorado Hotel/Casino in Reno. The family who owned the hotel, the Corona family, was a wonderful Italian family with three boys, one girl and father Don Corona running the family business. They were always good to me and all my memories of the family and casino are among my favorites. I was the Entertainment Director and did a show with my band at the El Dorado Hotel and Casino in Reno. I was also called the Swinging Ambassador of Good Will.

B.B. Morse: During the El Dorado days, Freddy had power of the pen, which meant he could get someone a room for the night, or a meal, or free passes to a show. He could even sign for them to get a marker to go play on the tables.

Freddy Powers: With the Power of the pen to buy anything in the hotel for anyone I chose. I kept half of Reno drunk for three or four years!! (laughs) I lived on top of the hotel in a suite and the party always wound up in my suite almost every night. Why not, the whole damn thing was free and everyone knew it. The hotel people weren't so dumb giving me the Power of the Pen, because these guests of mine would wind up spending half the night in the casino, drunk out of their minds gambling (shall I say more).

B.B. Morse: That penthouse, any time I was up there, it was always PACKED with people. He was right there on the backside of the banks of the Truckee River. He had a hot tub in his room, and there's always be a bunch of girls up there having a hot tub party.

Milton Quackenbush: Everybody knew who Freddy was, he was friends with everyone. The big thing for Freddy back then was the El Dorado Hotel, and we did 3 shows a night. Our schedule back then was usually you played for 6 hours, but you were on one hour, then off the next while another band played, and we usually started about 8 at night, and got off around 2 AM. It all depended on what shift you were on. They had a nice, cozy little showroom that would seat about 100, so you could be really close to the people in there. That was Freddy's main thing, interacting with the audience. Entertaining people, you've got to be right on top of them.

J. Gary Smith: I was an artist on RCA Records, then I was on Capitol, Elektra, I toured all over the country, played Vegas, and have played shows with everybody. I first met Freddy way back at the beginning of both our careers, and back then, all of the big Hotels had showrooms, the Ramada's, Hilton s, etc. We had them big in Houston, had our own circuit we all played on, and they paid us real good money.

We all did floor shows back then, we didn't do dance sets, so it was a Vegas-style presentation. I played the guitar and would work the floor taking requests, and my band played the house music for the dancers. So we'd do a dance set and then a 9 o'clock or 10 o'clock show. Freddy played some of those, but we never played them together. He loved the life of an entertainer – the babes, the booze, the whole thing he was always the life of the party. If you were in a room with Freddy, you were going to be having fun! He was just that way.

BB Morse: Freddy was KING of the strip! He drove a brand-new Cadillac every year, and it was generally a convertible as I recall, and held the title of Ambassador of Good Will. With his late shows, whoever was in town, even if they were in Lake Tahoe, they came down to Reno for Freddy's last show and his band hosted a litany of stars. If they were in the business, they knew Freddy and they knew if they saw Freddy's show, they were going to get their socks knocked off.

Freddy Powers
(live from the El Dorado Stage):

*Good Evening folks, we're going to treat
you this evening to a tribute to the great
Spike Jones and the City Slickers. The song we
opened with was called "Cocktails for Two" and
this next number is "The Führer In Space."*

*Alright Ladies and Gentleman, at this time,
we're going to begin our musical extravaganza!
I'm going to play a banjo solo, now before I play this banjo solo,
I would like to mention that last summer, I had the pleasure
of performing this banjo solo in Carnegie, Arkansas! (audience laughs)
This is my banjo solo, and I've been playing this for about 10 years
now and I never had a title for it till about a week ago.
I was driving down the road and it came to me,
the title for my banjo solo... Ladies and Gentleman,
I call this 'My Banjo Solo!' We ready boys?*

*One thing I would like to say, some people ask me,
they say "Freddy, would you mind showing us a few things
on the banjo, so I thought tonight, I'd give you a little lesson,
and if you play very close attention, I promise you
you'll play the banjo when you leave tonight!"
"Another thing you need to know is how to put a banjo on,
now I'm going to demonstrate for you now folks.
'Hey Banjo, you want to come up to my room and get high?'"
(crowd claps loudly) After instructing the crowd on the basics
of the up and down stroke on the banjo, Freddy closes with
"Down, up and with a hat trick!" (audience roars in applause)*

B.B. Morse: Before the show, Freddy and the boys would go out as a second line. Freddy had a banjo, and he had his trumpet, trombone, and saxophone players with him, and they'd walk through the Casino amongst the gamblers and Ragtime it through the Casino floor, then walk up on stage, plug in and start playing. I remember the first time when I met Freddy backstage at The Fitzgerald. I was playing in a different band and we were trading sets, so when we were getting ready to switch, we ran into each other in the hallway. It was show time, so I complimented him on the outfits they were wearing and how cool the show was.

Milton Quackenbush: During the show, we did all sorts of routines. We did a 1940s show where the whole band was unified in Zoot suits, talk about wild in color, we had all different colors up there! Zoot suits had replete pants that were real baggy with long coats that went with them, and then a chain that's hooked on the side where the belt loop is, and we wore two-tone shoes.

During the 40s show, Freddy had a strobe light in front of the banjo, and he'd be playing "*El Cumbuchero*" and then we'd go into "*Lady of Spain*," and then on the last chorus, we'd play it real fast and turn the strobe light up to its fastest setting and at the same time, turn the lights out, and it looked really cool! The audience would always say "Wow, is that awesome or what!" Then, for the Dixieland Jazz show, we wore Knickers with argyle socks, high-top shoes and burglar caps and did lots of Dixieland standards, like "*That's a Play*," "*Dixie One Step*," "*Avalon*," "*Farm House Blues*," and then of course his comedy routines. Then Freddy did this preacher routine. He was Brother Fred, who was a screaming preacher, but it was all comedy!

He was first class, a GREAT banjo player. Back when he had his banjo band before I started playing with him, they used to do all that Ragtime stuff, "*World's Waiting for the Sunrise*," etc. We had another routine where we all had Whigs, one was the Andrews' Sisters, and we also did the Ink Spots, and then we had a whole segment that was our tribute to Spike Jones and the City Slickers. Some of the songs we played were Spike Jones' "*Cocktails for Two*." The Spike Jones set is really where the comedy was, so when Freddy did "*The Führer in Space*," he wore a military hat with a swastika on it, Freddy was fearless on stage.

He did one where he was crying all the time, he would do all these one-liners, that was phenomenal, we'd all be cracking up in the band every time he did it. He'd deliver all these one-liners while crying, "I went to my doctor's office, he gave me six months to live, I didn't pay my bill so he gave me six more months..." Or "The doc asked me once, 'You ever suffer from

Hemorrhoids?' " Then he did a Boy scout Marching song, where he wore buck-teeth and the scout masters hat.

Freddy Powers
(live from the El Dorado Stage):

"Ladies and Gentleman, I'd like to change the pace a little bit for you tonight, with this second song, actually I'd like to dedicate this to my wife, who is no longer with us. She's in Nashville Tennessee with all my money and my car and a few other things!" (laughs) "She had been on this see-food diet for years: everything she'd see, she'd eat!

I mean, she got so big they finally gave her own zip code. The other night she got arrested going home. The policeman got her arrested, threw her in jail, woke her up the next morning and said 'Lady, you got one phone call...' She ordered a pizza!" (audience roars in laughter)

"One other thing I'd like to say about my wife that used to really get me, I mean, this one used to really get me. I mean, this used to really make me mad! Every time we'd start to make love, she always kept her eyes closed. She never could stand to see me having fun!" (laughs)

Freddy Powers: Many big-time entertainers came by to see my band back in those days, and a lot would sit in with the band, including Willie Nelson. I remember Willie was playing Harrah's when I was across the street at Harvey's Hotel/Casino once when he came over to sit in with me and my band. They wound up having to shut down the gambling tables around the lounge because it filled up with so many people that were crowding in to see us. It got so crazy so quickly that the dealers couldn't tell who was playing on the tables and who wasn't.

Milton Quackenbush: In 1978, we received the Best Lounge Act in Reno Award, and were doing a show and they stopped the music, came up on stage, and presented Freddy with a trophy.

Freddy Powers (right and Willie Nelson, late 1970s

CHAPTER 6: OVER THE RAINBOW

Freddy Powers: As a professional gigging musician, when you're a constantly traveling on tour to different cities and gigs, you share stage time or tour bills with plenty of peers and great players that you may enjoy sharing the stage with but typically expect you'll never see most of them again. You file those great nights of music you shared together away in your favorite Gigging Memories and move along to the next one. Those roles changed for me once I became the Ambassador of Good Will at the El Dorado in the 2nd half of the 1970s, where I had a steady headlining gig and would see my friends whenever they'd come through town.

Every once in a while, my old friend Willie Nelson would come through Reno headlining his own gigs across the street from the El Dorado at Harrah's or another Casino on the strip. The people that owned the Hotel and Casino were the Corona Family, and many big time entertainers came to see my band back in those days, and a lot of them would sit in with the band – including Willie. That was funny because it always drove the Casino floor managers nuts as half their gamblers would rush away from the games and tables and into the lounge as soon as they heard Willie start to sing! (laughs) Reconnecting with Willie would turn out to be the next big break in my career in the music business, and would mark my return to the recording studio for the first time in years.

The surprise invitation came one afternoon when Willie was in Reno, and he, I and another friend of mine, Nate Green, had all headed out to play a game of golf together. For anyone who doesn't know, Willie Nelson is not only one of country music's greatest golfers, but he would go on in the 80s to in fact own and live on his very own golf course, and hold his own celebrity golf tournaments for decades. While we were out on the course, Willie and I had got to talking about the old musicians we knew and soon got around to Django Reinhart. At the time, Willie was as hot as a Texas Tornado. The last thing I expected that day was his out-of-the-blue invitation at the game to help him produce, sing and play on his next studio album, which became the Grammy-Award-winning *Somewhere Over the Rainbow*.

Willie Nelson: *Over the Rainbow*, which Freddy produced, is one of my favorite albums. We've been in the studio many times together and I enjoyed all of them. He's a lot of fun to play with, and when Freddy was at his best, there was nobody better at what he did. I think *Rainbow* is one of the best albums I ever did because Freddy and Buskirk and Dean Reynolds were playing on it.

Freddy Powers: "I sang a little bit, on five or six of the tunes on the album, including '*I'm Gonna Sit Right Down and Write Myself a Letter*.' A lot of people didn't know it, because the disc jockeys that played it wouldn't say it, and a matter of fact, a lot of them didn't know that it was me singing on it. It was really strange, because every now and then somebody, they'd find out that it was me and they'd be real surprised because they'd heard it a lot of times and you know, somebody close to me sometimes, and all of a sudden, they'd find out two or three years later."

Willie Nelson: Freddy's strongest suit, I always thought, was his rhythm guitar playing. He was a great rhythm guitar player. I liked Django Reinhardt, and Django's brother was a great rhythm guitar player. Freddy and Paul Buskirk both were the two best rhythm guitar players – other than Django's brother – that I've ever known.

Freddy Powers: "The biggest influence in my life is Django Reinhardt. In the 50s, I was introduced to Django. I was drawn to that fiery acoustic rhythm with Stephane Grappelli on the fiddle. What people don't realize is Western swing was framed right out of that style of music. I'm not saying that Django is the king of Western Swing, but he's up there with Emit Miller. He had a band back in the Milton Brown days. Johnny Gimble gave me some Emit Miller stuff and believe it or not, that's where a lot of the Bob Wills came from. I also heard a song on an Emmett Miller tape '*Got a Feeling That Blue, Oh Lord*' just like Hank sang. Years before Hank did it!"

Rolling Stone Magazine 4-Star Album Review, June 11, 1981: "Somewhere over the Rainbow further establishes Willie Nelson as country music's preeminent conservator of America's pop tradition...Somewhere over the Rainbow is a lively acoustic record of simpler material, made in Texas, with no frills. Utilizing only a fiddle, a stand-up bass, a mandolin and guitars, the arrangements suggest a spontaneous musicale whose inspirations range from Django Reinhardt to Bob Wills to Les Paul. This all-purpose period sound perfectly complements Willie Nelson's Lone Star gypsy persona. Alternating with him on lead vocals is Freddie Powers, a Reno bandleader whose more casual swing style makes a nice contrast to Nelson's intensity...Somewhere over the Rainbow may be the most audacious album thus far in the revivalist phase of Nelson's career."

Freddy Powers: It was a proud moment for me and Willie after so many years to both still be here. By then he was a superstar, and almost as famous as Willie Nelson himself was his legendary guitar Trigger. The same guitar in fact he was playing back in the 50s when he and I were first starting out in the business together. I used to joke that I knew Willie before the hole. If you look closely at it when he's performing on TV, you'll notice there are names if all his closest friends signatures on that guitar, including yours truly. Funny, while some have rubbed off, because I was lucky to be around often. Occasionally I'd pick up Trigger and refresh my signature to the point mine is carved in there permanently. *Somewhere Over the Rainbow* went platinum, and Willie had credited me as the album's primary producer, so once it went to #1 on the Billboard Top Country Albums chart, overnight it was certainly a boost to my career.

The success of Willie's Grammy-winning *Over the Rainbow* album put a spotlight on me in the record business I hadn't had since the 50s. Willie and I loved playing guitar together off stage as much as on, and at first guess, while you might assume whenever he came through Reno that our favorite post-show past-time was partying, but it was actually PICKIN! Willie and I, both accomplished guitar players by then, would get together wherever he was staying, every night after the shows and sit around for hours smoking joints and picking on our acoustic guitars together! We had a regular flow of stars passing through town who would join us for those pickin' parties, and one day we were over at Bill Harrah's house, we were sitting around that afternoon when none other than Merle Haggard walked in the room!

Of all the country singers I had ever met, Merle made the greatest impact on me when I met him. That day, he was with his then-wife Leona Williams, and I'll have to admit Leona was the first one I saw, and I was thinking that she was a very beautiful lady. Then as Merle strolled in with his semi-cocky walk and all eyes in the room would follow him around, there was no doubt that he had a special "star charisma" about him. I laid my guitar down and walked over a little nervous, introduced myself, and to my surprise, Merle replied, "Freddy Powers, I love the work you did on Willie's new album *Somewhere Over the Rainbow*." He said that it was his favorite album at the time, and I must say I was so flattered that I didn't really know what to say. That same night Merle and I had started getting reacquainted, and as an interesting footnote: we'd actually met nearly 20 years before in the very early 1960s when we were both unknowns starting out on the Casino circuit when I was doing my comedy show and he was playing bass for Wynn Stewart.

> **Merle Haggard:** Over the years, I'd hear about different things, and as the years went by, things got good for me and good for Fred, and I don't think we ran into each other again for about 20 years. By then, around 1980, Fred had been working in Reno across the street from Harrah's at the El Dorado. He'd been doing mainly Dixieland up until that time, and was interested in trying to get deeper into country music, and I wanted to play guitar. We got together there, I think the first time we actually played together, we played for 18 hours up there at Harrah's in Reno.

Freddy Powers: After Willie had gone to his gig, we got our guitars out and began to pick. I had my bass player and best friend Dean Reynolds with me, we called him Deanie Bird. The two of us were the rhythm section with Merle and Willie taking turns on lead guitar. Merle really liked our style of swing and Dixieland jazz. Willie had to leave after a little bit to go and play his show, but the three of us – Deanie Bird, Merle and I – continued to play almost all night long, which turned into days and days of picking. Merle just couldn't get enough. I didn't realize it at the time but Merle was learning jazz from us. Not far out jazz, but country jazz.

> **Merle Haggard:** We really enjoyed playing together because he knew a thousand songs and I wanted to learn them all, and he wanted to write some country songs and he did. Then we looked at a clock and it was time for both of us to go back to work, and so we did- I did two full shows at Harrah's and Freddy did I think four shows. Then when we got off, we did the same thing and played together for another 18 hours, me and Deanie Bird and Freddy. After that, we played non-stop for about five years.

> **Norm Hamlet:** When I first met Freddy, he was working in Reno, him and his band were playing at a big casino there called El Dorado, and I guess Merle had gone in there and seen Freddy. At that time, we were working at Harrah's Casino Club, and were doing like 2 shows a day, which was quite a few shows actually spread over a week. When Freddy was off

stage, often he would be over visiting us while we were playing shows, and we really got acquainted with Freddy and his band.

Freddy Powers: From that day on, Merle and I were never too far away from each other. Little did I know that meeting Merle would be the start of another new step into the Country Music business for me on the heels of producing Willie's album. It had been over 20 years since I'd showed my songs to anyone because I'd gotten burned a couple times on people recording songs I wrote without crediting me properly as songwriter when they hit the charts. Still, I had more songs in me, I just didn't know if anyone else wanted to hear them.

One day, we were at Harrah's Hotel and Casino in Lake Tahoe in Merle's room before a gig of his when I grabbed his guitar and sang '*I Always Get Lucky With You*' for him. When I finished the song, he just stared at me for a moment saying nothing as if he didn't know how to tell me it was a shitty song! But instead, he jumped up out of his chair and said something about how the title of the song alone was a hit. When Merle said that, it was like a lightning bolt of confidence that hit me and that moment, unbeknownst to me, was the launching point of my songwriting career. One night not long after the phone rang and it was Merle's office manager Tex Whitson. He said Merle had re-arranged my song and played it over the phone to me on a little tape recorder. I couldn't hear it too good over the phone, but it sounded awful good from what I could hear. Merle recorded the song on an album called *Big City*, which was one of Merle's biggest selling albums. Later George Jones had a # 1 on it, and it was nominated for song of the year.

"*I Always Get Lucky With You*"

*I've had good luck and bad luck
And no luck, it's true
But I always get lucky with you*

*I've been turned on and turned down
When the bars close at two
But I always get lucky with you*

*I've had two strikes against me
Most all of the time
And when it's down to just a phone call
I'm minus a dime*

*There's been good days and bad days
But when the day is through
I always get lucky with you*

Oh, I always get lucky with you

I've had two strikes against me
Most all of the time
And when it's down to just a phone call
I'm minus a dime

There's been good days and bad days
But when the day is through
I always get lucky with you
Oh, I always get lucky with you

I always get lucky with you

(Written by Freddy Powers and Merle Haggard,
Copyright 1981, Sony/ATV Music Publishing Ltd.)

Freddy Powers: Merle sometimes showed his affection by writing songs about someone or even giving them a piece of a song's publishing. Unfortunately, as it turned out, we'd have to share the spoils from that song's success with some undeserving participants after our kindness backfired on us and some other writers tried to take partial credit for the song's writing. I wrote the first version of *"I Always Get Lucky with You"* awhile back before I met Merle, and after Merle and I got together, I played the song for him. Merle liked the title right off and thought the title alone was a hit. He took the song and after a few changes, we had a hit. For some strange reason, Merle and I thought it would be nice of us to give part of the royalties we made from the songwriting to a couple of friends and co-workers for all their loyalty and sticking it out with us. Merle gave Tex Whitson, his manager at the time, half of his part and I gave Gary Church, my trumpet player, half of my part. Little did we know that would come back to take a major bite out of our asses.

We had been out on tour and pulled into Redding, California to see a billboard that read: "Congratulations Tex Whitson! I Always Get Lucky With You." Merle and I walked off the bus and directly in to the middle of a party for Tex in his honor for writing this number one hit. Needless to say he never mentioned mine or Merle's name, the song's actual writers. One day he was bragging on the song and I finally had enough of it, and handed him my guitar and told him if he wrote the song to play me an A augmented. Well, with that, the conversation was over and I rested my case. Sometimes you have to be careful what you do, because some people start believing their own lies, especially in the music business, a # 1 hit is the kind of score that can corrupt anyone. I think that's one of many reasons why Merle and I trusted in each other so completely as songwriters, because there was such honesty going on in our natural friendship, that it showed up in our creative relationship and songs by natural extension. We shared in the successes that chemistry produced, and the occasional loss when we were taken advantage of by those seeking to get a free ride off Merle's name and stardom. Gary Church had even wound up with his name on a couple of other songs of mine he had nothing to do with writing.

> **Merle Haggard:** "*I Always Get Lucky To You*" there's a lot to that. We were sitting in somebody's bus, I don't remember whether it was mine or his, and Fred and I wrote the song. Well, there were two other guys there, and being stupid, we gave them part of the song. I said, 'Well, I've got publishing, so I'll just go ahead and give you two the writers' end, and I'll take the publishing.' Well, I got beat out of the publishing in bankruptcy, and when I look down at that song after it was recorded by George Jones, and my name ain't on it nowhere. That's the way life goes sometimes.

Freddy Powers: After that hit took off, even though I was still headlining in Reno, as Merle and I grew closer musically and personally, I would sit in with his band The Strangers whenever he played Reno, and even started traveling with him on the road a bit. The three of us became close and enjoyed playing so much together that if Merle wasn't in Reno, we were on our way to Redding, California to Merle's home to play. We kept spending more and more time up at Lake Shasta where Merle owned a marina and large houseboat plus a great showroom and night club. Deanie Bird and I started getting together with Merle anywhere we could and the three of us would pick for as much as 18 hours a day. Merle wanted to learn every song I knew, and I was in turn trying to learn every song Merle knew. This went on for months. Merle would come on my jobs and play guitar with me, and I would come on his jobs and play guitar with him.

> **Anne Reynolds**: Dean got his nickname way back when he had first been in the Grand Ole Opry when he was 16 and Uncle Dave Macon and Minnie Pearl were in the show. Well, after that, he went on the road with Uncle Dave Macon, and one day in between shows, they were bathing together in a horse trough, and Uncle Dave looked at Dean's legs and said, "My God kid, your legs are just skinny as a bird, I'm gonna call you Deanie Bird." Then Minnie Pearl took him under her wing and kept all his money for him, and they would sneak into churches at night – they were always unlocked – when they were empty, and she taught him to play the piano. She taught him math, and kept him on the straight and narrow while they were out on the road, because he was in the Grand Ole Opry on the road at 16 without his folks.

Freddy Powers: Finally, after the last show one night at the El Dorado, Merle asked me, "Would you like to give up a year of what you're doing and come live with me in Redding and write songs with me?" Merle was enjoying learning Jazz Swing guitar and I was learning a hell of a lot about writing country songs, so I threw caution into the wind and made the decision to split up my band and relocate to Lake Shasta. Two members of my band I felt that I couldn't let go because they had been with me through thick and thin, so Merle agreed to hire Gary Church for his band, and Dean Reynolds was still working with me when my band would play gigs opening for Merle when we weren't out at the Lake writing. At the time, the lounges of Nevada were getting to me, and already I had been writing a few new songs, so my decision was an easy one to come by. After a decade playing the Casino circuit, it felt like it was time for a change of scenery!

I couldn't have been more excited for this new adventure in my career and life to begin! It was 1981, I had just divorced my second wife and was free to go crazy – A 50-year-old playboy! Merle Haggard was working on a divorce and was primed for a party, setting the stage for the party of the decade. At the time, Merle owned a resort called 'Silverthorne' on Lake Shasta: they rented house boats, ski boats, and had a 400-seat club with live bands, a restaurant, etc., it was an unbelievable paradise. Even though Merle had a beautiful ranch just 10 miles away, he spent most of his time on his private 2-level houseboat he'd named The Hotel Troubadour. Shortly after I arrived, Merle approached me with the idea that I should have my own houseboat as well, but I told him I didn't have that kind of money to buy one, to which he replied, "Don't worry, that's the only thing I have plenty of..."

Within a few days, we located a 57-foot boat with everything (including the kitchen sink), Merle wrote a check out for $85,000 and bought the boat. He had it put in my name, even though I was worried about paying for the boat. Merle joked matter-of-factly that "Your only worry is taxes," and he said I'd be making a lot of money soon and advised me to hire a tax attorney, and from that day the now-infamous 'Spree of 83' was on! I named my boat the U.S.S.F. boat. You could hear the music and laughter ringing across this beautiful lake. My boat was moored next to Merle's about 8 to 10 feet away. It was about the same size as Merle's except for Merle's had a second story.

Merle Haggard: Of all the people I've met in my entire life in this business, Freddy is one of my closest friends. Some people thought we were homosexuals, we weren't, we both like women, and I can testify (laughs) that that's the truth. It was a gas. The Spree of 83, we called it that, had actually started out in 1980, and went on that way for five or six years I guess. The Great Escape is what it was really. We had some adventures; I don't think fear was in our vocabulary very much. We both probably wanted to bite the dust some other way than the way we're going to.

We'd become really close friends. We were both getting a divorce, and we were both happy about it, and Lake Shasta seemed like the likely place to go. So for about the next seven years, we had the greatest times. Sometimes we'd eat, sometimes we'd have a drink, but mostly, we played all the time. Living out on the lake there, we had the boats hooked up to the shoreline where we had phones down there so we could call up and get whatever supplies we needed while we worked. We really enjoyed it, we were in shape, our chops were up, and I don't think I've played that good since then.

Linda Mitchell: The guys would get into these long jam sessions out on the houseboats, they called it Pickin', and sometimes during the day, they'd have a concert right out there on the dock! Freddy's best friend Deanie Bird Reynolds used to come up to the lake a lot, and if you wanted Catfish, he cooked the best in the world, but Deanie Bird and Freddy and Merle and others would pick for hours. They'd play and play and play and play, and they spent a lot of time doing that. We'd get a phone call sometimes from Merle's houseboat after they'd been playing for hours, and he'd say "We're hungry," and I'd reply, "Do you realize it's two o'clock in the morning?" And he'd persist, "We're hungry, we want some biscuits and gravy," and everything. Well, because Merle was my boss, we'd get dressed, and go up to the kitchen in the resort and sometimes they would remember that they had called us to fix them something to eat, and sometimes they'd just keep playing and forget about all the food we'd cooked!

Milton Quackenbush: Whenever I'd go up to visit Freddy on the houseboats at Lake Shasta, Merle always loved to jam, and we'd stay on the guest boat, which he called the G Boat, and we'd all just be around in a circle playing.

Rattlesnake Annie: I used to go out there to visit Freddy and Merle a lot, because Freddy's family was my friend before I even met Freddy, so I was connected to the Powers family for 40 years. So I used to go up there and hang out with them on Freddy's boat, and in Vegas, and spent a lot of time at Merle's up there with him. That's where I got a lot of material of his. Freddy and I were like brother and sister, we had so much fun, we laughed and talked and just loved every minute of our times together. I spent a great deal of my time with Freddy just the two of us, and he was just such a great, great player and singer, and we just communicated. There was some kind of chemistry between us I believe, just as people and as musicians.

Merle had this little band house out behind his house. That's where one time Freddy arranged one night after supper for Clint Strong to sit in the corner of that band house with his electric guitar and play and play so I could pick out what Jazz songs I wanted to learn. For instance, the 12 bar blues played in Jazz form, and he was playing all these great arrangements and Freddy would say "Now you need to learn that one! That's a good one for you," like there was a great Jazz arrangement of "*Let it Be*" and he told me I should take that one. Then a couple days later, the wind blew all my arrangements off the deck of Freddy's house boat out into Lake Shasta, and I had to go get them all from Clint Strong again! (laughs)

We hung out quite a bit with Spud Goodall, and then I would go out to visit he and Merle out in California, and Freddy helped me build my relationship with Clint Strong, because Clint turned out to be my jazz professor and arranged a whole lot of songs for me. So Freddy and I kept crossing paths that way and working on songs, and Freddy was just one of the most kind and gentle and sharing musicians I've ever known. Jazz, because I don't see where Freddy had a more joyful relationship than he did playing with Clint and Deanie-Bird were all playing together. My god, we cut my album so fast you couldn't even believe it when them as my rhythm section! Then when Bill Monroe heard that version of "Blue Moon In Kentucky" that Freddy and I cut, I took it to Nashville and showed it to Bill, and his reaction was "Can I play on that?!" (laughs) I said "YEAH!" But I think Freddy enjoyed playing with Clint the most because he was the one person who could play anything, and he brought Freddy to the peak of his ability, I think, accompanying that Jazz guitarist.

Scotty Joss: The first time I met Fred was when he was up at the lake hanging out with Merle, and that was in 1983, and we became friends and I watched all those songs come to life out at the houseboats at Silverthorne. It was the best time of my life back then, one of the Top 3 of the best times I ever had! They'd sit on the boats for hours and hours and party and pick, and Freddy would come up with a title or a few lines, and then Merle would work on it some, and they'd include me and Deanie Bird and all of those people to be part of that creative process. I wasn't smart enough to create any lines, but being a fiddle player, I was there to lend some melodic help to the whole thing. For those two, it was pretty magical. Everything they threw back and forth seemed to end up in the song. I've never seen anything like it.

Troy Powers: Whenever Freddy invited me out to the houseboats for a weekend, we'd go fishing, we'd have jam sessions, and Merle treated us real good too. My band would play the Silverthorne, and we'd stay on the houseboats we rented, and Merle would pop his head in and say "Troy, get your guys together and come over to the houseboat, let's have us a little jam session."

B.B. Morse, Freddy's Bass Player: Those houseboat pickin' sessions were DAILY! At some point, you were going to definitely find yourself sitting in a pickin' circle.

Freddy Powers: Here we were, two single, middle-aged men, living in a near-paradise lifestyle. Merle was hot as a pistol and his career was at its peak. I was being treated like a king and I was thinking what in the world am I gonna do to justify this treatment? For the first three years or so, Merle was extremely protective of me. I traveled with that circus to every state in the country. From the beginning, Merle and I were almost inseparable. Where one went, we both went. We would do an occasional tour where I would play guitar and sing a few songs in the show. Somehow, I knew that it was more than just a friendship with Merle, it was a mutual respect for each other's talents.

Marc Oswald: Merle's life in the early 80s was insane, and it was such a crazy tornado around him all the time because of the fame and fortune and all the hit records, that Freddy was almost like 'Eye of the Hurricane' for him, where everything was still for a minute. Merle trusted Freddy no doubt with his life, and they were basically inseparable. Merle and Freddy were what I call running buddies, and the thing about Freddy is he's like the ultimate wing man! So for a guy like Merle, who's a fighter pilot and is going into dangerous territory 24/7 as a star of the stature he was and still is, Freddy served as sort of comic relief, Yoda – in that he always had a philosophical angle if you needed one. So he was kind of a filter, so when everything got so big for Merle, so many people were trying to insert themselves into Merle's life that I think Freddy was a little reality check for Merle. They would discuss what was going on, who they were meeting, what they were doing, and it gave Merle something to bounce stuff off that didn't have an agenda. Freddy always had Merle's best interest at heart.

Freddy Powers: When we'd come home after a tour we would head straight for the houseboats, and The Hotel Troubadour was host to many strange goings-on. There were a lot of people who partied on the Troubadour who cannot be mentioned by name. One was a young Hollywood starlet. We had met at the Universal Amphitheater in Hollywood. She came up to the boat and as so quiet all day long she never hardly said a word. She just watched us do whatever we were doing. Later that night when everybody left and I went back to my boat, Merle said the very minute the door closed she started stripping her clothes off and throwing them in their and hollering "Let's get with it." Trouble was, they couldn't get much sex in because she never stopped talking, all the way to the airport the next day. I'm sure if she reads this, she'll get a big kick out of it. Whenever we weren't partying on the houseboats, we'd load up with as many as six or seven girls and head up the Pit River, a great place on Lake Shasta to hide out.

Merle Haggard: The lake itself was just a different life than anything I'd ever experienced, and I think for Freddy too. It's one of the most beautiful places in the world when the lake is up. Then when it went down, it changed, so every time it dropped a foot or so, it was a different lake. There was a period while we were living there where for 500 something days it wouldn't rain, and every day it was exactly perfect. It went two years without raining a drop, and the lake dropped 237 vertical feet when we lived out there. They thought the damn thing was going to dry up, then one day it started raining and rained for four months straight and filled that lake up in four months when they'd predicted it would take three or four years. I remember one night the lake raised 13 inches overnight; that's a lot of water. We docked in places that are all underwater now, so you can't even go back out there to the same place and find them because they're not there.

Biff Adams: When he moved up to Lake Shasta, Freddy's houseboat was right across the dock from mine. We lived on our own private dock behind a gate. At the end of the dock was Merle's big two-story boat, and right across the dock from Merle's was Freddy's houseboat. My houseboat was on the other side and we had our own little circle there, and it was a real nice deal, it really was.

Marc Oswald: Silverthorne was a beautiful place, and it was Merle's field of dreams I think, and when you drove in there, you drove in this windy road into Lake Shasta, and when you first got in there, there was a restaurant and this beautiful nightclub there. They had stars play that place all the time; I remember I saw Wynn Stewart play there with Freddy and Merle, so when you came in they had this big parking area. Then they had the docks so you would walk down this one main dock that then connected to all the docks where the houseboats were. I think there were 100 houseboats there, and it was in this little cove called Silverthorne Resort, and they had a private dock that was Merle's dock that had this gate on it.

It was mesh metal and you could see through it, but it was really pretty; it had carpet on it and I potted trees on it, and on that dock was The Hotel Troubadour, and then Freddy's boat, and one other that was a guest boat. As fans would come down to try and look through that gate to get a look at Merle, he was super friendly with everybody, and people came by it all the time and would just stand out at the gate and look at the three or four houseboats they had on Merle's dock. So, your kind of like living in a fishbowl, and I also think that's why he was out at night so much, so he could have a little bit of privacy.

Linda Mitchell: No one, unless they were invited onto that private dock, got on it, period. That was the rule. That was their serenity, I guess is the way to say it. It was their downtime: it was their time to take deep breaths from the tours and crowds and hub-bub of having to travel and have people swarm all over them. So Silverthorne was their playtime, and they had fun. That was the neatest thing about them, they had fun.

We were out there in the snow, we were out there in the rain, we were out there when it was hotter than bloody hell, to put it very bluntly, and Freddy always wore pocket pants! As long as he wasn't swimming, he was always in long pants and that were always tan, and he always had a smile for anyone and everyone. Just the country gentleman that he always was, he was always so soft in his speaking, and the minute I met him, I fell in love with him. They were my boys, and I was like their Mom. He always had these twinkling eyes and this big smile and always a hug for you. He just had a Good Ole' Texas/Okie boy charming sense of humor, and he enjoyed everything he did, he just lit up: he enjoyed life on the lake, and songwriting, and performing and pickin' with other stars, he was enjoying his life.

Once we were all living out on the lake together, Merle started putting on his Merle Haggard Bass Tournaments, which brought in avid, professional fishermen: NFL football players, you name it, everybody who was anybody came out, and Merle and Freddy and the boys would jam up on top of Merle's boat out on the second deck. They just had a ball when we went out. In fact, Merle had a tour bus that was moored up there, and it had an actual recording studio built on board, and not only would they do the lighting and everything from there, but would record what he and Freddy and the boys were performing too.

Freddy Powers: There were lots of folks who came up to see us that were not part of the party life. Believe it or not, Merle and I and others around were pretty good about cleaning up our act when need be. So far, it sounds like we partied all the time, but there was a lot of business also going on. It had to be the greatest spot on earth to entertain people like TNN would send people up there to film TV shows about Merle. We had a guest boat right next to the marina, and that's where a whole lot of famous people stayed, all kinds of people who played the night club. Tammy Wynette, Ricky Nelson, Little Jimmy Dickens, Dwight Yoakam, Rose Maddox, Reba McEntire, and many others. I remember Tammy Wynette was a great cook and she always helped with serving up some good old Southern food.

Many times Merle and I would be alone and he would tell me stories about prison life and how many times he has escaped from the law. Merle Haggard was a young, restless renegade. The prison system almost ruined a life, the life of Merle Haggard, and I believe if he hadn't found success in music, he would be dead or in prison to this day. Those quiet nights on Lake Shasta fishing on the back of the Hotel Troubadour, telling stories about our past and making plans for the future will always be a source of my favorite memories.

B.B. Morse, Freddy's Bass Player: We'd go up Pit River sometimes and night fish. You'd tie off some place, usually around the mouth of the inlet. The Pit River was the main source of the incoming water there, but there were tributaries too coming off the sides, it was a very kind of surreal thing. You'd go out there with searchlights, and once you tied off, you'd put the search lights out on the back of the boat and go fishing for Bass and Trout. Generally, we'd have a guitar around, and sit and pick and watch the poles...

I remember catching the same fish twice, and it was verified because when I gutted him, he'd swallowed the previous rig that I had caught him with. When I'd pulled him in the first time, we weren't using very heavy line, and mine got tangled on the back of the boat so he got away with my whole pole. I had another pole sitting right next to it ready to go, and cast it right where he jumped in, and hit the middle of that little ripple and boom, he turned around and hit it. He was very hungry! (laughs)

Anne Reynolds: Merle never got up until four or five in the afternoon, because they stayed up all night playing, and they'd take the houseboats out on the lake at night and kind of put them in a circle and they would jam on the front porches of the houseboats. Everyone would gather round, all the other houseboats would come up and listen. They never interfered with us, but they were getting a free show.

Freddy Powers: Merle had the biggest houseboat on the lake and it was the command post for The Spree of '83. Downstairs, he had a large living room, a kitchen in the front, and a large bathroom and bedroom in the back. Upstairs was another large bedroom with a hot tub and big screen TV. Its looked like an old-style whore house, but an elegant one. On the front of the boat it had a big neon sign that read "Hotel Troubadour." Merle took great pride in his boat. That boat stood high above all the other boats out there. So when we went up the famous Pit River, everybody knew it was us. We used two-way marine radios to stay in touch with each other. Naturally, that meant everybody on the lake could listen in, and did. You could make phone calls from the boat, but that meant the marine operator had to hook you up, so everyone could still hear any and all our conversations. Through the night, you could hear the U.S.S.F Boat calling The Hotel Troubadour, ringing through all the radios on the dock. You could watch people on the dock run to their houseboats to listen to what we said. Being aware of this, we tried to watch what we said. We used codes such as, if some girl named Patty was coming by, we'd say things like "Your aunt Patty was coming by to bring you some cookies (cookies, ha ha)." Plus, sometimes we'd just say goofy stuff joking around to mess with the listeners, and you could hear laughter throughout the marina.

Marc Oswald: On Merle's boat, of course, they had every contraption known to man, it was kind of like a MacGyver place, they were always fooling around with contraptions. So on Merle's houseboat, his coffee table was electric, and you hit like this clicker that looked like a garage door opener, and it moved out of the way and turned into a fishing hole. They'd sit in the living room of his boat on the couch and fish through the floor while they were watching TV! Merle also had this thing called a hovercraft that was round and was like a donuts that came up on a little cushion of air, and had like a two-stroke engine in it and had handlebars, and it was maybe six feet across, and you'd get it up and it would hover four or five inches off the ground. It had a fin right, and then it had another fin and you could ride it across the ground and also across the water, it was bizarre looking!

Linda Mitchell: Sometimes Freddy, Merle and the boys would go up the lake to go fishing, and you just never knew where they were. In fact, one year, they all went out on the fourth of July back when they used to do the fireworks display out on Shasta Dam. Merle would take the Troubadour out and would have the band up on top and would serenade all the people that were watching the fireworks, but the Forest Service eventually shut that down.

Merle was always fighting with the Forest Service, let's just say they weren't houseboat friendly, and not wanting pollution and not wanting this and not wanting that out on the lake. We all had to have a permit, and give them their money too (laughs). I think the biggest honor I ever had was when Freddy and Merle asked me to put on a Willie Nelson Farm Aid event out at the lake. It was a big price he paid to the Forest Service, but they let us do it.

Freddy Powers: Its true, Hag was always fighting with the Forestry service. They were in control of the lake and what was allowed and what was not. That included the houseboats, their width, length, what you could have on them and what you couldn't. They made Merle take his side rails off because it exceeded the width rules. So as an act of defiance Merle started building upwards. When you thought he had gone as high as he could, he went and built a crow's nest. That made it about eight feet taller. My boat was moored next to Merle's about eight to ten feet away. They were about the same size, but I didn't have a second level. Merle's looked like a high rise houseboat going down the river. There was no doubt what was happening on our houseboats. You could hear the music and laughter, and the wild and wacky partying all over the lake.

Anne Reynolds: Merle is such a character, he was always up to stuff and you never knew what he was gonna do, and the same with Freddy and Dean, you never knew who was going to pull the next prank – I mean, the sky was the limit! Anything was game. Freddy was usually the joker, and Dean played right into it, but Freddy was usually the leader. Freddy had a great sense of humor, like one night, I remember he untied our houseboat while we were asleep and we woke up clear across the lake!

You never knew what was going to happen next. One day it was raining, and Merle, Freddy, Dean and I put on a play, we made costumes and everything, and they recorded it as we did a play on the houseboat. It was all just moving all the time, something was always going on. It really was like a family, I can't tell you how close we all were, and we just had such a good time. We were all like a bunch of crazy kids up there, like we didn't have good sense. We spent a lot of time just goofing around and laughing and doing silly things, we just had fun.

Freddy Powers: Whether it be partying, songwriting or playing music, we went after it with all we had to work with. I don't remember any day on that lake that wasn't magnificent. If there were bad days, they have somehow been erased from my memory, or maybe taking a line from one of Merle's hits, "There were the memories I choose to recall." But you better believe it was one big party for the rest of the 80s!

CHAPTER 7: THE SPREE OF '83 BEGINS!

Freddy Powers: By 1983, Merle and I were living on the boats full-time, writing and partying and 'The Spree of 83' was in full swing! Now, I've always been a pot smoker and beer drinker and that was about the size of my vices up to that point, but 1983, 84, and 85, were the wild drug years! It was as if we were deliberately trying to kill ourselves. We bought cocaine and speed by the bags and sometimes we would go for two or three days and never sleep. Merle was up one time I know for four, five days without sleep. It got to where he was almost afraid to go to sleep. Paranoia goes along with that kind of lifestyle, no sleep. I remember days of us both being paranoid of each other, peaking through our curtains like we were spying on each other. For my part, I don't think either one of us knew what we were paranoid about, we never had a cross word or gave each other a reason to think we were scheming against each other.

It seemed like we were living every day as if it were our last, which meant living for the moment. Sometimes we all got naked and stayed that way for days. It was just plain fun, and for the girls it was exciting as they always came back to do it again. We had these free spirits flying through us, and we chased the dragon on every adventure we could. The women were the fuel for our fires, and it seemed like they kept getting hotter and hotter, wilder and wilder till my life started to feel as surreal as a movie at times. I was definitely living the dream.

> **Biff Adams:** Some of the parties out there at the lake were pretty wild. You didn't know quite what to expect when you went out there, but they were always having a good time. It was a riot, it was a lot of fun, and the women always went gaga for Merle. There were some days where Freddy and Merle would be out on the lake just stark-ass naked passing some of these other houseboats waving at the girls.

> **Merle Haggard:** The Rat Pack in Vegas, they were jealous of us, we had more going on over there than they did, and they knew about it and called us every once in a while. Frank Sinatra called me while that was going on, and invited me to play on the White House lawn for the President, but I got out of it because me and Freddy were busy partying and writing songs.

Freddy Powers: It's true! Merle and I were having one of our wild parties when Frank Sinatra called and asked Merle to go and perform on the White House front lawn with him, an invitation Merle politely declined because we were having too much fun! During The Spree of '83, there was a party going on 24/7. We were flying girls in from all over, and if we wanted to play music and jam, we flew the musicians in. The word was out where we were living and people did amazing things to get to Merle. We had women take off their clothes and swim out to the boat. People in boats would flash us, it was really a kick. Our parties were at the height of their time. Almost everybody was doing cocaine regularly.

> **Merle Haggard:** We drank lemon water out there when a lot of guys were doing cocaine. Everybody had a little vile, and I remember before I quit in '85, it got pretty heavy. One time I was making a health drink, and it had all kinds of good things in it – fruits of different kinds, strawberries, blueberries, peaches and oranges – and I put it in the blender, got it all mixed up, and took that little vile and sprinkled a little bit of cocaine on it.

I'm not going to go into any of the prostitutes or hookers, it's not necessary, because you all know Freddy, and at that time in our lives, we were in between women. He would be up in his plane spotting fish and say 'Hey, there's a big school of bass located over here,' and we'd go over and catch the bass. Or he'd say, 'Hey, there's a bunch of naked women, and they're over just on the other side…'

Freddy Powers: Hell, why not! There were girls around for free, we didn't have to pay for pussy as long as there was cocaine around. We named my boat the USSF boat, and you could watch everyone run to their boats when they heard either 'USSF houseboat calling the Hotel Troubadour' or vice verse. So we used codes like 'Your Aunt Patty was on her way with cookies.' Cookies? Yeah right, you know the old saying if you believe that... The Hotel Troubadour was host to a lot of strange parties and lots of very famous guests, some of whom can't be named here.

One notorious groupie I still remember to this day was 'Little Rock Connie.' Merle and I being constant partiers thought we were pretty wild, had the attitude everything goes and never thought there could be a woman who could be too much for us. That was, until we met Connie, who back then was known as a famous groupie, and as we'd soon find out, for good reason too. She was a real good-looking gal, and actually a lot of fun, but she was WILD. Not realizing yet how wild she was, I got her phone number and called her up to invite her out to the houseboat for the weekend. I picked her up at the airport in a Limo with a sun roof- that should have been my first hint this woman was wild. The first thing she did was open the sun roof, take her top off, and stood up in the Limo flashing all of Redding, turning in all directions to make sure everybody saw her.

When the weekend was over and I was ready for her to leave, I talked the limo driver into taking her back to the airport without me. When he got back, he said "Boy that woman is wild! She was flashing everybody all the way to the airport, she nearly caused a pile up on I-5." Needless to say, it didn't help our reputation in the community. Later on, we saw her on a talk show. I was holding my breath, hoping she wouldn't mention my name and her weekend on the houseboats with Merle and I. She didn't, thank God.

We saw her again sometime later on at a concert in Little Rock. The famous 'Brown Sisters,' Maxine and Bonnie, were on the bus visiting Merle. Little Rock Connie showed up and just about the first thing she did was lift up her skirt and flash the Brown Sisters. Then she proceeded to tell Merle she liked him and he was a nice guy, but he, referring to me, 'is an asshole.' Merle liked that kind of stuff, but we preferred to be instigators at our own discretion. There were also people that did come to the party houseboat to see us that was not of the party type, and believe it or not, Merle and I and others around the marina were pretty good about cleaning up our act when need be. But when it came to partying, writing songs, or just playing music we went after it all the way with everything we had in us.

Linda Mitchell: There were girls, but I was Mom, so if any of the guys came up and said "You need to get rid of this person." Well, whoever it was,

I said "okay," went down and said "Young lady, you're going for a ride," and I'd already called her a cab, and gave her a bus ticket, and said "Don't come back." That was my job. I was mom like I said, I was kind of the mean one of the group I guess. There were even times when we had what Merle and Freddy called the Red Line Express, where these parents would drop their daughters off and I'd get a phone call from the houseboats, "This is jail bait, we need to get rid of them," and again, I'd either have a cab take them to the bus station or have the houseboat drop them off.

Freddy Powers: Early on in our life out on the lake, Merle got the idea to have a weekly wet T-shirt contest on our private dock, with the First Prize being $200; Second Prize was $50.00 and a free trip on Merle's private houseboat with Merle (you can guess what went on during those outings), and I mean, we had some BIG turnouts. We must have had 50 women enter each week, it was really something. Now, I'm not going to say the contest was fixed, but you could lay your $ down on this: the Second place winner would be a good-looking girl. One time we had a wet dress contest, but I'll just leave that one up to your imagination!" (laughs)

> **Merle Haggard:** The Wet T-Shirt Contests were a Thursday night thing. We were both single, going through divorces, so we had lots of time on our hands. We had a resort there, and 32 houseboats, several cabins, and we'd rent them out starting on a Wednesday night, then on Thursday, have that wet T-shirt contest to see if there were any new women. A guy named Lewis Tally was the hoser, we had to have a hoser and old Willie would hose 'em down (laughs). The second prize was fixed, so we would give that one the first prize whatever it was, $100 or something, and the second prize was a trip up the Pit River with us. We were going to build this flush unit, where if they said the wrong thing or acted the wrong way, we'd just drop the floor and flush 'em right out.

> **Anne Reynolds**, Deanie-Bird's Widow: Freddy and Merle used to call Dean "Jose" whenever they had wet T-Shirt contests, because Dean hosed them down.

> **Sherrill Rogers, co-author "Let's Chase Each Other Around the Room":** I loved Deanie-Bird Reynolds, he was just the best guy. He called everyone "Turkey Lips," he'd say "Hey Turkey-Lips!" We all were out there together for some crazy-ass parties! They had wet t-shirt contests all the time. They had five houseboats going down the lake, and the whole top part of Merle's boat would be topless women, it was crazy! There was a lot of cocaine, alcohol and pills going around. During the Spree of '83, he and Merle were playing pretty hard. LOTS of drugs, LOTS of

women, and lots of fun. Video cameras had just come out, and we would put on television shows we filmed on the houseboats, crazy funny shit. I remember one where Freddy was the announcer, and then we were all on a panelists were me, Debbie, and, Deanie-Bird and his wife, and Merle was video-taping. The game was called "What's that Object?", and it was so funny because we couldn't keep straight faces so we kept having to do it over and over again. So Freddy was talking in a British accent, which made it even funnier, because this was supposed to be a British television show, and we were all supposed to do our answers with English accents. Deanie Bird's wife played Margaret Thatcher, and we all kept breaking character because Freddy was so funny.

Marc Oswald: They would bring in CARLOADS of girls from the Bay Area, and all conceivable intoxicants, and everyone was just on fire the whole time! But when Merle was awake in the day time, he and Freddy would leave in their boats a lot and go up and fish the Pitt River. They'd go up there, drop their anchors and stay up there for two, three, four days.

Freddy Powers: I know it sounds like all we did was party, and we did a lot, but there was also a lot of business going on too. Lake Shasta, the houseboats, and having a club made it the perfect set-up for entertaining and having other entertainers come to play. We had a houseboat set up right next to mine for guests and other entertainers that would come in to play the club. We had many, many big stars up there and a gate to try and keep everybody out so we could try and get some rest. But that was hard because the women would just take off their clothes and swim around the gate and come on over to the houseboats. Sometimes I felt like we were the Beatles or Elvis, it was girls, girls, girls.

Traveling around the world with the show gave us lots of opportunity to meet girls. We would spend a small fortune flying them in. One time however, a famous night club owner sent a twin engine jet loaded with beautiful women up to party with us. There was six or seven. I and my bass player Dean Reynolds rode up to the plane to get them. They all looked like Playboy Bunnies, it was an interesting trip home. When we got back to Lake Shasta and got the ladies bedded down. Someone came running in saying Leona was on her way out to the houseboat. Leona and Merle were separated at this time, but Merle didn't want Leona to know about the girls, so we put them on my houseboat and headed up the river to hide out. Merle was supposed to meet us later. I spent two nights up there with all these girls. After the first night, you'll never know how much I wanted Merle to show up. He never did. The third day I took them to the plane and sent them back home. I don't remember if we ever said Thank You to our friend in Ft. Worth or not (but THANK YOU).

Linda Mitchell: Jack, the original owner of Silverthorne, was the pilot for President John F. Kennedy on Air Force One, and when he got sick with cancer, he sold the resort to Merle and Jim Jabalsie. Eventually, Merle bought out his partner and it became strictly the Merle Haggard Silverthorne Resort. Whenever Freddy and Merle and the original Strangers performed there at the resort, it was always old-time Country music. I was kind of in charge of the bar and the restaurant and booking the entertainment, and we had all sorts of Country & Western singers come up, and Freddy and Merle would jam with all of them, Little Jimmy Dickens even came up one time, and I'd grown up listening to him. You name them, we had them: Tammy Wynette, Dwight Yoakam, and Rick Nelson came up shortly before he died in that horrible plane crash.

Freddy Powers: I'd taken two members of my band with me of course – Deanie Bird, my bass player, and Gary Church, who played trumpet and trombone – when I'd moved out to Lake Shasta. Merle hired Gary into his band the Strangers and Deanie Bird and I with a great guitar player Clint Strong that my son had introduced me to. For the next two years, we toured with Merle as his opening act, and we'd also play shows at Merle's nightclub out there on the lake.

Biff Adams: In the evening, we'd all go to the upstairs bar at the Resort that Merle owned there on the lake, Silverthorne, and it was a pretty nice nightclub that held 200 people play at night and would have a lot of guest stars come and sit in with us. I did a lot of that booking of guest stars, and we had a lot of the players who worked the Northern Coast between San Francisco and L.A. that would come through in between tour dates and Merle would give them a free houseboat to stay at if they played at the resort. It worked out to be a pretty good deal for everyone all-around.

Linda Mitchell: The second floor of Silverthorne is where they performed, and when Merle and Freddy would put on a performance. I would always have to come backstage and tell them, "I can't put any more people in here," because the place was absolutely packed. You had people come from all over, they were on vacation and would hear that there was gonna be a concert. I remember one time The Strangers were performing and I had five cash registers up top working when we had a performance. 150 to 20ople was the capacity for the club, and we were always overcrowded up there because up to 300 people sometimes would pack into both floors, and you'd start to fear the roof was going to fall in! On stage, Freddy never wanted to upstage Merle. He never wanted to upstage anybody, that was Freddy Powers. Freddy didn't care if he opened or played background or if he was in a sense ever acknowledged, he just wanted to play his music. He didn't have to be # 1 and that's what made him # 1.

Scotty Joss: I was in the house band called The Sidemen At Work for a long time there in 1983, 1984. It was me on fiddle, Kevin Williams played bass, Randy Flom played guitar, Henry Pulkis played piano, and Leonard Camp played drums. We would open up for all the headliners, and if there wasn't a band headlining that night, we would be the main band playing. So I was so busy playing with all the local guys as the opening act, and usually the group would play 2 shows a night, and we'd play twice opening up for both shows.

Merle had turned that place into a beautiful showroom with wood and brass and you had that view of the lake, it was just a beautiful place to play. Merle treated everybody really well and we could stay there, and we just partied like madmen all the time! I got discovered by Dwight Yoakam out there playing in that house band at Silverthorne when he came through before Guitar and Cadillacs became a big thing. So we played every night it was open and opened up for everybody back then that came through, whether Merle was on the road or not. None of us were in the Strangers at that time yet, we were just a local band Merle was fond of and he let us have the gig. We got a weekly paycheck, and it wasn't bad, and lasted for the season.

Freddy Powers: When we played the showroom at Silverthorne it seemed like everyone we knew came out- especially the 'girls' – so we'd end up afterward with a party that lasted generally all night long. Most of the time, we'd party all night and sleep all day. By then, Merle wouldn't ever go near the Ranch. He said it was as if someone had died there, and he couldn't stand seeing memories of something that could never be. I truly felt for him because I had just gotten a divorce from my wife, who I dearly loved. What a setting for a bunch of hurting songs....

Merle Haggard: We were living on the houseboats when a lot of those things got written, and it was healthier out there. When you ride across country, a lot of people don't understand what I go through. I live out there, and every time I'd go to work, I've got to drive 2400 miles, and it can take three days to get over a trip like that. But when we were living out there on the lake, it would only take 24 hours. I got over it in one day. It's so much healthier because the air and the oxygen is plentiful out there.

Marc Oswald: I think it was a combination of things that made Merle and Freddy such a great songwriting team, I would say the primary elements were: Freddy is a great listener, he's just such a great listener, and he and Merle wrote a lot late at night, and they both lived next to each other on the houseboats. Freddy had the Aircraft Carrier, which is what we called his boat, and Merle had the Hotel Troubadour, and because they were next door to each other. Merle's kind of a night owl, they were right there in the same physical space, and Freddy was a night owl too. I would just venture to say that for Merle, the only time it was ever quiet was at two, three, four in the morning, when the spotlights had been turned off, and all the fans that used to come to Silverthorne just to try and watch them through the gate to the dock late at night when it used to be quiet.

Freddy Powers: For all the good times, many of the songs we wrote during that time were about lost loves or love experiences. Merle wrote a lot of songs about his love and feelings for Leona. When I'd first hooked up with Merle, he was married to Leona Williams. We all traveled on Merle's bus together. Their relationship seemed great at first. But before long, I began to see problems slowly starting to take place, and their marriage falling apart, eventually ending in divorce. I always thought Leona was a beautiful woman. She's also a very talented, singer and star in her own right. But she was always walking in Merle's shadow, and I believe that's what caused a lot of the unease between them. Merle was the successful star getting all the attention, and she may have felt unnoticed for her work as a singer and writer too.

I think given more time they could have been a great songwriting team, but as a couple they just had too many problems and their marriage just fell apart. He wrote a lot of sad songs during that time. At the same time, I was writing songs about my past life, which gave us both a lot to write about. We wrote a few number ones and some that should have been number ones that just got overlooked in albums. Songs we wrote during that time were like an audio biography of our lives, and of course, for me, writing songs with such a great writer was a terrific ego boost. With my confidence at this level, I was putting my heart into every song.

Merle was always looking for ideas for new songs. I remember I went up to the ranch one day to talk to him about a song I'd written for him, and he was walking all through this big house as naked as a Jaybird playing Bob Wills stuff on his fiddle (and Leona laughing like a hyena). I'll always love Merle's sense of humor.... After he put his clothes on, he and I and Leona were sitting around in the kitchen talking and he said, "Let me hear the song." I played him one I'd written recently called '*The Silver Eagle*.'

"Silver Eagle"

Well, he rides into town,
On the back of a big Silver Eagle.
Strapped to his shoulders are

The burden of stayin' on top.
And the lines in his face
Tell the story of an uphill flight.
You can tell how he feels day by day,
By the songs that he writes.
He's loved by millions,
Somehow, he's their prisoner, as well.

As he rides down the road,
In his 10-wheel aluminum cell.
Now he lives for the day
That the Eagle will carry him home
'Cause the glamour is over,
Nearly all of his seeds have been sewn
Let him go, Silver Eagle.
There must be a better way of life.
For this great, American poet,
Who's singing his songs about,
The every-day, working man's life
One night on the road,
Just south of the I-Dee-ho line,
We were smokin' some contracts,
And attempting to alter our minds
And just before daylight,
Hag pushed back his hat and he said,
"Are we put-tin' too much emphasis on ban' a star?
Can't we do a little bit of livin' instead?"

Let him go, Silver Eagle
There must be a better way of life
For this great, American poet,
Who's singing his songs about,
The every-day, working man's life
Let him go, Silver Eagle
There must be a better way of life
This great, American poet, Who's singing...

(Written by: Freddy Powers, 1982
Copyright Sony/ATV Music Publishing Ltd)

After the song was over, Merle walked over to the big bay window and stared out the window for a few moments. From where he was standing, I could see he had tears in his eyes and that he was truly moved by the song (again, he had given me more and more confidence). I started trying to think like Merle and find out where his mind was, so as to write things that he would relate to. The more I would find out about him, the more I believed that we were very much alike, in both background and our likes and dislikes.

Many of the songs of the time were about our love for someone. Merle wrote a lot of songs about Leona, as well as other experiences with love affairs. I too, was in that special time of my life where writing about the past seemed to help get over it. We wrote a few # 1s and a lot of good songs that didn't make it all the way. The songs of that time read like an audiobiography of our lives and of course, being able to write songs with such a great songwriter was a terrific ego boost for me. With my confidence at this level, I put everything into every song.

Merle Haggard: Me and Willie were both in a position to influence him and to guide him a little bit. He didn't need much, he just wanted somebody to assure him he was on the right track I think. Fred wrote his own songs, I didn't help him write '*Natural High*,' he wrote that one himself.

Freddy Powers: Merle first took notice of my songwriting when I played him the first song we ever wrote together, '*I Always Get Lucky with You*.' At first, it was real hard for me to just open up and let loose my words for fear he would have something much better. He is such a great and profound writer, and with that in your mind at all times, it was overpowering. And just think how I felt when Merle Haggard looked at me and said, "I like your writing." After that my confidence grew and I felt very comfortable telling him any song idea I had, and I'm proud to say we used a lot of them.

In spite of the good times, every now and then, Merle would drop into a deep depression for several days, and sometimes he was mad at me. I think it was a combination of loss of sleep and the drugs. Merle was never a heavy drinker. I've only seen him drink a couple of times. When Merle was in these moods, I tried to stay over on my own boat or go out for a cruise on the lake. I would always know when he was over it because all of a sudden you would hear him singing some really silly song at the top of his voice, as if to let everyone know he was over whatever had come over him.

I remember one day Merle came in and started talking about this Dr. who was a Nature Path or whatever you call them. We went to see him and he took a bunch of tests on us to see what our body was missing. Somehow we wound up with all kinds of vitamins, and he told us to drink at least a gallon of lemon water a day. So it seemed like we had bottles of lemon water everywhere. You couldn't walk on the boats without stepping on a gallon of water.

CHAPTER 7: THE SPREE OF '83 BEGINS!

We would squeeze two or three lemons per gallon of water. We really went overboard, one of the members of the band said we had drank so much lemon water that our farts smelled like Lemon Pledge. We were feeling mighty good, one time we were bragging about how good this Dr. was to a real doctor and he said the reason we were feeling so good had nothing to do with the pills or the lemon, he said it was because we were simply drinking tons of water. Plus, instead of drinking beer and whiskey, we were drinking lemon water. Along about this time, we decided to stop eating meat. We only ate vegetables, fruit and fish, even though we were doing drugs, we were watching our diet as well as we could. Still, no matter what we ate, we drank it down with (you guessed it) lemon water.

I, myself, had a love-hate relationship with cocaine. I didn't like the nervousness and uneasy feeling, but all the women loved it so Merle and I always had it around. If you had cocaine, the girls would come a running and be ready for anything. So I would catch myself doing another line even though I didn't like the feeling it gave me, I somehow thought it would get better. Either way, back then, it was the popular party drug and Merle and I for a while there both went through mountains of it – along with the girls of course, who always seemed to love it - during parties out on the lake. Our parties were at their peak at the time. Everybody almost, was doing cocaine regularly.

The government always puts marijuana in the same category as cocaine, heroin and speed. They lied so much about marijuana, but I found out cocaine was much more harmful and habit forming. I have never known anyone who has been harmed by marijuana but I can damn sure show you some harm when it comes to Cocaine. I personally have smoked grass since I was 21 years old. At the time, I wrote the book, I'm 71 and feel like I'm 40, and I know a lot of other people my age that have been smoking like myself. I know very highly professional people who smoke pot and get along fine in life and keep living on into the 70 and 80s. I won't mention names, but there are a hell of a lot of them. I'm not proud of my cocaine days, I'm glad I saw the light and gave that part of my life up and Merle will tell you the same if you ask him. Merle and I did it for a couple of years, then one day Merle came out of nowhere and said "Freddy Powers, you're the biggest asshole when you do that damn cocaine," and I said "You are too!" Then Merle walked over to the table and brushed a freshly cut line of cocaine into the trash can. After that, we stopped and as far as I know, Merle hasn't done coke since. I know I haven't. The music was always more important to us.

"It's seemed for a while like we could see a song in everything." – FREDDY POWERS

Freddy Powers

PHOTOS – MOLLY PARKES

CHAPTER 8: NATURAL HIGH

Freddy Powers: Merle and I didn't always just sit down and write a song together. A lot of times I would have an idea and I'd tell Merle about it, or I would start it and then give it to him and he'd take and finish it, or expound upon it or vice verse. Sometimes we'd pass a song back and forth to each other and make changes until we had a finished song. Together, we collaborated on some 40 songs he had recorded on albums as well as some that I wrote by myself. We had five # 1 hits, 'Song of the Year' and received the 'Triple Play Award' for writing three number one songs in a twelve-month period, and have since become what is called 'Members of the Million Air Play Club' for over one million plays on the radio. One of my favorite songs from this spree of hits was one I actually wrote by myself, "*Natural High*," that has remained one of the fan favorites throughout my career. It went to # 1 in 1985 and Merle included it on both his "*Kern River*" and "*All in the Game*" albums, cementing it as one of his biggest hits of the decade.

CHAPTER 8: NATURAL HIGH

"Natural High"

You stayed with me thru thick and thin
You watched me lose, you watched me win
You picked me up off of the ground
You never one time let me down
And you put me on a natural high
And I can fly, I can fly

I was drowning in a sea of make-believe
As helpless as a falling leave
You gave your hand to me that day
And you did it, 'cause you're made that way
And you put me on a natural high
And I can fly, I can fly

You always seem to let your feelings show
You love me and you let me know
Darling just remember these three words
I love you, I love you, I love you
And you put me on a natural high
And I can fly, I can fly
And you put me on a natural high
And I can fly, I can fly

(Written by: Freddy Powers, 1982
Copyright Sony/ATV Music Publishing Ltd)

Freddy Powers: "Merle did a marvelous job of that. I'm so proud of that song because, to me, you know Merle Haggard is the ultimate singer, the ultimate country singer."

Ray Baker: "*Natural High*" was a song that was so typical of Merle in that he led in my opinion a life that was destiny from one day to the next. He and Freddy were staying at the Opryland Hotel, and I went to pick them up around 1 o'clock because we had a 2 o'clock session at Larry Butler's studio, 11-11, and actually had 2 sessions booked back-to-back that day. So as we're walking through that lobby, there was a guy named Lloyd Lindroth up on that balcony NY who'd been hired by the hotel to play one of those great big harps like they had in orchestras.

This guy was a great musician, and Merle listened to him for a minute and told me, "Get hold of that guy, see if he'll do our session this afternoon." So I said "Okay," walked upstairs and talked to him, he said "Yes!" and sure enough, got hold of one of those cartage companies and had his harp brought over to the studio that same afternoon. Well, it just so happened one of the songs we were recording that day was "*Natural High,*" where you think about being up in the clouds or something like that. I couldn't have found – if I had searched – a better instrument to have on part of that song than that particular harp, it just fit perfect.

Janine Fricke: "Merle was at Shoney's Inn, on his bus, and he had just recorded these songs. He said, 'Come on up here, I want you to listen to some tapes.' We liked the songs, and he said 'Well, how about you coming in and doing some things on 'em?' So we went right on in and did it."

Ray Baker: Merle wanted somebody to sing harmony on it, so we got hold of Janie Fricke, and she came in and harmonized with him and it came out great. Merle sang live with the band on those sessions, so we did everything at once. The only thing we ever overdubbed is if Merle wanted to re-sing something, then we'd re-sing it, but as far as the music tracks, they were all laid down at once, so to speak. Very seldom did we ever overdub any musical parts because when you're in the studio with a great artist like Merle Haggard, he inspires you. The engineer I used on those sessions was a guy named Ron 'Snake' Reynolds, one of the best in Nashville, and he had a tube microphone he used that Merle liked that gave a real warm presentation of his vocals.

Freddy Powers: Against the backdrop of all this new found success and Lake Shasta itself, I felt myself coming alive as a songwriter again. To begin with, Merle to me is one of the greatest songwriters in the world. So to be asked by someone like him to co-write a song is the biggest honor a songwriter could ever ask for, especially because it was an untapped well of talent I never really knew I had before I met Merle. My confidence came from him in a big way, just as it did from Willie when he trusted me to pick the song list for *Over the Rainbow*. That was the first time anyone of that stature as a songwriter had ever trusted me to make that major a decision for him, and with Merle, co-writing songs together only made my awareness of that part of myself grow.

Linda Mitchell: Freddy and Merle were almost like twins, they knew what each other were thinking, is about the only way I can describe it, like they were one person. They were just in synch, they'd sit down and start doing something and all of a sudden, one would look at the other, and they would have a song, and it was just remarkable to watch how they worked together. They wrote from their experiences, and many a song that Freddy and Merle wrote, the inspiration came from out on Lake Shasta. It was something they lived. Music was just in their blood.

Sherrill Rogers: If you look at the songs that were written in that time, it really was a free time for both of those men. They were single and they were having a lot of fun! Merle had a fishing tournament every year. First of all, Freddy was a fantastic writer and musician in that, because he played banjo, he could do those triplets that you see in a lot of his music. He was extremely talented and banjo players can be pretty damn good guitar players, and he had a really good sense of jazz chords, which showed up a lot in his playing. Freddy was fun to play with. Merle always wanted to be known as a guitar player, that was more important to him than anything, because he knew he was a good singer but he wanted to be respected as a musician. He was one of the kindest, most generous people I've ever met. He loved his friends, and took really good care of Freddy.

Whenever we were touring on the road together, there was A LOT of pot smoking, some picking. Freddy had a bunk on the band's bus, but he would ride a lot on Merle's bus too. Especially once Merle got the big Santa Fe buses, those were custom buses, it was pretty cool. It was the first bus that was elevated, so it was up high like a locomotive. Underneath was his closet, it was like a rotating rack with all the clothes. He had a living room in the back, and in the front, had a table where we'd all play cards. That table would flip down to be a bed, and Freddy and I would sometimes sleep on that bed.

Freddy Powers: Even though everything was moving so fast and even in this hectic atmosphere, we were still turning out hit songs. I traveled with that circus to every state in the country. As in the beginning, Merle and I were almost inseparable, where one went, we both went. We were on tour coming out of Canada and heading for Nashville to the BMI Songwriters' Awards. It was probably around 3 AM, and we had our guitars out. The gal I was running with at the time, Sherrill Rogers, was singing in the band. In a joking voice, she said to me, "When we get to Nashville, I'm gonna chase you around the room!" Well, Merle and I picked up on that and it didn't take us long and in about 30 minutes, Merle and I had written the song *'Let's Chase Each Other Round the Room Tonight.'* It was recorded in Nashville shortly afterward and went to # 1 in the Country Music Charts with over one million airplay's, remaining on the charts for 14 total weeks! It was amazing how Merle and I could see a song in almost anything you said at that time in our relationship.

Sherrill Rogers: We were on a bus, and were having a conversation with Debbie Parret, and Freddy and I were playing cards. We'd just finished the Canadian tour and were on our way to Nashville to record *All in the Game*. That whole album is Merle singing sad songs about his divorce from Leona, and I was telling the guys a story about how difficult it was for a woman to go to a club and listen to live music and not get hit on. So I said, "It's funny, because the later it gets in the night, the more people get desperate and start chasing each other around the room, because they don't want to go home alone." Then Merle leans over to Debbie and says, "Let's just chase each other round the room tonight," and 15 minutes later, the 3 of us had a song. The first verse was the last verse, and the last verse was the first verse, and we didn't even change it till we got in the studio, but it became the first # 1 single he'd had since "*Big City.*"

Ray Baker: That song had what we called a '*Shuffle Beat,*' and with that one, I remember when we were recording it for the *All in the Game* album. I'd suggested to Tiny Moore and Jimmy Belkin, who played fiddle for Merle, 'Why don't you guys kick this off with Texas twin-fiddles sound?' and it was perfect, it just kind of set the stage. Tiny used to play with Bob Wills, and he played great Mandolin, but was just as great a fiddle player, and of course Jimmy can hold his own with anybody. That's part of that destiny thing I was talking about.

Freddy Powers: Until Merle, I had never had any songs really go anywhere and I had had a couple of real disappointments with songwriting that soured my attitude towards writing. One was a song I'd written that was recorded by the Wilburn Brothers back in 1953 called "*Nothing at All*" on Decca Records. I never saw a dime from that song. Another song that really hurt me and turned me off to writing was a song I collaborated on called "*There She Goes,*" recorded by Carl Smith. Eddie Miller – who wrote "*Release Me*" – came to Dallas and I met him at Jim Beck's studio on Forrest Lane, and Eddie and I became good friends (at least I thought). He stayed with my wife and I in our apartment for a while. He had an idea for a song and had it partly written. I helped him finish the song.

Eddie didn't have any money and neither did I to go in and cut a demo, so I borrowed the money from my dad to go into the studio and cut it. I sang it and we thought we had a hit. Thinking this was my chance to become a recording artist, I borrowed more money to send Eddie to Nashville to see if he couldn't get me a record deal. That turned out to be the last I ever saw of Eddie. The next thing I knew Carl Smith was in the same studio I first recorded the song in, and when I walked in and heard the song being recorded by someone else and while I was disappointed, I thought at least I would get credit for my part in writing it. But I was once again wrong, didn't see a dime from that song, much less did I even get credit as a writer on it. So with those kinds of disappointments and betrayals I didn't focus on writing anymore as much as I did playing and singing.

CHAPTER 8: NATURAL HIGH

I believe Merle has written more songs with Tommy Collins and me than any other songwriters he's ever written with. We had several other songs that I think should have been number one hits but they just got lost in albums. One Merle and I both agree on is a song off the 501 Blues album, "*Somewhere Down the Line.*" We had a couple that became famous and used in big albums or movies but we were never awarded. "*Texas*" was used in the James A. Michener movie 'Texas,' and it's also on the film's soundtrack for the album 'Texas'. "*A Friend in California*" was used as part of the *Marlboro* Album.

"A Friend in California"

L.A. traffic is bad this time of year
But there's a friend of yours in California
Sure wishes you were here
And as you lay your head on your pillow tonight just remember
There's a friend of yours in California sure misses you

You've got a friend in California that misses you
You've got a friend in California that sure misses you

Fort Worth can get cold this time of year
But this southern California sun is warm
You should be here
And as you lay your head on your pillow tonight just remember
There's a friend of yours in California sure misses you

You've got a friend in California that misses you
You've got a friend in California that sure misses you

You've got a friend in California that misses you
You've got a friend in California that sure misses you

(Written by: Freddy Powers, 1986,
Copyright Sony/ATV Music Publishing Ltd)

Merle Haggard: I like to write in the morning, my head is usually clear and so did Fred, so we wrote songs all the time. We didn't always have no reason beforehand, we just wrote songs and a lot of the sons of bitches we never heard again. Everything we wrote didn't go to # 1, a lot of them we threw in the God damn lake, because all of it was not good. We were always trying to write. We kind of helped each other sometimes when we'd have songs pretty well finished, then we'd give them to each other, and use each other's experience to see if we were on the right track. We did that a lot.

Biff Adams: Usually, the daily routine during those years when Freddy and Merle were writing neighbors was that one of them would get up in the morning. Freddy and I were usually up a little bit earlier than Merle, and if it was Fred, he'd usually say something to me like 'Boy, I had an idea for a song last night.' He'd go over to Merle's boat and tell him about it, and Merle would then typically tell me 'Hey, keep everybody away from the boat today, we're writing a song and don't want to be bothered.' So I'd say 'Okay,' and keep everybody off the dock while they went in Merle's boat and isolated themselves and sometimes they'd come out of there an hour and a half later with a hit song. Sometimes it wouldn't happen till maybe the next day or so and they'd keep working on it. I don't know numbers-wise how many songs they wrote over the years they lived together out there, but they wrote a lot of them.

Merle Haggard: My child Janessa was born while we still lived out on that boat, I think that was the year I wrote *"Twinkle, Twinkle Lucky Star."* Freddy had no idea that I was going to write a good song that day. One morning I ran over and beat on his door and said "I've got the complete construction for a # 1 song," and he said, "I don't feel good," and gave that little look that he gets (laughs). I said "Sick?" surprised, and he had the curtain pulled back, and said he'd been drinking the night before and he was serious because he didn't feel good that morning. I tried to get him out of bed, I said, "I'm serious Fred, I got a really good format for the song." See, there's been a lot of songs written about fiddle tunes, but *"Twinkle Twinkle Little Star,"* there hasn't been a song written about that, it's just a fiddle tune. I said "I'm telling you man, it's a hit song, the idea, I got the whole premise for it." Well, he said "Go ahead and write a little bit of it and I'll write some on it later around 12:30," but never did get over there. So I went back over to my boat and wrote *"Twinkle Twinkle Lucky Star,"* then went back over and sang it for him, and I thought I'd tell that story on him (laughs). It became a # 1 song. So he missed that one.

Freddy Powers: I'd come down with a sciatic nerve condition. That had me in a lot of pain. All I wanted to do was stay in bed. Merle came over and said he had the title for a song, *"Twinkle Twinkle Lucky Star."* The title didn't grab me as I said I was in pain, so I told Merle to come back later and maybe I would feel better. Needless to say, he wound up writing it without me and it became a big hit and won all kinds of awards and became a number one song. Alongside all the partying, Merle and I also had some quiet nights fishing off the back of the Troubadour, telling stories about our past and making plans for the future. I can't remember a single day on the lake with the Hotel Troubadour and the USSF Boat that was not a magnificent one.

"Freddy did a song called 'I'm Your Butter and Egg Man,' that was Freddy. Freddy's stuff was so off the wall, nobody wrote songs like Freddy's!" – J. GARY SMITH

"In Freddy's shows, he did a little bit of everything, all kinds of shows."
– MERLE HAGGARD

CHAPTER 9: THE BREAD & BUTTER BAND & LIFE ON THE ROAD WITH THE STRANGERS

Freddy Powers: Merle came to me one day on a whim and said, "Let's start another band. We'll call it 'Bread and Butter Band.' " He suggested we get together the jammers from our bands and tour playing more of my and Deanie's swing-style of music.

Merle Haggard: Fred was doing the singing and playing rhythm guitar, and had a guy named Gary Church who was playing the clarinet and trombone, and a good friend named Dean Reynolds that we called Deanie Bird. So that became a little four-piece band that we called the Bread and Butter Band.

Norm Hamlet: Merle really liked to play guitar, and he'd have Freddy sing some songs and he'd accompany him on guitar, he liked that when he didn't have to do all the singing! (laughs)

Freddy Powers: The band was built around my kind of music. Merle felt this would free him up to play more of what he wanted to and not pinning him down to just playing his hits. It wasn't the Merle Haggard and the Strangers show, and the public knew it when they came to see us. The band consisted of two members from my band, Deanie Bird Reynolds on bass and Gary Church and trumpet, and from Merle's band, Jimmy Belkins on Fiddle, Tiny Moore on fiddle and mandolin, Norm Hamlet on Steel, Biff Adams on drums, Merle on lead and rhythm guitar, and me as well on rhythm guitar. Merle said, "We'll book a California tour and split the profits right down the middle." I felt that was unfair and insisted that Merle take a bigger cut as, after all, he was the star, so it finally came out to be a 70-30 split. That was still a hell of a lot of dough for me.

The Oswald brothers, Marc and Greg had a booking agency called Luckenbach Productions and they had been booking Merle's shows. So we had them set us up a tour, as the 'Bread and Butter Band'. We toured mostly Southern California as far as I can remember because we were doing so much drugs and drinking during that time that it's all a haze to me. I could kick myself because this great experience even today is only a cloudy memory. I remember one time we were in Fresno and we went out and only did a 20-minute show. That happened a lot back then, whether it was drugs or something pissing Merle off, or he was just tired and wanted off that stage, and when Merle wanted to close a show he did.

Marc Oswald: In 83 when we did the 'The Bread and Butter Tour', it began as seven shows across California, starting in San Diego, then Bakersfield, Fresno, Visalia, Santa Barbara, and a couple more. It was supposed to be Freddy's band, and Merle was going to be a band member in it, so we weren't going to use his name in the promotion of the tour. 'The Bread and Butter Band', that's what they liked to call themselves as pickers, originally was just supposed to be Freddy, Merle, Deanie Bird Reynolds, and Clint Strong, the four of them, doing an acoustic show where they'd all be equal on stage. Because it seemed like Merle liked being in the band, more than he liked being the star, it seemed like, he liked being in the band because he was such a musician. So, of course by the time everybody in the organization got wind of it, it went from being the Bread and Butter Tour with the four of those guys playing small Theaters to Merle Haggard and The Strangers & The Bread & Butter Band. So suddenly we were playing large venues and running three or four Semis and God knows how many buses.

In the Bread and Butter Band, Freddy was the lead guy, and it was really cool because as a live performer, when he was on stage, it was hard to not watch him. You know how certain people just kind of draw your attention? Freddy was one of those players, because whatever he was doing, it was always interesting on stage. He was always understated, but always really confident too, he really had a sense of confidence on stage. Even when he was onstage with Merle – and Merle was such a presence on stage – Freddy was just fun to watch. It was like a rag-tag band going down the road, and Freddy and Merle were like Butch Cassidy and the Sundance Kid! Whether we were on the Lake or the road, Freddy was always the funniest guy on the planet. He surrounded himself with funny people like Deanie Bird Reynolds, and Merle, who's so funny and one of the best joke tellers I've ever heard. So Freddy and Merle were always up for a Shenanigan!

Freddy Powers: "My favorite food on the road, I'll tell you, I don't eat beef, I only eat bacon, like in the morning, I'd eat some crisp bacon sometimes. Otherwise, I eat chicken and fish. So on the road, yes, I had chicken sandwiches. It's usually what I wind up ordering in a restaurant. When I was on the road, I was always lookin' for a seafood restaurant too."

Biff Adams: Whenever those of us who were also members of The Strangers would go out and play with Freddy during one of his solo shows. It was a change for us, and that was welcome, because being in Merle's band for quite a while by that point. You can get burned out a little playing that catalog of hits exactly the way it sounded on record. With Freddy, we had the freedom to play different styles of music and it was a different show so we dressed different.

Anne Reynolds: Deanie and Freddy's relationship was awesome, and whenever they were together, the first thing they would do was to play. They would come out to the farm sometimes when it was just Dean and Freddy, and with Freddy singing and his rhythm and guitar and Dean picking bass, it was great. All my friends would gather around on the patio, and we'd have jam sessions on our farm. Dean and I would have barbecues with 50 people and live music with Freddy and Dean jamming, and everybody could bring their guitar because of course, in

Texas, everybody picks. Or they'd sit around and just watch Dean and Freddy, because even just the two of them was like a full-on concert all by itself, in fact, Dean was voted Best Bluegrass Bass Player for seven years in a row.

When they played together, it was just right, it was a love between those two. Dean would say, "It's just right Mama when I play with Freddy, it's just right." And Freddy always looked back over his left shoulder at Dean when they were playing, Dean was always off behind him a little bit on the left, and he'd always be looking over at Dean. It was magic between them when they played. Freddy and Deanie Bird opened for Merle for one whole season, and were very well-received: they were the best damn trio you ever heard. They were really tight.

Freddy's a great entertainer, he's just so in command of the show. He's just so sharp, his music is so good and his fans just love it, they'd always yell and scream and carry on and he's a great emcee. Dean didn't talk during the show, except for *"Sweet Georgia Brown,"* which was his show-off number, and he would do it in single time, double time and triple time and keep the flat bass going as well, so people would go crazy over that. And of course Clint Strong was just so awesome on the guitar, I don't know any guitar picker better than Clint, he's just an Ace and drove the audiences wild. So there was a lot of entertainment from three people, it was a great trio.

Freddy Powers: The road can be a tough place to be, it all depends on what's happening while you're out there. Most of the time, we enjoyed it. Think of how it can be there, you are traveling all over the country in real high style with a bunch of people, maybe 20 or so, who you enjoy being with in the first place, playing music you love to large crowds every night screaming and yelling because they liked the music. They came out of the woodwork to see Merle. When I would go out to sing a song, they liked me okay, but make no mistake, they came to see Merle.

Whenever we weren't doing Bread & Butter Band gigs were back on tour with The Strangers – Merle's band when he was headlining – we traveled in 3 buses and a big truck that carried the equipment. Merle's bus had two drivers, Dean Holloway and Biff Adams, the drummer for his band. Merle's band had their own bus with several of the members who could also drive. When I wasn't riding with Merle, Deanie Bird and I rode in the third bus with Lewis Talley and a guy who we called Steve Stone. His real name was Steve Van Stralen; he was the video man on the tours taping all our shows and whatever else we wanted videoed. ☺

Norm Hamlet: I actually started going out with Merle on the road in 1967, and worked with Merle for 49 years. He made me band leader after about 6 months, before that he'd been the bandleader, and finally he said "Hell, I need a band leader, I need somebody to take care of the band," and offered it to me and Roy Nichols. Roy looked at him and said "No it ain't." (laugh) He didn't want all that responsibility, and told Merle, "I'll take my amp and guitar in and play it, then take it back out to the bus and load it, and then show me my bunk!" So I wound up getting the gig by default, and during that whole 49 years, I don't remember one time of me and Merle having a cross word between each other. That gives you an idea of the kind of fella Merle was. He was nice and easy to get along with, all you had to do was do your damn job. We had some guys that came into the group, didn't do what they were told, and they didn't last long, but Freddy fit in real well with us.

Back in the 80s, we used Peavey amplifiers. We had a piano player, Mark Yeary, and we didn't have to use somebody else's piano, we carried around a piano with us, and at the time, had a semi-trailer truck that carried all our equipment. We had a lot of guys in the band, and at one time, had some of Bob Wills' guys with us, so we had to have that larger truck. Merle liked his bus a certain way, he had a bedroom in the back for himself, and then the kitchen and lounge, he had a TV back there, refrigerator, stove, it was a really nice bus for a million-dollar bus. He had some bunks on his bus where his son had a bunk, and whoever was riding on his bus at the time, Don Markham, one of the horn players, used to ride with Merle because he'd drive that bus some of the time. Gary Church, Freddy's horn player, would come out to work with us in The Strangers too on some tours.

On the road, Freddy road on Merle's bus, but I rode on the other bus because being the band leader, I had to keep some of those guys in line! (laughs) So I missed a lot of stuff, but Merle and Freddy were just having a good time over there. They were such good friends and really enjoyed each other's company. I really enjoyed when Freddy went out on the road with us, because he was opening shows for Merle, and he'd do some songs. Then after he opened the show for Merle, he'd bring Merle out and then stay on the stage with us through the shows playing rhythm guitar, and any harmony work that he did on any of the songs. Freddy also fit in good with our band because he could play those chords, and Merle was a big fan of Bob Wills. We used to do quite a few of his songs because they were like Western Swing, and Freddy could really get that rhythm going with Jazz. Any songs we would do, Freddy boy was right there on it! He was a good rhythm player. It was really fun with Freddy, he was great to work with and easy to get along with. When Freddy was out there with us, we had a great band and were really cooking!

Merle Haggard: When Freddy joined The Strangers, he fit in perfectly because – as a rhythm guitar player – he played what the band was playing, so he was able to play whatever he needed to. He played rhythm guitar real well, he had the ability to play a banjo lick with his right hand from his years playing banjo, and it worked real good. Freddy kind of needed a banjo-type rhythm because it was a swing band, and banjo was always kind of like the drums because it played to the snare drum. He didn't play banjo anymore when he joined my band, but he played with a banjo rhythm on the guitar. I've worked for Freddy as a guitar player in his band and he's worked for me as a guitar player in my band. I agree with the things that have been said about his guitar playing, I think he's one of the greatest.

Biff Adams: I think Freddy's style of guitar playing made The Strangers a better band. One thing I noted about Freddy as a guitarist right off was he was a damn good, solid rhythm player, he played real good stock rhythm. As a drummer, I always appreciated that, because the drums bass and a good stock rhythm guitar player makes a great rhythm section. At that time, though Merle was a good rhythm player, he was starting to play a lot more lead and getting off of the rhythm. So Freddy just fit right in there and I think it took a load off of Merle and in turn, he became a pretty good lead player.

Marc Oswald: When Merle was on stage, you never knew who was going to play a lead. One of the things Merle liked to do during concerts, and I've seen it a zillion times, and he would either do what he would or point at somebody with the neck of his guitar, or with a fiddle bow. But he liked to do these songs onstage with the whole band where he would improvise all the time, whether he was saying 'I want to have a guitar lead or piano lead or horn or fiddle', whatever it was, and would just toss the leads off to people when they didn't expect it. He liked to do that, and so the show was never the same twice, which is really unusual. So Merle would be playing a fiddle and all of sudden, would take his fiddle bow and just almost pop it over his head behind him. If he pointed at the piano, that piano player better be paying attention, because he was just throwing it all over the stage all the time. And Freddy of course could keep up with all that too, so they had fun doing that.

Willie Nelson: Freddy's strongest suit, I always thought, was his rhythm guitar playing. He was a great rhythm guitar player. I liked Django Reinhardt, and Django's brother was a great rhythm guitar player, and Freddy and Paul Buskirk both were the two best rhythm guitar players – other than Django's brother – that I've ever known. Freddy's one of the best guitar players, whether he's playing jazz or blues or country, all of it.

Freddy Powers: Merle has had some big hits in his catalog by then, like *"Mama Tried," "Okie From Muskogee," "Fighting Side of Me,"* and many more. But some nights, he would go out on stage and do Bob Wills' songs instead, or some new song that the public hadn't heard and his fans weren't familiar with and the audience would sometimes leave disappointed. They wanted to hear his hits and that's what they came for. Sometimes that would upset Merle, and he would then make the tour more work than it was supposed to be. Promoters back then I guess they half-expected it. Not just Merle but a lot of entertainers got by with more than they do today. Life seemed to be more of a party for everybody then. Now it's more business than party and promoters and venues are more likely to sue. One of my favorites on Merle: He had got into an argument with a promoter. He let him say what they had to, and then Merle said what he wanted to, and proceeded to walk out the door. The only problem is it wasn't the door to leave. Merle had accidentally walked into the broom closet. He walked back out like he meant to do that and waved his finger in the air, and said, "That's all I have to say," and walked out the door. The right door this time.

Marc Oswald: One of the funniest road stories I remember from my years touring with Merle and Freddy was the time we pulled in for a date in Worcester, MA about 2 hours outside of Boston. This was being billed as 'Merle Haggard & The Strangers w/Special Guest Freddy Powers', and we were playing the Theater in Worcester. Not surprisingly, because Merle was a huge superstar at the time, the show was sold out, and we were actually playing it as a make-up date because it had been canceled the year prior. Well, what was cool is not one of Merle's fans had asked for a refund in that year, so we stopped in Boston, MA with the procession of buses – two Semis and four buses. The reason we'd stopped was during that year in between the concert being canceled and our make-up date, the theater had gone bankrupt because apparently the theater manager had run off with all the money.

So this really nice elderly lady that owned the Theater lived in Boston, and had arranged for me to meet her at the bank so she could pay us for the show, which was like $40,000 or something large, so Merle wanted it done in person. Well, when we stopped in Boston, we parked all the buses and trucks around The Common, which is the central city park where they have the big fountains. All the street performers were playing music and doing mime acts, organ grinders with the monkeys, all of these little sideshows. So we stopped there right in the middle of a Saturday or something with a bunch of people hanging out in the park and all this activity going on. I jog on over the two or three blocks to the bank to meet the Theater owner, and I was going as fast as I did because we were running late for the show.

Well, by the time I got back, maybe an hour later and hopped on our bus to go, it was like a ghost town, I mean there was NOBODY on the buses, they were all gone, every last soul from the road crew, Merle's band, *everyone*. I couldn't find them, and it was really busy at that time of day, so I start looking around this park. Well before too long, sure enough I come across this HUGE crowd assembled around the fountain, and I'm talking 300 people. I couldn't quite tell what was going on yet, but I knew I was onto something. By the time I got over there and inched my way through all these people, there sat Freddy, Merle, Clint Strong, Deanie Bird Reynolds, and Tom Collins, all sitting there in their bus clothes – old t-shirts and sweats- picking. And the funny thing about this was, for as large a crowd as they'd attracted, because they all looked pretty beat up in their bus clothes, nobody knew who they were! Our buses didn't have the artist's name on them, so nobody had put two and two together, and again they looked damn near homeless the way they were dressed. But they had gotten out, set up shop and just started playing while I was gone. Well, they sounded so good that I threw my cowboy hat down right in front of Freddy just to see what would happen and threw a couple dollars in it, and before you knew it, the whole crowd started throwing money in the cowboy hat!

So as these guys played about three or four more songs – and they weren't playing hits, just jazz songs! Another funny thing happened when I turned around to see the guy who was the Mime, along with all his fellow street performers who worked that park every day, ALL watching these guys playing. And you could almost feel they were pissed off because here's this new act stealing away all the attention – and TIPS – that would have been going to them otherwise. (laughs) So as all this money was piling up in the cowboy hat, I snuck in and whispered to Freddy, 'Dude, we have GOT to leave', because by that point, we were running REALLY late for the show we were supposed to be playing.... So we get everyone back on the buses without too much hustle and bustle because no one had put together that Merle Haggard was sitting there. As we get on the bus, the final act of the comedy came when we're all finally sitting on the bus on our way up to Worcester, and it was Freddy, Deanie Bird, Clint, Merle and Me. Well, I had that Cowboy Hat full of tip money. I set it on the kitchen table, and it makes me bust out laughing when I think back about it, because the next thing I know, I'm watching five grown men straightening out these $1 bills – I don't think we got a single $5 – digging into this hat, counting up all the tips. We wound up with $143 dollars between singles and all the change. So I remember I took my booking commission, which was 10%, for laying the hat down, and then the band took the other 90% and sat there and divvied it up between them for this 'Gig' they had just played. Everybody made their $25 bucks, *Merle too*, and everybody was proud of that $25!

Merle got his cut too, because he was right in the middle of it, and what was funny to me was for all the fussing over this tip money they split up, the original reason we were in town was to pick up the fee for Merle's theater show, which was A LOT of money by comparison, and Merle NEVER asked me about it! So from the time we took off from the park to head to the show, it seemed to me that all he and the other guys in the band cared about was how they were going to cut up that $143 dollars. When I turned that $40,000 over to Fuzzy, Merle's manager, he found the whole thing pretty amusing too, because there was just something funny about that cowboy hat full of tips that everybody wanted to get a piece of, and it served for me as kind of a metaphor for the whole operation out there. Because leaving the bus and going and playing that park and then worrying about how to split up $140 was a bigger deal than going to play a sold-out show for thousands of screaming fans! They'd rather be in the park in their sweats and wife-beaters playing Jazz.

To top the whole day off, after all that – and being late and barely making the show –when we finally got up there, they got everybody loaded into the theater, and we're getting ready to start the show, and security comes over and says "There's been a bomb scare!" So they cleared everybody out of the theater – band and audience – and didn't find anything, then loaded everybody back in. We finally did that show that everybody had first wanted to hear a year before. It was quite a day…

Freddy Powers: We both had a love/hate relationship with the road. Not the performing as much because when we're not on the stage, we're still playing. With Merle, I think it bothered him more. We'd be gone for four or five days and he'd be ready to go home. He really longed for the houseboat, not to say I didn't too, but we'd get home and after a few days he'd be on the phone with the agents to book us a short tour, which generally ended up being lesser paying jobs because of such short notice and what venues were available. But Merle has also turned higher paying jobs down to come and be my guitar player on a gig that I had booked somewhere. Naturally I seemed to draw bigger crowds (laughs).

Biff Adams: A lot of times, Freddy would be the one to take Merle off stage at the end of shows, so he'd take the mic and thank everyone for coming. Merle and Freddy would make a beeline for the backstage exit door to get out of there before it got too crazy with fan frenzy. He would tell a lot of jokes and stuff. Freddy's timing was great for jokes, he always had a joke for everything. I watched a couple of his live shows from the audience and a lot of times, he'd tell jokes I'd already heard a couple years earlier, but the way he delivered it on stage just like I was hearing it for the first time. I'd laugh my ass off, so he was a natural born joke teller on top of being a gifted songwriter and guitar player.

That was versus Merle, who hardly ever talked on stage during shows. He used to say 'They're not here to hear me talk, they're here to hear me sing', and I'd say 'That's exactly right.' So a lot of times, Freddy would do cover routine things during Merle's shows like introducing the band sometimes, that's one example how much Merle trusted Freddy. He would always throw some humor in there too. For instance, I'm a pretty big guy, I weigh around 290, so when it came time to introduce me to the crowd, Freddy would joke and say 'And we've got little, bitty Biff Adams back there on drums…', and the crowd of course laughed because they could see me sitting back there.

Marc Oswald: Sometimes Freddy was just a musician up there, and other times, it almost seemed like he was a bandleader to a degree, especially on the songs he wrote with Merle. And sometimes he was a buddy up there, so it was like he played a lot of different roles up there on stage with Merle. He didn't just have one role, and it depended on what song was being played, but I think as a player, he gave sort of that Jazz 'Cred' and elevated the game on the stage. But of course, Merle's band was so freakin' good, that they were all Jazz players really.

Freddy Powers: Being a star can work for you as well as work against you. We were at a concert setting on the bus looking out and watching the crowd once when someone called it a circus. I told Merle when I was a young boy back in Seminole, Texas I had visions of running away with a circus. I said if the circus had come to town on a train, I would have hopped in a boxcar and went with them. Merle asked me, "Have you ever heard of anyone running away from a circus?" Of course, I had to reply no. Merle said, "That's what I feel like doing, running away from this circus right now." It was me, Dean Holloway and Deanie Bird. We all started agreeing, actually kidding saying, "Yeah, let's get the hell out of here and go fishing." The next thing I knew, Merle had convinced us to sneak off and get out of there. We were sneaking out the back and going up the ramp when I said, "Wait a minute, what are we doing, what are we running away from – our friends and our fans that love us and can't wait for you to perform your music for them?" Merle agreed and we all turned around and went on stage instead and probably played one of our best shows.

Biff Adams: On the road, Merle had his own bus, and Freddy would spend a lot of time over on Merle's bus and they'd sit over there and play a lot. I drove that bus a lot of times so I saw a lot of that, and it always kept them busy picking and writing songs. Freddy was a fun guy to be around, he always kept everybody in a good mood, and a lot of times Merle would come back after a show and might be complaining because something technical hadn't gone off quite right, and Freddy used to always be the one to cheer him up. He fit that part real good, and he did that both for Merle and for us in the band. If we were down or something, you could always count on Freddy coming by and saying 'Hey, what's the matter today Biff?', and he was a good guy to cheer you up or get your mind off something. He had a way with being able to get you off of thinking about it, and was always a good guy to be around, he really was. He always had a joke and a smile, or a good story to tell you because he'd had such a long, interesting life.

Catherine Powers: Freddy was always Merle's motivator, for instance, on tour, Freddy was generally the only one who could go on Merle's bus and wake him up to go out and play when Merle would be tired, and would say "Oh, I don't want to go do the show tonight." It was funny because Freddy would put his humor into it, and use Merle's old Prisoner number from when he was an inmate at San Quentin, and say, "Up and at 'em, on your feet!", acting like a prison guard, and Merle would do it! Merle used to laugh and joke with Freddy all the time about his time in prison, especially since all of Merle's crimes that sent him there were petty crimes. I think he broke into a restaurant that was open, so Merle would make jokes about it, and talk about how Johnny Cash had told him once, "Hey, you've been there, you've lived it, you let the world know it." There wasn't much Merle didn't talk about to Freddy, especially out there on that bus on the road. They spent a lot of hours just talking, and had a lot of really close, emotional, private moments together.

Linda Mitchell: Freddy would shake anybody's hand. Merle had an aversion to shaking hands because that was his livelihood, his fingers, and so Freddy was his surrogate out on the lake and road a lot of times.

Anne Reynolds: You have no idea how bad that was for Merle. People were so... women tried to force their way onto the bus, they rocked the bus trying to turn it over, and were so rude and loud and demanding. I've seen lots of this, and once Merle finally came out and said "Folks, this is my home, would you please leave my home alone?", because they just went wild.

Freddy Powers: One time on the road, I remember Dean Roe, Deanie Bird and I were standing outside the bus talking when I turned around and saw Merle watching us through the port hole of his bus. Merle just couldn't get off his bus and roam around the venues or in public like we could. He generally can't walk five feet before someone has stopped him for an autograph, and if he stops for one, it draws a crowd. The burdens of staying on top made him a prisoner in that bus, and that's how the *"Silver Eagle"* came about.

Merle Haggard: We used to talk about things like that, we used to talk about 'Let's just set up and play here at 7:30 rather than going to the gig.'

Freddy Powers: For whatever the headaches of the road, Merle's name was always magic on tour. If you wanted a hotel room when the hotel was full, all you had to do was mention Merle and they would move someone if they had to. If a restaurant was closed, they would sometimes open up for him. One of Merle's pet peeves was when a restaurant would stop serving Breakfast at 11 AM. Hell, the only time Merle got up at 11 was when he never went to bed. Whatever time he got up, he wanted breakfast (and nothing else would do), and I have been with him when he would really raise hell, but it always seemed to get him breakfast.

Traveling around the world as stars – especially Merle – gave us the opportunity to meet and keep girls around all the time and boy did we like that! Being able to pick and choose all the girls we wanted- and we did. We spent a fortune on girls just flying them in for an evening of partying. During the cocaine days it was always a party, even on tour. We'd party all night and sleep all day. When it would come time to do the show, sometimes Merle wouldn't want to go on. Everybody in the crew: Biff, Lewis, Deanie Bird and I – would talk with Merle till he would finally go on. But then sometimes he would only do about 45 minutes, then close the show. That would leave the audience pissed off and the promoters raising hell. Merle would then get mad himself and threaten to fire everybody in the band and go home.

Pot's about the only "drug" I put in my body after that. Even when I turned 75 years old and was still smoking, I felt like I was 40 or younger and I passed for mid-to-late 50s all the time. I know men half my age that are not in as good a shape as I am or as healthy as I am. My doctors tell me all the time they have 50 or 60 year old that would make me look like a kid. All my friends – men and women – who are my age or close are also marijuana smokers and have been since their young 20s and younger feel young and act young and most of them look as good as I do. I'm not bragging, it's just the plain truth. I see other men my age using canes or worse in wheel chairs, have false teeth and have had several bypasses or hip replacements, or some other health problems. And they damn sure aren't having sex, most of them have been only dreaming about it and living with the memories of sex since they were 55 or 60 years old.

So don't tell me marijuana is bad for you or addictive, and it DOES NOT get in the way of a professional career unless YOU let it. I can't and wouldn't mention any names but I have a lot of friends and acquaintances that are in high profile positions who show up for work every day and lead a normal life and are very successful in their professions. And if anyone uses marijuana as an excuse for committing murder, rape, or any other crime should be convicted because they are the biggest liars in the world.

I guarantee you alcohol or speed was probably in every case. Marijuana might make you hungry and kill you from the weight you gain, but 'Murder,' I can tell you no way. I'm not proud of my cocaine days and I'm glad I saw the light before it destroyed me and I ended that part of my life, but marijuana is something both Merle and I kept smoking regularly even after we quit doing cocaine in the mid-80s. Hell, I'll arrive at the Pearly Gates with a joint hanging between my teeth when I finally get to Heaven, a big smile on my face as marijuana has helped me live well past when anyone ever predicted I would.

Photo Chapter 1

Freddy as a Boy Soldier

Freddy as a Teen Marine in the mid-1940s

Freddy At Archery practice in the US Marine Core

Freddy in Service w/ Fellow Marines, late 1940s

Freddy and Don Powers as teens in Freddy's first car, later 1940s

Freddy as Teen in mid-1940s w/his trusty Rifle on Plains of West Texas

Freddy in the mid-50s in Barber School

Freddy out on the town with Marines, early 1950s

BROTHER PAUL BUSKIRK and his "Little Men" LIN RECORDING ARTISTS FREDDY POWERS

Freddy Performing on stage with mentor Paul Buskirk on first in-color program on WBAP TV

Freddy (center) and the Powers Family Band, The W Boys, mid-1950s

Freddy Autographed Late 1950s Fan Promo Photo

Norm Stephens, Freddy, Hank Thompson, and Don Powers

Freddy (center) Playing Banjo on NBC, late 1950s

'Be My Love 45'

Freddy Powers and Bobby Helms, 1950s

Freddy (center) and Willie Nelson (far right) playing Bass in Freddy's Band, 1963

Freddy shaking hands w/ Host on The Today Show, 1962

Wednesday, August 1, 1962 THE NEWS TEXAN Page 1

Arlington Scene

Scouts Set Ranch Trip

The Scouts of Troop 156 will leave at 2 p.m. Saturday for a trip to Palo Pinto county and the Worth Ranch.

There the boys will get a close look at the ranch and western life.

The troop, sponsored by the Sertoma Club of Arlington, will spend the night on the Worth ranch before making the return trip. Sunday they will attend church services provided on the ranch and on the two-day trip eat all their meals in the ranch house mess-hall.

Saturday night they will sleep in tents that have already been provided.

The troop is a special troop for mentally retarded boys. Boys making the trip are Ronnie Ellis, Billy Brooks, Gary Curtis, Buddy Strange, Billy Ots and Sammy White. Men accompanying the boys are Dave Ellis, assistant scout master, F. W. Ots, J. L. Strange, Bill Nolen, scout master, Kenneth Lee, chairman of the troop committee and Joe Houston, institutional representative.

NEW YORK BOUND -- Freddy Powers is shown shaking hands with John Chancellor following a taped segment of the show used on the National network while the "Today" crew was in Arlington. Powers and his band will leave Monday for New York. Others in the picture are Bobby Hollinsworth, and Ralph Sanford. Behind Powers is the groups business manager Arden Powers. --NEWS TEXAN PHOTO.

...and I Quote

AUGUST 10

Banjo Band Sets New 'Today' Date

BY UP INTERNATIONAL

BERLIN - An American spokesman, commenting on Russian threats to shoot down a U.S. helicopter if it flew over East Berlin:

"We certainly plan to continue to fly in accordance with our rights within the control zone."

Freddy Powers and his banjo band will leave Monday morning for New York and make final arrangements for their second appearance on the "Today" show. While in New York, the group will also make final arrangements to cut a record album and for appearance on the Dinah Shore fall show. It was not known if their appearance would be on a special or the regular weekly show.

The local group first gained recognition following an appearance on the morning show "Today" when it visited...

ALT Sales

Freddy Powers (second in from left) and Powerhouse IV – Early 1960s

Freddy, Today Show producer Don Silverman and company out at the legendary Copa Cabana, 1962

Freddy International Talent Agency Head Shot, early 1960s

Freddy Powers (second in from left) Playing Drums w/ his band the Powerhouse IV

Freddy's Mother Mary Singing On Stage w/Freddy Playing Guitar in Background late 70s

Freddy Powers (center w/Banjo) Headlining at the Showboat Casino, 1975

CURRENTLY APPEARING
THE FREDDY POWERS SHOW
thru October 26

THE MATYS BROTHERS
featuring Maria Carmen
thru October 26

VIC & DEE CARDIS

1975 Elko, NV Appearing - Freddy Powers

1974 Houston, TX - Freddy Powers Show

1975 Alexandria, MN - Freddy's Boat

1975 Elko, NV - Milton, Trout, Freddy

1976 Jackpot, NV - Matt, Freddy, Don, Larry, Milton

1976 Jackpot, NV - Freddy Powers

1976 Ramada Pool Scottsdale, AZ - Larry, Sandy, Milton, Freddy

1976 Fisherman Freddy Powers

1976 06 MN - Milton, Bob, Freddy, Larry - Jammin

1976 MN Horseshoes - Freddy, Milton, Larry'

Paul Buskirk, Freddy and Deanie Bird Reynolds

Freddy Powers and Willie Nelson (center left and right) at Gilley's Recording Studio During the "Somewhere Over the Rainbow" Sessions, which Freddy produced 1980

Original Set of Lyrics to Freddy's first self-penned #1 hit, "Natural High"

Floyd Tillman, Coach Darrell Royal and Freddy 1982

Freddy Powers, Larry Gatlin and DeanieBird Reynolds

Freddy Powers (far left) and Merle Haggard (2nd in) playing at Silverthorne Resort Live Club, mid-1980s

Freddy Powers and Merle Haggard (4th and 5th from left) on The Johnny Cash TV Show w Johnny and June (far right), early 1980s

Billboard Hot Country Singles Chart 1985 Celebrating 3 weeks at #1 for "Looking For a Place to Fall Apart"

Freddy's USSF Houseboat with his hand-built Natural High Airplane Mounted On Top, Lake Shasta, California, mid-1980s

Freddy Powers (center) at Willie 1984 Pedernales Invitational Golf Tournament

Merle Haggard (2nd from left), Sherrill Rogers, and Freddy Powers (2nd from right) at the BMI Awards Ceremony, mid-1980s

BMI Congratulations Letter to Freddy Powers for Joining the Coveted "Million-Air" Songwriters' Club after achieving over 1 million plays at radio for songs he'd written

Willie Nelson and Freddy Powers (center) Playing at Willie's Somewhere Over the Rainbow Headlining Gig on the legendary Austin City Limits TV Show, 1980s

Freddy Powers' First Pilot License

Freddy Showcasing his Silly Side on Tour with Merle Haggard, 1986

Actor James Garner, Freddy's Mother Mary and Freddy (left) at Coach Darrell Royal Golf Invitational, later 1980s

Freddy posing with his airplane, Air Fred, 1986

Freddy's Gyro-copter, which he taught himself to Pilot, mid-1980s

Freddy and Catherine Powers on their Harley Davidson Dyna Wide Glide with a Fatboy Front End, early 1990s

Freddy with special passenger Amelia, the Sheltie Catherine received in lieu of an Engagement Ring

Freddy Powers and Willie Nelson (center) back home in Austin, Texas on Willie's Ranch Picking for the Cameras, mid-1990s

Rogers and Hammerhead TV Show Set, Freddy and Catherine's Living Room, Austin, Texas, Mid-1990s

Freddy Powers with Rogers and Hammerhead co-host and biking buddy Bill McDavid, mid-1990s

Willie Nelson (far left) with Freddy Powers and Bill McDavid on Rogers & Hammerhead TV Show Set, later 1990s

Freddy Powers and Mel Tillis swapping jokes at the Freddy Powers Dirty Joke Night

Freddy and Bill McDavid with Legendary Dallas Cowboys Coast Barry Switzer (center)

City of Austin

Proclamation

Be it known by these presents that
I, Kirk Watson, Mayor of the City of Austin, Texas,
do hereby proclaim

April 30, 1998

as

Rogers & Hammerhead Day

in Austin, and call on all citizens to join me in recognizing that the Rogers & Hammerhead Show, an already well known interview series enjoyed by many people in Austin, has been nominated for the prestigious CableACE Awards presented each year by the National Academy of Cable Programming to recognize and promote excellence in cable television programming, in recognizing that the Rogers & Hammerhead Show, produced by Freddy Powers and Bill McDavid, also known as Mr. Rogers & Hammerhead, along with Ingrid Weigand of the Austin Music Network and TimeWarner Cable, was created to acknowledge songwriters and to give them a chance to talk about their work, and in congratulating all those involved in the creation and production of the Rogers & Hammerhead Show which can be seen in Austin only on the Austin Music Network, Channel 15.

Attest

Mayor
Kirk Watson

Austin, Texas Proclamation by Mayor that April 30th, 1998 was Officially Rogers & Hammerhead Day

Freddy and Catherine Powers on Location at Merle Haggard's 'Motorcycle Cowboy' Video

Freddy and Catherine Powers Out on the Town at Coach Darryl Royal Golf Tournament

Freddy and Amelia On Stage, later 1990s

Freddy and Willie (2nd and 3rd in from left) recording in the studio, later 1990s, recording the Freddy-penned Nevada Special Olympics Theme Song *'Everybody Has a Chance to Win'*

Freddy Powers w/Nevada Special Olympics Medal Winners Timmy and Debbie

Freddy Performing at the Aftershow to the Freddy Powers Celebrity Golf Invitational

Freddy Powers Signing Autographs for Country Jazz Singer LP, later 1990s

Freddy Powers Holding Willie Nelson's legendary guitar Trigger, later 1990s

Freddy Powers on Tour Bus with his Customized Ovation Django-Style Guitar, late 1990s

Freddy Powers and Merle Haggard Backstage Together, early 2000s

Freddy Powers and Merle Haggard Performing on stage together, 2004

Freddy Powers (left) and John Rich (right) out on the Town Together, early 2000s

**LISTEN WHILE YOU READ ALONG TO
BRAND NEW FREDDY POWERS MUSIC!!!**

(Portrait by Robert Hurst)

**Over 30 Never-Before-Heard Performances
Spanning Freddy Powers' 5-Decade Career!!**

**Listen for the first time to Freddy Powers & The Powerhouse IV
LIVE IN VEGAS & LIVE IN RENO!!**

STREAM ON SPOTIFY, DOWNLOAD ON iTUNES, LISTEN ON YOUTUBE, AND MANY OTHER DIGITAL MUSICAL PLATFORMS!!

Freddy's USSF Houseboat with his hand-built Natural High Airplane Mounted On Top, Lake mid-1980s

CHAPTER 10: AIR CRAFT CARRIER ON A LAKE

Freddy Powers: 'Natural High' was not only the name of a # 1 hit I wrote for Merle, but also of my ultra-lite airplane that I built myself out on the Lake. I found in flying a great form of relaxation, there was something very peaceful about taking off of the water and getting some distance from whatever was going on down below back on planet earth. I had studied flying years back and it was in my blood. I wanted to fly and own airplanes. Deanie Bird and I bought a little Gyro but we only went up in it a few times. I had heard about these ultra-light kits that you put together yourself, so I called the company and ordered one. With our celebrity status, they didn't want any bad publicity if something went wrong and if I crashed, so they sent one of their mechanics out with the plane to oversee me and make sure I was putting it together right.

Merle Haggard: I watched this man single-handedly build his own airplane on the dock out in front of my houseboat, I watched in amazement. After I watched him assemble this homemade aircraft, I had enough confidence in him to believe he could actually fly that thing and not kill himself because I watched him do it.

Biff Adams: I was with Merle actually watching Freddy build that plane by himself. Freddy was a good troubleshooter whenever we had problems out there at the lake with the boats or whatever; you could bring it to Fred, and he'd usually come up with some kind of useful solution or suggestion, 'Well, why don't you do this…', and I'd normally find myself saying 'Hey,

I never thought of that, I think I'll try that'. Sometimes it worked and sometimes it didn't, and with that plane of his, it did. I never trusted the engine on Freddy's plane, it sounded like a lawnmower to me!

Linda Mitchell: Freddy flew his Ultralight airplane all over the lake! You couldn't hide from Freddy, he'd find you if you were out some place.

Anne Reynolds: Freddy and Merle had a helicopter they would fly around in that Dean would pilot, because Dean started flying helicopters at 16, and for years, he flew helicopters from Grand Aisle out to the oil rigs during the week. So he was an accomplished helicopter pilot and would fly them around the lake while Merle and Freddy looked down on girls sunbathing on the porches of the houseboats. They were like little school kids, naughty boys, and were always goofing off doing stuff.

Freddy Powers: I originally built the way it came out on wheels. I remember I got out on the runway, and kept taxiing up and down it, just getting faster and faster until one day I just took off and flew. It was a great sensation: here I was flying, flying in a plane I built with my own two hands! Merle probably had more belief in my flying abilities than anybody else. He knew how much I wanted to fly and he believed I could. He said if he didn't believe I could fly and not kill myself, he would have been trying like hell to talk me out of it. So instead he became my air traffic controller. He would be on the dock with a two-way radio telling me what he knew of flying as Merle is a pilot himself and used to fly before I got interested in it. Everything went okay when I flew from the airport, but then one day I was going to land up at Merle's ranch and I lost air speed and crashed it.

Merle Haggard: Freddy wanted to fly that plane and I knew he was serious about it. I have my own pilot's license, I'm a pilot, and understand what it takes to fly, and I told him everything I could tell him about flying and I loved him enough that I would have tried to talk him out of it if I hadn't had confidence in his will to fly it. We talked a lot about it as he built this thing, and before he got his license to fly, I watched him learn how to fly on the lake, and his theory was: "Well, if I fall, I'll only fall 40 feet, and that water'll be soft!" Well, that wasn't true, anytime he'd have fallen, he'd have been dead.

We had this two-way radio from the boat to the airplane and I was the control tower with most of the flying experience, so most of the knowledge was on the ground. He did almost kill himself a couple times, and one of those times I remember clear to this day was when he took off in his airplane, got it up in the air. He tried to go out over Box Canyon and the trees were high on both sides, and he got back in there and could only turn that plane so much. Because the pine trees were about 100 feet tall and this was a little peninsula and he got in there and couldn't get out! I think he got the plane high enough to touch the top of the trees, but because it was an under-powered airplane, he had some of the trees hitting the bottom of his plane.

I thought he'd killed himself, and thought I was going to have to go tell people "Freddy Powers has killed himself in an ultralight aircraft that he built himself and I watched him do it." But he made it back in, and by some miracle, he finally got the plane up over that son of a bitch, came back around and landed and banged the shit out of the airplane – but he almost bought it that day.

Freddy Powers: I had the ranch hands load it up on a truck and as soon as I got back, I called and ordered pontoons. I decided right then I wanted something softer to fall on if I ever crashed again. I would rather be landing on water than the hard pavement any day. I took the airplane back to the hanger and redesigned the landing facilities, took off the wheels, and put the plane on pontoons.

Damon Garner: I sold Freddy the plane we did the "*Natural High*" video with, put it together and had it lettered, and Merle would put him on a private jet and fly him to Carson City and he'd stay with me while he was learning to fly this new little airplane that we built. So it came time, he wanted to get it up to Redding to Merle's ranch, and he wanted to put it on floats eventually, because I was flying on floats out on Lake Tahoe and he thought that was really cool. So I drove up to the ranch and Merle was there with his drummer Biff Adams, and Freddy and I had talked about where he wanted to land, down by one of Merle's barns, and so we went down and I told Merle and Biff after a quick look around, "Man, this is too rocky for him to land on, he'll blow a tire or something," and Merle said "Well, we'll just clean it off."

So we started moving rocks off this dirt path that was going to be the landing strip, and most of them we moved to the left, and we worked quite a while, a good half hour, cleaning off this dirt road. I mean, it was a job, so Freddy finally shows up and we're kind of waving at him to land on this little dirt road by the barn. Well, from the air, he must of thought for some reason that we were waving him off, but it was plain to see he needed to land on the road. Anyway, when he came down, he landed right in the rocks! When he did, he broke off the landing gear, and the expression on Merle's face was priceless, he turned to me and said, "We did all this for that?!!"

When Freddy was first learning to fly, he just couldn't get enough, so one morning, he came down and said "I want to fly out to the dry lake bed,' and I said "Okay, but I think the winds are gonna be coming up this afternoon," because the wind really blows around Reno." So he said, "I'm just going to fly out by Fallon, do some touch and goes and then come back," and I cautioned him, "Okay, but if you feel the wind picking up, get out of there." Well off he went, and I watched him fly off, had a couple students of my own and so an hour goes by and Fred isn't back yet, and then two hours pass and he wasn't back. Then three hours go by and he still wasn't back, and by that point, everybody at the airport was starting to worry, so we jumped in our trucks, drove the 20 miles over to where this dry lake bed was, hoping he was okay.

To my relief, as we're driving, I saw him up in the air, heading back to the air strip at Carson City, so we turned around, and when we got back, he'd already landed. When we pulled up to him, he was just shaking and I jump out and say, 'Freddy, what's going on??" Well, my eyes went wide when he replied, "My steering wheel fell off!", and I said "You've got to be kidding me?? How did you get the plane back?" With that, Freddy opens the door to the cockpit and says, "Well, look," and what had happened was, it came off while he was still in the air landing in one of those dry lake beds and somehow he got it down. Then he walked around in the desert on what he described as a scavenger hunt, found a piece of wire, and he wired the steering wheel back on and flew it home! Next he told me, "I'm lucky to be back here," and we both burst into laughter, partly in relief because we both knew what a close call it had been. Freddy was always adventurous.

Rattlesnake Annie: One time he wanted me to fly with him in his plane back from Reno, he'd gotten stuck there because of the weather. So on our way to go to the plane, he ran out of gas in his truck, and I said "I'm NOT flying with you! You can't get to your airplane without running out of gas!" (laughs)

Merle Haggard: As Freddy got to be a better pilot, he'd take his plane up and spot fish and women, and I was in the bass boat and he'd tell me where to go to find either one.

Marc Oswald: In his 'Natural High' plane, Freddy would fly over the lake and look for schools of shad that he could see swirling from the air. Then he'd land his plane, and taxi out toward the schools of shad, because wherever the shad are, the bass are, they're just swimming underneath the shad. So Freddy would find a spot he liked, land, shut the motor off, and he would fish right there, and catch fish every time because he could see where they were, it was great! He used to carry fishing poles on his plane, and he would cast right off the plane.

CHAPTER 10: AIR CRAFT CARRIER ON A LAKE

Freddy Powers: *"Ridin' High"* was a song Deanie Bird and I wrote. That's just a song, some ideas we had at the time. Merle and I both are pilots and I had a little seaplane there on the lake that lands on water, you know. And I had been flying around that lake all the time, and during the time when I was really hot into flying and Merle was also involved in it, you know, everyone up there was all involved in my big airplane adventure. But during the time we wrote a couple three songs that had to do with flying. That was just where our heads were at the time, but this was the ultimate one of them."

Marc Oswald: One day I was out there, just me and Fred, and I got in one of the bass boats and took off fishing by myself because I was killing time waiting for Merle to meet with me to approve some tour dates. So I was just out there all day, and I didn't catch a single damn fish, and I was out there by myself all day until I finally heard an engine coming, and looked up and sure enough, Freddy's circling over me in his plane. Well, he lands on the water in the 'Natural High' plane, and taxis up to this little bass boat of Merle's I'd borrowed, and asks me how I was doing, and I told him the fishing wasn't worth a shit that day. So he says, 'Well, hold on here a minute,' takes off on his plane, and comes back about five minutes later, unzips this little thing on the back of his plane, and pulls out a BIG OLD BASS. So then he flashes that famous Freddy Powers smile, and tells me to follow him, and took me over to this other place on the lake where the fish were biting.

Freddy Powers: So here I am up there flying as Merle had told me, most of the flying knowledge was on the ground watching. But I taught myself how to fly and land and take off on water. Merle's boat, The Hotel Troubadour, was the headquarters and command post for the 'Spree of 83'. It was also the Air Traffic Control center for me and my airplane. As I got more sure of myself as a pilot, I ventured out and began flying all over the lake. I quickly saw the advantages of low flying around the lake. Besides spotting the shad for a good fishing location, I could spot the naked women sunbathing. I would radio back to Merle and tell him where the naked women were, and he'd get in his bass boat, come out and meet me and I'd land next to him. Then we'd join the naked women for some sunbathing of our own.

Merle Haggard: He had a hydraulic lift built on the back of his boat where he could pick the airplane up out of the water so it came up about six – eight feet off the water, that sat on the back of the houseboat, sticking off the back end. People could see it for 100 miles. He did all that himself, I just kind of watched it.

Scotty Joss: The funniest thing I ever remember seeing was when Fred put that plane on the back of his houseboat with the lift that took it up and down, and I remember Merle just standing there looking at him like he was crazy! Merle thought that was just the funniest thing he ever saw, putting that pontoon plane up on top of the back of that boat.

Freddy Powers: I had an 80-gallon solar hot water storage tank on the roof of my houseboat and an electric lift Merle's son-in-law at the time had designed and built for me that lifted the plane on the top of my houseboat. We'd go up and spend several days on the Pit River and if we ran out of supplies or needed to make a phone call or something, I'd lower the plane in the water, take off for the marina and get whatever we needed before flying back. My houseboat was the only Aircraft Carrier on the lake.

Marc Oswald: On Freddy's 'Natural High' plane, there were no doors on the plane! So when he would fly it, it had a front nose on it and a little windshield, but was open on the sides. You wore a helmet and a ski-vest when you flew with him in it. But the thing about Freddy's boat that I think was the most awesome was that ultralight lift on the back that lifted the plane up onto the roof, because Freddy would taxi the plane right up to the back of this boat, and the plane would go into this little rack, almost like a jet-ski that you'd pull up to the back of the boat. And it had a cable and an electric motor in it, and it lifted the plane right up onto the roof.

Freddy Powers: Later on, I wanted something a little bigger so I could fly back and forth from Redding to Lake Tahoe, a Cessna 150. It was a cherry after I had it rebuilt. That one I called 'Air Fred', and it served its purpose for a while. I was making plenty of money then so I later bought a Cherokee 180, which went a little faster than the Cessna and seated four plus baggage. So depending on my trip I would choose the airplane I wanted to fly that day.

By this time, I had a lot of flying experience and had gotten my pilot's license. Merle hadn't flown in a while but wanted to fly over his ranch to look it over, and he wanted to fly my Cherokee. Knowing Merle was a pilot, I had no problem saying yes. So we went out to the airport and took off. Merle was at the controls. He was making low passes and turning too sharp of turns for that airplane, not to mention we were right on the verge of controlled air space. I kept telling him to get out of the TCA, and kept my hands close to the yolk at all times.

Merle Haggard: I got in his plane one time and was going to fly it, and all it had was a throttle and there wasn't no instruments or nothing, no way to tell when you had enough speed or nothing, I couldn't see anything on there. So I got it out one time, got it ready to take off, and then at the last minute I just taxied back up back and said, "I ain't gonna fly this plane like this, I'm not going to kill myself today." Well about a year or two later,

I was with Freddy, and he'd never seen me fly, so he didn't know if I was bullshitting him or not. So one time he came out to my house and he was flying his Cherokee 180, we went out to the airport. I told Freddy "I want to fly over my house for some building I got going on," then I surprised him and said "Let me fly your airplane!" He'd never seen me fly, so he said "Are you sure you want to fly this plane? This thing has a funny brake on it, how long's it been since you've flown?" And I said, "Well, I can fly this plane Fred," and when we got in the plane, I could see it had a brake that you pulled up with your hand. So you'd reach up underneath the dash, pull this thing up, and it'd stop the airplane.

See, most brakes in airplanes are foot pedals, but this one didn't have that, it had the brake up there by the hand, and I said "Damn Freddy, I've never seen a brake like this!" See, the brake's usually above the rotor, and he said "No you pull this one with your hand." So then I asked him, "Well, what happens if its pulled when you land?", and Freddy said "No, you don't do that, keep it down…" So we're taxiing out there, and we take off, and Freddy says "You're too low, you're too low," and I said "I want to fly over my house out here." We were only about 800 feet in the air, flying over my house, and I knew there was another runway across from the main one that was 120 degrees that way, and 300 and something that way. So we were up over my house, and I just kinda started steering us down, knowing that runway was there – but Freddy didn't know it! So he started screaming and hollerin' in there, "Hag!", as I'm going toward the ground, and just landed on the runway. I about scared him to death because first we landed on the wrong runway, and I kind of just let it go down real fast and scared him a little more. Then I squeezed it on him, and said "Look it there," and he said "You have scared the shit out of me!", and then says, "My God, you can fly, can't ya!" (laughs)

Freddy Powers: I must say that day scared the SHIT out of me and Merle knows it. I think he was probably just jiving with me, anyway, it did scare me but I do believe Merle is a good pilot.

Merle Haggard: I don't think we ever flew together except for that one time. I watched him fly, and there was about an 18-month period there where he was flying that I wasn't, but I was trying to give him all the knowledge I had when he'd go up. I remember another time Fred and Deanie Bird were flying once over Nevada out there and got into a bad deal where the wings started to ice up in the air. Freddy got frightened and couldn't fly it, and turned it over to Deanie Bird, who was an old helicopter pilot. So he nosed it over and took it down underneath the ice level, and the ice began to fall off the wings… he credited Deanie Bird with saving his life that day.

Freddy (kneeling, center) with his Air Fred Band and Airplane in the Background, later-1980s

CHAPTER 11: THE AIR FRED BAND

B.B. Morse: Freddy was a Jedi! I started work with him in the mid-80s after we went on a fishing trip together up at Lake Shasta, and Freddy Jr. and I had been playing together, sometimes in a trio, sometimes in a 5-piece band, and it was an in-between band kind of thing when we weren't booked with other guys. Anyway, over President's Weekend in 84, we went up to Shasta to go fishing and had jam sessions on the houseboats with Merle. Scotty Joss was always a part of those, and it became a regular thing. At that time, Freddy was looking for a new bass player because Deanie-Bird's health wasn't all that great, so one day he said to me, "You know BB, you're a good bass player, but that electric bass just isn't my sound. If you'll take what you know that you learned from Deanie Bird and put it on an Upright bass, I'll hire you full-time."

So the next day I showed up on his doorstep with an upright bass! I couldn't play it, or hardly hold it at the time. It was kind of an interesting time in my life musically and personally because I'd let myself get up to around 368 pounds and my arms were so heavy I couldn't even hold it or hold my arms up for an entire song. Those upright basses aren't heavy either, they're like an eggshell, they look big and massive but you can pick it up with one arm and just go straight up off the floor with it. But it's the change-over of the physical relationship you have in the physical relationship you have with an instrument. Being an electric player all my life, I didn't have to play in this vertical position. I was in a horizontal position with the electric bass, and that transition and the combination of being inspired, I lost over 100 pounds, and I could hold my arms up for 8 hours at a time.

I even slept with that bass at times because I used to lay down and practice because I couldn't hold my arms up at first, and would fall asleep sometimes with my fingers still in the position of chording. Before long, it was a kind of labyrinth rising from the ashes, because I was 39 years old and starting over with a new kind of bass style, because I'd grown up with the Rock & Roll/Psychedelic/Blues bass, and had never played Dixieland Jazz before. I did know a handful of cowboy songs because my dad was a cowboy. I played with Freddy the first 2 ½ years before he let me walk a pattern with the bass, because there's a correct method of pattern of avoiding any clashes melodically that when you walk a line properly. Then that line automatically is in synchronicity of its self to generate harmony to the melody, and to expand what the footprint of say just the said changes of the song are. It's also the flavor you add to them, and Freddy's players were always the most colorful. The people who were playing with Freddy, from Perry Shumer, John Gurten, Joe Manuel, Bobby Black, Jimmy Day, Ben Wilburn, Johnny Gimble, were all world-class musicians.

Scotty Joss: In the wintertime up at Silverthorne, obviously everything would shut down, so it was a spring-summer-early fall type of gig, and then it turned into a dinner house when the winter season came on. That's when Freddy would turn back into the band leader. I love that guy! He took me to Reno, and I played seven nights a week with him in Reno and Tahoe, we just had so much fun. It was all the Django Reinhardt thing, fast, furious and just keep it going and throwing solo after solo after solo, Clint Strong was in there a lot, Deanie Bird played bass, and various drummers if they could keep up. Freddy just turned back into Mr. Entertainer, and got to do what Fred loved to do, which was just GET IT and to that Swing thing he was so very good at. He'd slow it down every once in a while, but it was Freddy being cut loose again and it was so much fun.

Troy Powers: My dad got me a guitar when I was in the 3rd grade, and when I was in the 5th grade, I taught Freddy the chords to "*Joy to the World*" by Three Dog Night. I was 24 when I joined Freddy's band as a guitar player. Back then, we where were sometimes the house band at a world-famous club in Ft. Worth, Texas called Billy Bob's when we weren't playing as Freddy's road band when he was on tour. Hillary Hamburg was playing piano and Ernie Hager was on steel guitar. One day, Hillary came up to Freddy and said "I don't think it's fair that we can't have women on the bus but you can," and Freddy replied, "Listen, it's my band, it's my bus, I'm paying your salary. If you don't like it, go home… You know what, I'll just take you to the bus station in the morning." So I asked him, "Are you going to fly him home Fred?", and he said, "Fuck no, I'm going to put him on a bus," because normally Freddy would buy them an airline ticket to send them home.

I was just playing rhythm, but that was a hot little band man. It was me, Gary Church, Gary Xavier, Tom Neils, Freddy and Deanie Bird Reynolds. Once I joined Freddy's band, he taught me all sorts of chords, and how to play things over the top of major chords, everything, he taught me the business, how to run a band, road managing, and between him and my dad, they taught me everything. My dad taught me what he could teach me, and then sent me to Freddy, but you gotta understand, just because I was his nephew doesn't mean he cut me any more slack than the next guy. I'll tell you what Freddy did to me once: We were getting ready for one of my first shows playing with him, and he told me, "Now, I don't want you using any kind of effects on your amp," and I said "Okay." Well, it just didn't sound right to me man, so I reached over without him looking, and turned my re verb up a little bit, just a little bit. We had a packed house that night too, but here in a minute, Freddy reaches over and turns my amplifier completely off, and says to me, "Just play with it off until you can learn to take orders."

Milton Quackenbush: I linked back up with Freddy in 1986 when he called and asked if I wanted to play a gig with him and his band at the El Dorado. He had a great line-up, it was Bobby Black on pedal steel, Clint Strong on guitar, and me on piano, Gary Church on clarinet, Deanie Bird on bass, and then we had Chris Jacobs for a while on drums and then Teri Coté came in. We'd get a lot of musicians come out to Harrah's because the band was awesome!

Troy Powers: Freddy was off one night playing with Willie or Merle, and when he would do that, he'd hire someone like Joe Ed Jordan to come in and play, and I remember asking "What key are we in Deanie?", and he said "Hell, how do I know?," because neither of us read charts. That night, Gary Church was introducing the band in Freddy's place, and he made a comment on a live mic about "The only two things from Texas are steers and queers," and I pointed my finger at him and said, "About one more crack like that and I'm gonna whip your ass!", and I meant it too. Well, from that moment on, every time I'd come into work, there was this pink purse standing where I stood. It was a prop from backstage Gary had found, and I mean, I'd come in a couple hours early sometimes just to see if I could catch him, and that damn pink purse would be there! One night I took it, and made damn sure nobody was following me, and took it across the street to Circus Circus, went around back to the dumpster and threw it away, and even put some boxes over the top of it. The next night, that damn pink purse was back! (laughs)

Hell, there were jokes being played in the band all the time, especially by Freddy! One time it was Christmas Eve at the El Dorado and there wasn't hardly anybody there, and all the guys in Freddy's band were comedians of one kind or another, they all were. So Freddy and Church and Xavier went off into the comedian routine, and I laughed so hard my guts hurt and just finally put my guitar down in the stand, went out, sat down and watched the show. I'm so glad that they did that that night, because I laughed until I cried! I'd seen him do his comedy routine at a Pizza Hut in Houston once, a long time ago when I was a little kid, probably and I was going from table to table drinking everybody's beer while they were in fits laughing. He was hilarious man! We'd be playing and off the cuff, he'd go into something while the music was playing.

B.B. Morse: In the Air Fred Band, along with Clint Strong, we had Jimmy Day on a bunch of stuff on Steel, then Bobby Black, Augie Savage on piano, Tom Herzer, Perry Shumer, and Freddy Jr. playing drums, and his nephew Troy playing rhythm guitar.

Augie Savage: Freddy was real big at the El Dorado Casino, and he went all over in Nevada. I played with him back in between '86 and '91. He would travel up and down to keep the Air Fred Band going. I played keys in the group, and his son was in it playing drums, along with players like Bobby Black, Tom Herzer, Scotty Joss was in the group, and he would get who he could get – ALWAYS top players. B.B. Morse was in the group playing bass, and I tell you, Freddy is a musician's dream, because he sings his verse and then he lets his musicians just go like crazy. He lets them all play and lets them all do a lead, and that's what was so fun working with Freddy, he was a musician's musician. I think any musician will tell you that if they ever worked for Freddy, it was probably the most fun they ever had working, because he would let us play all the time. He completely let the band go, he would sing a little verse and would let the band go.

Troy Powers: Our dressing rooms were down in the basement of the El Dorado. There were 5 or 6, and you had to walk through the casino and by the snack bar to get down to the basement. I saw Freddy get mad at security once over a fan we called the Budweiser Indian, because the El Dorado lounge had a 2-drink minimum, so he'd buy 2 Budweiser's, come in, sit down, and whenever Freddy played a song he liked, he'd give a classic Native American whoop! Well, after a few of these, here comes security, and Freddy laid into them one night, "Wait a minute! Why are you running him off, he ain't doing nothing but having a good time in there?" It became a big deal, and I know the Budweiser Indian kept coming in. I sold the records at the Merchandise table after the gig, and if they wanted it signed, I'd go get the autograph from Freddy, and if they wanted to meet him, I'd go tell him, and he'd usually come over. Freddy was a very gracious entertainer. He had lots of famous fans who came through to watch him play, from Mel Tillis, Paul Revere from Paul Revere and the Raiders would come in, Roger Miller, Lacy Jay Dalton, Dottie West, Rose Maddox, etc.

Freddy was always a generous host with everyone, his band members, the guest players who would sit in with him, he was always treated like Royalty at the El Dorado and always made sure everybody had a good time. The maddest I ever saw Freddy was at me when he went to Alaska with his mom and family on a cruise of some kind in the very early 80s. I brought my band from West Texas, a bunch of crazy cowboys, out to Reno, and all of us ended up going to jail for one thing or another. Another time he got upset at me, I was over at the El Dorado with some of Freddy's friends, like Cadabra – the bar tender at the Pizza Oven across the street from the hotel – and he said "I got a new drink I want you to try out." It was vodka and stout, and I got so blitzed that I didn't know the way back to my room. I wasn't staying at the El Dorado, I was over at some motel on 4th street, but Freddy kept a suite there and he also had a condo on the skyline.

So I started to get in the elevator to head up to his room to crash, and when the elevator doors opened, I passed out and fell flat on my face and broke my nose. The elevator doors kept opening and closing on me because I was passed out between them, so security had to come and they called the police on me. So when Freddy got back to town, they bombarded him with all the shit his nephew was doing, and he called me up to his room and said, "I couldn't believe you did this! How could you come to my room?" So when I told him I'd been a mess and was trying to go somewhere without getting thrown in jail, he says, "Well, dammit, you didn't, did you?" So he didn't speak to me for a while, then after a while, Freddy came back out to West Texas, pulled me aside one day and said "I want you to join my band." Well, when I told him "I'd love to," all the bad feelings were gone.

B.B. Morse: Freddy mentored, and he led in the sense of the way band leaders used to. There was a very stern control of command of the ship, and that was a respect you gave to Freddy, and it wasn't that he demanded it, but earned it in that sense. So he led me from the 2-beat to be able to walk these massive patterns on the bass, and the ability to understand the melodic structure of the music we were performing. After the first couple years with Freddy, after I started grasping those bigger patterns and scales and melodic structures, I now had command of the entire instrument.

Now, when you weren't playing the way Freddy expected you to, he wouldn't single you out or yell at you in front of the band and embarrass you, he'd just throw you a look! (laughs) And when that look came down over his shoulder, whoever was the recipient of that eye contact, you knew it. His music was always the most challenging. All the rest of the stuff I might have done was just like a cakewalk, and it wasn't that his stuff was difficult in a sense of understanding. You could understand it, but then to be able to perform it is a different thing, so he always brought a very high standard to the stage and to life in general.

Playing with Freddy brought me to a real good place and time in my life personally as well as professionally. Freddy's ability to draw that lightning in a bottle out of you as a player was something that at the pinnacle of my ability to do that, never seemed like work. Being able to make decisions in the moment when the song is going breakneck speed, the next note and the value of that note that you assign to it is part of the directive of the movement of that melody, then it almost becomes Jedi kind of stuff. If you had to stop and think about it, you were behind. You had to be right in the crest of the wave with Freddy, and there was no other place on earth you wanted to be.

Troy Powers: Whenever Freddy was getting ready to put a new band together, he'd go out to one of those small towns in Nevada like Elko, Ely, Wells, and Winnemucca with his new people, and they'd rehearse and learn all the material they needed to. They come back to Reno because you don't want to be putting a band together in one of your bread and butter places. He took care of his boys in the band out on the road too, let me tell you! For example, we'd go out and play Jackpot, Nevada every now and then, which is right on the borderline with Idaho, it had a beautiful casino! Better than any showroom in Reno, there were like 6 rooms in the back that were all for the green room. They had showers! We were playing to a dinner crowd, so they had steaks, and if you were the headliner, that was it for the night. So Freddy's band would headline, and then on other gigs, my band would play the little lounge out there.

On one of those trips to Jackpot, there was a whore house in Elko called Mona's where Freddy and the boys had been going for years, and the lady who owned the place was named Mona. So when we were pulling in, Freddy said "Hey, I want to stop and say hey to Mona." Well, once we all walked in, Mona walked over, put the Closed sign on the door, turned to Freddy and said "I'm going to bed, y'all have a great time!"

Catherine Powers: Freddy had a young drummer named Allan Barnes who was pretty green to the road. One time they pulled into Mona's, Freddy always paid for the band, $20 per man, but once Al picked out his girl and got up to the room, suddenly Freddy from the first floor heard some loud voices going back and forth. So poked his head in the door after a minute of it to see what was going on, and Al said "Freddy, she says its $25." Well, now Freddy gets into it with the girl, "Oh no no no, I've been bringing my boys here a long time, and I know the price, its $20 and that's it." At that point, the girl gets up, comes to the door to talk to Freddy directly, and says the same thing: "Its $25 or no go," and as Freddy was holding his ground on the price, his drummer speaks up with a $5 in his hand and says, "Brother Fred, I'll go the $5!" (laughs)

Troy Powers: Mona loved Freddy so much, her and her husband, that when Freddy came through town there were nights like that where she'd put the closed sign up, and I mean alcohol, as many women as I wanted, it was all covered, I didn't pay a dime. One time we were at Mona's, and I was sitting there talking to this girl when Freddy says to me, "Troy, come here!", so I told the girl I'd be back, got up, and Freddy says, "Look at this!", and this girl was sitting on the bar butt-naked!

There was another place out in the middle of nowhere in Jackpot, probably about 20 miles down this winding dirt road, but when you got there, it was like paradise. It had this town that had a sidewalk with all the store fronts and the motel rooms all had hot springs running through them. Can you imagine being in a motel room and there's a hot spring running right through it, build up with wood. It was like being in a hot tub, it was just amazing. I've never seen anything like that before. One time Freddy and I were down in Seminole, Texas and he said to me, "Hey, let's you and me go to Mexico tonight." So we crossed the border into Juarez, hit the bars, and hung out.

Ralph Emery: "Freddy? I see we've got guitars and everything, are you and Merle prepared to sing something together here on the couch?"

Freddy Powers: "We're prepared for anything!" (audience laughs)

Ralph Emery: What Feels Good to You?"

Merle Haggard: "Oh, if I said that, the show would be over..." (audience laughs)

- RALPH EMERY SHOW, 1984

"A Place to Fall Apart" – Co-written by Merle, Freddy and Willie – Sheet Music

CHAPTER 12: "LOOKING FOR A PLACE TO FALL APART"

Freddy Powers: When we got to Nashville for the Award Show, we were staying at the Opryland Hotel in two big hotel suites, Merle, myself and Sherrill Rodgers and Debbie Parrett, at this time, Merle's maid and close friend... we were sitting around playing guitars. Merle had just finished writing a lot of songs about Leona Williams. Merle had been writing a lot of sad Leona Williams songs. He was working on one and I asked, "When are you gonna quit writing about Leona?!" Merle turned right then and said to me, "I wish I could write a song to Leona and explain exactly how I feel once and for all..." I replied, "Why don't you write a letter and tell her exactly how you feel, and then we'll try to make a song out of the letter?"

I could immediately see he liked the idea of a song where someone would write a letter saying once and for all everything he wanted to say to her and how he felt about the whole affair. When Merle sat down to work on the lyrics, it was written exactly like the letter. Sadly, we never saw the letter, some fan at the hotel ran away with it, but we had it on tape. It was also a # 1 song. The letter began: "Dear Leona, I'll probably never see you eye to eye again, and this letter is meant to be my last goodbye. I thought everything was over until your phone call. That call turned my life around…"

"Looking For a Place to Fall Apart"

I'll probably never see you eye to eye again
This letter's meant to be my last farewell
But you need to under-stand I'm nearly crazy
You need to know my life has gone to hell
Write me back and tell me why it ended
Send a letter that I can show my heart
I'll be somewhere between "I love you" and what you're feeling now
Lookin' for a place to fall apart
Looking for a place to fall apart

Trying to find a place that I can leave my heart
I need to be somewhere hidin' when I feel the teardrops start
Lookin' for a place to fall a-part
I can't seem to justify your leavin' me
I'm be-bewildered as to how it all came down
I thought everything was fine until your phone call
The call that turned my world around
Send me word and tell me why it ended
I need some final proof to show my heart
I'll be somewhere between "I love you" and what you're feelin' now (I love you)
Lookin' for a place to fall apart
Looking for a place to fall apart

Trying to find a place that I can leave my heart
I need to be somewhere hidin' when I feel the teardrops start
Lookin' for a place to fall a-part
Looking for a place to fall apart
Trying to find a place that I can leave my heart
I need to be somewhere hidin' when I feel the teardrops start
Lookin' for a place to fall a-part

(Written by: Freddy Powers/Merle Haggard/Willie Nelson, 1984
Copyright Sony/ATV Music Publishing Ltd)

Merle Haggard: We wrote "*A Place to Fall Apart*" right here at the Opryland hotel. Freddy got the song title from Willie, brought it up to me, and one day asked me if I'd ever written anything about my divorce, and I said "No, I don't want to write anything about my divorce, I want to forget it." I said, "I'd like to write a letter', and Freddy said "Well, why don't you sit down and write the letter," and I sat down, wrote the letter, and the letter became the song. That's how it came out. "*Place to Fall Apart*" and "*Natural High*" are good songs, once in a while I sing them both

Ray Baker: '*Looking For a Place to Fall Apart*' is another #1 Merle wrote with Freddy that we tracked that as part of the sessions at 11-11 Studios. That was a great studio, and they shared a parking lot with Waylon Jennings' studio. Those were such beautiful days looking back, we took our life for granted back then because that's just the way it was. Nashville was still kind of a small town and the music business was an everybody-knew-everybody type relationship. It was kind of a buddy-buddy system.

Freddy Powers: With "*Looking For a Place to Fall Apart*," we wound up with three number one hits on the *All in the Game* album, and all of a sudden money came rolling in, and LOTS of it! And we had no problem spending it. Everything from Limos to Jets, still I could see that through the success we were having and all the partying, Merle was a troubled man, it was always on his face. Sometimes he would open up and tell me things that bothered him. He would tell me about personal things, things about his family, the music business, and lots of stories about prison. The better I got to know Merle, the more I realized that his career and his life all has been an uphill fight for him. Growing up in a boxcar, the loss of his father, refusing school, his prison life and being a prisoner of the music business – the very thing he loves most, it's ALL been a battle for him and in some ways still is. You can listen to any Merle Haggard song and tell me how he was feeling at that time whether he was in a sad or happy mood. All his songs tell a story that could fit most anybody's everyday life. Merle is the poet for the common man.

On Merle's houseboat one day, I called my mother. At the end of our conversation, I told her I loved her. When I hung up, Merle said he didn't know if he'd ever told his mother he loved her. I asked him why and he said they just "Weren't that kind of family." Merle decided to call his mother and before they hung up he said, "I love you Mama." When Merle's mother got sick, he and I got on the bus and went to Bakersfield, California to see her in the hospital. We stayed in the parking lot for several days until she passed on. That was a sad time in Merle's life.

One thing's for sure, he did inherit his writing ability from his mother. She wrote her own Eulogy, which was the story of her life and read at her funeral by Ralph Emery. It was the most beautiful and heart-warming story I'd ever heard. With all the rough exterior, Merle's inside is still that of a little boy, with a heart filled with romantic dreams. His songs come straight from his mixed-up past. When Merle was a boy in Bakersfield, he was a restless renegade. He was in and out of reform schools all because he didn't want to go to school. All he wanted to do was get a job and that was against the rules of society. But the reform school only primed him for prison, and he tried to escape from there many times. The prison system almost ruined a life, the life of Merle Haggard. I sincerely believe that if Merle hadn't found success in the music business, he would either be back in prison if not dead. After living nearly ten years next door to Merle, today when I hear one of his songs, I'll remember the story behind it and know what part of his life he's singing about.

Merle had several old friends visit us on the lake over those years, most of them only a few days or weeks, but one woman had always stayed on the scene, Debbie Parret, Merle's maid and housekeeper. After Leona and Merle finally called it quits, Debbie moved out to the houseboat with Merle and started cooking and taking care of both of us. Debbie had been with us all the way: she cooked good, healthy things that we needed, she was a mother and sister and a wonderful friend to Merle, and also to me. I could gradually see Merle falling in love with Debbie, but I never believed it was love like between a man and a wife, but more like Merle needed a female friend.

It seemed there for a while like we could see a song in everything. Someone would say something and one of us would say, "That's a good title for a song." And most of the time, a few minutes later we would have a song. Debbie, she was a great person to be around. She understood we were songwriters. Knowing that, if she saw a song coming on, she would have pen and paper ready and made sure we had peace and quiet. We had a lot of women up there with us that were not so good to have around while we were working. They would do something to interrupt us, like "Request a song." I think songwriters have to have people around that understand, and Debbie is that kind of a person and I will always love and respect her for that, and all her devoted care she gave us. And I know Merle feels the same way, as he's told me so many times.

She had a cabin that she was renting just up the hill from the boats. She got to where she seldom ever went to the cabin. She was still Merle's maid, but they just kept getting closer and closer. Debbie did everything for Merle, and was somewhat like Merle. I've seen Merle with all kinds of women, but when things went wrong and he was down he always went straight to Deb. She was what he really needed and would baby him like he was a child, and then sometimes she would lean on him like he was a giant. It was a relationship I have never seen since. Debbie hung on instead of confronting Merle about the other women. Instead, she just worked harder and harder doing things for Merle, so the more Merle would see other women, the harder Debbie would work to make him happy. It was really something to watch her work, but with kindness, and love for Merle, she did something that a lot of women would have liked to do: become Mrs. Merle Haggard.

Merle Haggard: Debbie did a lot of things for us, she cooked for us, washed our clothes, did whatever we asked her to do. If somebody got out of line in the female department, she'd whip their ass and kick them off the boat, whatever we wanted her to do. She took care of that light work for us (laughs).

Freddy Powers: In a quiet ceremony at sunrise at Shade Tree Manor, Merle's ranch, Merle and Debbie were married. The wedding was held at Merle's ranch set on top of a small hill outside of Redding, California with a view of Mount Shasta 360 degrees to the north and Mount Lassen exactly 90 degrees to the east. It was a beautiful sunrise you would have thought had been ordered just for the occasion. Dean Reynolds, Steve Van Stralen and myself played a song that Debbie had requested be played at the wedding, "Natural High." It was so early in the morning that everyone was sleepy-eyed at first. I only cried at the wedding of my daughters, but I must say this one brought tears to my eyes. One thing we had agreed to is that Debbie would never, ever in a million years take more than she had coming from Merle in a divorce, an important topic since divorces had cost Merle so much money (including half million dollar payments he was making at the time to Leona).

When the ceremony was over, Gary Church – a trumpet player who'd originally played in my Dixieland band had come with me from Reno and joined Merle's famous Strangers band – stood up and announced: "The wedding omelet would be served at the ranch house!" Even after he was married, the partying on the boat was still full-blown, and people were often filming there, all the usual fan-fair that goes with being a superstar. I really believe that if Debbie hadn't been there during our party days, always serving good, healthy food and pouring vitamins down us, we probably wouldn't be here today!

"The proudest achievement of my career is to be able to say I have written No. 1 hits for the greatest country singer of our time, Merle Haggard."
– FREDDY POWERS, SEPT. 1989, HARRAH'S LAKE TAHOE RESORT CASINO

"Once I wrote my first No. 1 hit for Merle, people no longer looked at me as 'Freddy the entertainer' – they called me 'the songwriter.' It was like the entertainer part of me got lost in the songwriting. Singers are singers, but poets are forever."
– FREDDY POWERS, JUNE, 2006, TEXAS MUSIC MAGAZINE BY JASON HARDISON

Country Jazz Singer Cover

CHAPTER 13: THE COUNTRY JAZZ SINGER

Freddy Powers: I am very proud of my songwriting career and thankful to all my friends and to those that I have never gotten to meet that have recorded my songs throughout the years. If I were to complain about anything, it's that after I had my first hit people began to refer to me as a songwriter and somehow forgot I was a singer too. I've spent most of my life as a singer and musician and love the stage and enjoy the satisfaction of knowing people like my singing and my style of guitar playing. After I'd spent a few years writing songs for Merle and producing for Willie, I finally – with their encouragement I must admit – decided that it was time to put together an album that showcased my own musical roots, and "*The Country Jazz Singer*" was born, produced by Merle Haggard on Inorbit Records.

> **Stereo Review Magazine:** "Freddy Powers… appears here in an impressive, if quiet, performance of upbeat jazz and country ballads. A dexterous musician and adroit lyricist, Powers dedicates his album to Django Reinhardt, Haggard and Willie Nelson among

others, citing their influence on his music. Judging from this outing, however, it looks as if Powers may have been as much of an influence on Haggard as Haggard has been on him...This lovely LP is an eye-opener, revealing Powers as a remarkable country-jazz stylistic and songwriter worthy of far greater exposure on his own."

Freddy Powers: "I never thought about writing songs as to make a living or to make money. I started writing songs because I wanted something to sing, you know, in my band. I was a performer long before I was a songwriter. I couldn't believe it when my song became # 1 for the first time. George Jones recorded it. My sister and I wrote a Christmas song called '*Silent Night, Lonely Night.*' I wasn't real fond of it, but Merle was doing a Christmas album, and I got it in there. I was flabbergasted when I heard the song with a big orchestra, the London Orchestra and I fell in love with it. Songwriting is like a habit, like I'm addicted, and I didn't realize this until I got started. Once you write a song and when it's over with, you've finished it, and you've got it all done and you're singing it, then you have a let-down. You need another one; you need another one right now. Songwriters get addicted to the tension of a new song."

Merle Haggard: "He's a genius whispering in the ears of giants, never realizing that he's been a giant all along."

Freddy Powers: "When I'm composing, I never sit down to write. I get up every morning, have a cup of coffee and just play my guitar and if I'm ever gonna get an idea, that's when it's gonna come. A lot of songwriters ask, 'How can I get my songs out?', and I say 'If you've got a good enough song, you can't hold that song down. If the song is in the upper category, like Misery and Gin or Night Life, that song will escape. Just take it out and play it.' On the other hand, critique is important for a songwriter. If you ask somebody, 'Well, what do you think about that song?', that could just kill the song, he'll drop it right then and there. Just be your own judge. Because I've written songs, played it and gradually a metamorphosis happens. I don't know how many times it has happened to me, and I'll always have a doubt in my mind."

Willie Nelson: "You know a Freddy Powers-style song when you hear it... you know you've stumbled onto a good thing – something beautiful."

Freddy Powers: "The key to songwriting is having a story to tell. To me, it takes one of two things: you have to be devastated by something or overwhelmed by something to start a song. Be totally impressed with somebody or some action, especially over romances. All the good songwriters I know have real bad relationships, or rocky relationships. You go back and look at the songs from 1900 and they are all saying the same thing as today. They are saying 'I love you,' 'I'm leaving you,' 'I hate you,' 'I've got somebody else' or 'My heart is broken.' You know, there are just a few messages of love that can be portrayed.

    I always write the same, I don't write for the modern day, I never did. I never paid attention to what was going on with music. I wrote what I could write; I still do. What comes to me – my emotions or whatever stirs you up…. We write music as we go, and then there is the possibility that after we sing a song for a while we get tired of it. We just change it. There's an incubation period, you know, the song is born, but there's a rebirth. Within a month or so you begin changing the song. I have one song that I wrote yesterday, it will take three weeks or so before it is as I want it. Every day just foolin' around with the words and lyrics – it'll come fine."

Nevada Appeal: "Powers' speaking voice is like music itself. His pronunciation and tone have the lilting, lyrical qualities found in West Texas."

Freddy Powers: "As far as writing goes I guess I like Cole Porter, Johnny Mercer and one of my favorite all-time songwriters, Fats Waller. The stuff that I sing, that's all my style. What I write is reminiscent of that style of music. Most of my music you don't hear on the Country radio station, they're not as easy to pitch because that particular style of music is not in fashion right now."

Country Music Round Up Magazine, London: "Every so often along comes an album that's a little bit special and as far as I'm concerned. Country Jazz Singer is destined to be my album of the year, sheer musical magic is the only way to describe it with its deceptively simple feel due no doubt to the fact that the main instrumentation comes from the superb guitar work of Clint Strong, whose sensitive lead guitar on the slow ballads just has to be heard, while Dean Reynolds on bass adds the necessary depth to highlight the searing vocals of Freddy Powers."

Freddy Powers: "Deanie-Bird Reynolds has been my best friend, well, since we were kids. He worked with Willie Nelson years ago with the band. Willie, I and Deanie-Bird, a guy named Paul Buskirk and occasionally Johnny Gimble was working with us."

Music Row Magazine, 1987: "Powers aligns with a nice backing trio, including young guitar wiz Clint Strong…The songs are good, the playing wonderful."

Merle Haggard: Fred had a three-piece band and they recorded and made a really good record. I liked it a lot.

Freddy Powers: "I've always liked performing better than anything. Performing is where I learned to play music, and performing is where I learned to write, I guess. It's better for relaxation, you know. I live out on a houseboat on Lake Shasta and I stay up there most of the year, and it's a pleasant life that I'm living and writing. But I got to get out to the people every now and then. The trio is so pure, we don't use any gimmicks, it's all real, pure sound, and you can hear individual instruments. I don't know, it's just so pure, and the guitar playing of Clint Strong, is one of the best."

FRETS Magazine: "Powers is a gifted songwriter. The album's sequencing is dictated by tempo, with up-tempo swing tunes on side one and ballads on side two."

Freddy Powers: "I've some albums out over the years, but they were very obscure albums. When I was traveling with the band on the road and I didn't have any national recognition, and we sold them, kinda bandstand albums we'd call them. And I had an old album for Warner Bros. years ago. It was kinda with a Dixieland style that I played. But *The Country Jazz Singer* is my first big effort in the country music album field of any substance. It was just a lot of fun. It was all in stages, though, I'd written these songs a while back and a lot of them had become hits. Mainly by Merle Haggard, and then I decided, 'Well, I've written me enough hit songs now that I think I'll try to make me an album. So I put my trio together and we made this album. It's actually a 14-song album, and I did it a little different. I put seven slow songs on one side, my ballads, and seven of those up-tempo country-jazz style on the other side. It's almost like two albums, because you turn it over and you got a whole series of songs in the same style. It's really an exciting album, and something I'm really proud to be a part of."

Country Matters Magazine, U.K.'s first country music magazine: "Some inspired playing back in the mix by Powers and arrangements for the interplay between Powers' guitar and the fiddle work of Johnny Gimble.'"

Freddy Powers: "I have three favorites on there for different reasons. I like the song '*Texas and Oklahoma*' because I was born in Oklahoma and raised in Texas. It's something that I wrote about my memories of Texas and Oklahoma. That's one of my favorites, and then there's one on there called '*I'm Free At Last*' on the end of the album on the slow side. That one Merle and I wrote, and I really do like it a lot. I like the guitar playing on '*Texas Barbecue*' by Clint. It's as good as any guitar solo I've ever heard. Matter of fact, I like everything he did on that album. I can listen to it over and over. It's the only thing I've ever done in my life that I've never gotten tired of, and I've been listening to it for two years, before it came out."

Reno-Gazette Journal: "After years of opening for Merle Haggard and cutting albums with artists such as Ray Charles and George Jones, Powers brings his special brand of country-western jazz."

Freddy Powers: "I did this album with a strict, 'This is the first album I've ever done with no commercial thought in mind.' I just decided I'm getting to the time in my career where I've gotta do something for my art form for my own self, for what I wanted to do. So I did this album, and it seems I should a been doing that all along."

Austin City Limits, 1988: "Freddy Powers hosted two songwriter shows: on the first, a bearded Merle Haggard and Willie Nelson joined him, and the three traded solos, duets and trios. The concert turned into an impromptu tribute to Floyd Tillman, present in the audience, whose melodic complexities and popular lyrics had influenced both Nelson and Haggard. 'Pure magic', judged Darrell Royal, 'Pure magic.' The following year, Powers brought back Haggard and Nelson and expanded the circle to include Whitey Shafer and Spud Goodall in a program that crossed the borders between country and jazz. In the eleventh season, Merle Haggard repaid Freddy Powers' hospitality by inviting him to be a special guest on his own Austin City Limits show – his third."

Pauline Reese: When he played ACL, nobody knew who he was bringing, and he showed up with Willie Nelson and Merle Haggard, that's the kind of guy he was.

Freddy Powers: "The thing that I really like about Austin is that is an acoustic town. Quite possibly the acoustic musical capital of the world. It could be the people's ears are just blown up. But it's hard to have a local music scene when the radio stations do the stuff straight out of Nashville. It makes it difficult for an area to bust off its own music scene with that influence hangin' around – maybe good things are happening. I think people are wanting to go back to the old country style."

Lee Duffy: "Freddy is indefinitely in touch with how sounds affect the psyche and how lyrics touch the soul. When you see him perform, you know that he's breathing with the universe. He can cue the sunset as part of his delivery."

Freddy Powers: "When people ask for my opinion of their song, I always ask them what their opinion of the song. I always seemed to trust someone else's songs more than I did mine. If I had any recording to do, a lot of times I wouldn't trust my own judgment. I'd think it was a good song, but I'd be afraid to go ahead and play it. I felt I stood a better chance if I played something that was already proven. One thing that's helped me more than anything else with my songwriting is that I was finally able to critique my own material and not ask someone else to do it. Now, I like to critique my own material and I pay very little attention to what anyone else has to say. That is, until I perform it. If I play it a few times and I don't get any response, then I know something is wrong. The songwriter who performs also stands a much better chance of being heard.

I do believe there's a lot of great songwriters out there, it's a matter of believing in yourself. Believing, you know, if you think it's a good song, it's probably a good song. You know, believe in it anyway. Believe in what you write. I don't know what to say makes a successful songwriter, but I do know this: when I started believing and letting my own self judge what I wrote, if it's good enough for me to hear, it's good enough to play for somebody. Every now and then, I'll write something and I'll listen to it a couple times and it doesn't hit me, so I'll throw it out. But Merle Haggard gave me the encouragement or whatever you want to call it that started me writing, and I try to tell other people as much as I can. If somebody's got a good song, I try to tell them over and over again, because I remember that thing that if the song is good, tell them it's good. Because they need to hear that."

Country Music Television: "With the release of *The Country Jazz Singer*, there was finally a full album devoted to Powers' efforts as a leader."

Augie Savage: My all-time favorite guitar player was Django Reinhardt, and Freddy had that rhythm down where he'd just chunk out the rhythm, and it was just so solid, it was absolutely solid. He was probably one of the best rhythm guitar players around, in the Country field, he was absolutely the best rhythm guitar player there was. You couldn't fail, because Freddy was underneath you all the way holding you up. It was very musical, very, very musical. When he had the Air Fred band, we just got up there, held on and played like hell.

Rattlesnake Annie: He was a great guitar player, he was patient enough to show me exactly how to play his songs, and all the little tiny secrets some people don't even notice, and taught me exactly how to play the intros to his songs, so I became real familiar with his style of playing by him teaching me those songs. When he taught them to me, he knew that because when you study Flamenco, I was a disciplined learner, and that I would play them exactly as he taught them to me. When Freddy would show his songs to me, I'd make chord patterns so I could remember them, and I still have photographs of those! I had to go back to one the other day because it was such a complicated chord from one of his songs you don't remember. That's something else I learned from Freddy too: every player has their own inversions of different kinds of chords, and he definitely had his own.

Freddy took the whole process very seriously, and I was studying from 1984 on with Clint Strong and getting more and more into Jazz, and Jazz and Flamenco – which I learned to play in Spain – but they were very akin to each other. If you look back in history, all those great Flamenco players all progressed to jazz, so I would say my connection to Freddy was really Jazz. I look at his songs, for instance, "*Texas and Oklahoma*," that's what I think of as being Texas-Swing sort of chords, and my ability to play Jazz comes from learning how to play Flamenco and use my hands and all my fingers, and that's why great musicians – like Lonnie Mack and Freddy Powers and Clint Strong – have sat with me because I learned how to play all this stuff. So Flamenco was what brought a lot of guitar players to my table, and gave me the opportunity to learn from them. I love that song in particular because its fast and its challenging to play, not just everybody plays it like Freddy, he taught me exactly how to play it. It's just a great, great song and it's got really interesting chords in it, and it just suits me to a 'T.' I love it!

B.B. Morse: If you've listened to any 4-string plectrum style banjo music, say the Dixieland or Ragtime type stuff, not the 5-string bluegrass banjo, but the actual banjo they play chords on, that style of movement is based around melodic extensions to the melody of any particular song. So that, in essence, the chord that you play reflects the melody of the song that you do, and when you play one chord in 4 different stages, you've basically performed a musical scale. Whether that's in a major or minor tone, or augmented, diminished, any of these different values of the chord itself that there is also one note away, an alteration of that chord which expresses value in the melody. So when talking about Freddy chords, you're talking about a banjo-style movement of melodic structure that aren't there just to play a fancy chord, but are there to reinforce the movement and the melody of the song. Freddy was a hybrid of playing the roots and essence of both Country and Western music, and kind of took off where Bob Wells left off – it generated this whole other revenue of styles.

Scotty Joss, The Strangers Fiddle Player: Freddy's one of the last Django Reinhardt-kind of influenced rhythm players, which infuses immense amounts of energy into a song, and Fred was very, very good at that. He studied Django quite a bit, and that's where he picked up a lot of that. It was his rhythm, the chords weren't so much the issue as he had this right hand that would NOT stop, and that drove the rhythm of the whole thing. I think he taught Merle a lot of that, and Merle on the other hand turned around and taught Fred more about country guitar playing – slowing it down and playing a regular D chord instead of a big old Reinhardt chord. So that was an inspiration as well. Fred had an amazing amount of energy and love and life in his playing that was infectious, you couldn't keep from tapping your toe. Then at a moment's notice, he would just go off in a different direction than you'd heard anybody go before, at least at that time. I don't think anybody's done it since.

Ray Baker: When Merle and Freddy would write songs together, typically you would hear some chord changes in some of those songs that maybe Merle wouldn't have included. Most of Merle's stuff was pretty standard as far as the melodies, they didn't get into a bunch of minor chords or augmented or diminished chords. Freddy had such a diversity in his musical talents and also playing the rhythm guitar that he would throw in an augmented or diminished chord. I think *"Natural High"* has some of those chords. So Freddy was a catalyst for some of Merle's output.

Rattlesnake Annie: I very rarely saw Freddy where he didn't have a guitar in his hands, wherever he was, whether in a hotel or when I was in Vegas or when we were in Reno or Nashville or Austin, I would just hook up with him when I'd come back from Europe to see family or record, and it would sometimes be a year before I'd get back. We remained friends and we'd play together. Then we became acquainted musically, and he showed me a bunch of his songs, and how it all turned out is, we ended up recording in Nashville in 1982 or 84 when he was on the road with Merle, and he had Clint Strong with him. So we went in the studio and recorded one of Freddy's songs. Then we saw each other at a recording session down at Willie's studio later on, and I'd listened to all these different songs of his and said "Man, I love these songs, I'd like to record them!"

His reply was "Well, we can record them together but I'm going to have to have your word that you'll hold them until I see if I can get them cut by Merle." So I held them 5 years before I released any of them. Then I made them into an album called Crossroads! When you look at Freddy's music, he generously uses diminished chords, and the types of grooves that he chose, for *"Little Hotel Room"* and *"I Always Get Lucky With You,"* he taught me his special little intro into that song, and I've never heard anybody else do it. But I had the opportunity to hang with him and pick with him probably as much as I ever did any musician. George Jones said he never cut a song that had a diminished chord in it until "*I Always Get Lucky With You.*"

Norm Hamlet: Merle and Freddy really enjoyed playing with each other, and in fact, they'd get together with Freddy's bass player Deanie Bird and his trumpet player Gary Church, and whether it was out on the road or out on those houseboats and have jam sessions. Sometimes The Strangers would show up and a lot of them liked to do a little fishing but they wound up doing some playing too. They'd get into playing a little Jazz, Merle liked to do that a little on the side and Freddy was so good at it!

Freddy Powers: "I've gone to book myself in a club and they'll say 'Songwriter, do you do copy music?', meaning is it played on the radio? I'd tell them 'Hell yeah, just turn the damn radio on.' Sometimes I wonder what would have happened with my performing career as a singer and musician if I hadn't met up with Merle and left it behind for a songwriting career. I was pretty hot at that time and was becoming more well known for my own shows. I had already done several T.V. shows like the Today and Tonight Shows. Before that, I did the ABC Hootenanny Show with Paul Buskirk, and WPAB Serve-All Barn Dance television show with Pat Boone. So I might have been a big star myself, who knows…"

Marc Oswald: The Telluride Blue Grass Festival held in Colorado was one of the biggest Bluegrass Festivals in America, and it's still going on today. Well, back during the Spree of 83, I remember we all loaded up on buses from California, and went out to the Telluride Festival just to have fun, we weren't even booked on it. When we got there, Merle wound up deciding he wanted to go home and took off right away, he didn't stay very long, but we stayed for a couple days, and Freddy decided to play a set. Well, in that company, you're talking about guys like Sam Bush and Bela Fleck and Doc Watson, those were the kind of artists that play that show, and are HUGE stars in that genre, and when Freddy went out on stage to play that Festival, he wasn't known as a Bluegrass act. But with his Jazz licks, and all the skills he has on guitar, and the way he sings and all, he was a SMASH!

What made it so cool was, the day he played, the Festival was sold out and there were about 15,000 people there, and so whether Freddy was walking on stage at a Bluegrass show, or walking on stage in a country show, he was always one of the best players in the house. So that day, I remember Doc Watson was over to the side of the stage, and he's blind so of course he couldn't see Freddy, but he was sitting with Bela Fleck and Sam Bush and all those guys were all just transfixed! I don't think they knew much about him up until that point, not coming from the Bluegrass world, but it was just awesome to see, because once again, there was Freddy Powers showing up in a different genre of music, and just smoking the place, because people were going wild!

Freddy Powers: "I'm still not terribly well-known as a singer because my songwriting has overpowered me. Now every article you ever see out of Nashville, they always refer to me as a songwriter. I wonder what they thought I was doing for those 20 or so years before that."

Merle Haggard: *'Little Hotel Room'* is a great song off that record. I remember when Freddy was working on it!

Sherrill Rogers: I was with Freddy when he wrote *"Little Hotel Room."* The story was pretty much about as a traveling musician, or a person who travels for work, you get lonely in your hotel basically. There was a meteor shower that night, and we watched the falling stars, and he goes "Oh my god, 'From a window, I can see a falling star, I wonder if you see it from where you are?' The chord progressions are wonderful, they're really beautiful.

J Gary Smith: Freddy and I were sitting out front of the studio in Nashville on the hood of the car, and the President of the record label came out the door, and he said "You got any songs for Ray Charles?" That's when Freddy played him *"Little Hotel Room,"* I heard the whole thing, I was standing right there, and Ray wound up cutting it.

Freddy Powers: We were in Nashville and Ray was doing an album with some of his friends in the music business. Merle came in and asked me if we had anything Ray could do? I jumped and said 'Yes I do!' I had written this song, and the first time Deanie Bird heard it he said 'That sounds like a Ray Charles song.'

Songwriter Bo Porter: Once you hear a Freddy Powers song, if you listen to it enough, whether Merle Haggard is singing it or Ray Charles is singing it, the way he phrases things, there's just a certain way he can write a turn of phrase. One of my favorite stories Freddy told me came when we were talking about how you cue up the song, where they come from. I told him I'd been in a grocery store and heard a man talking about how his wife had left him, and the last thing I heard was "I didn't see that coming," and I'd gone out and wrote the story out in the truck.

So next I asked him, *"Little Hotel Room"*, how did you write that song? And he says, "Well actually, me and Merle were supposed to do this radio thing up in New York, and I got there and this was back before cell phones, and I just had a piece of paper with a number on it but I'd lost it. But they knew I was going to be at the Waldorf, and at that time, the Waldorf was under construction, they were renovating it. So I figured I'd just go to my room and they'd find me, so I got there and got settled in and decided to order a bottle of wine, called down to room service and they sent it up. Well, this older black man comes up to the room, and he has the bottle of wine and two glasses, and asks me, 'Do you need one glass or two?', and I told him, 'I just need one,' and the man said to me, 'Oh, it's a one-man celebration'."

Then he said, "That started my song, that's the way it starts: 'A one-man celebration, ain't what I had in mind, sitting here sipping on this glass of wine…' He said "So I sat in the room, and like I said, it was under construction, and I noticed the plaster on the ceiling was just about to fall, and there was a picture hanging crooked on the wall. And I wanted to be at home, there's no place like home, and its lonesome in this little hotel room." Then he told me, "Everything I needed was in that room, and anything you need to write a song is right there around you, you just have to pay attention to it and be in tune to it." That is the mind of a genius, and one of the greatest songs I think he ever wrote was right there. He was so descriptive, he knew how to describe things, and the way he timed things and phrased things, the air in between words, when I hear that, I know its Freddy.

Freddy Powers: My proudest song was one I wrote myself that was recorded by Merle and Ray Charles for the *Friendship* Album. I actually sat beside Ray at the piano stool and taught him the song chord for chord, word for word! It always bothered me that we weren't living back then in the era of cell phone cameras because it would have made for a hell of a picture!

Freddy Powers and John Cody Carter, Silverthorne Resort

CHAPTER 14: LAST DAYS ON THE LAKE

Freddy Powers: In the mid-80s, I'd met a sweet lady Anne Pinto and introduced her to Deanie Bird. They hit it off right from the start and began dating, then had been together for a while and decided to get married. They wanted Merle to marry them, so Deanie Bird asked him if he would do it. Merle said he would if they found out how to get the appropriate licensing he would need to make it legal. I guess it was Anne who did the research and found the necessary forms you had to fill out in order to become a minister and be able to officiate weddings legally, and the next day, Merle had his people at his office send off for some kind of a certificate to show he was a minister. Lo and behold, the certificate came back legal and all!

Merle took the ceremony very seriously and was very nervous about it. He felt this to be sacred and not to be looked upon lightly. So he put his heart into this and though he has had several failed marriages himself, he married two people who were together till the day they did part by death. It was a wonderful ceremony on the front of Merle's houseboat. The whole crew was there. I remember how happy Deanie Bird looked standing there holding Anne's hand as Merle spoke of the vows they were making, and I played and sang *"Ridin' High"* for them. I was very happy and proud for him.

Anne Reynolds: It was funny, because years earlier when I'd first met Freddy. He was a little standoffish at first because I don't think he wanted Dean to get interested in me because they were in all this stuff with Merle. I remember Freddy saying to him at one of the shows, "You better watch out Deanie Bird or you're gonna be married!" This was over a microphone at one of the shows, so he was a little bit nervous about me, but Dean and I were head over heels! We were inseparable and never a minute apart if we could help it, so soon, Freddy and I became like family too.

Years later, we were all on the road in Florida and we'd been carrying our marriage license around for like a year and there had never been any time to get married. So Merle called us up onto his bus, and the band only had one more gig left on that tour leg, and he said, "Why don't you guys leave tonight and go on back to Texas and get your things and then fly up to the lake? We'll meet you up there and I'll marry you on the houseboats." This was the first we'd heard about that, so we flew up there, and he televised it, and it was beautiful. Biff's wife made our wedding cake, and I ordered our flowers and we had a lovely wedding. My older son gave me away and my daughters were my bridesmaids and maid of honor, and my family was there, and all of Dean's older children and our friends. It was quite a big crowd there on Merle's private pier, and even then there were people pressed up against the gate watching.

The day Dean and I were married, after we left, three of my four grown kids were there, and Freddy entertained them as though he was back in the Dixieland era. Then as a stand-up comedian, for two hours they said, and the whole time they absolutely laughed themselves hysterically to death. They said he was great, talked like a Swede, and was just hysterical funny.

Freddy Powers: Deanie Bird was a special man; he was friends with everybody. Nobody was a stranger to him. He made everyone feel welcome and comfortable like they belonged there. I loved Deanie Bird and so did everyone around him. Anne is also a wonderful lady and still to this day is a very dear friend of mine, though I don't see her much anymore. I know Deanie meant a lot to her and she loved him very much and missed him like I do. I'll never have another bass player that could read my mind and understand my style of playing like Deanie Bird could. I miss my friend every time I set down to play.

Merle Haggard: I married him and his wife, I pronounced the ceremony. Deanie Bird, he played fiddle and upright bass, and he was voted six years in a row # 1 bass player, he was a showman and also a good bass player. He was also a helicopter pilot and built his own steam engine, so he was really an intelligent guy and cooked Cat-Head biscuits. He was a master at several trades.

Anne Reynolds: Dean was the most generous man, he grew four acres of produce when he came off the road, and would say, "It's just me and the good Lord on the tractor," grew four acres of produce and gave it all away. He'd get it all processed and bagged and then give it to old neighbors and everybody who needed it. It was his way of getting back in touch with the world. He was very earthy, there was nothing phony about him, he was very humble and always kind and happy.

Merle's father was an engineer and he adored his father, who died right at his feet of a heart attack as a young boy. He was so close to his father, and that's where he went wild as a boy, and took off and started riding the trains and getting in trouble. But he loved trains, and on his tour bus, he had a train etched all the way down one wall of the bus, it was beautiful. Not long after he married Dean and I, I remember one day he said, "Let's rent a train car," and it turns out you could rent them from a museum up there, an antique car, and he put it on the back of an Amtrak. Freddy, Dean, me and Merle and one of his sons, we pulled it across from Redding to Reno and then across to Chicago. They wrote some more songs, and I was the cook. He didn't want anybody else to cook, he was very particular about his food. So we had a retired General for a trainman and then a working trainman. We had the most gorgeous antique car you ever saw. It's lovely, it was crystal and china with fine linens and rugs that were woven and fresh flowers.

Freddy Powers: As time went by Merle and Debbie broke up. Strange as it may be they remained friends and she stayed on as his maid and also worked in his office Hag Inc. One day, this tall blonde showed up on the scene. She was with Clint Strong, the guitar player for both Merle and I. You could tell Merle was taken by her, and before you know it they were a new couple. Theresa Lane is her name, from Sacramento California. She was very quiet with a cute sense of humor. She ran with us for a while and the parties kept going.

Theresa and Merle kept getting closer and closer until they finally married in 1989. This time, Merle had a sunset wedding at his ranch, and believe it or not, Debbie – Merle's ex-wife- became close friends with Theresa and was Theresa's maid of honor at the wedding! After the wedding, she continued to work for Merle in the office for a long time after, but to me, even more beautiful than that, Bonnie Owens- Merle's second wife – also sang at their wedding. I say beautiful because I think it is really great when people can remain friends after a break-up. Theresa had already had their first child, a baby girl. With a baby, it was hard and dangerous to continue living on the house boat, so they moved off the lake and back to Merle's ranch. That ended the boat life as we knew it and the Spree of 83.

Merle Haggard: I moved off the boat to keep from dropping that baby in the water. She started crawling around, and she was six months old and starting to pull herself up on things, and I said "Well, it's time we get off the lake." So I was looking for a cabin to move into, and somebody said, "Well, you've got a cabin on your property." And I said, "I do?", went up there, found this old abandoned cabin and there was a cow standing inside the cabin when we found it. So we chased the cow out of there, and I said "Well, this is just exactly what I'll need," so we fixed it up and moved in.

Freddy Powers: I continued to live on my boat for a while, but it wasn't the same. When Merle moved off the lake so did most of the party...

Norm Hamlet: Freddy and Merle were the best of friends. Them working on songs together, I would say at that time Freddy was probably the best friend Merle had. Merle thought the world of Freddy. I could see why he did, because Freddy was just a nice guy to be around.

Scotty Joss: Fred made a huge difference in my life. I stayed with he and Catherine when they had their condo in Nashville, and they invited me to come out and stay. He was always the nicest man, he took me under his wing and taught me how to play like he did, not quite like he did but I'm pretty close when I cut to it. He taught me a bit about songwriting, and was just a really good friend and mentor for me. I still do his tunes today when I play my shows, and have recorded several of his tunes myself. On my latest record, *How Far to Georgia?*, I've got 2 or 3 of his songs on there. He was an inspiration and friend and I miss him terribly. I went off to play with Dwight Yoakam from 1988 to 2002, but Silverthorne is where I got my start.

Merle Haggard: I've got a song called "*Favorite Memories*" that was a number one song that came out of the lake life. It was very fertile song-writing ground. It was the right period of time in our lives. We were both healthy and both had a lot of experience.

Freddy Powers: Years later, I captured those days in a song appropriately titled "*Tom Sawyer and Huckleberry Finn.*"

CHAPTER 14: LAST DAYS ON THE LAKE

Vs 1

Well I'm watching the bubbles in my beer disappear
My mind is taken far away from here
To a better way of livin'
To a world much more forgivin'
We were just like children
Who had run away from home

Chorus

That old jukebox plays a lot of memories
And takes me back to 1983
Floatin' down the river, sailin' on the wind
Living like Tom Sawyer and Huckleberry Finn

Vs 2

I'm thankful for the memories I'm able to recall
Me and Huckleberry, we had ourselves a ball
Writing songs of broken love and places we had been
Living like Tom Sawyer and Huckleberry Finn

We called it the Spree of '83
Old Huckleberry and me
Floatin' down the river, sailin' on the wind
Living like Tom Sawyer and Huckleberry Finn

Bridge

Now if you see old Haggard
out there in the West
tell him Austin Freddy Powers
sends his family all the best
and take another quarter
and play that song again

written by Tom Sawyer and Huckleberry Finn

Freddy and Catherine Powers Newly Married, 1992

CHAPTER 15: THE BALLAD OF FREDDY AND CATHERINE

Catherine Powers: I fell in love with Freddy and knew in my heart he was going to be my man when I saw his picture on the cover of his *Country Jazz Singer* album. I took one look and said to myself, "Oh my god he is beautiful and I am in love, and I haven't even met him yet!"

Merle Haggard: The same time Freddy met Catherine, I met Theresa out there on the dock one day, and Fred had said to me, 'You know Merle, we can't keep these women,' and when I asked why, he said 'Because we're too fuckin' old!' They were young, and everything Fred said that day sounded right because I figured some younger fella would come along and run off with mine over the years, but it hasn't happened. And sure enough, he didn't know what he was talking about because we both still got 'em.

Freddy Powers: "I used to come where she was auctioning off clothes and I'd bring my girlfriends over there to buy clothes."

Catherine Powers: When I first saw him my heart felt like it had stopped for a moment and I couldn't breathe and my eyes had to be as big as silver dollars. It was a beautiful day, and Freddy was such a gracious host. He was very polite and I just hung on to everything he said all day (and in a very sneaky way I began to flirt with him, trying not to be obvious to anybody else). Freddy had a girlfriend he hadn't been dating very long, but he flirted back and made his move that evening when he and I finally had a moment alone walking up to the marina to get more beer. On the way back we were talking and walking along the ramp when, all of the sudden, he reached out and grabbed me by my waist and pulled me in close and said, "You and I would make a good couple."

It was a statement that would prove prophetic, but at first, I never really thought it would happen. Freddy's girlfriend was a singer also in the business, so I didn't really think I had a chance. But I was all over him every time he was around without being all over him at the same time (if you know what I mean). His girlfriend was generally with him so I had to be cool. But I think she knew. I'm sure my face couldn't hide how I felt about Freddy. This went on for about a year to a year and a half. Then one night we all went to see a George Strait concert. We all had passes where we could stay backstage or go out front to watch the show, and Freddy had asked me if I wanted go out front and watch the show with him. I agreed, and was lucky everybody else stayed back stage. I had been hoping for a chance to be alone with him. I thought to myself that if I ever had a chance to get him alone in a dark corner he would be in trouble.

We were sitting and talking, people were coming up and getting his autograph and he even introduced me as if I was somebody and they started getting my autograph too. It was fun, but he's a fun guy like that. Anyway we were waiting for the concert to start when he leaned over and whispered in my ear, "I want to feel your panties." Here I was finally alone with him and he's just blown me away with a line I never expected. At first, I moved away and looked at him like he was an old pervert, but then I thought "Wait a minute, this is what I wanted." So I scooched back over to him and said "I hope you do," and he did, feel my panties that is. He invited me up to his houseboat that weekend.

I snuck off up there and it was fabulous, he is such a romantic. I left overwhelmed and head over heels in love. Slowly, everybody began to find out we'd become the new item in town. It was pretty cool: he was an established celebrity and I was well known in the area for the RITZ fashion show I was in as the emcee and auctioneer. So I was a bit of a celebrity in town too. It wasn't long and we had moved in together. Our first place was a ski chalet on top of Kingsbury Grade in South Lake Tahoe. Freddy had never been a skier before, but he got into it because I loved it so much. He tried to go out there and just get after it. But he quickly found out it was not quite as easy as he thought.

Even with all the practicing on the bed mattress with skis on. The first time out the door on the way to the chair lift – which is only about a hundred yards or so – and he fell so many times, I thought about giving up skiing to keep him from killing himself! Thankfully, he decided to go and take lessons from a pro, and then we were on the slopes almost every day. We had so much fun skiing. Every ski resort had a view made for a romantic ride on the lift, and we were like teenagers!

Freddy Powers: "We traveled all over the world together, and I had a couple of airplanes and we flew all over the country together. I was on the road with Merle Haggard about 15 days a month, and she traveled with us sometimes."

Catherine Powers: Freddy was also a pilot with his own airplanes, so if we weren't skiing, we were flying around the country just for breakfast or lunch. We'd fly back and forth over the mountains from Redding, CA to Lake Tahoe all the time. He knew how much I loved flying, and we had talked about me taking a crash course in landing just in case we were up flying and something happened I would at least be able to get us on the ground. Well, one day, right after it had snowed the night before and the roads were still slick I wrecked my car. Being the sweetie he is, he cheered me up by getting me my first flying lesson. Every day just got more romantic and special with Freddy. We lived out on his houseboat for almost three years and those were the most romantic days of my life. He would do things like sneak the houseboat out of dock, anchor down out in the middle of the lake and wake me up with a cup of coffee singing "*Peg Of My Heart I Love You.*"

For all our good times, one of the saddest things about memories I have of Freddy and I together in the early days of our romance, the houseboat days or even times like the day Ray Charles recorded "*Little Hotel Room*" is that there are no pictures. People didn't walk around with cell phone cameras in those days and most people didn't carry cameras on them. Actually, when Freddy tells me about a lot of days with people like Ray Charles and the houseboat days with Merle, I wish there were more photos. I have very few pictures of the houseboat years on the houseboat and all the people we met back then. Even in the early days after we moved back to Texas living on Willie's golf course, technology still hadn't caught up with us. Funny, I remember Freddy and my first cell phone weighed probably 10 pounds and looked like a big box that we left in our van when we sold it. After all these years, the only thing that probably works on that phone any more is 9-11.

Linda Mitchell: One of the best things that ever happened to Freddy is the fact that Catherine came into his life, because I had never seen somebody so happy. The day I met her, I fell in love with her, because it was real.

It wasn't a one-night stand; it wasn't anything but pure love. Catherine was the first person I ever saw Freddy with where he wanted to be with her, I mean, literally, it was like the kindred spirits, they just clicked and there was not another man or woman in the world that could turn her face away from Freddy or his face away from Catherine. Catherine was a stable person in his life. I think she grounded him in a point that was just phenomenal. When she came into his life, that was it, that was totally it, and I'd seen the girls come and go but there was just something about her.

Freddy Powers: "We were driving through Lovelock, NV going camping, and I said 'Lovelock, sounds like a place to get married', and we pulled into a Justice of the Peace and got married on the courthouse lawn."

Catherine Powers: Freddy never really asked me to marry him. Actually we both had said we were never getting married again. But we both had friends who were writers for local newspapers and they were always writing about Freddy, especially when he was playing in the area. So the very mention of us as a couple would give them the hankering to announce we were engaged, though we were not. That had never even been mentioned between us (at least not until we went to his cousin's funeral), where with his son standing there he introduced me to his family as his fiancée.

We had moved to Nashville about three years into the relationship when we had an argument and I was feeling insecure with us. He had just given me a white terry cloth robe, but, a few days before he had told me a story about his ex-wife and a white stained terry cloth robe. It wasn't a good story, so I was wondering what he was thinking. I thought he was trying to tell me I reminded him of his ex. So during our argument he just yelled out, "You know I love you," I looked back at him and yelled "Well you've never told me, so how was I supposed to know?", and there hasn't been a day since then that we didn't said I love you at least once a day, generally ten times a day.

We were getting ready for a camping trip to the Ruby Mountains in Elko Nevada with his brother Don and nephew Donnie when he finally popped the question officially. Freddy was mapping out our route when he said "Hey, we're going through Lovelock Nevada, you want to get married there?" I thought he was just kidding at first so I said, "What else would you do in Lovelock?" The next thing I knew, I was out buying a little summer dress to be married in. The next day we were in Lovelock before a Justice of the Peace. We were such hippies about the whole thing: I had gone into the restroom to change into my dress when a lady knocked on the door and told me I needed to hurry because it was going to start raining. We had to get married on the lawn because we had our dog Amelia and I wanted her to be my Maid of Honor. So with my jeans and hiking boots on I slipped on my dress, put my hair up in a French bun and we got married. Just as we were signing the marriage certificate it started to sprinkle which left a memorable water spot on it.

It was beautiful: we were married on the lawn of this old court house, me standing there with a smile as big as Texas on my face and when the Justice told Freddy to take my hand, Freddy put his arm around me, pulled me in close and we looked like we had just been tied into a knot. The Justice of the Peace couldn't even look up at us without smiling. He knew he was marrying us for life. After Amelia finalized it with her paw print on the marriage certificates, we were on our way to join his brother and nephew for a romantic honeymoon up in the Ruby Mountains in Elko, Nevada.

Willie Nelson (left) and Freddy Powers (right) recording
'Road to My Heart (Catherine's Song),' mid-2000s

CHAPTER 16: ROAD TO MY HEART

Catherine Powers: Imagine this scene right out of a movie: Twilight, Ruby Mountains. A beautiful, scenic campfire backdrop, two newly married honeymooners sit next to one another, the open break in two mountain canyons and a volcanic lake before them with a perfect center view of the sun setting. The silhouette of their two heads leaning in for a honeymoon kiss when to the left, out of their sight, the shadows of several gun-toting men come trotting into the left side of the shot. The sound of shotguns racking interrupts the romantic moment, the two honeymooners' heads pull apart, look skyward toward the sight of a circle of shotgun and handgun barrels facing down at them.

That actually happened to Freddy and I while we were on our honeymoon!! A manhunt was underway for a fugitive trapper named Claude Dallas who had shot and killed a Game Warden, so we had our fire going and I guess some of the Indians who live up there saw the smoke from our camp fire and called the Sheriff. So just imagine, we're sitting there one day around that fire, sharing a kiss, getting ready to cook our freshly-caught dinner when I looked over to my right and here comes two guys with *Shot Guns*. I look over to my left, and there's *FOUR more* coming up the other side, and now they've got us surrounded!

At first, they thought we were this Claude Dallas guy, so Freddy – still holding his guitar – stops playing and says, "What's going on here guys?" So the head Sheriff is still holding that shotgun on Freddy while he's talking to him, and Freddy asks him, "Is that shotgun loaded?", to which the Sheriff replies, "It wouldn't do me much good if it wasn't." So next Freddy replied, "Would you mind aiming that thing away from my leg?" Their next exchange was even funnier, because Freddy says "I don't know what's going on but my name's Freddy Powers...", and the Sheriff says "Freddy Powers the Entertainer?" He'd seen Freddy's show at the Casino in Elko, Nevada. We were camped right outside of Elko, anyway, that's the only thing that got us out from under suspicion in a hurry was that Freddy's celebrity preceded him – even up in the mountains!

Don Powers Jr: My dad used to go up into the Sierra Nevada Mountain Range for health reasons every summer, and sometimes he would even stay all summer. So we were up there, and had already been for a couple of months, and Freddy and Catherine spent their honeymoon with us up there. We'd met Catherine only once before this, and it was funny because right about the time they were coming up there, my Dad and I were running pretty low on provisions, and were fixing to have to climb out of there go get stuff, and Freddy and Catherine looked like Santa Clause when they got up there! (laughs)

Catherine Powers: My honeymoon cottage was a hundred and fifty-year-old cabin with a dirt floor and half a roof. It was a ten-hour mountain climb that was supposed to be only a four-hour Hike. I thought it was going to take Freddy's life! It was so hard a climb that Amelia, our dog with four-wheel traction, laid down and looked at us like we were crazy and she was not going another step. Freddy gave his brother his backpack, picked up Amelia and carried her up this one steep hill. When we finally got to the top, Freddy said it was like he had stuck a needle in himself and it felt so good pulling it out, but it was worth it, it was so beautiful. We were in what once was a volcano with a beautiful lake and snow-topped mountains and this old cabin. We fished for our dinner that night and for the first time, I ate a fish that was looking back at me. The first couple of bites were hard, but they were so good that the eyes stopped bothering me and I ate at least ten little Brookies myself. He carved "Freddy and Catherine with Amelia 92" on every spot we visited in the ten days we were there. Our trip back down the mountain was a lot easier it only took about four hours to get back.

Don Powers Jr: They come up the hill and here they've got a guitar, food and all of that, and they spent 10 days up there near Overland Lake for their honeymoon. There's around 10 lakes up there in those mountains, and Dad used to go up to every one of them, but you couldn't drive, you had to hike up there. That was the whole idea, we were trying to get out of the Casinos and get some exercise, because you don't get much standing behind Black Jack tables. Freddy brought a solar-bag that you hung up that was supposed to give you a hot shower, he said that was the only thing he'd be missing when he come up there would be a hot shower. Well, there wasn't enough sun up there with so many trees so he never did get that shower! (laughs) Then Catherine, when she first got there, after we all got through hugging and saying hello, handed me a *padded toilet seat*, and she said "I don't mind roughing it, but build me something around this," so we built her a little toilet and put a shower screen around it for privacy. They had a sheltie dog at the time, Amelia, and she played with our dog, and those two had a ball up there in the mountains. Freddy and them would hike up to the lake and fish, and then come back down to where we were camped on a creek and cook dinner right there over the fire.

Catherine Powers: As a wedding present, Freddy wrote me a song "*The Road to My Heart*," which he snuck into my purse as I was going out the door to the store. When I got in my car, put my purse in the seat and saw it, at first I didn't know what it was, then I saw my name on it "*Road to My Heart (Catherine's Song.)*" I put it in the tape player and listened to it about ten times, crying every time. For our first anniversary, he wrote the words down on this pretty red material and framed it for me. Then when he recorded it in the studio for the "*Hottest Thing in Town*" album, Willie Nelson did a duet with him as I sat watching and listening. Willie knew it was my wedding song and how much it meant to me so he told me a story about his song "*Half a Man*" which is also a romantic story and how he got the idea for the song.

"*The Road To My Heart (Catherine's Song)*"

*You're on the road
On the road to my heart.
Just follow that old love light,*

*That brings you back to me.
You've found the way
To make me want to stay.
Make me want to stay around
And never part.
You read my mind I guess,
You're good at bringin' out my best,
And you're on the road to my heart.
Hey, you read my mind I guess,
You're good at bringin' out my best.
And you're on the road to my heart.
You're on the road to my heart.
... turn right at the mailbox!*

I love to watch Freddy when he's writing. There's just something romantic about him when he's all wrapped up in a song. I can see him and I can hear him, but at the same time, it's as though he's behind a glass wall and I can't touch him. I'd sit for hours watching and listening to him play and write and never get tired of it. His music is what he's all about, and what makes Freddy, Freddy – and not understanding that, one could never understand him. I am so proud to have someone like him in my life. His creativity is so profound that it almost rubs off on you, and makes you feel as though you could do it too. I have such great respect and admiration for my Freddy.

Freddy Powers: "I've told everybody in the business, don't offer me jobs on the road 'cause I don't wanna go on the road anymore. I'm sick of traveling, I won't even go to Elko. I made those fans when I was out there with Merle, I went out and saw my fans all this time. Now, my fans can come and see me for a while."

Catherine Powers: When we came home from our honeymoon a friend called to tell us about this little cottage for rent. It turned out to be a little house that had been built in the mid-1800s for a honeymoon cottage. It was perfect, though it needed some work. We grabbed paint and brushes and had a blast fixing it up. We spent the winter skiing Mount Rose, which our cottage was at the foot of. We'd pack a picnic lunch and a bottle of wine or Yukon Jack, which at the time was the party drink of our little crew. We'd ski and drink Yukon to keep us warm {that was our excuse anyway} until lunchtime, then we would find a little place off to ourselves for a romantic view as we ate our picnic. Just about every day in the spring and summer, we rode our bicycles to the two parks on Franktown Road to have breakfast and to feed the animals. We'd stop at the first park to eat and feed the chipmunks and the birds. Then ride to the next park and feed the squirrels. Sometimes we would lay out our blanket and take a nap, or just lay there and talk and listen to the birds singing and the wind blowing through the trees.

We both love animals of all kinds. When we lived on the houseboat, Freddy bought me a rubber raft. I would have all the houseboat neighbors save their food scraps, collect them and as Freddy would get the binoculars and sit out on the deck, I would row myself over to the beach and scatter the scraps all around. By the time I would get back to the houseboat, all these animals would come out of the woods to feast and we'd sit and watch them together. It was fascinating watching the different rituals and habits of all these different species of life.

The birds were the most interesting to us. While the vultures would span their wings and turn from side to side (we guessed to dry them?), the ravens would fly in, grab a piece of food, then fly over to the rocks and hide it.

We wondered how they remembered where they hid it, with so many hiding places. But we were sure that they got more to eat than the vultures. Besides deer, we also had a wolf that generally got there first to eat. He was also pretty cool. He would come out of the woods just a little before feeding time and come down to shore to drink and watch me load up my boat and head his way.

Right before I'd get there he'd mosey back to the top of the hill and watch me scatter out the food. Then when I'd get back in my boat, he would mosey back down and feast. I was really known as Ellie Mae around there. I feed every animal out there including the fish. They'd come up every night to an underwater light that we dropped down from the fishing hole Freddy had cut in the living room floor of the houseboat and eat right out of my hand almost. We never had to fish in the rain, just lift the stern wheel he had turned into a cover and set back and watch TV and fish indoors. Of course, we also had ducks, and if a door was left open, they would come on in and make themselves at home. Freddy was asleep on the couch one afternoon and the ducks, he said, must have been hungry, because they came in and got right in his face and let out a quack that demanded his attention. So he got up and led them back to the water with dog food that we bought every week for them.

We lived in the honeymoon cottage for about a year then we found our dream house: a little cabin on the side of the Diamond Mountain range in the Plumas National Forest. I could stand on our front porch with a hundred mile view and look back at the Lovelock Mountain range where we got married. It was a small cabin with no electricity or running water. Freddy and I put in the plumbing ourselves, and made our own electricity. We did this out of water from a spring in our back yard. Freddy was so proud of his electricity, and basically how it worked was: Freddy and the ranch hand Bunkhouse Bill had dug a hole at the foot of the mountain below the cabin deep enough to hold an old double-door refrigerator. They lowered it down in there, and it was connected externally by an irrigation pipe to that natural creek that cut down the mountain beside the cabin.

Freddy Powers: It was real simple: I attached the pelting wheel to one side of the fridge, drilled a hole through the other side and ran a rod through the hole, and then the water from the creek powered that pelting wheel, and it turned the generator hooked up on the other side of the cabin. That in turn was hooked up to 6-deep cell batteries we'd buried back there in the ground behind the garage so we could make our own electricity! Everything from your soap operas to the vacuum cleaner!

B.B. Morse: That was quite a rig of ingenuity, he devised a number of different devices and designed them to follow the gravity of the water to be able to turn spin turbines. He even reverse-engineered a refrigerator to become an insulated box against freezing so the main turbine had some place to run. He ran the pipes through it and connected the turbine inside the refrigerator and then closed the door on the refrigerator and it would never freeze up.

Freddy was always 10 steps ahead of everybody on what the big picture was going to be like, he had kind of a visionary ability to take it from his mind and create it into something tangible. He was writing, completing or starting a new song every day, if he took a day off it was because he was traveling. You can tell by the amount of people his music has touched, the biggest gift he left us is with the community of musicians and family that has developed as a result of his influence. He gave so innocently that there was something magical in the exchange of information when it came down from him that launched so many moments of grandeur.

Catherine Powers: We spent our first three months up there lighting the place with oil lamps and bathing in our wood-heated hot tub. We chopped wood, raised a garden, and I did laundry in a wash tub and wringer by hand. It was old-school and we loved every minute of it! Freddy and I were a great team all around, whether it be the outdoors or the music business, where we've worked together for the past 30 years. I'll never forget when Freddy and I first got together – the very first day we met – he looked at me and said, "We would make a great team," and it was true, we did, we just clicked right off the bat. I had already been in and around the entertainment business in fashion shows as a model, emcee auctioneer, and dabbling in the movie industry. As much as I loved being in front of the camera or on a walkway, I found myself drawn with equal fascination to everything that went on behind the scenes to make it happen. I was the type who was always I'm sure driving the producers nuts because I would ask them every technical-type question I could when I'm sure they wanted to say, "Lady, please zip it up and smile for the camera." Seeing I had that spark in my eye, they'd indulge me and eventually, I picked up enough of how a fashion show ran to begin putting on my own. I knew plenty of established and aspiring models to keep the runway busy, and by the time I met Freddy I was putting on charity fashion shows where I was acting as producer, auctioneer and emcee.

So I already had my foot in the door with all these Entertainment Directors and promoters around the West Coast who hired and booked entertainers like Freddy. So when Merle had his baby girl Janessa and announced he wanted to take a break from the road, Freddy handed me the keys and said, "Start driving mama!" I saw every bit of the star that he was, and versus going with some veteran – of which he knew many – he entrusted me to become his booking agent and gave me that opportunity. From that moment on, Freddy and I have worked together on everything we've ever done since, from booking Freddy's solo tours to his celebrity charity events and Concerts to our Pickin' Parties, to the Rogers and Hammerhead TV show and albums we've Executive Produced together behind the scenes for Freddy, Merle Haggard, Mary Sarah, and on and on. Freddy has always been equally considerate and supportive of the fact I still enjoyed doing my own thing in acting and modeling when I got a call from my agent. Whenever I had a booking, he would work his schedule around those dates where he could, and where he couldn't – though we hated to be away from each other or miss any of the others gigs – he was always supportive of me doing what I wanted to do.

Whenever we weren't on the road, we were back home at our mountain cottage, which was always an amazing escape because we also had forty acres with mountains to climb, small caves and mountain lions! For my birthday while I was in working on the movie *The Ty Cobb Story*, Freddy fixed up one of the caves that he had to take over from the mountain lions, and with wine, flowers and the dogs, that's where we spent the night. Freddy and I love the outdoors and love to camp. Every chance we had, that's what we did. Our camping gear was always ready. We have camped in some unusual and some dangerous places. One time, we had been driving out on this dirt road drinking blackberry brandy all day. The next thing we knew, it was getting dark and we hadn't found a camping spot yet and were over half drunk. So we pulled over on the side of a cliff and being too drunk to set up the tent, we just threw the tarp over the car and went to sleep. When we woke up later in the middle of the night freezing thinking it was cold outside, we jumped up to build a fire and found it wasn't really cold, it was the tarp holding in the cold from the night air.

One of our most dangerous camp outs, now that we think about it, was in an old abandoned mining town called Masonic. We had been up there a lot and never really ran across too many people, so we decided to camp out there that night. Everything turned out okay, but we were really taking a chance. We didn't even carry guns with us back then and this is miner's country and any escapee hiding from the law "haven." Our funniest story though was camping with bears in Twin Lakes, California. We got there early that morning, and after we set up camp, decided to go for a short hike. We were walking along and Freddy started telling me, "Now we are in bear country, so if a bear shows up, don't run, whatever you do *Don't Run*." Here we are walking along and all of the sudden, I see bushes moving. I stopped Freddy in his conversation and pointed out the moving bushes, he looks up and says, "Oh shit! It's a bear!" He grabbed my hand and tugged tight on Amelia's leash, turned, and did the exact opposite of what he'd just been saying and started high-tailing it out of there. I remember running alongside him in fear, but laughing at the same time, saying, "I thought you said you're not supposed to run!"

Luckily, we looked back and the bear was doing the same thing we were, though running in the opposite direction! That evening, we watched closely especially for Amelia while the bears walked in and out of the abandoned campsites looking for leftovers. The next morning, I went up to the bathhouse and after I took my shower and was ready to leave, went to open the door to only find {a couple of other ladies and I} were trapped in the bathhouse because there was a bear at the door going through the trash can. We started yelling for help, Freddy heard the screaming and came up to check it out. Here I was standing on the sink, yelling through this small window, which was more like a six inch slit at the top built that way to keep the animals out.

So now, with all these people yelling, Freddy and the Forest Ranger were outside trying to scare him off with his truck, and the bear just wasn't leaving until he was ready. He sat there on that trash can and ate until there was nothing left. Then, he slowly got off and moseyed on up the hill. Freddy said he'd never seen anything so funny as to see me with my head sticking out of this window screaming like a hyena. We still laugh about that weekend with the bears. Even as I write this story, I can't keep from giggling and at the same time I feel teary-eyed from the memory.

Freddy and I not only loved the camping for sleeping outside, but because hotdogs or scrambled eggs and bacon always taste better on open campfires. As I said, our cabin's property line backed up to the Plumas National Forest. There was this picnic area up there, so we and Amelia along with our hotdogs and buns would go up there and Freddy would dig out the campfire ring and with it snowing, us all bundled up we would have a picnic. While we waited for the fire to get started we danced to the crackling of the fire and the sounds of the falling snow. I got lucky, because most musicians don't dance, but Freddy is a wonderful dancer and loves to dance as much as I do. So we were always dancing. We'd be at parties and while everybody is laughing it up we are over in a little corner dancing all alone and being all romantic. I'll be in the kitchen cooking or cleaning and he'll come up and say, "You wanna to dance?", and I always accepted.

We set back and look at some of our camping days back then and thank God we are alive to tell about them, but I wouldn't take a single trip back. As newlyweds, we had so much fun and they were always so special. We would dance to no music but the sounds of Mother Nature by the campfire, or sit for hours watching our four-legged little fur doggie daughter explore the area. Amelia was kind of like our engagement ring. We made a commitment the night we got her that we would be together as long as we had her because we knew neither one of us would be able to give her up. It used to scare me, that if something happened to Amelia would our relationship survive (since she had everything to do with us making a commitment to each other). Though it broke my heart to lose her, I now know with all my heart Freddy and I will always be together, and there's nothing or no one can tear us apart. He's the man of my dreams. Freddy always went out of his way to do things that would make me happy or romance me all the time, and he's been that way since the day we got together.

He had a business trip to Oceanside, CA that he really wasn't interested in doing. He decided we would make this a little vacation and he would show me around since he had been stationed there when he was in the Marines and I had never been there before. He got this little beach condo that had everything a guest would need, including bicycles. We spent that morning with the accountants, which I thought would surely ruin the day. We left there and sort of walked down memory lane for him as he showed me Alameda Naval Base. We didn't get to go in because he had not made necessary arrangements you have to get. The guards knew of him as he had left his mark in guard stand with his military issued pistol. {By accident of course}. It was another one of those times he was goofing around and dropped his pistol and it went off and left a hole in the wall that hadn't been fixed. So he had a reputation there for being more than the ex-Marine that turned entertainer and songwriter.

He'd fallen asleep on guard duty one night standing up leaning against the guard building when the sergeant came by and accused him of being asleep on duty. Freddy jumped to attention and told him, "I wasn't asleep, I was just resting his eyes." The sergeant looked at him and said, "Oh yeah Private, it looks to me like the rest of your body joined in too!" From there, we left and headed over to this bar that he used to play at back then. When we walked in, Freddy said it looked exactly the same, so we sat down and had a drink and he told me stories of those days. After that, we went back to our romantic condo and had an eyebrow lifting evening. {umm bet your wondering}. The next morning after we had breakfast, we rented two of the property bikes and spent the day riding around town. Well, if you've seen that commercial where the man asks in the British accent, "Have you got any Grey Poupon?" Here we are riding bicycles when a stretch white limousine pulls up beside us and Freddy reaches over, knocks on the window and asks the same question! (laughs) Of course everyone cracks up laughing as they sped away honking.

That evening he had planned on us going out to a fancy restaurant and having wine and maybe some dancing. But I had seen this Der Wienerschnitzel hotdog stand that I hadn't seen since I left Texas. So I persuaded him into going there instead. We got back on the bicycles rode to the Der Wienerschnitzel and had hotdogs, at a picnic table on the street corner. Once again, it turned romantic having hotdogs watching the traffic go by and having a cross between a moonlight and sundown bike ride back to the condo. As the sun started setting in the West, the moon was already full and high in the sky (not to mention this was all with the beach right alongside of us). I've probably had more girl's dreams come true than any other women I know. So many things we've done, most would only be a dream.

CHAPTER 17: WILLIE'S HILL & COACH ROYAL'S PICKIN' PARTIES   141

Coach Royal Pickin' Party: (left to right) Ernest Owens, Jimmy Dean, Coach Darrell Royal, Floyd Tillman, Deaniebird Reynolds, Johnny Gimble, and Freddy Powers

CHAPTER 17: WILLIE'S HILL & COACH ROYAL'S PICKIN' PARTIES

Freddy Powers: After Merle and I moved off the houseboats, I'd moved back to Lake Tahoe and played around Reno and the surrounding area, but that had even changed because the Casinos had begun to feature lesser-known acts who would play for almost nothing, and most of the classy lounges were gone for more gambling devices. Entertainment became less than important to the casinos, and after trying out Nashville and our adventure living up in the Mountains, Catherine and I decided in 1994 to move back home to the Lone Star state. We set up shop on Willie Nelson's golf course.

Willie Nelson: He lived right there on hole # 7.

Texas Music Magazine: "Their home, the house where Willie Nelson hid out from the IRS when his taxes were just a tad overdue, bears a wall collage littered with enough accolades to satisfy every musician who ever graced the stage of the Grand Ole Opry, including a BMI placard recognizing more than a million radio spins of '*Let's Chase Each Other Around the Room*,' award nominations for the Rogers and Hammerhead Show he hosted through the '90s; and dozens of awards for hits covered by the business's brightest stars."

Catherine Powers: It was amazing how quickly our life in Austin blossomed once we had settled back in Austin. Personally, I could tell Freddy was excited to be living next door to another of his best friends and clown-around pals in the business, and let me tell you what, like Freddy said, Merle and he were more akin to Tom Sawyer and Huckleberry Finn. Once you added Willie Nelson into that club, no matter how much older he and Freddy have gotten over the years, whenever they got together, they were all like little boys! By that point, Willie and Freddy's friendship had gotten pretty intuitive like he and Merle's had. After knowing each other for so many years, to where Willie could start a joke and Freddy would finish it. And even when Willie was on tour, and it didn't matter if he was touring the U.S. or somewhere across the waters or down under, whenever he would hear a new dirty joke, Freddy was one of the first person he would call to tell. They'd go back and forth like that all the time, almost like a competition to see who could tell the newest joke first!

It cost a small fortune too, because I can remember more than a few times over the years being woken up out of a dead sleep at three in the morning to the sound of our phone ringing with Willie on the other end calling from overseas somewhere after after he'd just heard a new joke and couldn't wait to tell Freddy! I'm not kidding. Though Willie did a lot of the calling, I can honestly say I've sat back at times and looked at *our* phone bills and had to shake my head laughing at how many long-distance and international calling minutes were burned up with those two calling each other back and forth vice versa with new jokes! So alongside music, throughout the 60+ years they've known each other, another strong part of their bond has always been the joke-telling. They would crack each other up so hard it was instantly infectious to anyone else sitting there listening. I'm not talking where people were laughing just because it was Willie Nelson telling the joke, he could always see right through that, but because they were both genuine comedians. I swear if they hadn't been musicians, they could have had their own two-man comedy act!

Don Powers Jr: They all loved jokes, and to show you how quick a joke gets around, me and my dad used to write comedy material for Freddy when he was doing Dixieland Jazz and comedy. So we called up one time and told Freddy a joke, Freddy told Merle, Merle told Willie, and two weeks later we heard our joke on the Tonight Show! That's how quick a good joke got around between those guys!

Marc Oswald: Freddy's the funniest guy, he called me one time, and didn't even say hello. As soon as I picked up the phone, he said 'Willie's pissed,' and I said 'Fred, how you doing?', and he goes 'Not too good, Willie's pissed?' So next he says, 'Willie keeps calling me from the road, and everywhere he goes, he's hearing another joke,' because everyone wanted to share their jokes with Willie. Then Fred says, 'He's been calling me because I'm sick, and he's been cheering me up, and calling me every day or two with a new joke that he hears out on the road. Of course, I'm home sick here and can't stand it, so I've been out walking around the golf course, and every time I hear a new joke, I tell everybody here at the course the joke, and everybody laughs. Well, then Willie gets home from tour with all those new jokes, starts telling them, and I'd already told every single one of them, so he's pissed! (laughs) Willie and Freddy are best friends, and that little group of Willie, Freddy and Merle, they're a gang, they're a posse, and do like to help each other out and really care about each other.

Catherine Powers: Whenever Willie was home off the road, being such close friends and neighbors, it seemed like he and Freddy were always together. I've been there many times over the years when Willie and Freddy got stoned together where they would pick up their guitars and just pick and play for hours and hours, and sometimes days! It's funny too because from what I've seen, there's no real difference in Willie's personality from when he's not stoned to when he is. It's like he has said himself many times, he's been smoking pot for so many years that he doesn't feel like he's stoned even when he is. (laughs) It's the same way with Freddy, except now I notice the difference because of what pot does to calm his Parkinson's symptoms down.

    Freddy was at a video shoot years ago working with Big & Rich, Merle and Gretchen Wilson. Freddy and Gretchen were sitting in the back of the Limo – in fact there was a documentary film crew recording this – and it was funny because Freddy said, "I need to get high" and right there *on camera*, lit up and took a big old hit off his joint. Well, right about that time, Gretchen asked him, "Freddy, do you like getting high?", and he answered her with an expression that has long been a true inside joke among his friends: "If you see me, I'm high." Then he laid down out of view of the camera and said, "And if you don't see me, I'm high!" (laughs) With that, he raised back up in view of the camera again, took another big old hit and started coughing, and next Gretchen says, "Well, is it good?", and he leaned back and said "Shit yeah!"

    I remember one time when we were living on Willie's golf course when he called Freddy from home and asked him, "Freddy, do you wanna get higher than you've ever been in your whole life?" Well, of course, Freddy's response was "Well, hell yeah!", and Willie said, "Well, come on up," which meant going in our back yard because we were neighbors, he lived behind us. This was when the vaporizers had come out back when they were still these big old machines, and Willie had just gotten one. So Freddy goes on up there and a couple hours later, I get this hilarious call from him saying "Mama, I'm lost…" Now, you've got to remember, Willie lives right behind us up on the hill, and you could *see our house* from his with just a street between us. He insisted, "I can't find my way home." I chuckled and asked him where he was, in a worried tone. He continued, "I don't know, I just left Willie's and started driving and now nothing looks familiar, I don't know where I am." He and Willie had gotten so stoned that Freddy's literally forgot where he lived, and he knew that neighborhood well. We still joke about it to this day, and our punch line always gets the biggest laugh: "Now that's getting high with Willie!"

If they weren't playing music for hours on end, they played A LOT of golf, and stoned golf too because I'd be able to see them from our front porch when they were playing on a hole near our house. Routinely, I'd chuckle as I watched little clouds of smoke appear above their golf cart! (laughs) Willie had a pool table up at his house, and they loved to play pool together too. They were REALLY a hoot when they'd get high and had been drinking a little bit together, the two of them were so funny and would sometimes even go up to Willie's World Headquarters Ranch. There's actually a whole actual main street town designed like it was straight out of the 1800s Wild West where he, Freddy and Bill McDavid would play cowboys and bank robbers, they were a hoot!

Anne Reynolds, Deanie-Bird's Widow: The first time Willie and Merle got together to record, they had never been together. Freddy and Dean and I were there at the Golf Course, and Merle's bus came in and it was Thanksgiving. Somebody brought a catered dinner, and it was all of Merle's entourage – which was a lot of guys – and I was the only female there. We were staying at this one fellas house. So I was the cook, and then the day after Thanksgiving, we were supposed to be gone by then, finished with the recording, and we weren't because they were all getting on so well. Merle, Willie, Freddy and Deanie were all there milling around the house, and in-between these hours of what they called *Pickin*. I became the defacto cook and made my famous Turkey Soup recipe, which is all the left-overs from Thanksgiving put in a pot, and they loved it! Merle even took it on the road when he left.

Edith Royal: We started seeing more of Freddy after he and Catherine moved out there onto Willie's course. After the children were out of school, we had eventually moved out by Willie and had a house on the lake. So we all hung out together all the time, and Darrell played golf with Willie nearly every day. He always went to the studio with Willie after their golf game was over, and Darrell loved being around music. He either met Freddy there or at one of Darrell's golf tournaments Willie invited him to, but Darrell and Freddy became fast friends. Then, after the Longhorn games, we'd always have pickin' parties at our house, and Freddy was always there for those playing with Willie and the boys all night.

Larry Gatlin: You don't meet Freddy, you just encounter Freddy. He's kind of the grey ghost, Willie was out there, and Merle and Waylon Jennings was out there, these guys who all had a commanding presence, and Freddy was kind of a side-kick. He was Soncho Panza to Willie's Don Quixote, and you kind of felt his presence. I saw Willie play one night at the Desert Inn where the Gatlin Brothers were headlining, Willie was coming through town, stayed over, and he came to the show that night and Freddy was with him at that show. After that deal, we went over to Willie's hotel and hung out till about dawn, and sat around and smoked playing songs.

From then on, I'd see Freddy whenever I came to Austin. Everybody'd be at a picking session, and then Freddy would just knock you DOWN! I always thought he was one of the closest things to Mickey Newbury, he sang like Mickey, so it's like Freddy was always there, but then all of a sudden, he was REALLY there, boom! And you'd watch him play and say "Holy shit! Wow…"

Molly McKnight: Everybody got to know everybody from wherever they'd came from – Oklahoma to California – and James Garner would always play, and Don Cherrie, and Terry Bradshaw and his wife were there, just people who loved music. What they would do is: they'd play golf and one member of each group would be an entertainer, and they'd be teamed up with famous athletes, astronauts, and we even had a blind guy that played! So the pickers – like Willie and Freddy and Johnny Gimble, who was always there, Floyd Tillman, Sonny Throckmorton, and Whitey Shafer – all got to know all the celebrities, it was just a conglomeration of entertainers playing golf for charity. Then after everybody finished their golf games, they'd have time to come in and shower, then they'd have a dinner, and then the music would start,

J. Gary Smith: The thing that made it amazing was the stars were the songwriters! Not the stars that came to perform, but the Red Lanes and Sonny Throckmortons and Mickey Newburys and Whitey Shafers, so when we did the picks in the big room after the shows, there's be 100 people packed into a hotel room with the doors open to a little suite, all drinking and listening. Because when Darrell Royal said "Red light," that meant "Shut the fuck up, because somebody's going to sing a song." See, Darrell Royal was an amazing man, he loved Willie Nelson and Country music and pickin' and songwriters. It would always be an original someone was playing with just an acoustic guitar and the writer, and if you made too much noise, they'd throw your ass out. Darrell was like a Commando, when he spoke, we all listened.

Those tournaments that Freddy and I and so many others played over the years were an amazing networking opportunity on top of everything else. In fact, a lot of people take credit for this, but I called Darrell Royal at Freddy's request before they'd ever met and got him in one of those golf tournaments for the first time. Darrell knew who Freddy was, so the first time he came, he brought his little band with Deanie Bird and everybody, and they blew Coach Royal's mind! Freddy was a really fine guitarist, really solid, and they were invited to everyone after that. Fred and Deanie Bird would play during the picking parties, and Deanie would pick his stand-up bass and Freddy would play acoustic guitar and they'd play original songs. You didn't do covers in those things, they wanted to know who you were.

B.B. Morse: Those were magic moments. My favorite story from those days was the time Doug Supernaw and Matthew McConaughey squared off against each other! We were doing one of the after hours Presidential Suite Pickin' Parties at one of Coach Royal's golf tournaments. So this one jam was going along pretty well, Ed Bruce had been there and Aaron Barker and Doug Supernaw's turn comes and he gets up there and starts playing. Well, prior to that, when two or three other performers were playing, Matthew McConaughey had performed Body Bongos on himself shirtless. All the 16 year old girls in that place were going nuts, and he sounded good by the way, the guy sounds like a watermelon. So when Doug started playing, Matt continued body-bonging, and after one song, Doug expressed some dissatisfaction or disapproval with the fact that Matthew was stealing his smoke, so he said "Hey man, why don't you take a break," and he didn't say it that nice either! (laughs) You could hear a pin drop after he initially addressed Matthew, and Matthew responded in kind as you might expect someone to who was verbally assaulted in public in such a manner, and next thing you know he and Doug are face-to-face. They were stepping into each other, and got chest to chest before a "Hey, cool it" moment, and Doug wasn't invited from then on. There were sparks flying that night man.

Catherine Powers: Freddy grew close to another true original when he met Bill McDavid at one of Coach Darrell Royal's Golf Tournaments. In that spirit, Coach Darrell Royal was a key to a lot of people's relationships, especially in the music industry. A lot of people credit Coach Royal for helping launch or advance their careers, George Strait being one example. There are so many people who would just have to say if it hadn't been for Coach, they may not have gone on as far as they did, or had the support network that they had.

Edith Royal: Willie moved to Austin from Nashville in the 70s because he couldn't get any gigs, and one time he was here, he couldn't even pay the band. He said, "I'm gonna have to move back to Nashville because I don't have enough money this week to pay the band," and Darrell said "No, don't do that Willie because I'm gonna rent a place here for you, and everybody has to come and pay $25 for a couple, and that will include all the beer they can drink." So Willie said, "Well, I don't think anybody will come. They're not coming to my gigs, so why would they come to that?" And Darrell said, "Well, I'm gonna ask everybody in the Athletic Dept. to come, and they'll come and pay $25," and Willie got enough money to pay his band and stayed. So Willie was just amazed, because he wasn't getting any money from his gigs, but he got a whole bunch of new fans from that, because everybody in the Athletic Dept. started listening to country music after that and coming to his gigs. His friendship with Coach just kind of grew from there.

Sonny Throckmorton: Coach Darrell Royal was a great influence for music in Texas. He was a big part of Texas Music over the latter 20, 30 years, he had a big hand. He knew all the entertainers, and was always friendly because Coach just loved singer/songwriters, he just loved them and treated them good, and gave them breaks and invited them to do things they probably wouldn't have gotten to do otherwise. In fact, I met Freddy at Darrell Royal's golf tournaments down in Houston, he would come down and entertain and play golf, as we all did. First they were Coach Darrell Royal Golf Tournaments, then became Darrell and Willie, and then it was a Ben Crenshaw, Darrell and Willie, but those 25+ years of tournaments were all one in the same because they all had Darrell. So I got to be friends with him, and that was probably about 20 years ago. I dearly love Freddy.

Wayne Ahart: I met Freddy through the Darrell Royal and Willie Nelson jamborees they'd have at the annual Darrell Royal and Willie Nelson Invitational. They would gather up a lot of unknown as well as very well known performers and play golf in the day and music at night, sometimes all night! Generally, they'd go till 2 or 3 in the morning. I met Freddy through those events, and everybody knew I was very, very close friends with Darrell Royal, and he was all of their hero. The fact they would see me frequently with Darryl, they quickly took me as like one of them. I wasn't one of them, I wasn't a musician or singer or songwriter, I was a business man, and in fact, Darrell and I did a lot of stuff together and he served on my board of directors for 25 years or so.

First of all, Darrell Royal was a winner at whatever part of life he was participating in at the moment, he was a winner. He was a straight arrow, and everyone trusted him without ever questioning his thinking, they took whatever he said to heart as fact because that's how Darrell meant it to be taken. Darrell was the winning-est coach, and men just naturally like to be around and associated with Coaches. Especially good Coaches, and Darrell was one of the best ever. Darrell happened to love music, and he didn't just love music, he loved the words of music. I can't tell you how many songs he and Id be listening to where he knew all the words, like a singer knows them. Right away, after he got hired by the University of Texas Longhorns, he found out about this guy everybody was talking about named Willie Nelson, and a lot of times, after Darrell would finish all his coaching duties. Then, instead of going home like a lot of people would do, he'd take an hour out of his time to go some place and listen to music, a lot of times just by himself.

Then, in that fashion, people began to recognize who he was sitting in that audience, and so he and Willie got to be friends. Then later, when Willie really realized what kind of man Darrell was, and Darrell realized what kind of a guy Willie was, then they learned to really appreciate each other. So Darrell Royal and Willie became close friends, and I mean real close friends. Darrell would help Willie out when he needed help if Darrell could help him, and Willie would do anything for Darryl, then and would do it right now. So as a result of his friendship with Willie, Coach began to meet a lot of the big-time superstars in country music and he became their Champion and that of songwriters in general.

Darrell loves good singers, but what he loved more than anything else were songwriters. He loved the way that a person could take words and sometimes make them mean something entirely different than what everybody thinks that word means, and put it to music that everybody in the room could listen to and enjoy. Darrell LOVED songwriters, and that's one of the reasons he loved Willie so much, because Willie was a great songwriter, and he thought the same of Freddy. So Freddy and Darrell became very close because of Freddy's, and both he and Darrell were good old country boys with good hearts. Freddy had a beautiful way of wording things and putting them to music, and that's why he was such a good songwriter, so it was natural for Darrell and Edith to love the Powers.

Catherine Powers: Coach was a major supporter of musicians and football players, and Freddy first met Coach through Willie Nelson, who was living in Austin, Texas while Darrell Royal was the Coach for the Texas Longhorns. Well, once Willie introduced Freddy and Coach, they hit it off immediately and became very close friends. It was funny, one time, Coach rattled off our home number from memory to someone else who'd asked for it, and that shows you how close they were. Coach was even close with our dog Amelia, who was a singer, and he was fascinated by that, and even brought the current Coach Mac Brown of the Longhorns out to hear our dog sing. Well, as soon as Freddy started singing her song, "*Soldier Girl*," Amelia stood up and started performing, and when she would do that perfect for him, then Coach Royal would take her for a ride on the Golf Cart.

Edith Royal: Back when he was growing up in Hollis, Oklahoma, we used to listen to the Grand Ole Opry, that was about the only time we had any music there. Then he grew up in the Church of Christ where they didn't allow instruments, but they all sang A Capella without any instruments. So he grew up singing himself in church, and then after we were married, we still listened to Country/Western music, and we listened to all kinds of music. He coached in Durham, North Carolina at one time and Louis Armstrong came to town, and this was a dance – before integration, so the white people couldn't dance, they had to sit up in the balcony and watch and listen to the music. Then when we'd get a chance to visit New Orleans, we always went to hear Fats Domino and all of the Jazz people, so we just grew up loving music of all kinds. We never went to the symphony, but always attended the Jazz and Country Music events any place they were going on, we were there. So then when we landed in Texas and Darrell coached the Longhorns, country music was just a natural fit, and there was lots of it.

So Darrell loved music, and he loved all those guys – Willie, Freddy, Merle, and songwriters like that. They were all very interesting people, and the writing of the songs, he loved to be there to hear how they came about writing something and what it was about, and how it started. He loved all of that, he just loved the music and musicians. After games, they'd come over to my house – including Freddy a lot of times – and I'd have food for them there, and they'd stay playing until we'd go to bed. One time we had Mickey Mantle there, and all of the pickin' was going on, and when it was time to go to bed, we had extra beds, and put them all to bed. Mickey was the last one who wanted to go to bed so we had to make a pallet for him on the floor in front of our bed. That was an interesting night, there were lots of them and it was always fun.

Catherine Powers: We all used to say that his name was the most appropriate name anyone in his position could ever be given, because Darrell and his wife Edith were Texas Royalty. They are more loved and more respected and more well-known than anybody else in the entire state of Texas. You put Willie Nelson and Coach Royal in a room together and you have two of the most famous people in Texas, and Willie's going to get some of the attention, but Coach Royal would get all the attention.

Freddy Powers (right) Pickin' with Merle Haggard (center)
on the Rogers and Hammerhead Show Set

CHAPTER 18: ROGERS & HAMMERHEAD

Freddy Powers: We were sure living high on the hog, but I always used to joke that you could tell the difference between when a musician and a songwriter pulled out of our driveway because the musician's car only left one oil spot while you could literally follow the songwriter home because they left a trail of oil spots. There's another old but true saying among songwriters that you can have a bunch of hits, but if they're not on the radio playing, they're not paying! Luckily, we came up with the bright idea to start a Cable TV Show in our own living room! We called it the Rogers & Hammerhead Show, and actually filmed in our living room! My close friend Bill McDavid and I co-hosted the show!

Catherine Powers: Bill McDavid was one of the characters Freddy met at one of Coach's tournaments. They immediately hit it off and became best friends, and stayed close a good 40 years before Bill passed away. Around Texas, the McDavid family owned car dealerships all over the state. Bill opened his first one at 19 in Weatherford, Texas and branched out into Dallas, Ft. Worth, Houston, Beaumont, every big city had a McDavid-McDavid Pontiac. Their commercials would star Bill at the end of each one calling for his Great Dane Wide Track, who would bark back at him. That became kind of a signature everybody knew him by and Bill was definitely a one-of-a-kind just like Freddy!

Bill McDavid: "I was out there making money, but I was also hanging out with Freddy for 20 years. I can't remember exactly when we met, but it had to be at one of Coach Darrell Royal's Golf tournaments back in Galveston."

Catherine Powers: Bill came to one of our golf tournaments for the Nevada Special Olympics, and bought one of the guitars we were auctioning off that day. Bill had never played before and wanted to learn, so Freddy taught him two chords and spent the weekend picking with him to get him familiar with playing them and switching back and forth, the basics. Well, a few weeks later, Bill called Freddy back up and said, "I've written this song I want you to help me with," and they hung up. I remember Freddy saying "Hell, I'm looking forward to seeing Bill, but he's written this song and it's probably not going to be worth a shit, and I won't know how to tell him…" Even I could see he was real nervous about seeing Bill, and next thing you know, we're sitting in the room, and I watched this whole scenario play out first hand: Freddy had a plastic grin plastered on his face not knowing what to expect as Bill excitedly whipped out that guitar he'd won at our auction. With those two chords Freddy had taught him, shocked us all as he began playing this song. I could tell that Freddy was genuinely surprised by the end, because the first thing he said once Bill had stopped playing was "Holy crap Bill, you've written a great song!"

Freddy Powers: "I was visiting with Bill about two and a half years ago, and someone had shown him a chord on the guitar he had recently bought. I was really happy to see Bill learning how to play a guitar, so I showed him a couple more chords. Next time I saw him, he knew those chords real good, so I showed him a little bit more. In March of 94, I came down here to record and I've been here ever since. I started giving Bill full-time guitar lessons and he's wrote a song, '*Me and My Drummer*', which has now been recorded by two major artists: Willie Nelson and Doug Supernaw. It's like "*My Way*," only it's country. I had to march to the drummer in me. Willie Nelson and Merle Haggard said the same thing – it's a damn good song."

> **Bill McDavid:** "Freddy was the first person to take me serious, which he did a long time before anyone else did. Willie was the first person I sung 'Drummer' to."

Catherine Powers: After that, Freddy was now all of a sudden excited and right there, showed him a few more chords, and Bill – like Freddy – proved to be one of those people who, when he set his mind to doing something, he wanted to learn everything he could and become the best he could at it. He had been a Quarter Horse champion, for instance, and the next thing you know, the very first song he ever wrote based off those chords Freddy taught him wound up being recorded by Willie Nelson. After that, Freddy and Bill started writing together regularly, and as they started going out and playing a little bit together around town, Willie wound up watching one of their gigs and joking around afterward said they looked like a couple of Hammerheads. In fact, Willie was the one to actually give them what became their moniker as songwriters, music publishing company and ultimately the name of their Cable television show. Freddy and Bill started writing a lot of songs together after that first one, and even had a couple Christmas songs recorded by the Texas Girls' Choir. Freddy always was very supportive of the Texas Girls' Choir, in fact, we did a fundraiser for them one time hoping to raise $10,000 and wound up raising almost $300,000! What we all laugh about looking back on Freddy and Bill's working relationship is that Bill was 60 years old before he ever picked up a guitar, strummed his first two chords, or wrote his first song!

Freddy Powers: "We were sitting around discussing what to call our publishing company and just talking about songwriting when I said, 'Bill, you and I might turn out to be the next Rogers and Hammerhead of country.' You know, the country version of Broadway. That's where it started. Everybody laughed about it at first, but now nobody is laughing. We've got a TV show going once a week featuring major songwriters: there's Sonny Throckmorton, Gary P. Nunn, Doug Supernaw, Aaron Baker, Ray Wylie Hubbard, Rusty Weir, Steve Fromholz, Larry Gatlin, the Geezinslaws, Merle Haggard, Floyd Tillman, and our neighbor Willie Nelson."

> **Bill McDavid:** "We started it to provide a place for songwriters to get their songs heard. We're strong believers in divine intervention because we're not smart enough to have made this happen. I see the Rogers and Hammerhead Show becoming as popular as Johnny Carson. We market ourselves, we've got so many friends in the music business."

> **Molly McKnight:** I was freshly divorced, and had a little boy named Peyton who was four years old at the time, and he took to Freddy like a duck to water. He called him "*The Man With the Stars on His Hat*," because Freddy always wore this beret that had four stars on it.

Catherine Powers: Not long after Freddy and Bill first hatched the idea for the show, we met Randy Willis, who was one of those kind of go-getters there in Austin. He had quite a resume of production credits from T.V. and Film, and he and Freddy started about doing a T.V. show. Freddy and Bill's concept was simple: invite songwriters to come on and play their songs and then talk about the craft of songwriting afterward. So there was a performance and guest segment for the songwriters, which was a first-of-its-kind format. During the first season, sitting side by side with matching motorcycle caps and jean jackets, they had a policy where every songwriter appearing as a guest on the show had to have one hit or more under their belt. The guest would play their song, and then Freddy and his co-host Bill McDavid would ask them questions like, "What inspired you to write that song?" "How did you become a songwriter?" and, "How do you write your songs? Do you write your melodies first or do you write the words first?"

They talked a lot about structuring, and also talked a lot about the music industry: "How do you get a song out there to be plugged and picked up by a recording artist?" So the show focused on the whole songwriting process and the business of being a professional songwriter. It was an educational songwriting show, and they had everyone from unknown, up and coming songwriters to legends.

FLOYD TILLMAN, Rogers & Hammerhead, December 2nd, 1997:

Bill McDavid:

Hello everybody, welcome to the Rogers & Hammerhead Show. Me and Freddy have been having a lot of fun since we did one of these shows. We took a little motorcycle trip.

Freddy Powers:
Yes-sir.

Bill McDavid:
Freddy got his merit badge in Harley Davidson riding. They used to call him Moped Fred...

Freddy Powers:
Riding with the big boys!

Bill McDavid:
We had a good time, we went up 7 states Montana, Wyoming. You know, every time we do one of these shows, we're surprised ourselves at who we get to be guests, and this week, we're really amazed. I'm going to let Freddy introduce them, he's known them a *long* time.

Freddy Powers:
Boy have I ever known these guys
a long time. We are so honored today,
we've had a lot of songwriters on here
the last year, but this is probably the
best songwriter, certainly in my life. I've
always been a big fan of this wonderful
songwriter, ladies and gentleman,
we have with us today Floyd Tillman.
(audience applauds)

Floyd Tillman:
One of the first songs I ever wrote was
called "*Put the Rhythm in the Air*" back
when I was 14, and I didn't know what rhythm
was. I knew it had something to do
with music! (laughs)

Freddy Powers:
Do you remember that song?

Floyd Tillman:
Well, yeah...

Freddy Powers:
That'd be an appropriate way to start
us off.

Floyd Tillman:

This was during the Depression, and I got
a job as a night watchman at a cotton mill,
and you walk in the big old building where
the night watchman hung out all night, and you'd
see that one little old jet of natural gas coming
out, and it looked like Frankenstein's
castle! (laughs) So I would just set there
with my guitar and play, and thought one night
"Well, I'll just write a song..."

Catherine Powers: As a matter of fact, the last two shows that were ever done for Floyd Tillman was the one he did for Rogers and Hammerhead, and the same for Rusty Weir. Being a talk show hosted by songwriters, and of course, those would turn into Pickin' Parties.

Big Kenny Alphin: I met Freddy and Bill McDavid for the first time at Marc Oswald's house. They were traveling on the Rogers & Hammerhead bus around the country a little bit, having a good time. So I met him there, and then one of the next times I saw Freddy, John and I were on the road and stopped down there at the house where they'd perform and record the Rogers & Hammerhead shows. That was right near Willie's, and there were so many instances we got together in the beginning of our career. They would invite us if events were going on, and had us over to visit with Willie Nelson at his Willie's World Headquarters on the ranch. He and Bill became like older brothers to us both and were great, great friends.

Pauline Reese: I feel like people think of him as kind of like a Godfather-type presence in songwriting, and they're kind of nervous to go up and talk to him. I've watched other artists around him who are just meeting him for the first time, or are getting to know him or watching him, and they're just so humbled when they're around him that they actually get nervous! I remember John Rich and Big Kenny from Big and Rich, when they were around him, they were just enamored with his presence, every time they were around him – even up through his Parkinson's taking over. They just really respect him and would always listen to what he had to say, there was no talking over Freddy. Everybody listened to what he had to say, and that was another lesson he taught me was, "If you want people to listen, don't yell, don't turn up your amp, don't play louder, play softer, because then they have to be quiet to hear you because they hear themselves talking and knock it off." That was a huge lesson he taught me.

John Rich: He played "*Georgia On My Mind*" one time at a pickin' party, and I'd never seen that many chords put into that song before. I remember after he got through, I said 'Alright, you gotta show me how you just played all that!' So he said: 'Alright, well, here's the first chord, here's the second chord...' and as he started moving through it, he lost me after about the third or fourth move. And I watched him play it, and went 'Unbelievable!', because he was playing a guitar like people play a piano, with so many inversions of the same chords, and knowing how to move them around and create a new atmosphere around a chord is really something extraordinary that he does.

RAY WILEY HUBBARD, Rogers & Hammerhead
February 25th, 1997

Freddy Powers:
This is our 9th show!

CHAPTER 18: ROGERS & HAMMERHEAD

John Rich, Lonestar/Big & Rich: Our manager, Mark Oswald, along his brother Greg – and another guy named Bill McDavid– have kn Freddy since back in the early 80s when Mark, my manager, and C my booking agent, were promoting Merle Haggard concerts out o1 West Coast. They got to know Freddy then and all of Merle's band kind of became running buddies with these guys, and really got to 1 Freddy very well from sitting around jamming with them and wat Freddy write all those Merle Haggard hits, and hearing all the great st Freddy's a blast, Freddy's a party, he's hilarious! And at that point, s are still being made, back in the 80s was when Haggard was proba the peak of his career. That was as hot as he ever was, right through Freddy and him were hooked at the hip.

So when Mark and Greg started managing and booking Big & Ri were down in Texas for a concert, and Mark suggested we go over t(dy's house, he said "Freddy lives on Willie Nelson's golf course," to I replied "No Kidding!" And he continued, "Yeah, they live on ' golf course, and they have these big jams- let's go over there...." rolled over to Freddy's house, and the first thing we saw when we in was a giant Neon sign hanging in the living room that said R(AND HAMMERHEAD, which was Freddy and Bill's band.

I didn't really know Freddy very well at that point, only that he'd with Merle, and knew Willie and all that stuff. So we sat down, p the guitars, poured a couple of cocktails, and started going around i with everybody playing a song, and what'aya know, Freddy start off some of my all-time favorite country songs: *"Chase Each Other. Room Tonight," "Natural High," "A Friend in California,"* on and o could NOT believe it! I was just floored, being a songwriter mys was sitting in a room with the guy who had written all these song

Past that, watching him play the guitar was really something els was ripping jazz licks left and right that were Willie Nelson (was actually probably better than Willie, it was the real, real hi ucated jazz licks in these country songs. So I asked Freddy, " you start putting jazz licks into country stuff?" And he said, "A always done it." So next I asked him, "Is that where Merle ; his sound and his style?" And Freddy wouldn't take credit for ' said, "Well, we have sat around swapping licks for many, m and I was so intrigued by Freddy at that minute that I decidec Honky Tonk hero," and that I needed to dig down in him as f; and really understand this guy. I just had so much reverence had accomplished in country music.

John Rich, Lonestar/Big & Rich: Our manager, Mark Oswald, along with his brother Greg – and another guy named Bill McDavid– have known Freddy since back in the early 80s when Mark, my manager, and Greg, my booking agent, were promoting Merle Haggard concerts out on the West Coast. They got to know Freddy then and all of Merle's band, and kind of became running buddies with these guys, and really got to know Freddy very well from sitting around jamming with them and watching Freddy write all those Merle Haggard hits, and hearing all the great stories. Freddy's a blast, Freddy's a party, he's hilarious! And at that point, stories are still being made, back in the 80s was when Haggard was probably at the peak of his career. That was as hot as he ever was, right through there, Freddy and him were hooked at the hip.

So when Mark and Greg started managing and booking Big & Rich, we were down in Texas for a concert, and Mark suggested we go over to Freddy's house, he said "Freddy lives on Willie Nelson's golf course," to which I replied "No Kidding!" And he continued, "Yeah, they live on Willie's golf course, and they have these big jams- let's go over there...." So we rolled over to Freddy's house, and the first thing we saw when we walked in was a giant Neon sign hanging in the living room that said ROGERS AND HAMMERHEAD, which was Freddy and Bill's band.

I didn't really know Freddy very well at that point, only that he'd written with Merle, and knew Willie and all that stuff. So we sat down, pulled out the guitars, poured a couple of cocktails, and started going around in a circle with everybody playing a song, and what'aya know, Freddy starts rattling off some of my all-time favorite country songs: "*Chase Each Other Round the Room Tonight,*" "*Natural High,*" "*A Friend in California,*" on and on. And I could NOT believe it! I was just floored, being a songwriter myself, that I was sitting in a room with the guy who had written all these songs.

Past that, watching him play the guitar was really something else, the guy was ripping jazz licks left and right that were Willie Nelson on kill! It was actually probably better than Willie, it was the real, real high-end educated jazz licks in these country songs. So I asked Freddy, "When did you start putting jazz licks into country stuff?" And he said, "Always, I've always done it." So next I asked him, "Is that where Merle got a lot of his sound and his style?" And Freddy wouldn't take credit for that, but he said, "Well, we have sat around swapping licks for many, many years," and I was so intrigued by Freddy at that minute that I decided: "This is a Honky Tonk hero," and that I needed to dig down in him as far as I could and really understand this guy. I just had so much reverence for what he had accomplished in country music.

Big Kenny Alphin: I met Freddy and Bill McDavid for the first time at Marc Oswald's house. They were traveling on the Rogers & Hammerhead bus around the country a little bit, having a good time. So I met him there, and then one of the next times I saw Freddy, John and I were on the road and stopped down there at the house where they'd perform and record the Rogers & Hammerhead shows. That was right near Willie's, and there were so many instances we got together in the beginning of our career. They would invite us if events were going on, and had us over to visit with Willie Nelson at his Willie's World Headquarters on the ranch. He and Bill became like older brothers to us both and were great, great friends.

Pauline Reese: I feel like people think of him as kind of like a Godfather-type presence in songwriting, and they're kind of nervous to go up and talk to him. I've watched other artists around him who are just meeting him for the first time, or are getting to know him or watching him, and they're just so humbled when they're around him that they actually get nervous! I remember John Rich and Big Kenny from Big and Rich, when they were around him, they were just enamored with his presence, every time they were around him – even up through his Parkinson's taking over. They just really respect him and would always listen to what he had to say, there was no talking over Freddy. Everybody listened to what he had to say, and that was another lesson he taught me was, "If you want people to listen, don't yell, don't turn up your amp, don't play louder, play softer, because then they have to be quiet to hear you because they hear themselves talking and knock it off." That was a huge lesson he taught me.

John Rich: He played *"Georgia On My Mind"* one time at a pickin' party, and I'd never seen that many chords put into that song before. I remember after he got through, I said 'Alright, you gotta show me how you just played all that!' So he said: 'Alright, well, here's the first chord, here's the second chord...' and as he started moving through it, he lost me after about the third or fourth move. And I watched him play it, and went 'Unbelievable!', because he was playing a guitar like people play a piano, with so many inversions of the same chords, and knowing how to move them around and create a new atmosphere around a chord is really something extraordinary that he does.

RAY WILEY HUBBARD, Rogers & Hammerhead
February 25th, 1997

Freddy Powers:
This is our 9th show!

Bill McDavid:
Who would have thought that.

Freddy Powers:
We didn't think it was going to last the first week!
We've had so far ONLY Texas songwriters...

Bill McDavid:
That's right, we've had some good ones too.
We've got a great one today!

FreddyPowers:
I'll tell you what. Ladies and Gentleman,
our guest songwriter today from Poetry, Texas,
what a place for a songwriter to be from,
Mr. Ray Wiley Hubbard!

Audience Applause

Ray Wiley Hubbard:
Thank you!

Freddy Powers:
Nice to have you with us.

Ray Wiley Hubbard:
Glad to be here, glad to be here.

Bill McDavid:
You know, that is a great place to be from
if you're a songwriter.

Ray Wiley Hubbard:
The big occupation out there is (oil coot?),
it's a nice little place. There's a Baptist
church and a Methodist church, and a
graveyard and a place to get your tractor
tires fixed, and that's it...

Bill McDavid:
What else would a man need? (laughs)
This show is about Texas songwriters
and naturally your name came up the
first night we were talking about it because
you're a legendary Texas songwriter and
a real nice guy, and we're glad you're here.

Ray Wiley Hubbard:
I'm glad to be here.

Freddy Powers:
We're gonna just let you take the show
and do what you want to do.

Ray Wiley Hubbard:
Well okay, this is a new one I sang at a wedding
down in Carville about 3 months ago, and
when I wrote it, I didn't write it as a wedding song.
I actually wrote it about when there comes a time
in a relationship where it's time to fish or cut
bait! (laughs) So we'll try that.

Audience Applause

Bill McDavid:
Did you write that for yourself in a situation
Or for the people getting married?

Ray Wiley Hubbard:
Well no, I didn't write it for the wedding at all, which
I might as well take this opportunity to say "I'm
available if anybody else is…" (laughs)

FreddyPowers:
We got a nice studio audience here today.
Rattlesnake Annie, Darrell Royal…

Ray Wiley Hubbard:
My goodness, what a deal!

Bill McDavid:
We're doing alright here!

Catherine Powers: We wound up on Austin's Public Access Cable television station, and being that Austin has as large a musician and songwriter population as it does, the show quickly caught on and had quite a large viewing audience each week. We'd film three shows at a time, and it's kind of funny because if you watch the shows, you will see how we actually learned how to make a set look better and how to make the lights work better, more like filling up the room. It had gotten to where I almost hated to dust in there because we had so many books, candles and trinkets of all kinds stacked up on top of each other because it made the room look bigger and fuller. So we learned a lot about production tricks, those little things that would make the show look more professional, because we were trying to make it as special as we could. In fact, if you watch the first couple of shows, you'll see how the lighting was a little bit dim and the living room doesn't look full, and then as the shows go on, you'll see the room was getting fuller, and then we started panning over to the audiences.

We had three cameras, and would have an audience of 50, 75 people sitting out there – just like the Pickin' Parties – along with all the lights, we were lucky to have a nice-sized living room to pull all that off in looking back on it now. We had a great, big stone fireplace that was part of the backdrop Bill and Freddy sat against as they filmed, as a matter of fact, whenever tornadoes would come through that part of Texas and tear a house down, those big old stone fireplaces would be the only thing left standing. It was grand, and I would always keep that fireplace cleaned out and ready in case we needed a place to take shelter during a tornado, that's where we would go.

Applause Magazine, February, 1996: "Freddy lives in a big house on the edge of Willie Nelson's golf course. As I entered the room, I noticed Darrell Royal relaxing in a chair and in the center of the room, dressed in a jogging suit with a red bandanna, sat Willie Nelson. I had just entered into that sacred space where Willie jams with friends just because he loves it. Freddy Powers and Bill McDavid have Hammerhead Publishing Company, and they film a television show in this very living room, a show that features interviews with songwriters."

Catherine Powers: When we got nominated for a Cable Ace Award in 1998, we all loaded up with our production crew and producer from Time Warner, and went to the award show together. Well, when it got to our category, they called out the three nominees, and we were all sitting there like kids waiting for them to announce the winner. When they said "Louisiana Jute Box" instead of Rogers and Hammerhead, of course, all our faces collectively dropped down together at the same time, and our excitement left, but our table managed to be courteous and applaud the winner. I remember Bill McDavid was really visibly bummed out about it until someone said to us, "Hey, what are you pouting about, you were three nominated out of 500 entries!" So it felt like whether we went home or not with the award that night, that we'd still won.

I learned a lot on that show, because I'd done a lot of movies in Reno and had learned a lot on set about how to be a camera assistant and a make-up artist, so I was our floor director on the Rogers and Hammerhead Show. Rogers and Hammerhead – you would have to almost say – was a crew of Freddy and Bill and their spouses, Sheri and I, because the four of us always worked together on getting the guests booked. Just every end of the spectrum you can imagine has to be produced running a television show, especially considering that the set was our living room. So really we were all producers on the show, and we all had positions: I did the make-up, I was the floor director, I assisted with the cameras, I wore all kinds of different hats.

SONNY THROCKMORTON, Rogers & Hammerhead
October 17th, 1996

Bill McDavid:
Sonny, How are you doing man?

Sonny Throckmorton:
Shoot, Roger Miller once told me you couldn't break my heart if you tried, and that's about where I'm at.

Bill McDavid:
We've been getting to spend a lot of time with Puddin' lately – everybody calls Sonny 'Puddin' – and he calls everybody else 'Puddin'…

Sonny Throckmorton:
I call everybody Puddin' too.

Freddy Powers (singing):
He calls everybody 'Puddin'… (laughs)

Bill McDavid:
We've had a lot of fun the last few weeks with Sonny…

Sonny Throckmorton:
Don't tell everything we've been doing!

Bill McDavid:
I won't even tell a little bit of it.

Freddy Powers:
Well, we've got some stories to tell, I know that! Sonny, you're one of Bill and my heroes, we play your tape all the time down here in the car and everywhere else, and Bill has made me teach him every one of your songs off that tape he made, and he's got about 4 of them down real good.

Sonny Throckmorton:
What a mundane task that must be! (laughs)

Freddy Powers:
What are you going to play for us good folks over here in Austin, Texas?

Sonny Throckmorton:
I tell you what, like Coach Darrell Royal said, "I just dance with who brung me," and I'll just stick with some of the things maybe they've heard. Here's a song I wrote while I was sitting in a parking lot of a big mall one day and this lady come walking by the car. And I kind of watched her, and she gave me absolutely no response at all – which I'm used to – but this song came into my head as this occurred, and The Oak Ridge Boys cut this. I'll try to do ya two or three songs have been hits, this is *"I Wish You Could Have Turned My Head (And Left My Heart Alone...)"*

Audience Applause

Bill McDavid:
Sonny's got so many, we just don't have time to play 'em all.

Freddy Powers:
Tell me this, do you plug your own songs or do you have a publishing company that plugs your songs for you?

Sonny Throckmorton:
I had a good publisher, I was with Tree Publishing, they're now Sony Music, and I really give it to the boys who pitched my songs. I sat down and sang Merle Haggard *"The Way I Am"* when I pitched that to him, and I'm sure there's been times, but the greatest amount of my success was being with a great publisher.

Freddy Powers:
All the years I was out on the road with Merle, he did that song every night, he did that every night.

Bill McDavid:
When you write songs, are they mostly something you've experienced or witnessed or do you just dream 'em up?

Sonny Throckmorton:
I'm not smart enough to do that, and I don't try to do that. I'm pretty much a reporter, it's what I see people doing and what I feel in my heart when I see other people feeling. I just try be a big ole pad that absorbs all that.

Catherine Powers: We were honored to be the last television show the legendary Floyd Tillman, who had a whole career of # 1s, from *"They Took the Stars Out of Heaven"* to *"I Love You So Much It Hurts"* and *"Slippin' Around," "G.I. Blues," "Drivin' Nails in My Coffin," "I'll Never Slip Around Again," "I Gotta Have My Baby Back," "Each Night at Nine"* and on and on. Freddy was always particularly proud of the fact that Floyd made his last T.V. show appearance on Rogers and Hammerhead before he passed away, along with the distinction of the last show he ever played was being on stage with Freddy at the world-famous Broken Spoke in Austin. Our show was also the final interview for Rusty Weir, who was another big songwriter and Texas star best known for *"I Heard You Been Layin' My Old Lady"* and *"Don't It Make You Wanna Dance."* So that T.V. show, just by the stroke of luck, we had some of the last interviews with major Texas music stars, which was the whole point of the show really, to put a spotlight on Texas songwriting.

Along with our own television show, Freddy also stayed very active playing out on the live scene around town, and he would play shows with Bill, and even took him on tour to Europe with us. One really exciting filmed performance came on the world-famous Austin City Limits television show, where he taped an hour-long set playing with Willie and Merle where they each sang a verse, and one of our favorite moments from that show. You can still see it on YouTube today, the night at Austin City Limits when Freddy sang Bill McDavid's song live on the air. It was very touching to Bill, and I know it meant a lot to Freddy to be able to do that for him, and again, was another example of a great writer with a lot of promise that Freddy helped get started in the music business, something he always felt proud of throughout his career.

Freddy Powers, Austin City Limits, 1996: "My friend Bill McDavid wrote this song, I'm so proud of him because it's the first song he ever wrote in his life. Not only this, but Willie and the Offenders do it as the title song in one of Willie's new movies! (Doug Supernaw covered it too)."

WILLIE NELSON, Rogers & Hammerhead, April 2nd, 1997:

Freddy Powers:
Thank you everybody, we're back again.
This is I think our 10th week doing
the Rogers and Hammerhead Show.

Bill McDavid:
Freddy, what inspires you when you write songs?

Freddy Powers:
Well, isn't it funny, songs are either
about 'I love you,' 'I hate you,'
'I'm glad to get rid of ya,' or 'I'm glad
you're here.' There's all different ways
of saying that. Speaking of great songwriters
we've had lots out here, and we keep
seeming like we get better and better as
we go along. Ladies and Gentleman, our
guest today is a fantastic songwriter
and singer, and a longtime friend of ours,
Mr. Willie Nelson, and his sister,
Bobbie. (Audience applauds)

Bill McDavid:
It's going to be a little hard to
Keep getting better and better
after this one, isn't it? (laughs)

Freddy Powers:
Isn't it though?

Bill McDavid:
This guy really is a great songwriter
and I think everybody in the world
knows that, a lot of people say the
best ever, and we appreciate you
coming. Good neighbors.

Willie Nelson:
I'm glad to have sister Bobbie here,
back us up over there.

Bill McDavid:
Give us a little charm and grace.

Willie Nelson:
Makes the picture look a lot better.

Freddy Powers:
What do you got for us today Willie?
Here's my favorite guitar player too,
I tell you what.

Willie Nelson:
(strumming his guitar)

*Why do I have to choose,
and see everybody lose, and
walk around and sing the blues,
Well darling I refuse..."*

Freddy Powers: A funny footnote, the first time I signed Willie's guitar, I wrote my name in ink, then I noticed a few years later it was fading, so I went back over it again, and it became a habit whenever I saw Willie over the next few years, and now my name is as permanent as that hole is on Trigger. I've been told in the years since that show inspired a lot of songwriters, and I'm proud of that.

Freddy, Catherine and Steve Carter
(left to right) in France

Freddy and Catherine
anniversary

CHAPTER 19: THE ROMANCE CONTINUES...

Catherine Powers: On our tenth wedding anniversary we went to Paris and with Floyd Domino {a famous Texas piano player and Grammy winner}, went to the top of the Eiffel Tower and with Floyd acting as Minister, we re-announced of wedding vows. I couldn't believe I was in Paris, but to be re-marrying the man of my life I can't help from feeling like the luckiest girl in the world. As a footnote: Paris is my favorite place to get Escargot, just as long as I don't mix it with a glass of red wine, Freddy used to joke, because it spoiled my breath for when we got back to the hotel! ☺ We also went to Rome and Switzerland on that trip. Actually, that was not the first time Freddy and I repeated our vows to each other. We were best man and bridesmaid for some friends of ours that got married in Reno, and as the minister asked them to repeat after him Freddy looked at me and begin lip speaking, silently repeating everything after the Minister as if we were the ones getting married, so I did the same. When he said you may kiss the bride, after they kissed Freddy leaned over and kissed me.

All our anniversaries are something to talk about. We've only had one that we spent alone. Remember our honeymoon was with his brother and nephew camping in the Ruby Mountains, and our first anniversary was none other than camping, this time with his son and new daughter-in-law. Our second and third was with three hundred or so guests we hosted for a golf tournament in Freddy's name to raise money for the Special Olympics. Freddy has been a longtime supporter of the Special Olympics, and for years put on celebrity golfing tournaments and performances to raise money for this cause, which has continued to remain especially close to his heart throughout the years.

Reno Gazette-Journal: "You've got several world-famous friends, and dozens of your other buddies are fairly popular across the United States as well. Instead of bragging, or spending all your time schmoozing with your pals, you get them all together to raise money for charity – the Special Olympics. Well, that's what Reno resident Freddy Powers and his wife, Catherine, are doing for the second year in a row. Country music stars Willie Nelson and Merle Haggard will attend the Second Annual Freddy Powers Celebrity Golf Tournament Wednesday through Friday.

" 'Willie is like me, he's got more stamina than any other human being,' Powers said, 'It's super that he and all the others are coming here.' Powers' primary motivation in organizing the fundraiser stems from his childhood, where he was reared by a mentally-handicapped Uncle…Other faces some folks might recognize are Darrell Royal, a former Texas Longhorns coach, and ex-NFL star Lance Allworth and Fred 'Hammer' Williamson. Tickets for a Thursday evening Texas-style dinner-dance at the Flamingo Hilton Hotel-Casino are $75 per person and $100 per couple. The dance is to feature celebrity songwriters Whitey Shafer, Sonny Throckmorton and Mickey Newbury, plus comedians Norm Alder and Jim MacGeorge."

Ray Baker: I remember being out in Hollywood, recording a session on Merle out there, and Freddy was out there. I was up in Freddy's room and we were staying at the Beverly Gardens Holiday Inn, and there was a knock on the door and Freddy said "Would you get that? I'm shaving," and when I answered the door, it was the movie star James Garner standing there! He introduced himself and said "Hi, I'm James Garner, is Freddy here?", and I said "I know who you are!" (laughs) James was a big fan of Freddy's, he didn't come to see Merle, he'd come to see Freddy, and he came in and we had a nice visit.

Catherine Powers: Freddy actually wrote the official theme song for the Nevada Special Olympics. Freddy and I were heavily involved *with the kids*, whether we did Golf Tournaments or Bowling Tournaments, and especially with the Summer Special Olympics. We first hooked up with them back when Freddy was playing at the El Dorado Casino, and there was this couple that came in with their son, who had Down Syndrome. Well, the kid was just fascinated with Freddy, and they ended up becoming regulars at Freddy's shows. The child's name was Tim Young, and one night they asked to meet Freddy so I brought him over after the show and he sat down and got to know Tim a little bit, and he invited us to one of his events.

So we attended, and the next thing you know, I start volunteering, and we started talking to the event organizers, and they asked about us sponsoring an event. Freddy turned to me and said, "Mama, why don't we do a golf tournament for them and raise some money?" So we started working with the President and Vice President of the Nevada Special Olympics about doing this Celebrity Golf Tournament with Willie Nelson and some other friends of ours.

Freddy Powers: "We got more out of that experience than anything we've ever done. Deaf kids would come up and touch the instruments during the songs and feel the music."

Catherine Powers: That went so well that we started being hosts at a lot of their charity events. We would go to Special Olympics Skiing, Bowling and Track Meets with them, Freddy would get his band and we'd go play their dance parties. We got so involved that it became where on a weekly basis, we were involved in one way or the other with the Special Olympics, and we had a lot of the kids that just hung on us and became good friends with. Freddy was so moved by it all that he decided he was going to write a song for them, and that became the official theme for the Nevada Special Olympics, titled "*Everybody Has a Chance to Win*".

BB Morse: I became nonprofit President or V.P. of 5 organizations since my involvement with Freddy and the Special Olympics. It fostered that whole spirit in me and my wife Cindy, and we still do a couple of non-profits every year for those less fortunate. There was one dance I remember at a school for Autistic and Down Syndrome children where we'd go in acoustically, generally not even set up a P.A., and perform for the children. There was one child who was deaf, dumb, and blind, who would put their hands on the instruments because they could still feel their vibration. In fact, I remember one little girl hugged my upright bass and the look on her place of complete, utter blissfulness was the juice that made Freddy flow. This was before any inkling of him having any illness on his own.

I played bass on the theme to the Nevada Special Olympics, "*Everyone Has a Chance to Win*," and he got Merle, Willie, himself, Johnny Rodriguez and George Marriott, and they each took a verse like "*We Are the World*." We recorded that session at Grannie's House Recording Studio in Reno, Nevada, before they moved over to Sparks, Jody Peterson engineered it and Freddy had a whole choir of these Down syndrome and mentally-challenged children singing harmonies, and playing bells too on the song. The kids had a wonderful choral director, who was one of their teachers, and Freddy worked with her. I tell you, there wasn't one out-of-step child in that whole place, they all heard what they were supposed to do, had rehearsed it beforehand, walked in and just nailed it. I don't think there was any need for too much direction beyond where and when they were going to come in, that was it. That was definitely a golden moment.

I remember when ABC Sports retired Chris Schenkel after years of broadcasting, and they did this big tribute to him at a ballroom in Indianapolis, and it was quite a who's-who of Indiana and national figures. Dan and Marilyn Quayle were there, Dorothy Hamill, and Freddy was part of the musical bill. He'd known Chris Schenkel for a number of years and stayed in touch with him through his association with the Golf tournaments. I remember I was dressed in tie-dye with a beard hanging half-way down my chest and my mojo bag hanging around my neck. I remember Freddy had alerted Coach Darrell Royal to the fact I didn't have a tuxedo like the rest of the band, and Coach said to Freddy, "B.B. is B.B." To play the hippy is to be the hippy! (laughs)

Wayne Ahart: I'll tell you one thing that impressed me about Freddy: I was with him at the Woodlands one year when the Darrell and Willie Golf tournament was being held there. After it was over, I had one of my corporate directors on my board in Indiana, who was ABC Sportscaster Chris Schenkel, and Chris had invited me to come to Indianapolis to a huge birthday celebration on his 70th birthday at the Hyatt Regency. So I took one of my sons, and attended a little dinner the night before the big party. Then went to the big celebration the next night and we were sitting pretty close to the front table and the announcer came on, and said "Ladies and Gentleman, it's time for us to have a little entertainment here, and so we've invited Chris Schenkel favorite Country and Western entertainer, Mr. Freddy Powers."

So here comes Freddy and all his band, and they walked right by my table, and as they got pretty close, he saw me, came over to my table and said "I just left you in Houston!" So he entertained the crowd that night, and I thought it was pretty neat that it was announced that he was Chris's favorite, and he was a favorite of a lot of people.

Reno Gazette-Journal, Sunday, May 22, 1994: "Money also was raised through a silent auction that included a golf bag and guitar autographed by event participants. Organizer Catherine Powers coordinated the evening's activities. The Freddy Powers' Celebrity Jam included the Tex Mex of country music Johnny Rodriguez, jazz artist Don Cherry, and members of Haggard's, Nelson's and Freddy's bands. Also appearing were songwriters Whitey Shafer, Sonny Throckmorton and Mickey Newbury, who have 50 or more No. 1 hits among them. The shows and tournaments will benefit the local chapter of Nevada Special Olympics... Powers wrote a song, *'Everybody Has a Chance to Win.'* "

Norma Powers–Marlowe: Freddy did something quite nice when he did a big benefit for the Special Olympics, that song that Freddy sang was so precious, and he's raised a lot of money for children that are challenged, just out of the goodness of his heart.

Catherine Powers: We ended up taking Merle, Willie, Johnny Rodriguez and George Marriott along with like a hundred Special Needs children and we went into the studio and recorded that song. We had cassette tapes made and would sell them there after all the Special Olympics events we were involved with. Of course, all the proceeds went to their cause, and we had 51 Major celebrities from men who walked on the Moon to Heisman Trophy Winners to Major movie stars to Freddy's usual cast of Major Country Music stars. I remember one of the most beautiful things I've ever seen happen came on the night of the show when we had made up these medals to give to the celebrities, but we had the Down Syndrome group go up and hang the awards on all the celebrities. I'll never forget, the entire stage of 51 people up there, men and women, were all bawling their eyes out, the whole room was all crying. To see those kids and the excitement they were having of putting the medal on somebody instead of receiving the medal was absolutely unbelievable. Those kids just lit up the room with their smiles!

Another favorite time of Freddy and mine came when we were down in Las Vegas for the Summer Special Olympics, and we're sitting there watching all the events. So Little Timmy was running in this race and Freddy's watching Timmy, and all of a sudden, he's leaning forward and it looks like he's gonna fall over and trip on his own feet. Well, that made Freddy nervous, so now he goes running out there next to the track, yelling and screaming, "Slow down Timmy, slow down," and he gets all the way up there right beside Timmy, "Timmy, slow down!" Right then, Timmy looks back over at him while he's still running and says "Fweddy, I'm wunning in a wace!"

One of the other reasons it touched Freddy, especially the Down Syndrome children, is that he was raised with an Uncle Slim who was mentally handicapped, he'd been kicked in the head by a horse. Slim was in some ways younger than they were mentally, so when we did the Special Olympics, we did all that in honor of his uncle. He wanted to share his love for his Uncle and honor him with the Golf Tournaments. Another time, we were up there with the kids at one of their Skiing events, and we were all skiing together, and whenever Freddy would call me "Ma," I'd say "What Pa?" One of the kids looked up at me and said, "Mrs. *Catherine*, if his name's Freddy, why do you call him Pa?" So we were very close and very involved with those kids.

B.B. Morse: We started a little support group, The Grateful Freds, and we had a legion of people who worked on his behalf on fund-raising goals Freddy had set out for the Special Olympics. That spoke beyond the famous names he could put in a room at the same time, he had the ability to do that many times over all in the name of charitable fund-raising, and they raised a lot of money and it went where it was supposed to. It gave a real sense of community and involvement and the levels of just how much one person's efforts can affect a whole organization, to be able to bring the attention and talent together, and make things better for everybody. It was contagious, and as much of the allure from the music that was being generated, it was also a spirit of kinship and family. Catherine was a big part of that, as a team, and they weren't profiteering for themselves, they were making everything better for everybody.

Catherine Powers: We would bring people to play at homes, and the Special Olympics kids dances and parties, and got more musicians involved in different organizations. At one dance, there were all these special needs boys lined up, and I thought they wanted to dance with me, but they wanted to dance with Freddy! (laughs) It was the most beautiful scene, because during a band break, here Freddy is slow-dancing to a rap song with a little boy, and he's just looking up at Freddy. Then all a sudden, Freddy looks down with tears in his eyes, and the band couldn't take it. They left the room in tears in their eyes!

On another of our anniversaries, Freddy was playing a gig with Bill McDavid {pre-Sherry} his songwriting partner. On their break Freddy came over to join me and before he could set down next to me, Bill got in between us, forgetting it was our night. I leaned over and whispered in Bill's ear to give my husband a kiss for me and tell him I said Happy Anniversary. That was nothing, the next year for our fifth anniversary Bill talked Freddy into going to a Stag party with him. So I stayed home and watched I Love Lucy and Dick Van Dyke with Bill's girlfriend Sherry. The sixth he was playing a private birthday party for a friend of ours. So as everybody celebrated and toasted our friend's birthday we celebrated our anniversary and toasted to each other privately. I also spent my seventh wedding anniversary with Sherry. Freddy and Bill were out on tour with Merle, so Sherry and I along with the dogs Amelia and Sugarbam went camping in Spearfish Canyon outside of Deadwood, South Dakota.

Our eighth we actually spent alone at a very romantic restaurant not to mention expensive, which we realized when we got the menu with no prices on it. But my Freddy never worries about money until he needs it, so he's always the big spender and just smiles and says "Momma it's our anniversary, so eat and drink almost all you want". And we did $275.00 later for just the two of us. We spent a little larger celebrating our ninth wedding anniversary with my first trip to Europe. We – along with the whole band – went to Amsterdam before going to play a country music festival in Col-des-Roches, Switzerland where we spent four days in this old farm type bed and breakfast with the nicest people, that basically gave us the run of the place. They had a room set up for the band to practice in and served us all the wine, bread and cheese we wanted. They didn't speak English and we sure don't speak Swiss but somehow we seemed to communicate and became friends I'll never forget.

As a bonus, from there, we went back to Amsterdam for a couple more days by ourselves; where I got Freddy on this Ferris Wheel, the tallest Ferris Wheel I've ever seen! You could see the next country once you got to the top, and though Freddy hates rides mind you, it was our anniversary trip and he knew it was what I wanted to do so he ventured the ride with me. It was worth it too because it was beautiful up there, but like I said, it was the highest Ferris Wheel I'd ever seen! I never get scared on rides but this one scared me so bad that I had to hold on and I begged Freddy not to rock it (and with a "No matter what you do, *"DON'T ROCK IT"* attitude). Being the natural prankster he was, Thank God he didn't want it to rock any more than I did. Our hotel room was right on Demark Square and we had two big bay windows that opened up to overlook the square. All the street dancers and musicians were down on the street in front of us while we sat in the windows drinking our special tea we got there and watching all the entertainment wrapped up in each other's arms.

Freddy and I have married each other five times and never been divorced, including our 20th Wedding Anniversary, which was amazing. We returned this time back to Lovelock, Nevada where we'd first married, and decided to actually have the "Big Wedding," something we'd not done till now. My daughter and sister stood up for me, and my son in law and youngest grandson stood up for Freddy. One of Freddy's fiddle players Ben Wilburn and his wife were there – people came from everywhere! One of our longtime friends Jody Peterson along with Ben Wilburn sang *"Catherine's Song (Road to My Heart)."* To top it all off, the City of Lovelock made arrangements for me to be picked up in this unbelievable 1930s Ford Coupe that coincidentally matched the colors of my red wedding dress with gold trim, and Freddy donning a red shirt with a golden necktie. Freddy was in his wheelchair by then, so I keeled down on a pillow when we renewed our vows. The next day, the town took our whole wedding party on a tour up into the mountains and old mining towns. It was all so wonderful!

Wayne Ahart: We had a good time at the re-stating of their 20th Year vows, and the whole trip was a lot of fun. We went from there further up into Nevada and then into California, and we mainly did it just to be there with Freddy and Catherine

Catherine Powers: Freddy is never boring. He is one of those types of people who is always witty and has a great comeback that generally cracks you up. I've always called him my personal CO-MO-DIAN as he has a thousand jokes. Even though I've heard them all by now and he knows I have, he'll tell me again and I'll crack up again. He's always been playful throughout our 30+ years together too. I could be sitting there watching T.V. and he'd start walking in circles around the room and every time he'd walk in front of me he'd change his walk into something weird and funny, but all the while would never look at me, acting as though this was normal.

Freddy and I have always kept our natural sense of adventure alive throughout our life together too. I remember when he got a Harley Davidson motorcycle for his sixty-fifth birthday – which I like to joke knocked about ten years off him – I kept telling him if he got any younger, I was gonna have to find an older man! (laughs) We've gone on four-thousand-mile bike runs in twenty-one days: from Albuquerque, New Mexico to Saskatchewan, Canada over to Alberta, Canada and back to Albuquerque! We loved our bike and rode as often as we could before Freddy's Parkinson's started making it too dangerous to ride. Every time we'd get on that bike, he just turned me on. We'd be riding down the highway with my arms wrapped around him and we're kissing while he's patting me on the leg. I'm so grateful to have so many wonderful memories with him.

Freddy Powers: To top off the decade, I went into the studio to make another solo album, *Silver Eagle*, with a few of my buddies, and the great Ray Baker produced it for us!

> **Ray Baker:** Freddy had a couple of guys back in Houston who wanted to back him to do an album on him. He got in touch with me, and it turned out one of them was a guy named Bill McDavid, who was a friend of Freddy's and I had known Bill from back in Ft. Worth when I worked in radio back in the early 60s. They came up here, and I gave him the budget for the album, and he said "Let's do it!" So we did a whole album on Freddy called *Silver Eagle*.
>
> I hired my regular guys that I use on sessions, and Merle wasn't there when we recorded Freddy's record so I didn't use any of Merle's band. Freddy had told me "Hire whoever you want and let's just do it." So we went in there and recorded 10 songs and they all turned out great. We recorded a few of the songs that he and Merle wrote, and one of them "*I Had a Beautiful Time.*" Freddy was real pleased with it and I thought it was one of the best things we ever did.

Merle Haggard (center) Roasting Freddy (far right)
at his 70th Birthday Roast, 2001

CHAPTER 20: FREDDY POWERS' 70TH BIRTHDAY ROAST

Catherine Powers: Everybody turns 70, but when Freddy's birthday started approaching, rather than a quiet affair, I and his friends like Coach Darrell Royal, Merle Haggard and Bill McDavid, decided to go in the opposite direction and throw Freddy the 70th BIRTHDAY BASH OF ALL BASHES in the Darrell Royal Ballroom at the Barton Creek Country Club! It took 7 months of careful planning, and was THE EVENT to be at, a virtual who's who of Texas Country Royalty showed up to tribute Freddy with funny anecdotes and live performances of his greatest hits. During the planning, so many people had to be in the loop on the date and invites that they'd call our phone and if Freddy answered instead of me, they'd have to hang up so he didn't catch on. Thank GOD they had email by then as that made life a bit easier planning this whole event! I ran out of excuses after a while for why we were getting so many hang-ups and even had to talk Freddy out of calling the phone company to change our number!

As a ruse, I had Merle Haggard call Freddy up and ask him to play a birthday party he had no idea was his own and of course Freddy agreed. Freddy showed up that night thinking this was just a paying gig, and before the party, Coach Royal met up with us outside on the Rogers and Hammerhead Tour bus, which wasn't unusual, and kept Freddy occupied while we were getting everything set up inside. I remember when Freddy walked in the room, he had NO IDEA at first that the party he was at was for him. Everyone played along beautifully because it took a moment before he caught on, so much so that he didn't even realize at first it was his own band standing up on stage playing. Freddy even turned to Coach before they'd walked as he heard the band playing and said "Coach, I can't go in, they've already started!" Once Coach Royal finally got him to walk through the main doors, I was grateful he didn't have a heart attack when everybody stood up and all started singing "HAPPY BIRTHDAY FREDDY!" because it blew him away!

Below are some live highlights from this very special night:

Catherine Powers:
There is Rogers and Hammerhead, but if
there is a Mrs. of either, I am Mrs. Rogers!
(Audience Applause) Because the true hammerhead
is about to take the mic, introducing Hammerhead
himself, Mr. Bill McDavid.

Bill McDavid:
I should have known better than to let her
Get her hands on that microphone. Spud Goodall
once stole Freddy's boots right off his feet,
and never gave them back. He said to tell you
he'll leave them to you in his will! (laughs)

Spud Goodall:
My name is Spud Goodall, I'm an ordained
guitar picker! I'd like to say a few words
about a great humanitarian. A man whose
outstanding in his field, recognized by his
peers of being one of the all-time greats.
He has played all over the world with some
of the biggest stars – pop and country – and
he has also appeared before Presidents and
Kings. Now, that's enough about me… (Laughs
Who is it that they're honoring? Freddy?
Freddy who? Oh, Freddy Powers! What did he do?

(audience laughs and claps louder)

I first met Freddy Powers over 40 years ago,
and it seems like last week, and you know
what a lousy week last week was! (laughs)
Shortly after I met Freddy, I found out that
he'd been dating my cousin, and I didn't even
know he knew Walter! (laughs) Freddy, my daddy

told me, he said "Son, if you can't say something good about anybody, just don't say nothing." So I guess that's about all I got to say! No, Freddy, people will call you 'a lousy bastard' and 'a no good S.O.B.', and a 'cheap M.F.,' and there are others that will lie about you! (laughs)

No Fred, I'm just kidding you, but I would like to say right now that Freddy Powers is one of the best guitar players in the country, he don't do too good in town, but out in the country he can play the strings off that thing. Freddy Powers is the best guitar player I've ever played with in my life, and I've played with most of them. We would go down to Willie's for 3 or 4 days and meet down there and set around and pick guitars all day and night for 3 or 4 days, what a wonderful thrill it was.

J. Gary Smith:
The first time I heard Freddy perform, my Father took me when I was a small boy, to see Freddy perform, and told me many stories about his dad taking him to see Freddy perform! (laughs) Freddy's been around a little while. From the very beginning, music was first in Freddy's life, it was so important to him. Music was first, then the soft lights, a couple glasses of wine, and two hookers he picked up at Denny's! (audience laughs louder)

I always kind of felt Freddy knew his place in life. He knew his job, what he was cut out to do, and his job was spending all his time trying to figure out how the hell to keep from ever having to get a job! (laughs) And he's done it for, how long now Fred, 100 years? (laughs) He's the king man.

Freddy's the guy who's played everything from pizza joints to stadiums, coliseums, and some of the sleaziest places you've ever seen in your life! One night in Vegas, it was a tough night, and I actually saw him begging

a hooker for money. It wasn't her money,
he was begging her to take his!

Paul Buskirk:
Well, Happy Birthday Freddy, surprise,
surprise, surprise. I was thinking about
you the other day, in Europe, when we started
to come home from Germany on that little tour
we did over there, the Military thing, and I
thought about you sitting at the airport saying
"Why don't I catch this plane? They got one
seat on this other plane, why don't I catch this
plane and come on in on my own? I can bring
the car around in New York! (laughs) Boy,
your 70th Birthday, what a trip.
(laughs)

Catherine Powers: Freddy was clearly moved as Paul's video finished because he had his hand over his mouth and tears in his eyes. Paul was 90 years old at the time and we all lost him shortly afterward. I remember Coach Darrell Royal tapped Freddy on the shoulder, leaned in as the two warmly embrace one another. They'd grown to be such very close friends by then.

Coach Darrell Royal:
That was beautiful.

Freddy Powers:
Thank you Coach, the whole
night has been!

Sonny Throckmorton:
It's good to be with y'all tonight.
I have the job of trying to roast a
marshmallow! (laughs) One night we were
at a party at Coach Darrell Royal's house,
and I'll tell you what a nice guy he was,

we were all there kind of waiting to get
in the bathroom, and there was a pretty good
line. Ladybird Johnson, and I don't know
who all was there that night, and there's quite
a line, and Freddy had waited a pretty good
time there, and as it became his turn, he
started to go in and this couple ladies walked
in with him, you know. And old Freddy, being

a nice guy, didn't say one word, he just walked right on in with them, was in there about 15 minutes, he comes out and didn't say a word. I know it was 15 minutes because Lady Bird come out and she was rapping on the door, and said "Freddy Powers, you come out of there right now, you been in there FIFTEEN minutes!" (laughs)

Bill McDavid:

I was playing golf with Freddy one day and Freddy loves dogs, as everybody who knows Freddy knows, and Poodie – a guy who works with Willie – has a dog named Einstein, and he just loves Freddy to death. So we're on the # 5 hole out at the golf course and we're teeing off and here comes Einstein, and he's not a 3-legged dog but he can only use 3 legs because he's crippled, and Freddy's bent over and I'm trying to hit the ball, and he's calling the dog and everything, and I hit the ball, get in the cart and drive off before the dogs get there, and it's just breaking Freddy's heart because he didn't get to pet the dogs. So I'm looking over at Freddy and he's waving at the dogs as we drive off. That tells the whole story of Freddy Powers, how do you roast a guy like that?

Merle Haggard:

Sitting at this table are two of my very favorite friends in the world, Johnny Gimble and Freddy Powers. Ray Benson, Norm Stevens, anyway, I'm real honored to be here. Of all the people I've met in my entire life in this business, Freddy is one of my closest friends. Some people thought we were homosexuals, (laughs) we weren't, we both like women, and I can testify that that's the truth.

I'm going to quit talking about Freddy, but before I do, I want to give him something that's very special, and I don't know why I want to show it off, but I'll tell you what, I designed this guitar myself. It's a Martin guitar that's

built out of the same wood Jimmy Rodgers' guitar
was built out of.

Catherine Powers: To top Merle's headlining roast off, I remember, standing behind Merle to his right and to Freddy's left, our friend Ray Benson snuck out a guitar case, opened and presented a beautiful acoustic guitar made from the backs of some original Jimmy Rogers Blue Yodel guitars, there were only 35 of these Martin guitars, they were all numbered individually because they were so rare. Merle had personally designed it for him, the guitar had Freddy's name in Mother of Pearl up and down the neck, and he was visibly SHOCKED when Merle presented it to him at the roast! The whole night couldn't have come off better!

CHAPTER 21: THE ROYAL KNIGHTS OF THE RACCOON

Freddy Powers: Just as people have often joked that Texas could be its own country, my home state has its own rich history of local traditions. The Fraternal Order of Eagles for instance, or The Texas Elks, The Knights of Columbus, The Loyal Order Moose. Perhaps the most prestigious up in Bee Caves, Texas, is induction into the Fraternal Order of Coondicks, officially known as The Royal Knights of the Raccoon!

Catherine Powers: It's quite a prestigious little club actually, including other legends like Sonny Throckmorton, Coach Royal, Willie Nelson, Billy Bob Thornton, Lee Roy Parnell, astronaut Charlie Duke, the list goes on and on alongside Freddy.

> **Wayne Ahart,** Fellow Member of The Royal Knights of the Raccoon: The Royal Knights of the Raccoon needed to be shortened and somebody suggested the Coondicks, and it caught on.

> **Terry Booth,** Coondicks Founder: This little piece of land that the Coondicks Headquarters is on, otherwise known as the West Pole, and has been in my family since I was just a child. It was formerly a ranch, and what remains today is about 4 ½ acres I inherited from my Daddy's sister when she passed away. I took note that the property was right on the 98th Meridian. The 98th Meridian, as noted by Walter Prescott Landon and other Texas historians, is the beginning of the West! For example, Ft.

Worth and other famous towns along there was the beginning of where all the action was in the old West, the Indians, and all of that. And being on the 98th Meridian made me think about the idea of having a designation, which would not be unlike the North Pole and the South Pole, but if there's those two, there should be an East Pole and a West Pole. I just took the West Pole, went to the Texas State Legislature, and they thought it was a clever idea. So I had a resolution in 2007 passed with the West Pole being claimed by Texas and designating up here where we have our club house of the Benevolent Knights of the Raccoon, which is the formal name of our Coondick Organization.

So now, I've got this little piece of family land, and I had the designation from the Legislature. How the Coondicks came about was, I was sitting out here with a few of my buddies one day, and when you're a kid, I grew up rural on a farm, you grow up hunting, and you get the pelts of your different raccoons, and rabbits, and you could sell them. Well, when you got a male raccoon, you got a bonus because they have a bone for the penis called the baculum. So the crotch on several animals – the Walrus, the bear, the minx, and it goes on down the line over a number of animals – but the Coon is the most abundant in this part of the world. So when you kill a Raccoon, you have the pelt, you have the tail of course, and then you've got the baculum, and you can wear it on your neck, wear it in your rear view mirror, put it on your key chain, and when we were kids, you could tease the girls, "Look, I've got a Coondick!" (laughs)

It was funny, having that as a kid, so fast forward, I'm in my 50s, and my buddies and I were out there, deciding that if we were going to have a fraternal organization at the West Pole, what were we going to call it? When I was building a house up near the fort, I'd gotten a catalog that sold antlers and all kinds of bear skins and all types of deer out of Idaho, and they had a dozen Raccoon pecker bones for sale. I thought, "What a novel idea, I'll buy a load of those and just give them away as gag gifts." So I bought a dozen of them, and they came in plastic bags so I fixed them up on a little shelf in my closet. Fast forward another half-dozen years, and I'm talking to my pals here, and they asked "What are we going to call our organization?", and it dawned on me, "Guys, I just happen to have a bag of Coondicks down at the house, and we could wear those Coondicks around our necks, and be benevolent. We could be the benevolent knights of the Raccoon."

Now, if you were old enough, you'd remember Jackie Gleason and (Art Carney and Audrey Meadows) in a show called the Honeymooners, and in that show, they had a brotherhood where they were the Raccoons of some sort. So we formed, and Freddy instantly became a ring leader, it was right up his alley, that kind of dirty satire was all he needed to get started. Nearly every Friday, depending on the weather – sometimes it was every other week – we'd all get together and hold court and tell stories, and Freddy was always the ringleader. He was not only an elder, but a celebrated character, but so we were all the Coons! There was a saying, that "To be a Coondick, you had to be just a little bit sorry, but not too sorry," and sorry means outrageous.

Wayne Ahart: The Royal Knights of the Raccoon was kind of a funny little group who would get together sometimes just to tell jokes and Freddy used to come out to those. And of course, what he wanted to do was tell jokes, and he was a natural comedian! He got his start as a stand-up comedian, but his joke telling was legendary!

Terry Booth: For our Membership certificate, we used basically an old Code of Arms from England, and then the shield had 3 Raccoons' heads, and then the phrase "Hear No Evil, See No Evil, Speak No Evil," it was funny as hell. Then the top is pulled off the sign on the chuck wagon from the Lonesome Dove film like the Hat Creek Cattle Company. Then on the bottom of this code of arms, it says "Friendship, Health, and Benevolence." The membership reads "Whereas, in recognition of one who has demonstrated steadfast dedication to celebration of life, while upholding commitment to friendship, health and benevolence to women and children and sissy men, it is hereby declared that (Freddy Powers) be heretofore and in perpetuity certified as an official member of the Benevolent Knights of the Raccoon." Then underneath that, it says, "What has been declared here, let no man put asunder without fear of a severe ass kicking."

Catherine Powers: Along with the honor of joining the Coondicks, starting back in the late 1990s, Freddy's legacy status as a living legend within Texas Country Music had officially kicked off a formal ceremony where Coach Royal and family members like Freddy's brother Don and nephew Don Jr., The Air Fred Band. Joined by other local country music and public personalities who were on hand as the Mayor of Austin Kirk Watson announced that "The City of Austin is proud to declare a Proclamation that October 31st, 1998 is officially FREDDY POWERS DAY!" Freddy as usual was pretty close to speechless, but I could see by the smile on his face how much the acknowledgment meant to him after 60 years in the Entertainment Business. By this time, especially because even though our house was already full of BMI, ASCAP, and CMA Awards, by the early 2000s, Freddy was also beginning to be recognized on a Legacy level in Texas by some of the big Hall of Fame organizations, including induction into the prestigious Texas Heritage Songwriter's Association Hall of Fame!

Terry Booth: When I first met Freddy, I was involved in originating an organization called the Texas Heritage Songwriters, and it is exactly what it says it is: it acknowledges the importance of Texas songwriters, historically all the way back and continuing obviously into the future. I got to be very good friends with Freddy right off the bat, he loved what we were doing with the songwriters, and of course, he had an illustrious career as a songwriter. The whole idea when we started this was, there is no pecking order. All Texas songwriters are important, because of the contribution to our culture and becoming a member of Texas Heritage Songwriters was an acknowledgment you were important to Texas. We've had nearly 30 honorees over the past 15 years.

I'd always had an intense interest in songwriters, really more so or equal to the vocalist, so that was instilled in my heart and soul. I had been looking for probably 10 years to do something to commemorate Texas songwriters. It just didn't line up until Bob Cole re-opened an old Texas roadhouse out on Highway 80, or what is now South Congress, in Austin called Hills Cafe. We went to the Texas Legislature and got a favorable legislator to write a resolution recognizing the Texas Songwriter, and acknowledging Bob Cole and I as the stalwarts of the organization. So with that little document, we went forward and founded it in 2005. Sonny Throckmorton, Freddy Powers and Kris Kristofferson were our 3 initial inductees into the Texas Heritage Songwriter's Hall of Fame. They ended the night up on stage together.

Catherine Powers: That night was special in so many ways, just like Freddy's 70th Birthday Roast had been! There were so many amazing friends and fellow musicians in the audience, including Ronnie Dunn, Leroy Parnell, Scotty Emerick, Toby Keith, and Michael Martin Murphy, who leans in to give Freddy affectionate greeting, and told him "You know Freddy, you've always heard that saying, 'Someone can make you feel six feet tall, but when I'm around you, I feel 10 feet tall!'" It felt like another big family reunion, because the Texas Heritage Songwriter's Hall of Fame Induction of Freddy, Kris Kristofferson and Sonny Throckmorton on the same night! It was incredible, because they all got up and performed "*Goodnight Irene*" on stage together!

Terry Booth: When we came up with the WILLIE, we'd been racking our brains at a group trying to figure out we could present to the Honorees. At that point in time we just had a plaque, but we were in touch with Connie Nelson, and Willie allowed us to use his image for our presentation piece which would be a statuette not unlike the Oscar, only it's a statuette of Willie Nelson. So instead of getting your Oscar, at the Texas Heritage Songwriter's Hall of Fame, you get your WILLIE! A funny footnote:

once you've been awarded one, the saying goes "DON'T TOUCH MY WILLIE!" (laughs)

The night Freddy got inducted, it absolutely made him happy to get his, who wouldn't want a statuette of Willie Nelson on their book shelf. It's a significant honor in respect of their songwriting status. Freddy deserved one because he was not only brilliant, very-talented individual but absolutely one of the most humorous and man of depth and character. He was outrageous, but amidst the outrageous persona was a man of immense character.

Freddy Powers: While I appreciated all the acknowledgments starting to come in for my past achievements, I and all of the guys on that stage with me still LOVED making new music. Along with Willie, throughout the next few years, I continued to play live and in the studio with Merle Haggard. We produced albums with each other in the studio during this wonderful period in our friendship and 25-year career together as collaborators – Merle in the studio producing my *Great Escape* album and my producing his '*Unforgettable*' album.

Stomp and Stammer Magazine: "Freddy's songwriting skills are in evidence on *My Great Escape*, his latest album. Also there are his laid-back vocals – very informal, but very skilled with plenty of jazzy phrasing. His last album, 1997's *The Hottest Thing in Town*, had a Hot Club of France feel, with its wall of rhythm guitars, classic material ('*I Can't Give You Anything But Love,*' '*Sweet Georgia Brown*'), and Grappelli and Reinhardt-influenced soloists. For *Escape,* Powers went ahead and found a guitarist named Django. Django Porter is more than an audacious name – the guy plays remarkably in Reinhardt's style, right down to the tone, and really adds a lot to the album. The album is the first non-Merle Haggard release on Hag Records... (and) the result is a great batch of songs, from the romantic '*Angel In My Arms*' to the camaraderie of '*Tom Sawyer & Huckleberry Finn*'."

Freddy Powers: "He's a young kid here in Austin named Django Porter I sort of discovered. He doesn't play just like Django Reinhardt, but he's got that fire. He's got a little Hispanic blood in him and I think that's where that fire comes from."

Catherine Powers: When we produced the *Unforgettable* album for Merle Haggard, that was another really special project for Freddy because he'd picked, written and performed on stage together with Merle for many years. With his condition getting steadily worse, all those abilities to interact with Merle creatively were being stripped away one by one. But *producing Merle* was something Freddy had never done yet and could still do, and we were just so grateful that Freddy got the opportunity to let that side of his talent shine on this record. It meant the world to Freddy to get back in the studio with Merle one more time.

> **Merle Haggard:** "Freddy and I are great friends. We play that kind of music—just kind of sitting around. Freddy's an old Dixieland player; he knew all those old songs like I did. He and I had what we call a sidebar band called the Butter n' Egg Band, and for years we've been guitar buddies: we'd sit around the house and pick guitars like everyone else in the United States. Those songs are some of the songs that we'd started doing in the circle. So Freddy wanted to add two or three new ones and do an album of them all: a standards album. And that's the outcome of it, even after this period of retrieving the record after it being stolen—we would have been first with it before Rod Stewart (whose *Great American Songbook* series has sold millions of CD's), but Rod Stewart got out there while I was chasin' the thief."
>
> **Billboard Magazine:** "Warm, relaxed and laid-back, impeccably performed, and pleasurable to hear…what makes *Unforgettable* work is Haggard's easy, assured delivery. He may not reinvent these songs, but he sings them as if they were his own, making this a small, romantic gem for listeners who love Hag the singer as much as they love Hag the writer."
>
> **Country Line Magazine:** "This new release from Merle Haggard is not only *Unforgettable*, it's unbelievable. One of the most perfect albums I have ever heard, from the vocals that are like fine wine, to the fantastic production that pairs Haggard with legendary singer-songwriter Freddy Powers. This is a classic gathering of pop standards done like no one else on earth could do them…Intricate, amazing arrangements and tasty compliments from the strings, horns and fiddles, this is a Grammy-bound collection that will go down in the history books as one of the finest albums ever produced by an American singer, Country or otherwise… Four stars and two thumbs up."

Catherine Powers: I remember the first time I heard it playing on the radio, I kept saying over and over out loud, "Oh my God, it's playing on the radio!" I was in shock because I was a part of that, I helped put that whole project together, and all of a sudden, to turn around and hear something I'd been a part of being played on the radio, it was just like so many times I've been sitting there when a songwriter or artist heard their song for the first time being played over the radio. I was just overwhelmed, that was such a beautiful record we all made together. Freddy was very proud of that one.

Freddy Powers: I was lucky enough to be staying in the spotlight thanks to a new generation of country superstars like Big & Rich who invited me to star in the opening scenes of their hit music video, "*Coming to Your City.*" I played the grumpy old man in the very opening of the video sitting in the lazy boy yelling at the TV, "*Them Big & Rich fellas are a slap in the face to Country Music with all that Rock & Roll!*"

Big Kenny Alphin: That was all of our idea, Mark and John and myself, we said, "We've GOT to have Freddy in this video!" We wanted to have an old dude in the beginning talking about how these guys ain't country, and Freddy was always game to do anything we threw him into! "Filthy Rich" was another one of those only-Freddy moments where we were hanging out in Deadwood, South Dakota, up at the north end of Main Street. John and I'd been up there hanging out with Freddy and Bill McDavid, and Sonny Throckmorton was up there and here we are sitting down the three of them, (laughs), all of us talking about people trying to make it off of somebody else's smarts, and it just fit right in. That was kind of a swing-style song in Freddy's style, and to hang out with Freddy, Bill and Sonny, it just kind of naturally came together. "*Cause, everybody's trying to get filthy rich off somebody else's money, Hey, me and my friends we were talking 'bout that, ole Freddy, Bill and Sonny,*" what a great lyric, he's memorialized right there in the chorus of that song.

John Rich: When we wrote "*Filthy Rich*" together, I remember me and Big Kenny, and Bill McDavid and Freddy were sitting in Deadwood, South Dakota, and I believe it was Freddy who said: 'Everybody's trying to get filthy rich on somebody else's money,' and we all just laughed about how hilarious that line was- and it's true. So we tore into it, and I think it took 45 minutes to write that song, and from there, we put it on a Big & Rich record and millions of fans heard it, so that was a really cool thing to do. Every now and then Big Kenny and I will tear back into that just for old times' sakes, and rip it out.

Big Kenny Alphin: One of the most predominant memories I have is when John and I had written "*The Great Escape,*" and Freddy fell in love with it and was recording his new album with Merle and invited us to come out to Redding to be there to help him record the song. Of course, when an opportunity like that happens for a couple up and coming fellas in country music, then John and I took what we could gather together as far as a couple plane tickets and got ourselves out there. That was another vibrant experience where the only way it happened is because we knew Freddy Powers.

John Rich: To feel that Freddy has respect back towards the new generation of country music is pretty unbelievable too, the song "*The Great Es-*

cape," Big Kenny and I wrote that, and Freddy heard me sing it one night at a party and asked if he could record it. So to have one of the greatest songwriters in the world want to record something they didn't write, is HUGE, and not to mention you wrote it! To have a guy like Freddy sing something that Big Kenny and I wrote was just one of the biggest compliments and shows of respect you could ever have as a songwriter.

Country Music Planet, Dec 2004: "This past weekend, the William Morris Agency, Muzik Mafia, and CMT were in the Austin area filming a CMT special with Big and Rich. Legendary songwriter, Freddy Powers was a part of the festivities. Big and Rich's next DVD will be focusing on Big and Rich's relationship with Freddy, and Freddy's induction into the Godfathers of the Muzik Mafia. Additional footage featured Freddy and Willie Nelson with Big and Rich at Willie's World Headquarters. Freddy will be joining Big and Rich in Las Vegas and Reno Dec. 8th and 10th. Big and Rich also have a dedication to Freddy on their CD Super Galactic Fan Pak. The title track of Freddy's new Smith Entertainment CD, '*My Great Escape'* was written by Big Kenny and John Rich."

Catherine Powers: For as well as things were going for Freddy's career in 2004 in his early 70s, it was Big and Rich who first helped me see that something was bothering him physically that none of us had really paid any attention to previously. Among other early warning signs we were starting to catch, one day John and Kenny were coming over to hang out at our house in Spicewood so we could all watch the debut of the "*Coming to Your City*" video on CMT. John and Kenny, when they walked in, had both done so in choreographed fashion each with one leg moving normally and the other arm and leg moving stiffly. When I asked who they were imitating, Kenny said "We're doing the Freddy Powers strut!" Little did we know we'd need A LOT of humor like that in the coming years given what Freddy was about to be facing...

Freddy playing with Stop the Truck band early 2000s

CHAPTER 22: PARKINSON'S DISEASE

Catherine Powers: Looking back on it now years later, it's kind of strange because I know so much more about the disease as it got worse, but the truth is: Freddy had Parkinson's Disease ever since we got together. There were early signs, I remember one time he was sitting on the houseboat, and he had his leg propped up on a coffee table, and I just looked down and noticed that he had this little ripple going down the side of his leg. I remember I reached over and I touched it and it stopped, I asked Freddy, "Did that bother you?", and totally unaware, he said "What?", when I moved my finger away, it started again, and I said "That!" he said, "No," when I asked him what that was, he shrugged and said, "I don't know, I see it all the time but it doesn't bother me."

Then, every so often when he'd be flying, he'd put his foot on the pedals of the airplane and his left leg would just start shaking, and he couldn't control it. But once again, he didn't think nothing about it because we'd never heard of Parkinson's before, so we never even thought of anything like that. This was before Google where you can look up a symptom on your phone and have an idea right away of what it is. Back then, because it didn't really seem to bother him that much, we didn't go to a doctor or anything where we might have been able to catch it early and at least be aware or possibly slow it down.

Freddy Powers: "When I first got Parkinson's, the thing that scared me was that I got to thinking back to when I first started noticing it, and it's been a long time back that it started bothering me. My left side has always been a little weaker than my right side, my left arm didn't have as much circulation, and my left leg was weaker. It was little things, nothing that we considered important."

Catherine Powers: The first time I realized something was wrong even though Freddy hadn't been diagnosed yet with anything, live on national television, on The Tonight Show with Jay Leno no less. Freddy always waved to me whenever he was playing on TV, and it might sound silly, but I knew when he didn't that something was wrong. When he got his cast off, the urgency really started to set in because he noticed his fingers wouldn't move the way they were supposed to, and that the little finger had a little twitch, and he couldn't make chords on the guitar like he always had. We thought at first maybe something had been wrong with his hand and the way it healed up. After that, Freddy and I went back to see his hand doctor, and when he showed the doctor what was going on, the doctor looked at him and said, "Freddy, you need to go see a neurologist friend of mine and have an MRI..." That's when they first officially diagnosed him with Parkinson's Disease.

Freddy Powers: "At first, it didn't dawn on me just how serious it was, you know? When we finally came around and realized what it was, the impact was already over with kind of."

> **Norma Powers-Marlowe:** My father had Parkinson's, and my husband had Parkinson's. When I found out that Freddy had it, oh My God, I knew what Catherine was in for, because this is a disease that bothers you like you wouldn't believe.

Catherine Powers: Following the trip to the E.R., for as strong as he was trying to stay physically and in spirit, in his heart, I knew Freddy had fallen into a depression as he began to see the little tolls his disease was beginning to take on and from him. Our moment of truth as a couple came one day while we were still living out there on Willie's golf course, and Freddy by then had already gotten to the point where he was no longer able to drive himself into town, and only able to drive anymore down to the little store. Even then, he was starting to have little, small wrecks, and after a while of this, he got really, really depressed to the extreme that all of a sudden, he was just laying in bed, not wanting to get up anymore. The best I could get from him was to get up in the morning, go to the kitchen, get himself a cup of coffee, and then the next thing you know, he was right back into bed and lay in there watching T.V. until he fell back to sleep all day. Well, I let this go on for about four days before the 5th morning, when I'd finally had enough. I stormed into the bedroom wearing only a long t-shirt with my hair wrapped up in a towel, but I couldn't stand it anymore! I flipped the lights on, looked at Freddy and gave him an ultimatum: "Are you gonna get up and live with me?" At first, he just kind of moaned, and I said, "Freddy, either you get up and live with me, by God, or I'm outta here! I can't live this way, I'm not going to sit here and watch you do this."

At first, he just rolled over and turned his back to me. I'd just gotten out of the shower, and had my hair still wrapped up in a towel. I jumped in my flip-flops, grabbed my dog and purse, stormed out the door and peeled off in the car. Well, I got about a mile and a half, two miles down the road when my phone rang and it was Freddy. When I answered, he said, "Mama, I can't do this without you," and I said, "Are you gonna get out of the bed and live?" When he said "Yes," I told him I was on my way back and never left his side again. Neither of us knew fully what we had in store over the next 10-plus years, but as hard as Freddy was ready to fight for his life, I was ready to fight that hard alongside him.

> **Merle Haggard:** I can't stand to see Freddy like that, it's hard for me to look at him, I'm sure he don't want to be that way and I don't want to see him like that. I hate that, it hurts me....

Catherine Powers: At first, Freddy could still play guitar, he just kind of changed up his chords, because he always had his special chords that were complicated. Still, there's also ways of simplifying those same chords, so he would change their structure in order to be able to play the chords. He continued to work and continued to go out with Merle and travel – and even went out on tour with Big and Rich a couple of times. But by the middle-to-end of 2005, Freddy's ability to play the guitar had weakened in his hands to the point where he couldn't make a chord at all anymore with that left hand. That's when he came off the road with Merle, and his condition continued to spread and worsen to where he eventually had to have somebody with him to just do basic things around the house or on stage. That's when it got to be too hard for him to play in Merle's band anymore.

Freddy Powers: "The most disturbing part about it for me is I can't play the guitar anymore. It's very difficult, and my left hand doesn't work real good. There's a lot of things we have to give up and it's kind of hard."

Catherine Powers: As word started getting out, a really sad moment of realization for Freddy's friends came on Thanksgiving, 2006 where we'd gone out to Merle's. We were going to do the Agatha Christie Holiday Party, which we all did, and I was shocked that Merle actually played a part in this Agatha Christie Mystery where we all dressed up in costumes. It was kind of funny because I actually won the best costume of the day, but we all had character roles they give you before you arrive, and you show up to the party in the character you're going to be playing. Freddy and I went as a 1920 mobster and Flapper.

Later that night, after the game was over, Merle and Freddy and everybody from The Strangers were all sitting there still in their costumes picking on guitars like they always did, and Freddy was struggling really hard. He was wanting to play and be a part of it, and all of a sudden, he turned to Merle and said "Merle, I just can't play my guitar anymore. This Parkinson's is taking the love of my life, what am I gonna do Merle?" Of course, Hag and everybody got tears in their eyes, and that's when Merle reminded him, "Freddy, you can still sing." But it was very emotional for everyone, and you could see it hurt Merle really deeply, and it was heartbreaking for all of them. It was just a big slap in the face to everybody in the room to look at Freddy and realize they'd never be able to play or pick with him again *either*.

Freddy Powers: "I can't play guitar anymore, it's indescribable. It was hard to give that up."

> **Rolling Stone Magazine:** "Just a few days before wrapping up their Last of the Breed tour, Willie Nelson, Merle Haggard and Sixties Country Star Ray Price played a sold-out gig at New York City's Radio City Music Hall. Seeing these three on one stage (accompanied by backing band Asleep at the Wheel) is a once-in-a-lifetime opportunity, and the show itself was a master-class in classic country music. Although the audience provided a diverse cross-section of the country music fan base -- yuppies in suits and pearls, aging hippies in t-shirts and cowboy hats -- by night's end, everyone was moving (and boozing) in unison. The rest of the evening, Nelson and Haggard, along with Price and Freddy Powers, tossed lead vocals back and forth on familiar songs highlighted with instrumental solos and an occasional jam-out. Together, the group focused less on tracks from the new disc *Last of the Breed* and more on popular hits such as Patsy Cline's '*Crazy*' (originally written by Nelson) and '*On the Road Again.*' No one seemed to mind."

Catherine Powers: It was really hard on Willie Nelson when Freddy told him and it hit home that he would never be able to play guitar with Freddy again. So when he realized Freddy was losing his ability to play, Willie was spending every opportunity he could there toward the end of Freddy's playing to pick with him. Every time he was home, they went back to that routine of almost playing 15 hours a day like they used to in the beginning.

Willie Nelson: He's a lot of fun to play with, and when Freddy was at his best, there was nobody better at what he did. He's a great singer too, especially when he was singing what he was playing, he could accompany himself very well, he could sit down with just the guitar and keep you very entertained. We were always telling each other our latest jokes; we were joke tellers.

Catherine Powers: Freddy had been out of the hospital two days shortly after a life-threatening bout with his condition, and we went to see Willie up at his place, World Headquarters. Right there in front of he and I, Freddy had his first seizure. I remember it took both of us by surprise, and as we turned around to look at Freddy, he'd stiffened up in that wheelchair and jerked a little bit and his head just fell completely backwards and he was totally motionless. Both Willie and I thought at that moment that he had just died. He'd been standing on the opposite side of the bar from Freddy and I, and came running around from behind that bar FAST like some young whipper snapper, ready to face the situation head on. We were both on top of Freddy like you wouldn't believe trying to wake him, and all of a sudden, he came to, and looked at us both like, "What's going on?"

Well, both of our faces at that moment had gone totally white with shock, Freddy laughed at both of us, but it was quite a freaky situation. We both just about panicked, and Willie said, "We gotta get him to the hospital..." It was amazing Willie actually helped me lift Freddy in that wheelchair, down a flight of stairs, and into the car. As you can imagine, here I'm now concerned about Willie getting hurt too because he was only a year younger than Freddy! But I got Freddy to the hospital, and then once we got to the hospital, everybody there in the E.R. knew who Freddy was right away. In fact, this one nurse when she saw Freddy's name on the medical chart said, "Is this Freddy Powers?" When they told her yes, she started jumping up and down in the E.R. going, "Oh my God, I'm such a big fan!" It was hilarious under the circumstances.

Freddy, knowing his neurologist was his main doctor, didn't say much to the first wave of doctors and nurses that walked in. When the neurologist walked in the room, the first thing Freddy asked was before she could say anything. "Am I going to be out of here by Saturday night, I'm supposed to be honoring Ray Price?" Then she said, "We'll talk about that later," and began running him through a battery of tests that day, from things as simple as, "Can you tell me your full name?" and "What year is this?" and "Do you know where you are?" Then, after a series of questions that honestly scared the shit out of me because I was worried about what impact the seizure had if any on him mentally, the doctor finally got to "Can you tell me what brought you into the hospital? Why am I seeing you?" Freddy responded, "Well, I was sitting at Willie Nelson's..." and before he could say another word, she politely interrupted him and said "Just a minute Mr. Powers." She laid her clip board down on the edge of his hospital bed, got right over on top of his face and kind of straddled him with her arms, and said, "Now Mr. Powers, were you really at Willie Nelson's or are you just imagining you were at Willie Nelson's?" I couldn't tell if she was suddenly star-struck or just thought he'd legitimately been hallucinating from the seizure. Then from behind her, Freddy's guitar player Steve Carter – who'd met us at the hospital – started laughing and said "Oh no ma'am, he's telling you the truth! This is the legendary Freddy Powers, he's supposed to be honoring Ray Price this Saturday night, and was definitely at Willie Nelson's house...."

After hearing that, the neurologist stepped back and said "Well oh my Gosh, who's my patient now?", and Steve proceeded to give her Freddy's history in Country Music, so that was of one of those funny stories that came out of the tragedy. It was like that at most hospitals we've had stays at over the past 10+ years. I remember in Nashville when Freddy wound up in the E.R., the whole staff was extra-alert – not only because of Freddy's condition – but because throughout his whole stay, a steady stream of country music stars would drop in to not only visit with Freddy. In some cases, Tanya Tucker or Big and Rich would play for him as they did when they put on an impromptu concert for him right there in his hospital room!

Big Kenny Alphin: Freddy knew it was happening to him, but was always just so gracious about it, in that he'd still do the best of what he could. I can remember many a time of him saying "Oh, my hands just aren't working like they used to," but he'd still give it his best. I think he handled it as best as anyone possibly could, he never let it stop him. I think he accepted what the task was in that terrible disease, and did it with as great a humility and graciousness as you could. I think he still tried to live each day as grand as you possibly can. He was a great lover of life and living and gave it everything he had till his last breath.

John Rich: Writing with Freddy is a party! You pour a cocktail, and Freddy, he'll smoke something, and you sit around and you basically just start talking about what's been happening and what's going on. The next thing you know, Freddy's over there riffin' on something or he says something, and everybody just kind of looks and says, 'Yep, that's brilliant, let's follow that', and you jump in and get rollin'. Freddy's direction in a song is unbelievable, and I'd have to think when he wrote with Merle, that it probably worked like that. I'm sure Merle was the bulldog in the song, but I guarantee you he was following Freddy's direction on every twist and turn. And Freddy is a twister and a turner, which makes his stuff really interesting.

"Medley of a Hillbilly Jedi" was another one in there that Freddy wrote on, and *"Let's Don't Say Goodbye"*, we wrote that song the same night we wrote *"Filthy Rich."* We were getting ready to leave Deadwood, and Bill said, "Man, I just hate saying goodbye, I don't want you boys to leave, I hate this part of it," and Freddy said, "Well, we don't have to say goodbye, just say see you later gator." So we said, "Well, let's write that while we're here, let's write a goodbye song, an 'end of the show' song." So we wrote *"Let's Don't Say Goodbye,"* and once again, it has that Rat Pack – Vaudeville thing in it that really only Freddy can do.

What Freddy brings to the table as a songwriter is timeless, it doesn't ever change; the equation of what he does in music is not bound by any time element whatsoever. So any real serious songwriter would want to know as much about Freddy as they could. And whether they realize it or not, they know the man's songs. That's the position I was in all those years ago when I met him, I didn't know who he was but I knew all his songs, and so when I sat down and started getting into the guy, I was just more and more blown away by the minute, uncovering all these things and sitting with the guy that wrote all this stuff that impacted me so much. To know that I sat around as a kid learning all those licks and those songs, and those are his creations, and now you're sitting with the guy. It's pretty unbelievable.

Freddy's melodies move like horn sections, is the best way I put it. There's no redundancy in what he does, he could play the same chord progression 10 times in a row and sing 10 different melodies over it back to back to back, you hear that in his guitar playing too. He's a real jazz guy, and we all know about Jazz: it's free-flow and doesn't have the parameters around it that other forms of music do, and that really applies to the way his melodies hit too. It feels free-form, but after you've heard it twice, it's a hook that's stuck in your head.

Catherine Powers: Writing with Freddy was just one of Big & Rich's contributions to trying to keep Freddy's name out there with the Millennial country fans. It helped him get some music publishing going to put towards our rising medical costs as his condition worsened and he couldn't perform live on a regular basis to earn the same living any longer even though he kept performing.

Freddy Powers: "I want people to know that the disease doesn't mean I'm dead or dying, and neither is my career."

Catherine Powers: After reality set in that we were going to have to learn how to live a different life, because Freddy and I had been troubadours our entire marriage and Freddy his entire life, I knew the most important thing we needed to do was keep him on the road. Thankfully, one of the first of many angels on our shoulder would appear when his youngest sister Norma Marlowe-Powers stepped in and bought Freddy and I our beloved bus. That allowed Freddy to stay out there working vs. just sitting there in the house withering away. By then, though Freddy wasn't fully bound to a wheelchair yet, he'd already started having problems with balance where his legs would randomly buckle under him when he was standing or walking, and was starting to fall down a lot. That was dangerous not only when Freddy was doing something as simple as crossing a street or some other every-day activity. He and I both took for granted before this, and equally so when he was standing on stage performing. Sadly, after a while, it got bad enough to where he'd actually broken a couple of ribs during one of these random falls. He hit his head during another fall so hard it left gashes, and eventually got to where it was so frequent he'd have bruises all the time, and was always getting banged up from falling.

> **Joi Vinson Davis:** Freddy's Nurse, Whenever some new medical situation would pop up, I'd get a phone call, I knew something happened when she'd call me and say "Okay, well, they're telling me this, what do I do?" Every time I would just teach her everything I knew about anything that was going on – and she knew more about the Parkinson's than I did and I'm a nurse – but as far as taking care of everything, I would show her: "Well, this is how to do this," and she would improve it every time! (laughs) Seriously, she got it all quickly, and there was nothing that I taught her that she didn't improve ten times better by the next time I was with her and Freddy – and she taught me a lot actually. She was his best possible caretaker because she cared most about his quality of life and care. It was hard to keep up with all the medical supplies too, she'd have to take oxygen and suction tanks, and pills, and syringes, and extra tubes, but she juggled it all.
>
> Day to day, it was wake up in the morning and the first thing she would do was clean his mouth out. Then feeding him, and she went from spoon-feeding him every day – and it took two hours to feed him a bowl of anything. It was always organic smoothies and fruit – to eventually feeding him cans through his feeding tube in his stomach after he couldn't swallow food easily anymore. Then every 3 hours it was pill time, and every two hours, she would change him, and would roll him over every

couple hours in his hospital bed. So it was something every hour: he had to be suctioned, he had to be changed, he had to have medicine, he had to be dressed, groomed, and it would take 15 minutes just to set up to have his teeth brushed for instance. So she did it ALL by herself except when she was lucky enough to have me or Cass or someone come occasionally to give her some relief. But 90% of the time she did it all by herself, from daylight to dark, taking care of him. I've never seen nothing like it.

So our friendship grew as I helped her with him, and now, it's just like they're my family. I never wanted Freddy to miss anything, and if I knew there was something going on and Cass couldn't do it, I would always make sure if there was any way possible she could get him to an event or concert and I could get there to make sure he got there. I was going to do it. And if he had any extended stay in the hospital, one way or another, I got there. One time, John Rich had me flown out to Texas where it was a 16-day stay.

Catherine Powers: The final fall that prompted us to put Freddy in a wheelchair full-time came when we were in Nashville staying at the Fontanel, which at one time was Barbara Mandrell's mansion and grounds that Marc Oswald and William Morris had since bought and turned into a museum and concert venue. We were frequent guests when we came through town, and on that trip, once again, with no warning or clumsiness on his part, Freddy had fallen on the bus and this time hit the ground so hard he broke his nose! The only funny part of the whole thing is, for his whole life and the 20 years I'd spent with him before then, Freddy was one of the toughest people I ever knew, and would have bandaged that broken nose up himself and considered it nothing more serious than a scrape on the knee. He'd been brought up in that classic Great Depression-era generation where you only went to the doctor if you had a broken arm or something serious. So I knew it drove him nuts to now have to make so many routine trips to the E.R., neurologists, etc. because of his condition.

Well, that day, before we'd even gotten him fully into the ambulance and out of there, I was already being inundated with concerned phone calls from all over town, and remember thinking, "My God, news travels fast." So we got him to the E.R., they sewed his nose up, and they discharged him without anyone realizing he'd gotten a staph infection. By then, we'd gotten so used to hitting hospitals on the road that with Freddy's "*The Show Must Go On*" attitude, there was no taking a few days off to recuperate so we'd hit the road for a show in Gainesville, Texas to honor Mickey Newbury. Being the professional he was, he'd gotten right up on stage with a broken nose and sang and everything, but after the show, I noticed he wasn't feeling well, and over the next couple hours kept getting sicker and sicker. So without missing a beat in what had become reflex by that point, I peeled out of there and headed straight to the E.R. in Austin. The only difference in outcome that night once we arrived at the Hospital came when they told me his fever had gotten so bad they didn't think he would make it through the night.

It was the first time since his diagnosis and downward spiral of his condition worsening that I'd been faced with the prospect of losing him, and not over time but so suddenly. By the grace of God and Freddy's own resilient strength and spirit (and a very top notch hospital staff), he not only made it through the night but wound up fighting the infection for the next eight days in the Intensive Care Unit and eventually pulled through. Still, by then, because Freddy was pretty much losing the ability to walk independently and I was now having to literally carry him on my back or assist him where I'd have to constantly walk behind him and help him walk even just across the room. I knew this was taking a huge toll on his independence psychologically, especially coming right on the heels of accepting the reality that he could no longer physically play his guitar. And by the time he'd been discharged from the hospital and entered into physical therapy, it became clear to everyone that the atrophy and everything had set in and he was no longer going to be able to walk on his own.

Joi Vinson Davis, Freddy's Personal Nurse: When he first started going downhill, once his feet started going, Catherine would be his feet, and when he couldn't pick his feet up all the way, she would just kind of kick the back of his heels, so he could walk. Then after that became impossible to do, she would actually hold him and have him walk on her feet to try to keep him walking. Then he had to go to a walker, and then he got the motorized wheelchair. He used that by himself for a while, then got to where he couldn't control it using that arm, so she would walk beside that motorized wheelchair and take him everywhere he needed to go. Then when he got to where he couldn't use the motorized one anymore, it was just a regular wheelchair pushing him everywhere he wanted to go, up hills and dang near across valleys – wherever he wanted to go.

Then she started carrying him like a baby down the steps of the bus, putting him in his wheelchair, then when they'd get back, she'd carry him back on the bus, then when that became impossible, she started piggy-backing him. So every step, she had a solution to keep him active and that's what kept him going for so long.

Catherine Powers: The day Freddy was being discharged from rehab, another miracle of generosity from his peers when I found out that, initially, they were not going to let me bring him back on the bus. First off from a safety point of view, they didn't like the way I was having to get him on board piggy-backing him in on my back. Then once the medical professionals came on and saw that his bed was all the way in the back of the bus and that I was having to again piggy-back him all the way back to the bed, and then walk backwards in order to be able to set him down. They immediately told me, "Mrs. Powers, you're going to have to make some other kind of arrangement because this isn't going to work." To my relief, they told me if I could get a hospital bed installed up in the front of the bus, he could stay, so I called up this old-boy-type club, starting with the Coondicks!

Well, thankfully, as with so many others, once they heard what Freddy was facing, they raced into action and the *very next day*, showed up with a hospital bed. It was quite a sight, because then, right there in the hospital parking lot, cut off the base of the bed – which was the wheels – built this wooden box up in the front of the bus, brought that bed in three pieces and put it back together on the bus! It was nothing short of a miracle, the next day, I was able to bring his physical therapists back on and they were impressed too, after a quick inspection, they signed off and said, "Okay, you got it," and I was allowed to bring Freddy back on the bus. That made a life-changing difference too, had I not been able to bring him back on this bus, he would have been stuck in a home and his quality-of-life would have ended back then. But because of that hospital bed and his attendants, I have been able to keep Freddy out on the road and a part of this world for the better part of the last decade.

Wayne Ahart: I don't know of anybody who was a friend of Freddy's who wouldn't have done anything they could to help Freddy when they asked. Catherine had mentioned she was having difficulty, she was his caregiver and boy, she was like an angel. I told Freddy one time, "Freddy, I'm sure you know, but boy, you're so lucky to have someone like Catherine, that loves you and takes care of you the way she does. So she mentioned one time that she was having trouble so one of the guys said, "Let's get him a hospital bed," so we just all chipped in until we had enough money to get it for him.

Terry Booth: Mike Burke found that hospital bed and had to rearrange it a little bit to get it on the bus. We were just trying to do anything we could to help Freddy and especially Catherine. She's is like a humming bird. She's all over the place all the time, and quite a character herself, and a delightful woman. The determination and dedication she showed when Freddy got ill was more than I've ever seen before. I couldn't believe the dedication that woman showed, it was impressive to anyone and everyone who had any contact with Freddy, and/or Freddy and Catherine over the years.

Catherine Powers: Following the reality setting in that he was going to now be hospital bed-and-wheelchair bound for the rest of his life. Once that hospital bed was installed on the bus, I would still have to carry him like a baby or piggy-back him just to get him on and off the bus everywhere we went, and knew at that point, God and Freddy were both counting on me to stay strong for both of us.

Tanya Tucker: She works so hard! I've seen her lift him up over her shoulders and carry him, and she's just a little thing, she's not any bigger than he is, but I have never seen anybody work so hard and be so dedicated and so loving than Catherine. Bar none, she's got to be an angel, there's a song right there! (laughs) You don't see that kind of love very often. I saw it with my parents and I see it with Catherine and Freddy. That kind of love is hard to find.

Big Kenny Alphin: Catherine is just as gracious and loving as you can possibly be. She loved that man so much, and wants to make sure his memory continues on and that his music never stops playing, and I've got to give her credit. The little thing she is, how she would handle Freddy in the toughest times of his life, just being able to physically move him around and all the things they dealt with, I never saw anything but a joyful love between the two of them. They would crack each other up or give each other a hard time, just like best friends. I never saw anything but a woman that was standing by her man every moment she was given, every day they had together. She'd done volumes for him during and after he's passed, anytime I'm around and see Catherine, before or since, Freddy's always been on the front of her mind.

Moe Monsarrat: I never seen anybody love somebody that much. She'd literally pick him up, put him on her back and carry him in and out of that bus. I couldn't pick him up, it's hard, I remember I tried one time and it was like trying to pick up a bag of potatoes. I was afraid I'd break him or something! (laughs) So we just all have so much respect for Catherine because we all saw how she was with him, and you just couldn't be more devoted to someone. It was almost like a movie. To love someone that much, that doesn't happen to everybody.

Freddy Powers: "We've had a wonderful relationship. Everybody notices it, you know. She does everything for me, and I do everything for her that I can, that's the way it works."

American Music Project: "As we…come upon his rebirth, not all Parkinson's victims have a savior – someone powerful enough to give them new life. Through Catherine however, Freddy is, in many respects, reborn. Her will power nurtures and preserves him. At a time when he could have quickly passed she united with him closer than before and helped him adjust to a new, dark, foreign world and remain. She is a cell of immense love, energy and light. She is the keeper of his new cell. On the couch inside their camper our conversation carries on and goes deeper. She levels with me, quits with the facts and begins to express the true feelings and emotions she has tied to her husband. In these expressions and in her deep commitment to him she propagates his tale and his spirit. Like a surrogate she carries on his story and his personality with impeccable depth, accuracy and care. No one can ever replace Freddy yet she carries on his flame. True to her name Catherine is his catharsis: his release, purification, his restoration, his chance. In my pursuit to understand Freddy I never expected that one of the most compelling pieces of the story would be his wife."

Catherine Powers: When Freddy was first diagnosed with Parkinson's, we went to several different doctors to get different opinions, and at the top of every one of those consultations, Freddy was very open with them about the fact that smoking Pot seemed to help with his condition more than anything else. Well, these were five of the top Neurologists in the Austin area, and every one of them told him, "Freddy, I can't officially prescribe you to smoke marijuana, but if it helps you, I'd advise you to keep doing so," because off the record, they did know it made a helpful difference. Thankfully, in the last few years, Medical Marijuana has continued to gain acceptance by society and the medical profession at large. Without a doubt, Freddy is an example of a success story there because I can personally give you timeless examples where pot has had a calming effect on his day-in-and-out condition physically.

One powerful example that might sound kind of funny on the surface but that in reality proved to be life-threatening came when Freddy got the hiccups, and it got so severe that we thought we were going to lose him because it wouldn't stop. He wasn't even having a chance to breathe and was turning blue. It got so bad that I had to call his hospice nurse, who came right over. The only humor we could take from the whole thing was, "Oh my God, everybody's going to say 'Freddy Powers died from the hiccups!" She gave him a muscle relaxer that didn't work, so I finally decided, "Look, I'm going to try this," and gave him a big old hit. At first, I'd been afraid to try it because he was having so much trouble with just his basic breathing, but within TEN MINUTES, the hiccups stopped! Then when it started up again after about an hour and a half, I gave him another hit, and it stopped. The kicker was, I smoked so much myself that I got tired of being high. So, before the next hiccup fit started, I actually had to call in a Mayday to one of our friends to come take over smoking with Freddy! (laughs)

Near the end of his life, Freddy had developed a problem with swallowing due to the Parkinson's had gotten so severe he was now permanently on a feeding tube. He even had a hard time with something as basic as swallowing his own saliva, and because he couldn't swallow it, it all got built up in the back of his throat to where he was constantly struggling to clear it. Well, I'd suction him to help, but when I couldn't get it all out and still hear him gurgling, all I had to do is give him a good ole big hit and he'd give me one good cough and all that stuff comes right up.

Privately, in the first couple years after we'd received the formal diagnosis, my heart broke every day for and with him as we both absorbed the permanence of our new reality and learned to do the most within the boundaries of the disease's increasing restrictions. Whenever Freddy would have this kind of a breakdown during those early years after he was officially diagnosed, I'd try whatever I could to break it up by giving him simple tasks to get his mind off it, sometimes even the simplest tasks that I knew he could still physically do would give him even the slightest sense of completion.

It was brutal to watch somebody as accomplished as Freddy, who'd always been able to physically do whatever he set his mind to, have a mind that was still so capable but a body that wasn't able to keep up anymore. It tortured both of us, and some of the depressions he went through during that mid-2000s period were very dark. He'd always tell me I was his sunlight, but you never quite feel you're doing enough, and it took a heavy toll on both of us. By now, I was wearing so many hats and juggling so many roles that I was going through a whole learning curve of my own: acting as Freddy's full-time nurse and caretaker, our tour bus driver, his manager (as I was still determined to keep him as active with and around musicians as much as possible), and would even carry him on my back onto stage to set him in his chair to sing!

Freddy Powers: "I've got Parkinson's, but Parkinson's doesn't have me yet. You know what I mean? It affects everything about our lives, but we're not letting it… We're still doing everything that we do, we're just doing it a little slower maybe."

Catherine Powers: "*The Saddest Goodbye*" was a song Freddy started working on before he lost his ability to play guitar, as he knew he was fixing to lose that ability. He could still write and play through the basic chord structure, but every time he sat down to work on that song, he would get very depressed. It was a reminder of the totality of what he was losing in the ability to translate the music he heard in his head physically into those classic "Freddy Powers" triplet chords on the guitar. It took him three years to finish that song where he would have previously had it written and finished in a quicker time than the length of the song itself!

It was so hard to watch him go through that too, because every time he'd get the inspiration up to sit down and work on it, he'd get through no more than two or three lines before the Parkinson's made his hands shake so bad he couldn't form the chords to keep writing on to the next verse. It was heartbreaking for both of us, every time I'd come in to check on him once he'd stopped playing, he'd always have these big old tears in his eyes and his head hanging down. As a matter of fact, if it hadn't been for a fellow Texas songwriter and guitar player named Gary Nicholson sitting down with Freddy to work on it, I don't know if that song would have ever been finished.

Don Powers Jr: The last video Freddy was in was called "*Last of the Breed,*" and it had Willie Nelson, Merle Haggard and Ray Price, and Freddy sang back-up in it because his Parkinson's had started to set in, and in the video, you can see Freddy's hand just shaking like crazy. As sad as that was, it was a real treat for my Dad when Freddy called us up in Oklahoma, and said "What are you gonna be doing for the next couple of weeks?" When my dad said "Just staying here tending our garden," Freddy chuckled and replied, "Well, you wanna go on tour with me, Merle Haggard, Willie Nelson and Ray Price?" So he went to check with me and I laughed and said, "What's the decision? I can hold Oklahoma down, go!" They played in Tulsa, and picked up my dad from there and went to Missouri, and he got a kick out of traveling with Freddy one more time on the road and all those guys.

"We never thought Freddy would live as long as he did because of his Parkinson's Disease."
– NORMA POWERS-MARLOW

"I don't force it, I'm too far along to write something trivial, I try to write something more profound." – FREDDY POWERS

Freddy singing Parkinsons Era

CHAPTER 23: FREDDY'S 2ND ACT

Catherine Powers: By 2007, Freddy had lost complete ability to play the guitar at all, but by the grace of God, he was still singing, so we kept the shows going on, and that's when Freddy started bringing his comedy back as part of his act! Once word had spread about Freddy's diagnosis, I think it inspired his friends and fans alike to see him out there on the road and in the world so much, and that led to all kinds of new creative doors opening. Freddy could not only still sing, and tell jokes too, which became a new mainstay of his act for the rest of his years on the road. He performed at Willie Nelson's July 4th Picnic in 2008!

Freddy Powers Live, July 4th, 2008:

Most people know I've got Parkinson's, it's why I'm shaking like hell. It's not cause I'm nervous about being on stage. I've been doing this 55 years and it doesn't scare me. What scares me is when there's nobody in the audience!
(crowd laughs)

There's one thing about Parkinson's that
you need to understand, you see, I'm kind
of lucky because I am a human vibrator!
(crowd laughs louder) Girls sit in my lap
and go 'Wooooooh!', no batteries needed!
(audience applauds even louder)
Merle Haggard told me one time, he said
'You know Freddy, with your Parkinson's,
it may come in handy for you because you
have to shake so many hands and you're
always warmed up!' (laughs) When I lay
in the sun to get a sun tan, they call
it shake and bake... So much for
that joke! (laughs)

I had a few drinks tonight and I'm feeling just a little
bit woozy! My wife, she hates my drinking. One time she
was trying to trick me into stopping my drinking, she was
trying to scare me, because I came in drunk one night and
she had this sheet over her head, and she jumped up and
said 'I am the devil! I am the devil!', and I said 'Shake hands,
I married your sister!'" (laughs)

Catherine Powers: Those were inspiring cheers for Freddy to hear, and he was right too because that opened the next door in Freddy's career as a performer as we took that bus on tour for the next few years solid, playing to loyal audiences everywhere we could. It was truly touching and really a miracle for both Freddy and I to see how the country music community rallied around him after word got out that he had Parkinson's. Freddy was determined not to hide from the spotlight, but to step proudly into it wherever he could so fans could still see him perform, and to set an example for anyone with Parkinson's that you didn't have to stop living in spite of the challenges and limitations of this debilitating disease. That inspired a lot of musicians who silently were battling Parkinson's too.

One of our proudest periods of productivity throughout Freddy's deteriorating condition came with the progress we made in fighting the disease through the Freddy Powers Parkinson's Foundation. We started the foundation with the overarching goal of spreading awareness about the disease, Freddy and I didn't know anything about Parkinson's when he was diagnosed, so that was # 1. But secretly, in my heart, I wanted Freddy's name to LIVE ON. He had done so much for so many people, and I never want him to be forgotten. Over the years, we've been able to call on Freddy's celebrity friends and relationships to host high-profile fundraisers in partnership with prominent local Parkinson's organizations like CAP (Capital Area Parkinson's Society), which serves greater Austin and Central Texas and make a sizable donation. That was always a huge honor and big thrill for Freddy and I to be able to do – for as helpless as he felt in many ways because of the disease – to still see we'd been able to succeed in making real contributions to the cause. This gave Freddy one more thing to live for, and some of our favorite highlights from those adventures received major press coverage as well, which helped all parties involved. Everyone involved proudly referred to themselves as 'Grateful Fred Heads,' a term affectionately started during our Special Olympics days.

Freddy Powers: "Most everything we do is for the Parkinson's (Foundation) now. That was Catherine's idea. She's the spark plug behind the whole thing."

Catherine Powers: So through the foundation, we have been able to help people and bring attention to a disease using Freddy's name, which would mean he'd never be forgotten – That was and still is the most important thing to me to this day. That's why I live on this computer, that's why I spread his name and keep him out there as much as I can at all the Hall of Fame Induction ceremonies and concerts, because he deserves it. He deserves to be honored and remembered as much as you would remember anyone else of importance in country music. That's the way I feel, and fortunately, that was a shared sentiment too by how successful a run we had during the foundation's heyday.

Wayne Ahart: When they started the Freddy Powers Parkinson's Foundation, they asked me to be on the board, I said "Sure," and did all we could to help promote the Foundation. Then Freddy occasionally – even though he got to the point where he shook so much he couldn't hardly get up and perform – sometimes would, especially among a crowd of people who were basically his friends.

Country Music Television (CMT) News: "Big & Rich, Willie Nelson and former U.S. Attorney General Janet Reno will help Texas music mainstay Freddy Powers celebrate his 75th birthday during an Oct. 16 charity event in Austin. A noted songwriter, guitarist and record producer, Powers has recorded with Nelson and toured extensively with Merle Haggard. As a songwriter, his No. 1 hits include George Jones' '*I Always Get Lucky With You*' and Haggard's '*Let's Chase Each Other Around the Room.*' Nelson and Reno will appear at a roast prior to a performance by Big & Rich. All proceeds from the event at the Barton Creek Art Center will benefit the Freddy Powers Parkinson's Foundation. Diagnosed with Parkinson's disease in 2004, Powers created the organization to fund research and assist Parkinson's patients in Central Texas."

Catherine Powers: Sadly, Janet Reno had to cancel, and a couple of days prior to the show, Willie had gotten busted, and graciously backed out because he knew that if he showed up, all the attention would have been focused on his bust instead of on the Freddy Powers Parkinson's Fundraiser. Willie did host one later at Carl's Corner.

The Lone Star, June, 2008: "Willie Nelson To Host Benefit Concert. Country Music Legend, Willie Nelson will perform a private concert, Monday, June 30, as a preview to the completion of Willie's Place at Carl's Corner, the new state-of-the-art truck stop located on Interstate-35 between Dallas and Austin. Those attending the June 30 benefit will enjoy a private concert by Willie Nelson, great food and beverages, and preopening guided tours of Willie's Place. Platinum sponsors will also be invited to an exclusive meet-n-greet in the Saloon with Willie Nelson. This exclusive event kicks off a week of pre-opening music and celebrations. On July 1 and 2, David Allan Coe and Ray Wylie Hubbard will be performing live from 8-12 p.m. July 3 will be filled with live performances by Merle Haggard at 6 p.m. followed by Ray Price at 8 p.m. and Willie Nelson at 10 p.m. These concerts are free to the public. The private concert is a benefit with a portion of proceeds going to the Freddy Powers Parkinson's Foundation. The foundation was founded in the name of the award-winning singer, songwriter and producer, Freddy Powers, who suffers from the disease. The foundation benefits Texans with Parkinson's, as well as their caregivers."

B.B. Morse: Willie and Merle were spoofing on him one day, talking about how having a shaky hand like that has opened up a whole bunch of new opportunities for brother Fred, Salvation Bell Ringer is one of them!

KXAN.com: "Parkinson's Patients Find Relief In New Treatment" Monday February 11, 2008

Michael J. Fox, Katherine Hepburn, Pope John Paul II, Muhammad Ali, the Rev. Billy Graham, Johnny Cash: All have been victimized by Parkinson's disease. For musician and songwriter Freddy Powers and his wife Catherine, the journey through Parkinson's disease has been grueling. Parkinson's is degenerative, depressing and deadly. It starts in the brain, where cells that make dopamine begin to malfunction. Dopamine is the chemical messenger the brain sends out to tell parts of the body to move. "Freddy was really walking very slow, moving real slow and his arm was clenched up real tight," Catherine said. "But the two main things were that he had really lost his smile, and his eyes had become real cloudy and really despondent."

But doctors may have stumbled on a promising new treatment. After only 10 daily treatments with a machine that electronically stimulates acupuncture points, things changed. "It was like I brought home a new husband," Catherine says. "He went from just, you know, almost not with me half the time, or it didn't feel like or look like he was with me, to all of a sudden, he was back; he was back to my Freddy." Dr. Donald Rhodes was working on a machine to help alleviate chronic pain in his office in Corpus Christi when he noticed symptoms of other kinds improved in Parkinson's and diabetes patients. "Diseases that respond to this treatment are grouped together by circulation," Rhodes said. "If we can improve circulation, good things happen."

Freddy's neurologist Rob Izor said the treatment is like acupuncture, but with a kick. Intrigued, Izor followed up with a 30-day pilot study with five patients, each of whom experienced some kind of improvement. "When I lay on the beach to get sun, they call it, 'shake and bake'," Freddy says. "He came back home with his smile," Catherine said. "You got your smile back, is that true?" Swift asked. "Well, it depends on if you say something funny," Freddy said.

Catherine Powers: Looking back now, as proud as I am of what we accomplished, in the same time, it breaks my heart that we eventually had to shut the foundation down due to overhead costs growing because of its success to the point where we had to hire someone full-time to manage the day-to-day operations. We did A LOT of good while it was running at its peak. It was amazing, all of the different songwriters and musicians that came out of the woodwork that didn't even want anyone to publicly know they had the disease, but were so inspired by Freddy's example that you don't have to be ashamed or don't have to give up what you love doing. As importantly, that you can find other ways to make what you love doing work in spite of the obstacles of the disease. That has been one of the greatest pleasures and achievements for both Freddy and I, to see him inspire that hope in fellow musicians facing the same struggles.

Still today, I will get people on the internet who have been struggling with the disease or equally often, folks who are newly diagnosed and scared out of their minds that will reach out to us – kids as young as 32, 33 years old – who write and say, "I have Parkinson's and I'm gonna be like Freddy and I'm not gonna give up. I'm gonna keep fighting and working and living until I can't anymore," so that in itself is a true honor that he's become an inspiration to so many. It should ultimately be the goal of any type of organization like ours to inspire people to come out and accept the disease and learn to live with it and still lead productive lives – what else could be a higher honor? We even held our own Freddy Powers' Parkinson's Cruise For the Cure in 2008, where Freddy stole the show with a mix of his singing and joke-telling, just like he did back in his Nevada heyday!

Freddy Powers, Live, Cruise for the Cure, 2008:

Thank you Ladies and Gentlemen, I wanted to
Tell you a funny story before we begin
our next song. I remember one night years
ago, I came in drunk as hell and
slipped on the front porch trying
to get my key in the door, and
and busted a half-pint of whiskey in my back
pocket. I cut myself all up, punctured
myself in quite a few places where the
glass broke, and I snuck in the bathroom
and took my pants off, backed up
to the mirror and put band-aids on
the proper spots, you know and went to bed.

Well, the next morning she woke me up and said,
"You was drinking again last night, wasn't you?"
And I said, "What makes you think that?", and
she said, "Well, for two reasons, there's blood
all over the sheets, and there's band-aids
all over the bathroom mirror!"

I come from a long line of drinkers, my Uncle one time
went to the doctor and the doctor told him if he didn't
quit drinking, his liver was pooping out on him and he was
going to die. So he decided that every time he would
have a drink of whiskey, he would take a Carter's
Little Liver Pill. "He lived to be 97 years old, and
when he died, they had to take a stick and beat
his liver to death!" (audience laughs/claps)

Moe Monsarrat: We used to always go to Freddy's room to smoke weed in the daytime because you couldn't smoke inside the ship. They kept coming in the room to make up the bed, and they'd go through the drawers, look in the ashtray, and I remember they found Freddy's brother Don's weed in his room and they told him he couldn't get off the ship! But in Freddy's room, there was a balcony where we could all go out and smoke, so that was all good. We played the cruise, and the thing to realize is we were playing for the Freddy Powers Parkinson's Foundation, so we played in a private ballroom for this particular group of people who had contributed and bought tickets. So the rest of the people on the ship, they'd never seen us play, they didn't know we were musicians or anything. We played our shows the way we were supposed to do them, and Freddy did his part and it was great.

Catherine Powers: I still remember that night, after the show, Freddy and I were staying in the Cruise-ship's Presidential Suite, standing out on the balcony with the moon shimmering off the water. I remember Freddy turned to me and said "Mama, we may be poor as a couple of Church House mouses but we sure do live high on the hog!"

John Rich: Freddy's a very visual guy, and he's also a comedian, so he loves the set-up and the payoff, he's all about the set-up and the knock-down, and that works for a joke and it also works for a great country song. And I think you can see the similarities between the way he tells a joke and the way he tells a song, they're really one in the same, it's just one has melody around it.

One thing Freddy has that is really interesting in how he writes is that old Vaudeville thing in his approach to writing country music, which is really interesting, and unless you're part of Vaudeville, or just a huge fan of it, you're not going to write that way. So, I'm a big fan of the rat pack and big band kind of music, and Freddy being such a great jazz player, he almost sings when he's writing a song so that you can almost hear horn parts moving around the chords and the melody that he's throwing out.

Its real simple what he does, but he doesn't come at lyrics in a kitchy kind of way, he comes at them in a real clever way but they still got a lot of class, and that's a hard thing to do. It's hard to be funny and still maintain the class, and not get cheesy with it. So for instance, when you talk about '*Let's Chase Each Other Round the Room Tonight*', that's a funny thing to say, but it's also very true and it rings a bell with anyone who's ever heard it, and millions of people now have heard that song. Its written in such a clever way that you don't feel silly singing it, and when you hear those moves and those pockets that he comes up with, it's really a classic way to go. So whether it's a sad song or funny song or drinking song or whatever, they've all got that classic set-up and knock-down, like Johnny Carson or some of our greats that we've had in country music.

Catherine Powers: Freddy was always so funny! I could be sitting in a chair watching T.V. at home and he'd come walking out into the room acting as normal as ever and then all of a sudden, get right in front of me and moon me or something goofy, and then continue with whatever he was doing like it had never happened. Then if I did mention it later, he'd act innocent as if he had no earthly idea what I was talking about, and say something funny like, "I think you're hallucinating over there!" So he was always a prankster, and just loved to see people laugh and never really could escape that comedian-side of his personality, but in what's maybe a testament to his talent as a performer, it never got old.

It gave him great joy to put a smile on anybody's face, whether he'd known you his whole life or you were a complete stranger, and I loved that part of his personality! Freddy was naturally very witty, and some of his comebacks would just crack me up – or the whole room if there happened to be anyone else present. As a natural entertainer, Freddy loved an audience, which is not to say he needed one all the time, but I loved it all and was his biggest fan. Over the years, I've even used a lot of Freddy's humor and it never gets old, his jokes always crack people up, and I'll say, "I stole that one from him." That's why he was always such a dynamic performer throughout his career too because he was extremely quick on his feet, and always kept his crowds entertained. He was definitely a character. In fact, to this day, our dear friend, songwriter Cass Hunter, has a literal pocketbook full of what she calls "Freddy-isms," things she has witnessed and watched through his Parkinson's while she was on the road traveling with us for two years.

Cass Hunter: I started traveling with them the last couple years they got to travel before settling in Flora-Bama, and we'd go back and forth between Nashville and Austin, and down to Perdido Key, pretty much anywhere we could get the bus in without hitting limbs. Catherine felt it was very important to keep Freddy moving even though he was stuck in his hospital bed, and to get him to as many different fans and friends around the country who still wanted to see him, and we would go stay in the driveways of our friends' along the way. If I had a gig somewhere along there, she'd plan around that and take me to it, and when we would travel, a lot of times, we'd take scenic back roads. One of my favorite trips from that time was when we took Natchez Trace Parkway through Mississippi, Alabama and Nashville. It was a far prettier drive than the interstates, and it was more relaxing for her, less traffic, and we would basically drive for a couple hours then pick our rest stops along waterfalls. We highlighted the ones that were 10 minutes or less walk from the bus to the attraction and back because we couldn't leave Freddy alone for more than 20 or so minutes at a time.

So instead of gas stations, we tried to maximize the historic or scenic stops as much as possible when Catherine had to stop and stretch her legs and feed and change Freddy. Freddy couldn't get out of the hospital bed on his own, so he never could come with us unfortunately, so on one of these trips where we stopped at a waterfall along Natchez Trace, and it was literally like an eight minute walk so we were literally back in like 15 minutes. It was the only time he was alone on a 12-, 15-hour bus trip, but when we got back to the bus, as soon as we got on board, Freddy blurted out to both of us: "Good thing you're back, I was about to leave you!" He had a wonderful sense of humor, and he tried to use it whenever he could to put a smile on our faces.

On that same day, she was having to pull the mattress pad thing out from under him, and had to roll him over on his side to get it out, and then roll him over the other way. So she's up on the bed, and went to turn him over again and rolled him over too far to where the side of his face was pressed up against the window. Well, I was trying to make light of the situation and make him laugh, so I said, "Good Lord Freddy, you just gonna let her throw you around like that? Ain't you used to that yet, she does it all the time," and he said, "I'll never get used to that!" (laughs)

One of my favorite Freddy road stories is one I call "Malfunction Junction", which was definitely one of our big adventures, we were on our way to Key West from Nashville. On the very first night of that trip, on the way down, at a rest stop at the edge of Florida, at two o'clock in the morning, I'm sleeping on the couch beside Freddy's bed. All of a sudden, I wake up to the sound of someone pounding on our door as hard as they could. Well, Catherine came running through the bus in just her t-shirt and panties yelling "Holy Toledo, holy Toledo!", we open the door, and the cops go, "Get out of here now! Get out of here now, it's a fire!" So we look out the window, and sure enough, the truck parked right next to us was on fire, an 18-wheeler, and the whole cab was engulfed in flames 20 feet high! I've got pictures of this.

This trip to Florida was supposed to be eight days long, there and back, and it wound up being a 17-day trip because the bus broke down right in the middle lane of a five-lane Interstate in Miami. There's Freddy in the bed, Catherine's driving uphill, when the bus broke down, our emergency brake wouldn't work, and we had to hold the brake down the entire time for hours with our feet in the middle of rush hour traffic. We were getting cussed by everyone, and we had to stay up there at the front of the bus taking turns keeping pressed down on the brake while we waited for help to show up.

They had to block off traffic and eventually got us off the middle of the road and next to a guardrail, and poor Catherine's a nervous wreck, calling tow trucks trying to find somebody who can tow that big of a vehicle. We had three different companies come, and we were waiting hours in between each of them, and *all three* couldn't do the tow. So this took 12 hours before they finally found one that could tow us, and then they told us we couldn't stay in the back of the bus with Freddy – who bless his heart this whole time is stuck in his hospital bed watching all this chaos happening around him – because they weren't allowed to tow a vehicle for insurance reasons. We even showed them, but it didn't matter, we couldn't ride in the wrecker and we couldn't ride on the bus, so Catherine had to call a cab, which was another hour and a half wait. To make matters worse, the bus was pushed off the road so near to the guardrail that Catherine could barely get out the door herself, let alone get Freddy out by herself.

That girl is strong! She had to carry him on her back by herself when she was alone and needing to move him from one part of the bus to another or to his wheelchair. When I was traveling with them, to help her, I would hold him up from behind by his knees while she carried him on her back and try to take the weight off of her a little bit. On that bus, you can't get through the door side by side carrying him, so one person had to go after the other.

Here we are these two little girls and there are two big old wrecker guys who refused to help us because of insurance reasons, so we're trying to squeeze Freddy out the door while he's shaking and everything. I was on the other side of the guardrail trying to hold onto his legs while Catherine carried him out by the arms. We wound up getting towed to some dealership in the middle of the night, and the place wasn't even opened anymore! In the morning, Catherine and I went to get a rental car and it turned out the wrecker people had locked the keys on the bus! So she had to climb through a window to get that opened, then to top the whole day off, Freddy wound up locking us out of the rental car, and Catherine had to go find a slim Jim to open it! What a nightmare, but we had so many good times out on the road too!

Catherine Powers: That bus became our Hospital on Wheels after the tens of thousands of miles and all the people who traveled with us on and off over those years. Luckily, I had a loyal crew of Road Warriors, because they didn't just keep me company, while I was driving, they were my all-hands-on-deck Freddy crew! We had a gang of girlfriends that included Cass Hunter, my sister Debbie Langham, Freddy III and his mama Carrie, our friend Joi Anderson, who we called our daughter from another mother and father, she used called us Mama and Papa, and she also acted as Freddy's nurse, and in fact she is a Surgeon's Nurse. At times, John Rich would even fly her out at his expense when we wound up in hospital situations where I needed help. At one time, Tanya Tucker was even on the road with us! As Freddy's care became more 24-7, they helped me out with everything from preparing medications to helping me suction his mouth, and by then, Freddy already had a feeding tube in his stomach.

Thank God he was lucky enough to still be able to sing his songs and call on the comedy all those years and every once in a while he would throw in a little short joke in one of his shows, when he'd laid the banjo down, he'd pretty much laid his comedy down. At first, even though he couldn't play the guitar anymore, he would still strap it on and walk out on the stage and make the motions of trying to play the guitar because he didn't feel comfortable singing without the guitar. It was always a part of his show, having either a guitar or a banjo in his hands, so he did use it as a prop, but once he couldn't play the guitar any more, he just felt he needed to add something back in there, and that's when he started bringing his comedy back. That started making it easier for him to stand up there without a guitar and we kept him out there performing as long as he could.

The Austin Chronicle, August, 2008: "Perched uneasily still on a stool center stage, Powers delivers his long-familiar songs with the subtle touch only their writer can. His arms jerk in slight involuntary shudders, and his hands tremble as if still fretting across his absent guitar, but Powers' voice unfolds with calm, rich control. With his band supplying gently rippling jazz tones, Powers closes the set with his plaintive '*All I Wanna Do Is Sing My Song*,' echoing lonesome through the wooden theater to a hushed audience."

"All I Wanna Do Is Sing My Song"
All I wanna do is sing my song
It's the only way to pacify my mind until I'm strong
The very thought of losing you chills me to the bone
And all I wanna do is sing my song
All I wanna do is sing my song
Don't wanna think about the times she done me wrong
I just wanna ease my mind but the memories are much too strong
And all I wanna do is sing my song
All I wanna do is sing my song
Maybe I'll find somebody else to help me sing along
There's something bout the melody makes the nights not seem so long
And all I wanna do is sing my song
All I wanna do is sing my song
And when the show is over I'll be waitin' by the phone

And if the phone starts ringin' with "Honey, please come home"
Who knows I might sing my way back home
(Written by Freddy Powers)

Catherine Powers: The Freddy Powers New Year's Day Party was another fun show he did that year that still continues today in the Freddy Powers Pickin' Pavilion at La Hacienda.

Freddy Powers Live from New Years Day Party:

I was just telling Rattlesnake Annie about this song, Rattlesnake Annie has probably recorded more of my songs than anybody. I got one I want to do here that's a little bit different style of song, for me anyways, it's called '*Like a Movie Star.*' Mama, come up and do this one with me.

Vs 1

She's like a movie star
Always shining so divine
For these eyes of mine

Vs 2

She's got a heart of gold
And the one I love
And hold when the night is cold

She's got more going than Cleopatra had
And she's so good and she's so bad
That's so good

Catherine Powers:
He's got more going
Than Clarke Gable ever had
And he's so good and he's so bad
That's so good

Freddy and Catherine Powers:
She's got a heart that's true
And I know that you'd approve
If you knew her too

Catherine Powers: It even got to a point where we weren't even sure any more how well he was going to be able to perform physically at the shows, but both Freddy and his fans still wanted him to be out there, but a lot of venues didn't want to hire and pay him if he wasn't going to be able to play. So I would make a deal with the clubs that, "Okay, you don't have to pay him, I'll take care of the band and will pay everybody, just let me have a place for him to perform." That's how I kind of got into the financial trouble that I did, because I was trying to keep the band paid and keep him on the road, putting fuel in the bus, and I kind of made that priority more important to me than paying bills. Willie had heard about it and he called me and then Willie Nelson and Merle Haggard stepped up and – Thank God for them – paid off all the credit cards, paid our car off, and gave Freddy and I a fresh start.

Of course, I turned around and pretty much did the same thing again, but I wanted to keep him out there working and a part of the music world as long as he wanted to perform. Most importantly, to give him something to live for as his Parkinson's continued to worsen. But Freddy's friends really stuck by him, from Merle and Willie to Big and Rich, I have to say, those two guys have been absolutely wonderful to Freddy and I over the years, especially right after they all started to realize that Freddy's ability to perform was changing. In bigger picture terms, the reality that we didn't know how much longer he was going to have on the earth with us.

John Rich: When you talk about his illness, there's no crueler way to take a guy like Freddy out than with what he's got, for his hands to go away and his dexterity. He can't really talk and to be as great a singer and picker as he is, and a great people person, for that to be what takes you out is just a crazy irony to me. We always tried to have as much fun with him as we could when we were all together.

Big Kenny Alphin: I can remember times playing Casino shows, where after show, we all wanted to go out there and play a few hands, and we'd roll Freddy up there and set his arm up on the Blackjack table. He could at least wiggle a finger to tell the dealer whether to give him a card or not. You could still see him laughing and see the excitement in him just by looking at his eyes.

We hung out A LOT! If there was any event we were playing that fit into his travels, he'd hang out with us a lot. He was one of our great friends. John and I, from the days we first got to know Freddy and hang out with him, was also in the heyday of the Musik Mafia starting up, and Freddy really fit right into that whole world of music without prejudice. He really enjoyed and appreciated all of it – and to hold his own with it too.

CHAPTER 23: FREDDY'S 2ND ACT 215

Joi Vinson Davis: When we went down to Mobile with John Rich and all of them, Freddy had a slew of Marines pick him up and put him on that stage when he was honored by Big & Rich, and that was a really cool trip. All these Marines wanted to take pictures with him, and pushed him up and down the street in his wheelchair, they made a path for him and us going down that road, it was just amazing. Then, after the show, we went to New Orleans for Big & Rich's next show, and John and them got Freddy up to the table, and gave him some chips, and John Rich was helping Freddy put his chips out to place bets because Freddy wasn't quite able to. Every time Freddy would ask him to put down a certain amount, John would say, "Are you sure buddy, you sure you want to do that?", and Freddy would always say "Yep", and he wound up winning like $4000 playing Poker with John!

Catherine Powers: In the fall of 2011, Freddy turned 80, and I wanted to throw him the sexiest birthday bash I could, so at the La Hacienda Freddy Powers Pickin' Pavilion. That night, in front of a packed crowd, I came out on stage dressed in a Dance hall Girl Red Dress with Feathers in my hair to introduce Freddy's birthday gift: "This next thing that's coming up is a little bit wild, so you may want to close your eyes, but this is a birthday present from John Rich, Big Kenny and Mark Oswald, so Freddy, Happy Birthday! This is nothing too because for Marc Oswald's birthday, they had Freddy sit in a cake for 45 minutes with a topless young lady who popped out after Freddy!" (laughs) It was classic because as I introduced Freddy, the audience started clapping, cheering him on as Freddy was wheeled onto the stage flanked by 3 scantily-clad women in just a halter tops and red plaid mini-skirts, who proceed to give Freddy a lap dance in front of the entire crowd! Freddy was clearly smiling and enjoying himself because the whole performance culminating with one rubbing her breasts in Freddy's face and grinding her backside while he spanks her 80 times in rapid fashion!

His friends weren't all just trying to help him out professionally, they loved to put a smile on his face too, and Big Kenny and John were both always joking and clowning around with Freddy. Then when John Rich cut his first big hit, "*Save a Horse, Ride a Cowboy*", he was one of those guys – and probably the first one Freddy or I've ever heard of – who went back to all his "Honky Tonk Heroes" as he called it and gave every one of them $10,000! Well, when our check arrived to us, it was like a miracle because we were to the point financially where it was like heaven just opened up its gates and rained down money on us, he knew that we needed it. That was not the only time John Rich ever opened up his check book for Freddy, and far from the last, there's been several times – I couldn't even start to add up – the tens of thousands of dollars that John Rich, Big Kenny, Willie, Merle Haggard and Marc Oswald have personally taken out of their pockets to help Freddy and I and keep our bus running and those wheels a-turning!

Big Kenny Alphin: Freddy deserved that. He had a natural instinct for Swing. I was inspired by Freddy to take *"Save a Horse, Ride a Cowboy"* and turn that into a swing song! So instead of how we were doing it, he inspired me to take any song and put it in that style also. He really opened my whole world up to the concept of it. I'll probably never to my dying day be the player Freddy was in that school of music. Freddy being a multi-instrument musician also – from guitar to banjo to pretty much anything with strings – it was just always so fun to sit down with him, with any kind of song we'd be playing, he could play along to it but in his own style. It was kind of a moving progression that kept it within the same realm no matter what you're playing.

Catherine Powers: Our dear friend Tanya Tucker has been another Country Music star who stepped up to help Freddy out, also Gretchen Wilson and Susie Cochran, Hank Cochran's widow. All of the financial generosity they have contributed, and it's been everything from helping out with a bus breakdown to buying $3000 or $4000 in gas cards they sent us to be able to keep Freddy out on the road. That allowed him to keep going to songwriter Festivals and concerts where, again and again, friends like Merle, Willie and Big and Rich would bring Freddy up on stage in front of thousands of fans to sing when he couldn't even stand anymore and was wheel-chair bound. They knew how much it meant to Freddy to feel like he was still part of the show, and still had a place in the fan's hearts.

I'm quite sure we would not have been able to keep the show on the road all those years and giving Freddy not only quantity but quality of life, and who can keep track of everything Merle and all of them did for Freddy. It wasn't always financial support either, a lot of times, it was just moral support, where we'd show up at their shows and while he was still able to perform and even when he couldn't anymore, they still made a big deal when he was there. Freddy drew his strength from that as much as anything else that kept him fighting all those years.

John Rich: I think the thing about him is, no matter how much it hurt him physically, he didn't say a word. They picked him up and set him on my bus the other night, and those old crazy, blue eyes open up and look at ya, and he didn't have to say anything, you just start bustin' out laughing because you know what he's thinking. And if you really know Freddy, you can read him just by looking in his eyes and watching his expression, he's a real communicator even now.

Joi Vinson Davis: Catherine called me the day that he went to the hospital, and she said he was really sick and they didn't think he was going to make it two days. She really needed me there and didn't feel comfortable with what was going on with him in the first place. She didn't feel Freddy was being treated the way he should have been treated by the V.A. hospital staff. So I called John Rich and he booked me a flight to go out there and personally take care of Freddy while he was in the hospital. I didn't make it there till 10 that night, but I'm glad I did when I did because there was a lot of bad things going on. He was getting the wrong treatments, his doctors were back and forth saying, "Don't trust this doctor", "Don't trust this doctor", so it was just a really, really bad experience.

They'd given him the wrong medicine and wrong I.V. Fluid. Upon laying eyes on him for the first time that night, I honestly didn't think he was gonna make it. So every time a nurse or doctor would come in, I would automatically start researching everything they were doing, because they'd made so many mistakes. I truly thought we were gonna lose him, but he pulled on through. Freddy lasted a lot longer than most Parkinson's patients do, and it was all because of Catherine.

While we were at the hospital, we were all doing anything we could to get him to do simple things like swallow his pills and food. Affectionately I've always called Catherine and Freddy, Mama and Papa. One day during this 2012 trip, they were trying to get this tube down Freddy's nose, and we couldn't get it down. They were trying to get Freddy to bend his chin forward, and when Catherine realized what they were trying to do, she looked over at me and said, "Joi, show Papa your tits..." Well, immediately, every doctor's eyes in the room got really big and they started taking their focus off Freddy. I looked up at Catherine, and said "Now, Mama?" And so I said, "Look Papa?", and those doctors, Catherine still swears to this day they were all about to lose it, but that tube went right on down! The doctors said it was the first time they'd ever been treated doing a treatment.

Cass Hunter: When they came to Nashville in 2012 when he was hospitalized, and they said he was going and we thought it was going to be Freddy's very last walk, so Joi – who's a nurse and a very close friend of theirs – Catherine and I were rolling Freddy around the hospital and grounds in his wheelchair boo-hooing. He could still talk, but it took him a little while to get it out, and a lot of times, he would scream things because he'd work it up. Freddy and I used to tell each other jokes all the time, and he would always know mine. I never could find one that he didn't know already. So on that little spin around the block at the hospital, I said, "Tell me a joke

Freddy," just trying to get him to talk. So he said, "This drunk was standing on the side of the road, and this lady walked by carrying this goose, and a man walks up and says, 'Where did you get that pig?'"

At this point in the joke, Freddy stopped talking and didn't finish the punch line. So it got silent again, and we were all so sad that the mood stayed that way for the rest of the walk, and as we made our way back up the elevator. Well, by the time we got back to his hospital room, we were all feeling super-gloomy, and as the nurses were getting him back in the bed. Mary Sarah and her parents were now in the room – a whole new audience who hadn't heard him start the joke and not finish it – all of a sudden, out of nowhere, Freddy yells out, "I was talking to the goose!" Whenever he was yelling when he'd talk, he'd look at you beforehand and his eyes would be going crazy because you knew he had so much he was trying to say, and when he was finally ready, he blurted it out LOUD because he'd worked it up so long.

Catherine Powers: There were several of those times where he'd start to tell a joke and then freeze up and we'd have to wait for him to finish it all. Freezing up is a common thing with Parkinson's, whether it was with talking, walking, etc.

Freddy Powers:
I came in one time and caught my wife in bed
with this guy, naked as a jaybird, and I said, "What
in the hell are you doing in here?", and she turned
around to this guy an says, "I told you he was dumb!"
I said to her, "I play second fiddle to no man!", and she said,
"With your instrument, you're damn lucky to be in the band!"
Then, the other day I went in for a check-up, and the doctor
said "Take off all his clothes," and I said "You first!"

Big Kenny Alphin: I've never seen a guy who could sit down, and tell 20 to 100 jokes in a row, non-stop. Just going from one to the other to the other, not many people can do that. Every time I think of him I smile because he was just so much fun to be around. Freddy stole the show at Dirty Joke Night up at John's house. That was just a get-together with a bunch of friends and everybody would bring their best joke and get up and tell it. Freddy was a positive encourager and great wealth of knowledge of music and influence, and especially in the realm of Country and Swing, and he appreciated everything we did. We were so full of joy and jokes, and was always laughing, and you'd crack yourself up every time we were around.

B.B. Morse: We were up at Mount Richmore, John Rich's house, one night, in Nashville overlooking Broadway, there was a panorama of 248 degrees of glass going around the top floor of that place. It had its own elevators, and it was packed with everybody from George Jones to Mel Tillis to Larry Gatlin of the Gatlin Brothers, Bill Anderson, and they were all there for Freddy Powers Dirty Joke Night.

Moe Monsarrat: Especially the first time you heard the joke, the audience reaction would always crack us up as well as the joke. Freddy's just a funny guy. Like one time we went to John Rich's house in Nashville, they flew us up to play Dirty Joke Night. Freddy's up on stage, and it's the end of the night, and every big star that's there who wanted to get up had told a dirty joke. So you've heard 50 dirty jokes by the end of the night. John Rich gets up, and Freddy's sitting there in his wheelchair, and he says, "Freddy, tell us one more joke to send us all home, to finish off the night." There wasn't a half a second between when he stopped talking and when Freddy started the joke: "I was fucking this guy up the ass the other night and he reached around and started jiggling my balls, and the thought crossed my mind, 'You think this sonofabitch might be gay?' " (laughs) It brought down the house! He was that fast, he didn't even have to think about what kind of joke he was going to tell.

Joi Vinson Davis: We were all having a good time one night after that, and Freddy at this time wasn't able to eat anything solid – he could have ice cream and smoothies and stuff like that. So we're all sitting around but he wasn't speaking or anything, and was setting up on the couch, and Catherine said, "Papa, what can I get you? What do you want?" And he was looking at us mad for hours, because he'd kept saying he wanted crab claws for like two days before that evening, and he'd kept repeating, "I sure would like some crab claws, I sure would like some crab claws," and we just kept ignoring it because we knew he couldn't have them. So that night, we're all sitting around, having a good time, and then I said, "Freddy, whatever we can do, what can I get you, anything?" He finally broke his silence, and said "Can you say FUCKING CRAB CLAWS?!!" (laughs)

Catherine Powers: During that September 12th hospital visit, Joi had to leave in a couple days, and kept saying, "Papa, I'm going to have to leave in a day or so. I really want to hear you talk, I just want to hear you say anything," and just kept on and kept on the nurse came in to check his vitals and everything. About that time, Freddy screams at the top of his lungs, "I want some pussy!" You could hear him all the way to the nurse's station! SO of course, Joi turns around and says, "Papa, I wanted to hear you talk, but I wasn't expecting that!" (laughs) The nurse kind of jumped back and stared at me, not knowing what to do, so I jumped up and walked over to him and said, "I'll tell you what Papa, you get yourself better and we get back on that bus and we'll talk about some Pussy!"

Joi Vinson Davis: Then he kept saying it, because he would get stuck sometimes trying to get the same thing out, so for the next 20 minutes or so, that's all he kept saying: "I want some pussy!" I mean, the nurses and everybody heard it, it was hilarious!

Catherine Powers: At the same time this is all happening, Sonny Throckmorton calls Joi's phone, and he's on the golf course out there with Willie, so he hears Joi laughing, and naturally asks her, "What are you laughing at?" So she tells him the story, he relays it to Willie, and they both hang up the phone laughing their asses off. Well, of course, being the joke tellers they always were, Willie picks up his phone right there on the course and calls Merle to tell him about it. It didn't take very long to make its way all around the Country Music circles that Freddy's first words after being through this horrific near-death experience in the hospital was to belt out, "I want some pussy!" Merle and Mark Oswald even made a video for Freddy about it:

Marc Oswald:
Hey Frederick P. Powers, this is
Marc Oswald, reporting from Deadwood,
South Dakota. We're here with Merle
and Theresa Haggard, and the crew,
here's a message of love and hope and
inspiration and horniness.

As Oswald concludes speaking, the phone camera flashes to Merle Haggard's wife Theresa and then over to Merle.

Theresa Haggard:
Hi Freddy, love you, Catherine,
give him a little will ya.

Merle Haggard:
I understand you've been wanting
some pussy. I'd give you some but
I ain't got any.

John Rich: When you play a Freddy Powers song, whether it's one we wrote with him or one of his, when you play something with him on it, for the rest of my career, as long as I'm singing, we will tell a story about Freddy Powers, or we'll tell one of his jokes, or we'll do something like we did when we were down in New Orleans one time recently. We played '*Let's Chase Each Other Round the Room Tonight*' and told the crowd, 'That's the guy sitting in the wheel-chair right in front of the soundboard who wrote that, go over and tell him thank you for all the great country music!' Then 10,000 people turned around and just started applauding, standing up and going crazy because they understand what he means to country music in a world that keeps becoming more and more shallow and shifting, you got a guy like Freddy who's just an absolute icon!

Catherine Powers: It's so amazing the way people have just come out of the woodwork that loved Freddy and have respected him and what he has given them over the years. Freddy was always such a contributor himself and spent so much time raising money for charity and advancing other people's careers. Even Freddy's Dentist, Dr. Charles Anderson of Spicewood, had appreciated Freddy for all he'd done and would never accept money to get his teeth cleaned! The first time that happened, he said, "Freddy, I would never let you pay me for a single thing I do for you. What you have done for so many people, this is my way of giving back." So because Freddy has done so much throughout his life and career for so many other people, that now they've been happy to step up and help him now in a time of his need.

Freddy and Co in Europe

CHAPTER 24: THE STOP THE TRUCK BAND

Catherine Powers: During all those years on the road in the last leg of Freddy's career, he was backed by one of the TOP live bands in Austin, known as the Stop the Truck band. At the time, the group featured Steve Carter on guitar, Moe Monsarrat on bass, Ed Ferguson and Pat McCann on lead guitars, and Miguel Pankratz on drums. These were ALL power players in their own right, and in the way they could credibly pull off Freddy's catalog live on stage! It was so important to Freddy to be able to perform, even touring EUROPE with them! We'd first gone to Switzerland and Freddy played before thousands of screaming fans. As a footnote: it just happened to also be our 10th year Wedding Anniversary and we re-announced our wedding vows for the fourth time.

Even as his Parkinson's worsened after that, Freddy's fans still came out around the world to see him perform. I don't know that either of us had realized until then that the full stretch of his popularity and influence had spread beyond the U.S. all the way across the Atlantic into Europe. You see, in Europe, it was different there. Freddy was always referred to as a master craftsman in the press, and being as well known over there as many of the stars who made his songs famous, and you really saw that whenever he played live. They have a high respect and admiration for songwriters where here in the States, fans often don't have any idea who wrote the song.

B.B. Morse: Freddy has a very big footprint in Europe, and the European listening audience is an educated audience, if they want to find something out, they knew who both wrote and sang the song. Freddy had a very good inroad there, aside from his association with Willie and Merle, he had his own following over in Europe. The outline of his presence, so to speak, is more than just the U.S., European country fans knew Freddy as master craftsman. It was great, the Colossal Tour! At the time, that had been my first trip to Europe, and we performed at this picturesque-mountain alcove up in Col-des-Roche, Switzerland. Everybody was dressed up like cowboys and Indians. The girls all looked like Pocahontas and the guys all looked like Daniel Boone, the crowd and the band. Black Powder Pistols and blanks are a big deal up there, this was a festival and with all these Texas acts coming in, to them, everything from Texas is Cowboys and Indians, and if they liked your song, everybody would pull their pop guns out and fire them off. You had black powder smoke hanging in the air. They were really big into line dancing too.

Steve Carter: My band Stop the Truck became Freddy's band when we took him to Europe. B.B. Morris, who was Freddy's bass player for years, once he left the band, I replaced him playing bass for about two years. The whole time, I was just watching Freddy's rhythm guitar playing, I was watching him like a hawk and stealing everything that I could. B.B. told me years later that it was good I replaced him because otherwise, they never would have found somebody who would learn Freddy's guitar style. So when he got sick, I was right there doing what he did, and so for the first two years I was playing bass, I was really learning those Swing chords and Jazz chords and how he went from one chord to another, and how he strummed and kept time. I was already a pretty good rhythm guitar player and was about 50 when I met Freddy, but he elevated what I did.

We took him to France twice, and it was after Freddy was too old to go in a way. Traveling wasn't easy for him, the first time in 2008 he was in a walker, the second time in 2010 he was in a wheelchair, and we played at EquiBlues Rodeo in France. I remember the second time, when Freddy's Parkinson's was getting so bad that he'd started to scoot, so we all whipped off our belts and strapped him in the chair to perform on stage! The crowds loved him over there, they knew the words, and didn't even speak English. We had my protégé Ruby Jane on tour with us, and she was standing on stage looking out over the audience and was stunned that these people adored him and cried because it was one of the best things she ever saw. To top the trip off, Freddy and Catherine renewed their vows at the top of the Eiffel Tower with Floyd Domino performing a Jewish Ceremony!

Moe Monsarrat: Steve Carter was playing with me in Stop the Truck, which was an original country band. In the prime of that band, preceding Freddy, there were other players involved – Boomer Norman, Wally Dogget, and Steve Carter and I – and when we started playing with Freddy, we'd replaced Boomer with Ed Ferguson, and Wally with Miguel Pankratz. So the first incarnation of that band sounded different than when we played with Freddy, and that band was really good.

Steve started playing bass with Freddy, and when Freddy got to where he wasn't able to play the guitar as well, Steve started to take over some rhythm guitar and Steve kind of brought the rest of us in. He brought me in to play bass, and Miguel to play drums, and Ed Ferguson, and Pat McCann eventually. We definitely changed our style to play with Freddy when Steve brought those songs in, "*Road to My Heart,*" "*A Friend in California,*" "*Always Get Lucky With You,*" "*Texas and Oklahoma,*" and I played with Freddy from when he could sing to when he couldn't at the very, very, very end of it.

My Reggae band was called the Mau Mau Chaplin, before and after Freddy, and Freddy and Catherine would come see the band and dance at our shows. I've been playing Reggae since 1973, and I was playing Reggae, and had been playing for years playing rock and jazz in my younger years, and Freddy's music was completely different from any of that. I considered it to be Jazz Swing with kind of a Country bend to it. Realize Freddy grew up listening to Bob Wills and guys like that and was greatly influenced by them. Those guys didn't play three chord country songs, they played Jazz Swing, Stomp, Western Swing, and the guy who taught Freddy – Paul Buskirk – had a big influence on Fred and the way he played. And the fact that he played Banjo, and then came from Banjo to guitar, he had this rhythm...

I've never heard anybody play rhythm like Freddy Powers, let me just say that right off the bat. If you listen to Django Reinhardt, the guys playing with Django played this real fast, strident guitar, and in a way, it's like you hear people play banjo. That's where Freddy's coming from, so that was totally new to me, and frankly, at the beginning when I started playing with Freddy, I was replacing people who were really, really good at what they were doing. I didn't know anything about that style of playing and he was real, real patient with me and I know I screwed up a lot, but in the end I got it, and it broadened my musicianship A LOT.

Learning something new that's really cool is always fun, or at least it should be, and it certainly was for me. Just learning all those chord changes that he had and used all the time, luckily Steve Carter helped me, and following guys like Deanie Bird and BB Morse, were a WHOLE lot better players than me. I'm a singer who plays bass to back himself up basically, and what I do now with Reggae music is very difficult to do, but it's certainly no more difficult than what those guys were doing behind Freddy for all those years.

Steve Carter: What made Freddy's style of guitar playing so unique is his rhythm was militant, he didn't need a drummer, he wasn't playing along with anybody, and militant's kind of a Reggae term, but it was just kind of no letting up. There was no doubt where the groove was when Freddy was playing, and he even made jokes that "It took me 25 years to get a perfect band, no drummer." (laughs) So he was the snare and the hi-hat and the bass player was the bass drum, and he was very much up on his time, there was never any relaxing, or any doubt about where it was. And by that, I don't mean he was pushing, but it was what we came to call digging a trench. If you dig the trench deep enough, the singer can't get out of it, the lead guitar player can't get out of it. So it's a very high-walled trench that you're creating that gives them the freedom to play, and that's kind of what Freddy taught us. He was a natural band leader, he led from the guitar, not from the things he said.

Moe Monsarrat: Freddy was always carrying the other musicians in his band, as good as they were, and as his conditioned worsened, it was important for us to keep in mind what his bands and records sounded like before we got there. So you'd listen to *The Country Jazz Singer* and it's just incredible, and you try to get up to that level of playing, and I'm not sure we ever made that. But I tell you what, we got some good recordings and made a heck of a tribute album for him, which is a really good album. I'm real proud of that album and how we treated his songs because with the ones he actually played with us, we stayed real true to the way that he wanted them.

Catherine Powers: I remember one particularly-touching time where we'd actually been able to arrange for Freddy and I to fly to Europe and perform.

Once we were at the venue, they'd known ahead of time about his condition and had set up this nice, big chair on stage for him to sit in while he performed. Well, bless his heart, but that night, right there in the middle of the stage, he was having trouble sitting steadily in that chair because of the Parkinson's shakes, and it got so visibly bad to both the audience and the musicians he was playing with they stopped the show in mid-song. What happened after that was so heart-warming it still brings tears to my eyes, because next thing you know, all these cowboys and country musicians are taking off their belts and a bunch of the band proceeded right there to fasten Freddy sturdily into that chair so he could continue his performance. Sure enough, he sat up there belted into a chair and finished the rest of the show, and the packed house went crazy! Afterward, the owner of the venue said to us with a broken French-English accent: "First time I ever sell out!"

Moe Monsarrat: I remember he kept sliding out of his chair, and when we had to strap him into his wheel chair, lift him up and put him on a platform in the middle of the stage, and then we'd go ahead and play, and on that gig, he sang magnificently, he was absolutely fantastic. He went on and on. Then this lady out of the crowd got down in front of him and held onto his shoes to keep him from sliding down. I thought that was the most touching thing, that was almost Biblical when that happened.

Steve Carter: I became his hands and his voice after he couldn't sing, I'm the keeper of the key. I was always a bass player and guitar player, and a friend of mine said, "You need to go meet Freddy Powers," so I did. I'd seen Willie and Johnnie Gimble and this guy in a Motorcycle hat on PBS shortly before that playing all these old Swing standards out on Willie's ranch. When I walked in, at that point, I didn't know Freddy by name but I realized he was that guy from the PBS special that was playing rhythm. I'm a rhythm guitar player, and it's almost a lost art. I don't care about solos at all. So I walked in and my first thought was, "Oh no, I can't do this, this is Jazz, this isn't country songs." When I auditioned, I literally thought he'd say, "Thanks for coming out son," and send me home, but instead he groomed me and taught me how to play Swing.

Moe Monsarrat: One day when he was going on, this was during the time when Freddy was getting hard to understand when he spoke. I couldn't understand a thing he was saying but I said, "Freddy, I love you man," and just as clear as day, he said "I love you too man." That was the first thing I could understand, and it just broke me up man. He popped out of his illness long enough to tell me he loved me! When I was there and Pat was there, we were the only two left who could go to the Flora-Bama. I remember the last show we did with him at the Silver Moon, Freddy could barely sing anymore but the audience still loved him.

Before the gig, we were on the bus and Sonny Throckmorton was there. Sonny and I were smoking a joint, and I said "Sonny, what the fuck do we do? Do we play in time and just I'll sing over whatever he doesn't sing? How do we do this?", and he said, "You know, they paid to see Freddy, they didn't pay to see you." (laughs) So what we did was, Pat and I would play in time together, then we'd stop for him to sing and then kind of just play the chord a little bit so Freddy could sing, and he would sing real slow. Then we'd play in time again till the next time he was supposed to sing, then we'd stop again, and we got through the gig like that. So Freddy didn't follow us, we followed Freddy.

At the end of that gig, every person there was in tears – I mean, the band, the people who worked there, the audience, everybody there was in tears, and I said "Oh my God, I've never seen anything like this in my whole life!" A normal person, being as sick as Freddy was, would not get up there and do this anymore. They'd submit to the disease, but Freddy Powers was a Marine, # 1, so they ain't known for submitting to anything, but the courage he showed to get up there, and way past when anyone else would have quit, I was proud to be up there with him.

Catherine Powers: In 2011, while Freddy could still travel on an airplane, we took what would be his last flight overseas to France where he played the Equi-Blues Festival. He could still sing and tell jokes, but he was no longer really able to walk so he was in the wheelchair full time. Freddy in that way became a different kind of hero than he'd even been as a songwriter because now he was an inspiration to so many who were also battling Parkinson's around the world.

Freddy Powers' Pickin Parties

CHAPTER 25: FREDDY POWERS LEGENDARY PICKIN' PARTIES

Catherine Powers: The roots of the Freddy Powers' Pickin' Parties are LEGENDARY! That tradition runs throughout his entire career, that's always been a part of Freddy. It's something he's done all the way back to when I first met him while he was still living on Lake Shasta. He and Merle would have big pickin' parties where there's be five, six, seven houseboats all loaded down with musicians and friends and we'd go up the Pit River there and have big picking parties right there on the water! Of course those Pickin' Parties never stopped, and so when Freddy and Merle both moved off the houseboats and we came back home to Texas, it's remained a common past-time with Willie and all sorts of different circles of musician friends of his. So whenever he wasn't out there working and was at home, a steady stream of musicians was always coming out to the house to play with Freddy. After a while it sort of took on a life of its own into what has now become an annual *South by Southwest* staple.

We lived in a HUGE house owned by Bill McDavid on Willie's golf course when Freddy threw his first official *"Freddy Powers' Pickin' Party"* back in 1995 and we started out just having smaller, private picking parties that first year. Not surprisingly, as word quickly spread Freddy was now back in town and we got more and more plugged into the Austin music scene, in 1996 we opened our doors to the public for the first time to host the first official Freddy Powers Pickin' Party. In classic maverick fashion, because our event was happening during the *South by Southwest Festival* in Austin and Freddy wasn't into the tradition of having to go along with the pay-to-play route where all the local live venues charge bands and artists/songwriters attending the Festival to showcase in their clubs. Freddy rebelled against that by sarcastically calling his event the "Freddy Powers South by *So What* Pickin' Party!"

It really did set the tone for what to expect whether you showed up to play or listen. He wanted our Pickin' Party to be more in the spirit of playing just for playing's sake, no matter who was sitting next to you in the circle, because it could run randomly from an unknown songwriter to a legendary one, or an up-and-coming country artist to a legend like Willie Nelson and of course Merle Haggard, Michael Martin Murphy, Tanya Tucker, Stu Cook and Doug 'Cosmo' Clifford from Credence Clearwater Revival. There were always lots of big songwriters, like Sonny Throckmorton and Monte Warden – who wrote #1s for George Strait – songwriters have always been a central focus since Freddy is a songwriter.

Freddy Powers: "Sonny Throckmorton is one of my hero songwriters. He has written 15 or 20 No. 1 songs, and he is very prolific. His stories – his songs are stories you know."

Sonny Throckmorton: I know Freddy's rhythm playing, every time I've ever heard him play, he's just the greatest player I've ever heard in my life on rhythm, he's amazing. If he was going to be on stage, and you were Merle Haggard, you wanted Freddy. If it was Willie, it'd be good to have him because he could play anything that Willie could sing, he was an amazing guitar player. He's the kind of guitar player that these young people are not going to get to hear that particular style that he played because there's not many people who can do that, or they don't want to because if they're good enough to play rhythm guitar that way, they want to be a lead guitar. So they're not going to exhibit a lot of that rhythm, where his was concentrated rhythm and it was unbelievable. I know when he dies and goes to heaven, they'll have a real good rhythm player up there.

Molly McKnight: We all love Freddy, what a talent! If you could have known him back then, he had more energy than anyone in the room. I remember the first time I saw him, he was playing the banjo, and boy he was a wonderful guitar player. He and his guitar player Django Porter would just sit out at a picnic table and Freddy would do a run then Django would do a run, then they'd put it together.

Catherine Powers: Originally, Freddy would sit in the center of a room full of musicians – 20, 30 musicians all sitting around – all pickin' with Freddy giving everybody opportunities to shine, and then when Freddy no longer was able to play, that's when we turned it into a party honoring Freddy. That was a very special celebration of Freddy's signature playing style, because there were so many unknown, up-and-coming guitar players throughout the years that have attended these parties to play with and learn from Freddy. It was pretty funny because usually when they'd first walk in, they'd be scared to death! He'd invite them to sit down and play with him, and at first, they'd say "Oh no, I can't sit down and play with you, I'm not good enough to play with you guys," and Freddy would coax them out. He would tell them, "Play along, just play along as best you can with what you can, follow my hands," so even during these Pickin' Parties, he was giving lessons to new players all the time.

To create as intimate and stripped-back-to-basics performing atmosphere as possible, we decided to hold the party in our living room, which really succeeded in making everyone feel at home and very respectful of the players performing at any given time. We used to always joke seriously with everyone, "It's the funnest, quietest picking party you'll ever go to," because when a performer was playing, there was *NO TALKING*. In fact, that became our number one rule on the wall. We used to call them the Coach Darrell Royal Rules, because of his Pickin' Parties at his golf tournaments where Freddy was pretty much always the host for many years.

Edith Royal: Freddy used to have a lot of pickin' parties at his house too, and Darrell would always be there, and I remember going to Freddy and Catherine's for those, and everybody would bring a dish. Freddy has had a lot of people who met him at our and he's and Catherine's Pickin' Parties over the years, everybody who could get in those rooms would come, if they were invited. Freddy was well known as somebody who helped whoever he could.

Catherine Powers: It would stay busy the entire day too, we had so many songwriters and pickers wanting to be part of what was going on that we'd start at one in the afternoon and at four o'clock in the morning we're still playing! I think in part because it was structured and themed so differently from everything going on in town, and because of Freddy's legend in Texas looming as large as it did. Over the next three or four years, our Pickin' Parties grew from 50 to 500 and spilling out of the house because our living room was only big enough to seat around 200 people in that living room easy (which still would have been considered a large audience given the setting). So by the first decade of the Millennium, it got so popular that every year there would be people spilling out all over the place, and the vibe was so infectious that out in the yard, there'd be little circles of players picking together everywhere. Then on our back porch we had this big old picnic table, and there'd be groups of people sitting out there smoking and picking.

Once we'd moved out of the house and over to the La Hacienda RV Park, who knew what we were going through with Freddy's condition, kept a permanent spot for us to be able to come in and out of town as we pleased, so they took good care of us. As we were downsizing, thankfully we were lucky by then that the Whitliff Museum at the Texas State University at San Marcus, Texas inducted his memorabilia into their archives..

We've kept the Pickin' Party tradition going over there for years to where it's become such a tradition that they honored Freddy by dedicating the venue the FREDDY POWERS PICKIN' PAVILLION, where we began hosting the pickin' parties shortly after moving off of Willie's golf course. We'd been invited over by the owner Ken Butschek to check the pavilion out as a possible new venue to start hosting the parties. It was supposed to be just for the weekend, but we parked our bus and never left. Not everyone realizes it either but R.V. parks are a BIG draw for singer-songwriters and even bands because those pavilions can pack 300, 400 people in for a concert, and Freddy had played that circuit for years before we became residents. Lucky for us, this is one of the finest RV resorts in the Austin area. In fact, when word got into town we'd moved over, the Austin Statesman came out to do a story on the resort and featured Freddy and our new home:

The Austin Statesman, 2010: "A few yards away, at a party building, a band is rehearsing in the middle of the afternoon. Freddy Powers, a singer-songwriter who toured for years with Merle Haggard, is preparing his band, Stop the Truck, for an appearance at Willie Nelson's Fourth of July picnic. Powers and his wife, Catherine, donated his memorabilia to Texas State University in San Marcos after he was diagnosed with Parkinson's disease. They are now living the RV lifestyle."

Catherine Powers: I get inundated each and every year with fans emailing and calling me to inquire about whether there will be a party this year, I always say "I plan on keeping these parties going for the rest of our lives, as long as there's a place to have a Freddy Powers party, we'll have one." Thankfully, the new owners of the RV resort have proudly continued on what has now become a proud tradition of hosting the annual Pickin Parties, and so as long as there's a Freddy Powers Pickin' Pavilion standing, there will always be a Freddy Powers' Pickin' Party! It has never lost its lure with fans either, and it's funny because on the day of the party every year, you can see cars lined up down the road pulling into the park looking just like outdoor amphitheaters during the summertime, so the demand has sustained itself.

Singer/Songwriter Lee Duffy: I met Freddy Powers through Rattlesnake Annie and became an immediate fan of his. I got to go to a picker's circle and hear Freddy do all these songs that he'd written for Merle Haggard. Freddy had moved back to town and Catherine was very kind and encouraging. I was petrified; she was saying "You're doing great. Don't let them see you sweat. You look good." She helped me out. She didn't just open the door for me, she opened the door, put me in the damn car and drove me there. Freddy invited me to Coach Royal's golf tournament with all the best singer/songwriters in the world. Freddy was coach's side-kick; Freddy runs the Pickin' part of the show. He knew how shy I was, if I'm in front of a microphone, I can't speak. I was petrified that I wasn't good enough.

Freddy was in the middle of singing *'Riding High'* from his *Country Jazz* album. The first line is "They told us we would never reach the top, they told us we would probably not." I love it. I had jammed with him a few times at his house because he was just really pulling it out of me. I would show up there every day. He leaves the guitar and microphone out 24/7. He would get up early and play until lunch. I would just ask for every song I knew. Catherine found this satchel of a couple hundred songs that he had written, which they found under a bed in Tyler at her mom's. He would just sort through them; he'd forgotten about five hundred of them, like diamonds.

So Freddy knew I would never sing out loud in front of all these people. He's in the middle of his show, in a room of singer/songwriters, trained professionals, and I'm minding my own business talking to Coach Royal, so excited that Freddy was singing "Riding High." I heard him introduce me as this wonderful singer and friend of his. I was melting. He doesn't play this in the same key I sing, and I heard him say to the band, "We're going to change this to the key of A." He just looked at me and smiled. You can't say no to Freddy, what could I do? I had to sing.

Catherine Powers: Freddy and I are especially proud of the fact that through our parties, we've had artists land record deals, songs get picked up by publishers, performers get picked up to go out on tour, so through Freddy's parties, once again, he has opened the door for other musicians to move upward in their careers. I remember one year NPR Radio was covering the *South by Southwest Festival* in Austin. The first week of the Festival is all about the movie industry, and then the second week, which focuses on the music industry. They got into talking all about who was in town and what was going on, and the NPR journalist covering the Festival closed his segment with the following nod: "And *renegade* Freddy Powers had his own star-studded South by Southwest Party at his home!"

Theresa Figg, Co-Curator Freddy Powers Pickin' Parties: When I first met the Powers, my sons were playing baseball, and one of their team mates' dad was Kelly Gruber, a pro Baseball player for the Toronto Bluejays. He saw my passion and interest in music, and said "You need to meet Freddy and Catherine Powers, and take this group you're promoting Jason and Charlie Caraway, you need to get them to the pickin' parties. That's who you need to meet!" Back then, a lot of local musicians and songwriters just starting out, if they wanted to get discovered, getting seen and heard by Freddy Powers, that was sort of the buzz in Spicewood and throughout Austin that Freddy could hear you and help. So getting bands I was promoting back then on the list was important so Freddy could hear them.

So I first started attending the Pickin' Parties when they were still held up in Spicewood in 2007, 2008, 2009, and then when they moved over to the La Hacienda Pickin' Pavilion. Back when I first started attending, I also met local artists who played them like Evelyn and Eugene Brown, who had put a little band together called Merry Go Round, and Eugene was a really good friend of Freddy's. Some other local acts playing those parties was Andrea Marie, who introduced me to Sonny Throckmorton, who was sitting right next to Freddy the first time I met him. Others I met included people like Pauline Reese, Bo Porter, Carl Hutchins, George Ensley, and eventually Mary Sarah and Michael Martin Murphy, who wrote my favorite song "Wild Fire." It felt like home.

The first time I met Freddy, I was really shy, and he looked at me with his big blue eyes when I told him I was a songwriter was invited me to play at his pickin' party. So I signed myself up, and was last on the list, and was shaking the entire time, terrified surrounded by all these good musicians, I could hardly breathe! So when my time came, it was 10 PM, and I was just about to go on when someone on the production side said "Sorry, its 10 PM, we have to shut down…" I had this 16-year-old guitar player with me, Dylan Robichaud, and this was at La Hacienda, and we sat down on the fireplace and started playing anyway, and Freddy and Catherine stayed and listened to me.

A week later, I checked my email, and Catherine invited me back to play again, and the fact she was still there after 10 o'clock and was paying attention to a nobody telling me "Everybody loved your music, next time we're going to put you in a better slot." It was so humbling that Freddy and Catherine were paying attention, and because she cared, I fell in love both of them. I knew there was something really, really special about them – more than just music – and I was hooked on them as people!

Wayne Ahart: One year, Freddy got up on stage at one of he and Catherine's Pickin' Parties, and he was sitting in his wheel chair, and once he started singing, he began to shake pretty violently. I had helped get him up there, and was standing next to him so I just reached down and held his hand to keep it from shaking, and he sang 2 or 3 songs and did a real good job. That was quite a moment though. Then there was a fella in our group, Mike Burke, and his wife and my son Kevin, who is a singer-songwriter, and Freddy was an encouragement to him and a lot of help to him, and he's one of Freddy's little offshoots who has learned a lot from him. I always appreciated Freddy's interest in doing what he could to help young people and he helped a lot of them. Young people would naturally come to him for advice, and he freely gave it.

Catherine Powers: Once they caught on, we were having pickin' parties all the time throughout the year. The other one that has become the most famous within the Austin and broader songwriting community worldwide is the New Years Day Black Eyed Pea and Cabbage Pickin' Party, we've actually had people travel from England, Switzerland, France and even as far as Barbados to make their vacation around our pickin' parties. The New Years Day Black Eyed Pea and Cabbage party got its start in the 1990s while we were still living back at the house on Willie's Golf course when somebody asked us one year if we were going to have a New Year's Eve pickin' party. Freddy said "Well, most of the musicians will be out working that night, so we probably wouldn't have a very good party, so why don't we have a party on New Year's Day, and we'll serve black eyed peas and cabbage." So we started hosting those, and they were such a hit that the next thing I knew, we'd moved over to the Freddy Powers Pickin' Pavilion and people were bringing their own versions of black eyed peas and cabbage! (laughs) It was like having a tasting party with black eyes peas and cabbage and wonderful, talented musicians playing from all around the world in the background.

Theresa Figg: I've been helping Catherine run the Pickin' Parties from 2012 through the Present. I remember the point where Eugene – who'd helped organize the pickin' parties – was dying of cancer, and Freddy's health with Parkinson's was starting to go downhill. And Catherine – this beautiful lady trying to keep this man alive, was also trying to keep his dream live, which were these Pickin' Parties – and she was doing it all by herself. She was running over here taking care of this, running over there taking care of that, getting on stage to announce acts and taking care of all these musicians, encouraging and supporting and helping them, and I thought "She needs help… Can I help you?", and she replied "ABSOLUTELY! Here's the list, it's yours!" So for the past 10 years, I've helped run the Pickin' Parties, and I remember praying to God for the strength to do this, after 20 years of their love poured into all these people, because Freddy had been holding these

Pickin' parties since they'd moved back to Austin in the mid-90s! It was a hollowed tradition round here, and this was their baby, but there was something inside of me that said "You can do this!"

So I started helping with the list and the introductions and Catherine trained me on how to run all of it, and Freddy would keep coming in the years after that. But he couldn't talk by then, so he'd just watch me with his big blue eyes running the Pickin' Parties with Catherine, and I could see he was telling me "Help keep my spirit alive, pass on the torch, keep this going..." Then I remember the first year Catherine called me and told me Freddy was too sick to make the trip, and that was the first time I had to run it by myself! I prayed so hard, because I didn't know if I could do this, but I knew the show had to go on and that Freddy was still fighting on to keep himself and this alive. We had Chris Newbury in that year, and Sonny Throckmorton, and we all pitched in and pulled it off, and I've been running it with Catherine since – Waylon Payne has played here, and I feel like we haven't even gotten started!

One of the beautiful things about the Pickin' Parties while Freddy was still alive is he loved to help young musicians, so I'd met some young musicians and saw their passion, and invited them to the Pickin' Party. Because they went there and saw other musicians and songwriters and bands up on stage playing, it inspired confidence in them that they could too. This one boy Lucas Sousa was 15 and told me he played guitar and sang, so I told him, "At the next pickin' party, you get up on stage and play 3 songs," and he'd never sang or played on stage before. But he felt safe, and got up there on stage with Freddy sitting behind him, and out of 30 bands, he was the only artist who got a standing ovation. That's how special the Pickin' Parties were, and that boy was invited from there to play the Grumpy Saloon, and that launched his career. Lucas Sousa is now opening for Rick Trevino on the road and on his way to becoming a star! One footnote that was really cool is that, because by the nature of the Pickin' Parties, people play their original songs, between Lucas' first and second pickin' parties, he wrote an E.P. of songs, and one of them is a Tribute to Freddy. Every show Lucas would play – no matter the venue – he'd put Freddy's picture next to him on stage.

DO512.com: "The Lucas Sousa Band is three high school seniors (& 1 slightly older friend) from the Austin/Round Rock area who have been close friends since childhood. They love music, fishing, hunting, and showing their livestock animals at FFA shows (Future Farmers of America)! Do not let their age fool you—their musical talent and high energy, power-packed performance will blow you away! Their debut was at the legendary Freddy Powers SXSW pickin' party less than 2 years ago. Besides playing clubs in and around Austin, they have also been featured on Songwriters Across Texas Radio Show. Not only on the radio part but also on the TV show. Their songs ring out with the tried and true country classic sounds of George Strait, Garth Brooks, Johnny Cash, also red dirt radio Randy Rogers and many more!"

Lucas Sousa: The Pickin' Party is a huge part of everything, its where I started, and the great thing I really loved about it was, I started out playing my first one at 15 years old, and most of the performers were in their 50s all the way up through their 70s sometimes. So I got to experience a traditional, old-school side of Country, before I went into doing any other kind of country music you have to play now-a days just to get on the road. I appreciated that my first audience was kind of that Freddy Powers audience.

As far as getting on stage to begin with, it's really hard to be 15 and have that opportunity, and as far as songwriting, the Pickin' Parties are the place to do it because the audience is going to listen to every single word of what you say and play. The respect that's in that room whenever you're singing to a song, especially with Catherine in the back, you DON'T talk in there, you listen! You can see that DEEP sense of respect she has for musicians and songwriters and to actually appreciate their performance in the moment. Take me for instance, at my first couple Pickin' Parties, I would play cover songs, and the more I attended and listened to other songwriters, I started to realize "Man, this is the place for originals, let me bring originals here, and try them out here." That was an important part of getting me to start writing songs, and I might have stuck to covers for a long time if I'd not had that kind of environment around me.

I come back every year to play Freddy's annual Pickin' Parties in January and March, no matter where else we're playing, whether being on Songwriters Across Texas or Coke FM, and Catherine pushed some buttons to help make that happen. Or opening for Rick Trevino or Mark Crowe or Sam Riggs or Cory Marrow, and I've fallen in love with just the process of becoming a really good musician, and that's another thing from the Pickin' Parties that you learn. You listen to players who are SO talented, not just that write songs but can play the HELL out of a guitar! I like to help keep that music going because there's such a large audience of people who still appreciate it so much.

Catherine Powers: That has continued to be a special feature of the pickin' parties is it was a great place for local musicians and bands to get gigs from the promoters and club owners and managers and Austin record industry people who would be sitting in the audience at any given time. Lots of artists got discovered by going to Freddy's Pickin' Parties. Songwriters Across Texas for instance would talent scout there, and like Lucas with other new artists on the rise would get TV spots on that show because they played at the pickin' parties, sometimes for the first time as Theresa was saying.

Theresa Figg: We have artists who wind up on radio shows, get opening act slots on bigger shows, who got their start right here on this stage at the Freddy Powers Pickin' Parties. A really cool thing happened with a picking party one year. I got an email from this band I'd never heard of called Pendulum Heart, and they said they'd just heard about the picking parties and were already doing Freddy Powers songs! They said he was their idol, and style of music, so we invited them to come out and play, and they BLEW US AWAY! They were a younger generation playing Freddy's music in Freddy's style, so the power of his influence is reaching younger bands and permeating in the younger generations and they're regulars now at every annual Freddy Powers Pickin' Party. Then Jessica Meuse, who went to # 4 on American Idol, she played here on this stage, so there's A LOT of talent, Katie Lynn from America's Top Talent, played in 2019.

Because Freddy has an international following, another thing they did with the Pickin' Parties has had a liaison with a Country Music Festival in France, and Freddy's played at it, his band Stop the Truck has played there, Mary Sarah has played there, and they come and bring artists from France here who play the show. We average up to 500 in the audience and 30 acts each year, all in one day! It's like a big family reunion every year, especially because people travel from far and wide to attend, be it driving across Texas or even the country over the years to see Freddy. A lot of them still make the trip because it's really grown to be a big family! There's residents at La Hacienda who only live here certain times of the year, so this is something really special they look forward to, and being part of the history. It's really transformed my life in so many ways and the friends I've made here are some of the most beautiful, incredible, warm, loving people on this planet. The Pickin' Parties have gone international, and now in 2021, we've started broadcasting them on Facebook's FACETIME, and SKYPE and ZOOM so fans can watch them each year all over the world!

Tanya Tucker: I went to a Black Eyed Peas and Cabbage Pickin' Party on New Year's Day, the one they do every year, and at this point, Freddy was already in the wheelchair, and we spent the night out there and I got to see how cool it was to go to these things. A lot of great writers show up and sing and play, and you could almost get your whole new album just from going to one of those Pickin Parties!

It was so cool, everybody brings something they've cooked, and there's no egos, everybody just has a good time, and a lot to drink and a lot to eat, and you hear a lot of great music: stuff that's never been recorded, stuff that has been recorded, big records, and you get to see where a song really came from. That's what I like about it. I love the fact too that you can go and hear new stuff, because that's what I'm always up for: hearing new songs and just songs that I've never heard before, that haven't been recorded or haven't been hits. It's a great way for an artist to get new songs, and I have done that for years, gone to events like Freddy's, that's where we used to write, was with a group of people that liked each other, were talented, and would get in a room with a few guitars and start writing something.

Moe Monsarrat: I just loved the way everybody passed the songs around and when it came to Freddy, the band would play one of his songs. You got to meet a lot of interesting people there, you never knew who would come. I remember meeting the bassist from Credence Clearwater Revival, that was like meeting Willie Mays to me! As time went on and it got to where Freddy was more and more ill and could just sit there and sing, and we'd play some of his songs and everybody would jam on them. Then, once it moved over to the Pavilion at the La Hacienda, instead of us all sitting around passing the guitars, it became a thing where acts would get up and play one after the other, and try to play for Freddy. Its act after act, it's not so much a jam session like it once was but everybody was there in his honor, and that's where it is today.

Catherine Powers: Those pickin' parties became and still are to this day a huge event, even to where people tell us they book their vacations around our Pickin' Party dates. Still to date, the droves of songwriters especially that come each year to play for Freddy, and it's really quite touching to watch because it's really like an event within an event. Where they used to play with Freddy at the parties, now they come to play for him, and often will perform Freddy's own songs for him that he can't play or sing himself anymore. That really has helped us come full-circle with the spirit of what the Pickin' Parties have always been about: a circle of songwriters, playing their own new songs as well as the classics, including Freddy's.

Our main goal every year is that Freddy is sitting out there watching and hearing these songwriters pay homage to his legacy and perform his hits, both for him and for the wonderful audiences that always wind up attending year after year, and hopefully still will for years to come. Even now, I take him over to the Flora-Bama, and you can see the energy and light in his face when they play one of his own songs to him, that became quite special in his final years that people were playing for instead of listening to Freddy. They continue to keep his music alive today in the same spirit, so even though he's physically gone his songs and legend live on.

Photo Chapter 2

Freddy Powers (left) and legendary Country Songwriter (center) Floyd Tillman on Stage Playing Together, early 2000s

Freddy and Catherine Powers Presenting Check to the Capitol Area Parkinson's Society from the Freddy Powers Parkinson's Foundation

Freddy and Don Powers 2000s

Capitol Records President Letter to Freddy for Co-Production Work on Merle Haggard's 2004 "Unforgettable" LP

Freddy and Amelia

Freddy and the Spoiled Doves of Texas with Catherine center in front of Freddy

Freddy and Catherine w their new dog, a piano-playing Russian Toy Terrier, Olga

Freddy Powers' Bullshitter's Bullshitter Award from the Royal Knights of the Raccoon, aka Coondicks, April, 2010

Whereas:
Texans are known the world over as bullshitters without peer, and Texans take pride in the fine art and nuance of Bullshitting, and Texans understand that one can inspire to high morals, ethics and be held in highest respect while remaining a Bullshitter par excelance, be it known throughout the Great State of Texas and all other sovereign countries, that

Freddy Powers

Has been declared and shall heretofore be acknowledged as a

BULLSHITTER'S BULLSHITTER

And from this day forward be allowed to wear his pants tucked inside his boots, the international symbol of the Master Bullshitter.

In witness thereof, this certificate is issued at West Pole Bee Caves, TX, on this day, April 21 2010

- GOD BLESS TEXAS -

Empresatio

Texas State University Official Invitation to the Prestigious Wittliff Collections' Freddy Powers Exhibit/Archives Reception, April, 2011

Freddy Powers in the later-00s while he could still play Guitar

Freddy Powers and Merle Haggard in the later 2000s at a Freddy Powers Parkinson's Foundation Fundraiser event

Freddy Powers NSAI Award

Family photo brothers Jerry, Freddy, Wallace and Don Powers (back row), and sister Mary Lou, Mother Ninnie, and Norma Powers (left to right)

Freddy Powers, Whitey Shafer, and Curly Corwin

Freddy with Big Kenny Alphin & John Rich

Freddy Powers Dirty Joke Night at John Rich

Freddy with friend Gretchen Wilson

Freddy w Gretchen Wilson, John Rich, and Mel Tillman, at the Freddy Powers Dirty Joke Night

Ray Price, Freddy, Owen Wilson and Poodle Locke on set for Willie Nelson music video 'You Don't Think I'm Funny Anymore'

Freddy and Catherine dressed for the Agatha Christy game at Merle Haggard's Thanksgiving party

Freddy, Coach Darrell Royal, Randy Willis and Rattlesnake Annie

Freddy, Kris Kristopherson,
Texas Heritage Songwriters Hall of Fame Recipients 2006

Freddy with Coach Royal and his hero
Charlie Duke who walked on the Moon Apollo 16

Freddy's custom-made
Gibson guitar front

Freddy's custom-made
Gibson guitar frontback

Pauline Reese, Freddy Powers II, Sonny Throckmorton, Freddy Powers, Kris Kristopherson, and Lee Duffy

Texas Heritage Songwriters Induction

THE TEXAS HERITAGE Songwriters' ASSOCIATION

Join us in a Texas Homecoming Celebration honoring Texas Legends

Freddy Powers **Kris Kristofferson**

Sonny Throckmorton **Coach Darrell Royal**

as they are inducted into the Texas Heritage Songwriters Association.

Featuring performances by the honorees and many other notable Texas musicians.

Sunday, March 12, 2006
3:00 p.m. - 6:00 p.m.
Hills Cafe
4700 South Congress Avenue
Austin, Texas

Limited number of tickets available online at:
www.texasheritagesongwriters.com

Pickin' Party in our living room

Joi Davis Anderson, Freddy and Bruce Channel

Leroy Parnell recording Freddy singing

Country Star John Rich Playing for Freddy on the Powers' Bus, 2013

Freddy and Catherine Powers and Country Star Toby Keith (far right), 2013

Freddy Big & Rich and Tanya Tucker, 2013

Freddy and Catherine Powers at "Nashville Songwriter" Book Release, pictured w/ fellow legendary country songwriters Neil Thrasher, Sonny Curtis, Bob DiPiero and Kelley Lovelace (top row) and Jeff Silbar and Craig Wiseman (1st and 2nd in, bottom left) 2014

Freddy and biographer Jake Brown working on book on bus on Freddy's 82nd Birthday

Freddy at legendary Poodie's, Spicewood, TX

Freddy Powers' Certificate of Baptism, Aug 2012

Freddy being kissed by the girls, JoBell Smith and Catherine

The Teacher and his students

Freddy with Cass and Mary Sarah

B.B. Morse, Freddy (front row),
Mike Burke, Michael Martin Murphy, and Pauline Reese (back row)

Freddy and Catherine 2015

Catherine and Olga with Freddy Powers on Florida Waters in his last days, 2016

Freddy's Full Marine Honors Burial w/ Handing Catherine Folded Flag, Flora-Bama, July, 2016

FREDDY POWERS
Legendary Singer • Songwriter • Producer
"A Hero to the Heros"
1931 - 2016

Freddy Powers "A Hero to the Heroes"
In Memoriam Picture, Summer, 2016

COUNTRY

HOME > MUSIC > COUNTRY MUSIC

JUNE 24, 2016 4:09PM ET

See Hayes Carll, John Doe's Moving Merle Haggard Cover

Singer-songwriters perform "I Always Get Lucky With You," written by the late Freddy Powers

By **STEPHEN L. BETTS**

L.A. punk legend **John Doe**, of X, meets Texas troubadour **Hayes Carll** for an acoustic version of the 1983 honky-tonk classic "I Always Get Lucky With You," and the results are profoundly moving. The pair's poignant in-studio performance of the tune will begin airing this weekend on Sirius/XM's Outlaw Country channel.

Penned by Merle Haggard with the late Freddy Powers, along with Gary Church and Tex Whitson, the song was covered by Haggard in 1981. Two years later, George Jones took it to Number One. Doe and Carll, while emulating the sweet spirit of the original versions, add mournful vocal touches that serve as a fitting tribute to the country icons.

Songwriter Freddy Powers **died Tuesday** after a long battle with Parkinson's disease. His string of Haggard Number Ones also includes "A Place to Fall Apart." *The Spree of '83*, Powers' authorized memoir, penned by Jake Brown with the songwriter and his wife, Catherine, will be published in February 2017.

The *Hayes Carll: Lovers and Leavers* special will air Saturday at 9:00 a.m. and 5:00 p.m./ET and on Sunday at 12:00 p.m. and 9:00 p.m./ET on SiriusXM Outlaw Country.

Freddy debuting Lauren Beller on KOOP Radio Station

CHAPTER 26: MENTORING A NEW GENERATION OF STARS

Catherine Powers: Something Freddy and I do laugh about a lot is that in more recent years, it seemed like girls were coming from out of everywhere wanting to learn from and be mentored by Freddy. One of our favorite early examples of that was Pauline Reese, I remember the first time she walked up to him she was 15 years old with a little boom box. Well, she set that boom box down and started singing for Freddy, and right there he told her, "Honey, you've got a great voice but if you can't play for yourself, if you can't back yourself, you'll be a slave to a band, and probably go no further than you and this boom box." So immediately Pauline went out and Molly McKnight bought her a guitar, and she played a little bit of guitar but not much, and before too long came back over that same day to get her first lesson from Freddy, and it was like she almost moved in! She was there every day taking every opportunity she could to just sit there and pick and play with Freddy all day long.

Pauline Reese: I've spent 22 years of my life with Catherine and Freddy, who is like a Grandfather to me, he's by far one of my biggest influences in my career. My friend Molly McKnight, her father was a State Senator from Texas, Peyton McKnight, and she had known Freddy for years, and Peyton was one of those people in Government who got Willie and Merle and Freddy all these gigs with Government offices, because they just loved that crowd of guys, for good reason. So she introduced me to Freddy thinking that he would help me out musically, I already played guitar, but he really took it to a different level.

Molly McKnight: Pauline came to me when a friend of mine had brought her to me, and she was 15, and I had a son and a daughter, but sort of adopted her as my other daughter, and she was playing just here and there at the time. So we went to dinner one night and I said, "Pauline, have you ever heard Willie Nelson?" And when she said no, I asked if she'd like to, and of course she said yes, so I we went over to where Willie was playing, and of course it was packed when we got there. She was saying, "We'll never get in," and I said "Hush" and went to find Willie's road manager at the time Poodie. So the bouncer went to get Poodie, and of course he let us in, and Pauline could not believe it! So a little after that, I took her out to Freddy's for a guitar lesson, because Pauline didn't play the guitar at all, and of course, she learned to play the guitar with Freddy, and everybody sort of fell in love with her like I did.

Pauline Reese: So when we met, the three of us fell in love, and he and Catherine took me under their wing and into their house. I literally spent most of my teenage years going to their house and learning chords from Freddy, we'd write songs, I'd stay the night because it was so far away from where I was living in Leander at the time. My parents knew them, and thought it was great that I was working with this wonderful songwriter who was really taking the time to teach me the craft and about the business and everything else about it. I always wondered what his motivation was to take a 15-year-old girl under his wing, I will be forever grateful for a guy like him and his wife. I mean, what a cool wife to have to say, "Yeah, that girl's got some talent, let's help her out!" And I mean, it just wasn't helping me, I literally stayed at their house for years on and off.

Invariably, Willie would come over in the mornings and have coffee with Freddy, and I would just be a fly on the wall listening to these great stories and them just talking about the business and music. I was so fortunate to be in a position that I was in soaking everything up like a sponge. Freddy would talk to Merle every couple of days on the phone, and Merle knew who I was because of Freddy, Willie knew who I was because of Freddy, and I credit my duets with Willie to Freddy, because I wouldn't have known Willie the way that I do if it weren't for Freddy and Catherine. He

LOVED to play jokes on people, and I think a big part of his and Willie and Merle's friendship was telling jokes back and forth, whatever the latest ones they had heard. So it was just constant joke telling, and I had to start categorizing all of the jokes so that I could keep up! (laughs)

Molly McKnight: So I introduced her around to all the people I knew, but Freddy really took to her and she to him, and it's not hard to like Freddy Powers. One thing led to another, and she called me one day and said, "Guess what I'm doing?", and when I told her I had no idea, she said "I'm playing golf with Willie Nelson, Sonny Throckmorton and Freddy!" I replied, "Well, you're in high cotton, aren't you!" So that's sort of how she got started out in the business, and Freddy was a big part of that.

Catherine Powers: Pauline from those lessons with Freddy learned a lot about songwriting and playing the guitar, and she went on to become a star in Texas. She's won every major award that an entertainer can win, and it's kind of a best-kept secret as a recording star, you don't have to leave the state of Texas to be a star. Texas is its own country, so you can have a huge name and make a living in the state, play large venues that would only be headlined by stars, and Pauline plays all the big shows and gets major radio play. In fact, she and Freddy had a hit they wrote together, *"One Less Honky Tonk"* that went all the way to the Top 10 on the Texas Music Charts.

Pauline Reese: With guitar playing, he taught me songs that had every chord in the book so that I could play anything, that was really important. Another thing that was really important Freddy did for me during those years is he would come out to my shows and watch and critique and say, "Let's video you so you can go back and watch yourself to see what's going on," so we would do that all the time. And I've gone through every old video tape of his old bands, and Catherine loved it, she loved that I was so into the old days of what Freddy had done. I think I heard every story about his life because I wanted to know more about him and how he ended up where he is, and how he wrote those songs because I wanted to be a great songwriter like him.

He was a great entertainer too, and he would also say, "When you walk in the back door, you better be walking straight onto the stage," and this is kind of an old-school thought process. But then he'd say, "You don't wanna be talking with everybody and doing all this stuff, you need to be getting on to the stage to perform: be a star and they'll treat you like a star." That was something he was really adamant about, and would get mad at me if I walked in to visit with people, which was difficult for me because I love people and love my fans and they've become my friends. So if I was out on the floor talking to somebody before a show and Freddy saw that, he would always come and gently lead me over toward the stage, and say "No no, you get on stage the second you walk in that back door, what did I tell you?"

Catherine Powers: He didn't give a whole lot of lessons, but was never one that gave lessons and then charged for it. I have seen Freddy take two guys, two guys who never played an instrument before, and gave them a guitar and six months later, he had them not only playing guitar, but had them singing and writing songs and performing with him. He gave them the courage and the ability to get up there and do what they really wanted to do all their lives, especially with some of the players that have come up playing in Freddy's band over the years. That includes players like Gary Church – who was just a 19-year-old kid when Freddy took him on, and he went on to play with Merle Haggard, and Mel Tillis and Ray Price – or Clint Strong or Django Porter. So when it comes to musicians, Freddy has worked with guys as young as a 16-year-old guitar player named Tommy Bell, and the Manuel Brothers, they called Freddy their mentor, there's so many.

Pauline Reese: One thing that I really soaked up and I think the only two people that really got this were Django Porter and I: it was the triplets, because Freddy – when he was in a band called the Powerhouse IV with three banjos and a tuba – was playing banjo and that's a lot of triplets to be playing and is a different style. So he brought that style of playing over to his guitar style, and that's what really made him stand out as a guitar player, because it was a very Django Reinhardt type of thing, but even more so because he played banjo for so many years. My grandfather played banjo as well, so I was like, "Well, yeah, that's killer," because it fits perfectly in swing music, it makes perfect sense, and kind of mimics the banjo sound.

So I do that still, even in the music I just wrote on my new record, it's kind of part of who I am as a player because I heard it in my ear since I was a kid through Freddy. I've even had other peers of mine, like Steve Carter, say "Can you teach me that thing that Freddy does? I never really took the time to learn how to do that", and his style really stands out – comparatively speaking – with other rhythm guitar players because that is its own instrument. I saw all these guys come along over the years, like Django when he was just coming into his own, when I first met Freddy he was just learning how to play from Freddy, and Steve Carter, who didn't come along till 2001. But I just remember all these people coming along into Freddy's life and just watching him embrace everybody, and what that did for their lives. He really deserves to be acknowledged for that from so many of us he helped along the way in our careers.

Catherine Powers: I can proudly say that out of all 30+ years I've been with Freddy, in a business where life-long grudges can be made off of a single bad encounter let alone the bad blood that can build between band mates, etc. over time. I've only run across a SINGLE, solitary example among any of the musicians who've worked for Freddy in bands or business, from unknown artists to superstars. Only one, and it was a situation where we had a former member of the Powerhouse IV, who we asked this former member to be part of a reunion performance since Freddy couldn't play himself anymore. Everybody in the band had signed on except for this one nameless member, and his excuse was over some gripe he made that he'd called Freddy years ago after he'd hooked up with Merle and claimed he wouldn't call him back.

Well, that was just not Freddy because he never met a request for a favor he didn't try to come through on, and I was in such disbelief that I finally called the guy myself, wanting to get to the bottom of what this was all about. He told me, "Freddy hooked up out there with Merle and I called him one time about a song, and he never got back with me." Well, I had to tell him, first of all, at that time, Freddy didn't have an assistant or personal secretary for himself, and more importantly, he was living out there on his houseboat with no phone! That was part of the point because there was a strong possibility he never even got the message, so next I asked him, "How did you try to get in touch with Freddy?", and he was very ugly – and obviously a little bitter – because he replied, "I don't care if he got the message or not, he never contacted me back."

That just ran contrary to history because throughout his career, there have been literally hundreds and hundreds of musicians who have played with Freddy. Every one of them still to this day will pay him compliments for the things he has done for them individually to open doors and make introductions that resulted in their careers getting a lift of some kind, and whether professionally or just musically as a player in what he taught them. They all appreciate it, and have thanked him years later for it because it made such an impact, because Freddy's word has always been gold when he referred a young up-and-coming player to a band for an audition or an artist considering opening acts or a promoter for a gig, it's been endless.

As a matter of fact, Freddy was one that was so loyal to his band that he would even put their name on a song he'd written when they didn't have anything to do with writing it so they could share in the revenues as a writer. He's even pulled his own song off a Merle Haggard album to make room for a writer he saw potential in, and lost money over it. But he never had a bad taste in his mouth or turned his back on them, he continued to help anyone out that he could, even if it cost him money. I've always been proud of how loudly that speaks to his character. He's always been someone who inspired people, whether it was an aspiring songwriter looking to learn how to write a song good enough to sell, or hit songwriters like Merle, who was the first one to see something special in Freddy as a songwriter, enough so to enlist him as a co-writer when Hag had thousands of songwriters banging down his door. Throughout his whole career, he's always been someone musicians felt comfortable enough to come to when they needed advice or guidance or a favor where contacts and making a call was concerned, because they also knew Freddy had enough respect among the live promoters, club owners and band leaders that his referral made a big difference as a foot in the door.

I remember a story Freddy told me about one of his band members who had asked him – with an obvious mix of admiration and envy – "Freddy, I work as hard as you do, don't I?", and Freddy said, "Yeah," and next he said, "I put in as many hours as you on that stage, don't I?", and again, Freddy answered, "Yeah." So then he got right to the point of his frustration: "Well then Freddy, how come I don't make as much money as you do?", and Freddy gave him a constructive and honest response – he was never disrespectful. But, Freddy had told him because I booked the job, if you book a job and hire me then you'll make more and I less. I remember Freddy said because it was one of those rare situations where at first, what Freddy said didn't satisfy him when he quit the band. He must have let what Freddy had told him sink in, a couple years later, sure enough, the phone rang with an apology from this player, and he said, "Freddy, I never knew what it was like being the leader of the band until I *tried* to be a band leader myself. That was probably the best thing you could have ever done for me, was to tell me that." What Freddy had told him had ultimately turned out to be exactly the kick in the ass he needed at that point in his career.

Moments like that were why many people came to Freddy for advice over the years, first and foremost because he always made himself approachable and accessible. Equally and maybe more importantly, because they knew there was enough wisdom naturally woven into his conversational response that they knew they'd walk away better for it. Professionally, as a player, and if you want a real measure of all the people Freddy's helped throughout their careers, to this day, I get strangers – to me – calling to check on how he's doing. People I've never met, but even if it was back in the 60s or 70s, there was something substantial enough about their connection with Freddy that it lasted their whole career. I never get off the phone with any of them without them telling me how much Freddy means to them personally, as much as he has professionally because he always made time for everyone.

Another one of our favorite mentor moments came when this friend of ours sent us a video over the internet of this little girl who was five years old at the time singing a song of Freddy's. It turned out as fate would have it that she lived right down the road from us. So we go to meet her at her house, we're visiting and all of a sudden, she grabs Freddy's hand and says, "Mr. Freddy, I want you to come to my bedroom," which got us all laughing. She takes Freddy back there, and hanging over her bed are two framed pictures: one was of Floyd Tillman – and how many five-year-old in their lives have ever heard of Floyd Tillman? (laughs) The other was of Freddy, those were the two pictures of her country heroes she had hanging in her bedroom.

Well, immediately, right off the bat, Freddy tells her dad, "She's gotta learn to play an instrument," and the next thing you know, she gets her hands on a Ukulele and with that ukulele, this little girl by the time she was seven years old, was writing songs, winning songwriting contests with adults in Austin, Texas! She probably is to this day the closest one who can play Freddy's riffs, even more so than Steve Carter, who became what we have always called "Freddy's hands" once he lost the ability to play guitar. But that little girl's name was Lauren Beller, She copied Freddy and learned all his songs. After two years she was on T.V. with him doing performances. So little Lauren became a pretty well-known household name right there in Texas before she was even 10 years old.

"The King of Country Dixie Swing"
(Written by Lauren and Jeff Beller)

Vs 1
He came from west Texas
With a pen in his hand
Writing and singing songs so grand……..so grand

Vs 2
A guitar on his knee
He plays a song and sings
Country, Dixie or Swing, hear him sing…….hear him sing

Bridge
You can tell by the company he keeps
He's in a league of his own
With all the greats who come to play with him
Paul Buskirk, Willie Nelson, Merle Haggard, George Jones

Verse
He's got a style all his own
He's got a style all his own
That's why Freddy's the King of Country-Dixie-Swing

Bridge
He's a master with the country sound
I tell you brother that's no lie
It's solid gold on your radio
A Friend in California, Texas, Silver Eagle, Natural High...

Verse
What more can we say
About the King of Country-Dixie-Swing
Well, maybe just one more thing,
Freddy we love youuuu Oh, Oh......Yea

Outro Verse
Hey, listen Freddy Powers
The pleasures been ours
Cause Freddy, Freddy,
We've Always Been Lucky With You............

Catherine Powers: Because Freddy could still share his creative opinion, this meant he could still produce too. That led us back into the studio for a number of special new projects over the past decade, perhaps most notably when out of the blue, future THE VOICE finalist and country star-on-the-rise Mary Sarah first came along. Initially discovered by Sharon Dennis and who has always referred to Freddy as her father in the music industry Sharon's first gig was playing drums for Freddy when she was just 18 years old. So she brought Mary Sarah to Freddy to meet him, and he liked her vocal style and thought he could work with her. Of course, the first piece of advice Freddy tells every girl – which he told Pauline Reese, who is another of his major protégés – is, "Honey, you got a great voice and you'll go really far, but you'll really go far and farther if you can play an instrument. You need to learn to play guitar," and he explained to her that if she didn't know how to play guitar, she would always be a slave to the musicians and would be singing to them, instead of them backing her. So Mary Sarah got a guitar, took some lessons, and is a great songwriter as well, a talent Freddy has also helped her develop over the years.

Mary Sarah: I first met Freddy in Austin, Texas. Freddy and Catherine asked if I could sing the national anthem at a charity function they were hosting. We had breakfast the next day. Freddy was not speaking much at the time but he was able to convey to Catherine... things he wanted me to know. Freddy was adamant about not just being a singer, but being a musician. I would say that I began to take guitar playing much more serious after meeting Freddy.

Catherine Powers: When we first had a meeting with her, it was just to hear her sing and Freddy was so blown away that when the thought came up with an idea of having Merle Haggard do a duet with her and he made it happen. That concept blossomed into what became Mary Sarah's *Bridges* album. Freddy has always said that the greatest achievement and honor for him as a songwriter or producer is to take an unknown and give them their start in the business. He couldn't play or perform any more at this point but could still produce, he became the Executive Producer on the project, and helped line up a lot of the major stars she did duets with throughout the record, including Willie Nelson, Ray Price and Merle Haggard. Between Freddy, Sharon Dennis and the Oak Ridge Boys, who also immediately wanted to be a part of Mary Sarah's career, doors started opening doors for her.

We were able to get 12 famous legends of country music, including Dolly Parton, Lynne Anderson, Ronnie Milsap, The Oak Ridge Boys, Neil Sedaka, Big Kenny and John Rich, Tanya Tucker, and she closes the album in a duet with Freddy titled, "*All I Wanna Do is Sing My Song*". With Freddy as the Executive Producer on the album, I wound up getting a crash course on record production during the making of the album after Freddy's ability to speak failed him completely. I had to become his voice on the album, which included things like reaching out to the artists and/or their management on all sorts of different management teams and personalities, and on and on. It was a lot to juggle while taking care of Freddy at the same time. In the long run, great training for the reality that I was having more and more to take over speaking on his behalf in matters of business, medical, personal, and musical decisions.

Mary Sarah: Freddy and Catherine were instrumental in pulling together *Bridges*. Without them... the heart of the project would have been missing. Ray Price, Merle Haggard, and Willie Nelson agreed to help Freddy finish this final project. Vince Gill also agreed because he knew of Freddy's work and artistry! I was humbled by the fact that he was putting his reputation and his friendships on the line for me. I know he believed in me enough to reach out to his closest friends and that faith changed my life. Freddy also gave my previous album, "*Crazy Good*" two thumbs up and that gave me the confidence to venture out in to more songwriting.

Catherine Powers: Everybody involved knew this was going to be Freddy's last project, his last big go-around, and I remember it was so touching. Ray Price had called us about it to check it out, and said, "Well, I'll do anything for Freddy," he went in the studio with Mary Sarah and they did the duet together. Mary Sarah's album took three years to complete, and she's still getting major publicity from it, and it's another project that is also bringing Freddy's name back out, because he hasn't worked since 2010 as far as going out on the road.

You have to refresh people's memory, and that will always be my goal, for the rest of my life, is to keep his name and music out there and current. That's why it's also great to have so many fans of his out there re-cutting or singing songs of his. For the first time as a cut, like "*Day and Nighttime Blues*", that song had only been cut by Freddy until recently, but now it's being made a favorite around here because it's being performed by Chris Newbury. Songs like that, that aren't his best known hits are making their way into the public by all these new artists performing and recording his songs.

Country Music Association CMA Close Up: "At just 18 years old, Mary Sarah is making herself known among Country Music legends. After years of performing and growing her own fan base through social media, Mary Sarah…with the help of executive producer, Freddy Powers…was inspired to create her latest project, an album titled *Bridges,* which features duets with some of Country's biggest names including Dolly Parton, Willie Nelson, Merle Haggard and Vince Gill."

Mary Sarah: My favorite song is "*Let's Chase Each Other around The Room Tonight.*" I love the playful lyrics and the melody. But I also was honored to sing, "*All I Wanna Do Is Sing My Song*" this song more than anything told me who Freddy was without him speaking. We connected in that song because that's all I ever wanna do is sing. Music heals and I could see it in Freddy.

Houston Press: "*Bridges* certainly has its heart in the right place. It's dedicated to Freddy Powers, the longtime Austin singer-songwriter and an old running buddy of Haggard's, who spotted Sarah early on and basically set this whole project in motion. Their tender closing duet, '*All I Wanna Do Is Sing My Song*', could choke up your average stone-faced DPS state trooper. (Now battling Parkinson's disease, Powers is also credited as an executive producer on the album.)"

Billboard Country: "All of the artists recorded live with the singer in the studio – a rarity these days. She says she knows they get tons of such offers all the time, but thanks to Freddy Powers – a longtime songwriting collaborator of Nelson and Haggard, the artists all signed on for the project."

The New York Times: "A salute to the latter, Ms. Sarah's mentor, whose voice has been silenced by Parkinson's disease."

Mary Sarah: I was able to spend many of nights singing to him as the Parkinson's was progressing. In the hospital, on the bus and even in the studio he would cry when I sang to him. His favorite song is *How Great Thou Art* and it was something he requested often. Those times will always remain very special to me. His eyes would light up and by the time I was finished he would be in tears. No doubt it was giving him strength!

Tanya Tucker: The first reason I did it was because Catherine asked me too, and I was glad to do it for her, I'm glad to do anything for her. She never asks much, but when she does, I'm ready to do it, and it was very cool that Mary Sarah was a new artist. You always want to give back and try to help out the new acts come along, and that's the other reason I did it, and they made it so easy for me. So I was proud to do it for Freddy and Catherine. I'll pretty much do anything they ask.

Catherine Powers: Mary Sarah's collaboration with Freddy would even inspire her boyfriend at the time, John Byron Carlton, to make him the subject of a truly touching College Entrance essay:

It was a Sunday night—September 16, just over a month ago—when I had one of the most influential, touching, inspiring, and emotional experiences of my life. As we walked into the hospital room, my girlfriend, her parents, and I looked at an 80-year old man; he was sitting in his bed, wrinkled, quiet, no more than 110 pounds. This man was Freddy Powers, a talented country artist who has played with many of the legends: Willie Nelson, Merle Haggard, you name it. He was also the executive producer for my girlfriend, Mary Sarah Gross, which is why I was there.

Mary Sarah was making a visit, her last visit, to Freddy; he was dying of Parkinson's disease—a degenerative disorder of the central nervous system—an illness that takes you from the inside, one in which you know what you want to do, but you physically cannot do it. I accompanied her because she told me he was an amazing man who had impacted her life greatly, and she wanted me there with her during this emotional time. I made my way over to him, said hello, patted his hand, and walked across the room to a chair. And when I turned around, I noticed something; his eyes, an extravagant sky blue, were still fixed on me. At this point in time, I had no clue why, but I was soon to find out.

I watched as Mary Sarah hugged him, kissed him, and then proceeded to sit down on the edge of his bed and hold his hand. She spoke to him softly, telling him that she loved him so much. But when he tried to speak back, his mouth slowly moved, and no words came with it. She looked at her father, Todd, and he said, "Well, Freddy, Mary Sarah wanted to sing you a song. Is that okay?" His reply, a low mumble, an understood 'Of course.' She sat there, still holding his hand, looking straight into his eyes. Todd began playing the chords of a song which was Freddy's favorite, a song which touched his heart, "*How Great Thou Art.*" Mary Sarah began to sing as Freddy stared straight back at her, and I will never forget when I saw the tears roll down his cheeks as she sang to him:

> *Then sings my soul*
> *My Savior, God, to Thee*
> *How great thou art*
> *How great thou art*

He may not be able to speak, I thought, but he can still, as strong as anything, feel the love of our God deeply in his heart. The rest of us listened 'til the end of the song, and when it was finished, we watched as Mary Sarah leaned on Freddy's shoulder, as they both cried. Then it came time for me to leave, and I felt the sadness as I walked towards him, knowing it was probably the last time I was ever going to see this man, who, even though I had only known for a short time, had made such an impact on my heart I could hardly explain it. And as I walked towards him, I noticed those giant blue eyes were again fixed on mine. When I reached the side of his bed, I didn't know what to say. I mean, I barely knew the man; what all could I say? So I laid my hand on his and said "It was very nice meeting you."

I turned to walk away, but as I turned, I noticed something out of the corner of my right eye—Freddy's hand was outstretched towards me. In complete awe, I turned my body back towards his and took his hand. As we stood there connected by a handshake, we also connected by a stare, right into each other's eyes. As I stood there, we just looked at each other, and that's when my tears began flowing. He observed my face and seemed to know why I was crying. I felt a small pull by his hand, and so I leaned in close, putting my ear close to his mouth, listening for anything he may have to say. And that is when I heard one of the most touching things I have ever heard in my life. "Take care of her, son." Another wave of tears came racing down my face as I replied, "With my life." As I squeezed his hand, I pressed my forehead against his, and then I said, "I'll see you again someday." And I left.

An eighty year old man with Parkinson's disease...can't hardly move, can barely speak, but he can love. That is what really influenced me that day, when I saw a man going through so much pain I cannot even imagine it, yet he still uses all the strength he has to show he loves someone an unbelievable amount. When I saw a man shed tears at such a beautiful song, knowing and showing how great our God really is. I've been having troubles in my relationship with Christ lately, and seeing this man helped strengthen my heart. It helped me listen for the voice and the love of God I've been striving for a while now. And through just that short amount of time, Freddy managed to influence me to love others with everything I have. He influenced me to never pity myself, to always protect the ones I care about. And on the night of Sunday, September 16, 2012, Freddy Powers influenced me to always love my God through anything and everything because I know that my God will always love me, and one day, I'll be coming home to him.

Catherine Powers: We were all so proud of Mary Sarah with not only the success of her *BRIDGES* project, but then watching her star rise even higher as she headlined at The Grand Ole Opry in 2016 – where she's appeared 5 times since. Then appeared weekly singing before MILLIONS of new fans as a contestant on Season 10 of THE VOICE television show on NBC, becoming a finalist. It made me and Freddy both so proud.

TasteofCountry.com: "Blake Shelton team on the 10th season of *The Voice* is off to a strong start with throwback singer Mary Sarah, who performed '*Where the Boys Are*' during the Blind Auditions on Monday night. The '60s tune took on new life as the young lady put her spin on it and showed off her classic voice, reminiscent of the decade gone by. From the first few notes of her performance she had coach Adam Levine on board — he spun his chair as quickly as she started singing. Next came Shelton and Pharrell, and finally, Christina Aguilera threw her hat in the ring, giving Mary Sarah her pick of all four coaches...Blake Shelton complimented: 'You actually sound like you came from that era. It's gonna be so refreshing to see somebody bring that era of music back to a stage like this. And then the Grand Ole Opry in Nashville — let's do that!' "

CountryRebel.com: "On Monday's episode of *The Voice*, 'retro-inspired singer' Mary Sarah competed in the Knockout round against fellow Team Blake teammate, Brittany Kennel. Both performed country songs, but only one could be named the victor. Kennel sang Shania Twain's '*You're Still The One*' and Sarah took on Loretta Lynn's '*You Ain't Woman Enough (To Take My Man)*.' Sarah performed the song as though it was an original and completely took charge of the stage. The attitude she brought to the song was perfect and her stage presence alone made it feel as though we were watching her headline a concert! Her performance had fans calling her a contender, frontrunner, and even offered her some song suggestions...All that we know is that she is an incredible vocalist who enjoys classic country as much as we do. This isn't the last you'll see of Sarah. Blake Shelton named her the winner of the Knockout round."

Mary Sarah, Carrie Powers, Catherine, Carson Bryan,
Flora-Bama co-owner Joe Gilchrist, Sandy Laird, Wayne Carson and Chris Newberry

CHAPTER 27: THE FLORA-BAMA

Catherine Powers: When I look back over the last 20 years, I still shake my head because I was in my late 40s when all this started, and was still young and strong as a blue Ox. By the time I got into my later 50s and early 60s, I started to feel the weight Freddy's condition was taking on both of us physically: over the years, I've damaged my shoulders and my back from carrying him everywhere so many years, and there came a point where I couldn't get him in and out of this bus myself anymore. That was a struggle in and of itself because it made us more dependent on others around us to pick up that slack, which is again why I'm continually so grateful Freddy had so many fans, friends and sympathizers around the country that – no matter where we pull in to – that were waiting to help us out with whatever we need.

We definitely had some adventures and misadventures along the way too that these dear friends of ours witnessed up close and personal, like Freddy's follies with golf carts! The first one of those happened when it was getting to that point where Freddy shouldn't have been driving. I didn't really have to take his license away from him, because one day when he was trying to back out of our driveway, and trying to turn, every time he would try he couldn't do it until he finally ran into the back end of our neighbor's truck. That's when he realized he didn't need to be driving the car anymore, but he could still get around okay on the golf cart until one of the craziest near-death experiences Freddy went through during his final pre-wheel chair days. It was horrifying at the time, but in hindsight, is downright funny because he survived it at all! Knowing how important his independence was to him, I went along with him driving the golf cart by himself for as long as we could till one day when Freddy was leaving to run up to La Hacienda's club house for his morning cup of coffee. I helped strap him into the cart with our Moscow Toy terrier Olga strapped into the passenger seat beside him – it would have made for a cute Face book photo looking back on it now.

As soon as they took off, Freddy's Parkinson's caused his foot to press uncontrollably against the gas pedal as he rocketed down the road, smashing through the front door of the La Hacienda R.V. Park's welcome center/kitchen building! From the inside looking out, you can imagine the poor counter clerk as they watched the front door blow off hinges as Freddy's golf cart crashed through the front of the store. That was all before he wound up plowing through the entire store, tearing down shelves and racks all the way through the building till it smashed through the back door! The mini-tornado of a mess that crash left in its path told me his golf cart driving days were over once and for all. It always broke my heart whenever that had to happen because it was like one more freedom Freddy was having taken away from him as the disease got worse and worse.

Cass Hunter: I remember back when Freddy could still get around some, he had this scooter at the Beach house at the Flora-Bama. There was like 10 girls, all of us, walking together, and he hit the gas, and he couldn't control his hands very well, so his hand gripped down and he couldn't release it and he went FLYING full-blast heading straight towards the road! We were all running and going, "Oh God, he's going to run right into traffic", and right before the highway, he suddenly turned, did a U-turn and flung gravel everywhere! (laughs) Scared us so bad we didn't know whether to laugh or cry!

Catherine Powers: Another of our golf cart adventures actually sent Freddy to the hospital. We were on Willie's golf course, and Freddy was letting Sonny Throckmorton drive, but Sonny was up on the green, and Freddy decided he was gonna pull the golf cart up to where Sonny was, and once again, he put that foot on the gas pedal and was sitting on the wrong side, trying to do it from the passenger's side. Well, his foot froze up with the Parkinson's, and when it did, he plowed into two golf carts totally destroying them, and if it hadn't been for them, he would have hit a tree head-on. Still, the impact threw him out of the golf cart and left him lying on the ground next to the wreck. So we had an ambulance come right down the middle of the fairway of Willie's golf course, before we'd even gotten out of that parking lot, it was already on KVET Radio that Freddy's had a wreck on Willie's golf course! After that, I started pushing him everywhere in his wheelchair, it was safer for both of us.

Tanya Tucker: Seriously, I think Catherine is a real angel, really, I really do. She is just unbelievable and it was so great that Freddy has someone like her, because anybody else, there's no way they'd still be around. There's nothing she wouldn't do for that man.

Catherine Powers: Thank God for the Flora-Bama because Joe Gilchrist and John McGinnis provided us a place to stay with all of our needs taken care of over what was supposed to be, according to doctors, only 3 or 4 months that lasted the last three and a half years Freddy was alive. I had help getting him out of the bus, and on days we couldn't get out where it was pouring down rain for instance, Freddy had a view and could sit there and look out his front windshield to watch the dolphins, watch the boats go by, and the Blue Angels when they fly by overhead. The Perdido Key Island, where Flora-Bama is located, is known as the Songwriter's Paradise because there's been a lot of songwriters who have made their home here, or who have their summer homes here, so it was a fitting community for Freddy and I to join. The island is loaded with musicians and songwriters who live all up and down this area, and there's been many songs written referring to Flora-Bama as the songwriter's paradise or the musician's paradise.

One thing that really makes this a paradise for songwriters and musicians is that they get paid. They get paid down here, where in Nashville and Austin, they're working for tips and for meals or the free drink. Here, they get the paycheck, the tips, the meal and the free drink. It's very fair the way they treat the talent down here. They've always been very respectful of songwriters of Freddy's stature, and Hank Cochran, and Red Lane – who's written major hits – we're all part of the Flora-Bama Family of songwriters and musicians, and of course, Kenny Chesney made it world-famous with his song "Flora-Bama."

Flora-Bama founder Joe Gilchrist is the co-founder of the annual Frank Brown Songwriting Festival, which Freddy played in previous years along with hundreds of songwriters from everywhere. They get paid vs. having to play for tips, and they're playing for an actual audience, which is one thing most songwriters don't get a lot of. A lot of these songwriters, people don't even know them by name, all they hear is a recording artist singing the song that the songwriter wrote. So when they come down here, they get to perform their songs and play on the same bill with songwriting legends like Wayne Carson – who wrote "*Get Me a Ticket for an Airplane*" or "*Always on My Mind*" for Willie Nelson. Then there's stars like Dean Dillon, Randy Brooks,

Buddy Cannon, Marla Cannon-Goodman, Bruce Channel, Mac Davis, Craig Dillingham, Rock Killough, Troy Martin, Jim McBride, Jim Rushing, Jerry Sally, Don Schlitz, who co-wrote *"The Gambler,"* Mark Sherrill – who co-wrote Blake Shelton's *"Ol Red"*, and on and on – so it's a great mix at the Frank Brown Festival.

Co-Owner Joe Gilchrist: Freddy had – and continues to have – a lot of musicians here that respect his history. For so long, I've been thrown in the middle of such wonderful characters and great music, and I mean, you can't make up people like Freddy and Hank Cochran: 8th grade education but communicates better than most anybody I've ever met with a PhD. Mickey Newbury, who gives words and music a feeling kind of like Ernest Hemingway's "The Old *Man in the Sea*," where you can feel the rope slide through your fingers. People who can transmit those kind of emotions through their songs deserve to be appreciated, and Freddy is one of those.

With Freddy in particular, and most of these people that create music, they should be appreciated because they are the kind of folks that make the burdens in life more bearable. So what I like to say is, "These folks express my feelings because I don't know how to", so when I listen to certain songs that affect me, I say to myself how fortunate I am to have people who can express emotions I wish I could express better, and Freddy's one of those people. It's infectious to have people do things that make your life more fun, not to mention more mentally stimulating, and I just feel fortunate to be a friend of Freddy and Catherine's. What could you want more of in life, than to sit down here on the coast with people who make the world a better place to live.

Catherine Powers: As a matter of fact, Freddy's final show was here at the Flora-Bama at the Frank Brown Songwriter's Festival, which was also sadly during the time when Freddy was starting to lose the ability to have the wind to be able to completely sing a song or tell his jokes. So even though Freddy would get most of the song out, most of the line out, then he would kind of fall off. But the audience, who'd been hearing and listening and watching Freddy for so many years at the Festival, that when Freddy was falling off on his words, the audience was picking him up and helping him. It was really a beautiful thing to see that audience connected with Freddy so well that they all knew the words to his songs. With the jokes, he still had the wind for talking soft, but his jokes were getting softer and softer, but the audience quieted down to hear every word he said.

At the end, I remember that crowd stood up and gave Freddy one of the most beautiful standing ovations. It wasn't just your standard stand-up-ovation and applaud – if there had been a roof, they lifted it. It was just so special. Freddy's a legend on this island, and he's highly respected and loved and looked up to. He's considered a hero, and the songwriters play his songs for him: Jack Robertson, aka Big Earle, does *"Natural High."* It was even the first dance at he and his wife's wedding. The Perdido Brothers, that's with Pat McCann who was one of Freddy's guitar players, do several of Freddy's songs, including *"Little Hotel Room"* and *"Daytime/Nighttime Blues,"* and Chris Newberry, whose father is Mickey Newberry, who performs *"I Always Get Lucky With You."* There are a lot of artists here on this island, and when we go in the room, they make a major deal and let everyone know that Freddy Powers is in the room.

Gulf Coast News Today, April, 2013: "Wednesday night was cause for several celebrations at the Flora-Bama. The iconic Lounge and Package Store marked its 35th year of existence, founder Joe Gilchrist celebrated his 71st birthday and a tribute was put on for legendary songwriter Freddy Powers. Perhaps Powers' most popular hit was, '*I Always Get Lucky With You*,' which was a smash hit for George Jones and Merle Haggard. Powers wrote numerous songs for and with Haggard. Another fellow who knows a thing or two about songwriting was also in the house, Wayne Carson, a member of the Nashville Songwriter's Hall of Fame. He penned the smash hit, '*The Letter*' for the Box Tops that reached No. 1 in 1967 and was subsequently redone by several famous artists. He was also a co-writer on '*Always On My Mind*' made famous by Willie Nelson but also recorded by numerous other artists."

Catherine Powers: Freddy didn't even have to be in the room over there, and someone would play one of Freddy's songs, and they'll make a big deal out of Freddy, even if he wasn't over there. They talk about Freddy as if he were there, and the audience knows all of his songs. That's what was so amazing with Toby Keith and Scotty Emerick, they were playing obscure songs, down deep cuts in the albums, not normally known by many, and songs that no one would normally sing. When other peers of Freddy are playing, someone like John Rich, would say, "This is a song Freddy and I wrote together", and tell the audience about Freddy, and writing with him and what a great experience it was.

The last song Freddy wrote, was right next to the Metropolitan, and he, Mary Sarah, and Mark Sherrill wrote it together. By then, Freddy had lost a lot of his ability to talk very well, but when he got over to that room and they started setting up to write, Freddy just started spilling out words. Thankfully, Mary realized what Freddy was doing and grabbed a paper plate and a pen, which was the closest thing she could find as Freddy started spilling out the words so quickly, she was writing them down just as fast. Then, when it was all done, and Mark and Mary called me in there and asked if I wanted to hear it, all of a sudden I realized I'd been hearing some of those lines in the days leading up to that write. Freddy would just blurt out, and I'd say, "What are you talking about?", and he'd go "I'm just thinking." So when I heard that song, I realized then, "Wow, that's what Freddy's been doing. He'd been lying over there in that bed, unable to speak very much, but he was still writing a song."

Mary Sarah: Writing "*Dreamin'*" was a very supernatural experience. Catherine would tell me he would try to talk and some of the lyrics to "*Dreamin'*" came out. She told him I think you have at least one more in you. I had made a trip to the Flora-Bama for songwriting with Mark Sherrill and the next thing I knew... we walked in the door of the condo and I had to grab paper plates to write the lyrics down because he was just saying everything so fast. He was mumbling but yet I could hear him clearly. It was an amazing night. Catherine confirmed when she heard what we wrote that he definitely was telling her he had one more song!

Catherine Powers: Freddy and I had so many good times down at the Flora-Bama, from the Mullet Toss – which is a huge event down here – and draws 30,000 people down to the beach to throw dead fish, that's a big huge event here. With boats stacked up all over the gulf beach and the Old River Bay. Then they have the Shin Dig on the Beach, which Mary Sarah played. They also have Bulls on the Beach, and the Barefoot Ball, where everyone dresses up in Evening gowns and attire but wears their flip-flops, so it was a Black-Tie affair beach-style.

Musically, there's a little bit of everything playing at the Flora-Bama at any given time, and Freddy and I enjoyed music playing everywhere around us at any given time. In the dome tent, referred to as the Bra Room, they will have anywhere from a single-to-duos to full band, and music starts in the morning, usually single songwriters or a duo, and runs all the way through the evening with the full bands playing. Then upstairs is basically the Listening Room, where songwriters exclusively play, (and No Talking is highly recommended). They will have singles, duos, or a round of writers playing together, then there's the tent stage, where the kids go to hear Rock & Roll. So the dome stage and tent stages are where you see the dancing happening, but it could be everyone rocking to country in the dome, and then over in the tent it might be straight Rock or Reggae. Then you have to bring it all the way across the street where they have two stages at The Flora-Bama Yacht Club, where they'll have either music playing on the inside or during the day outside on the beach stage. When you go over to the Flora-Bama Old River Bar and Grill, they have another two stages, one upstairs and one downstairs, so on this Island, just within this little conglomerate of clubs. I call it our compound: it's a total of seven different stages where music could be going on all stages on the weekend at the same time.

Co-Owner John McGinnis: Joe Gilchrist and I have been friends for a long time, probably 20-something years, and we worked a lot in the community together. Years ago before I got involved, he'd invited me to the songwriter festivals at the Flora-Bama, and I didn't go because I didn't think it'd be any fun. Then finally he drug me in there one day and I sat there for two days with him listening to songwriters and I fell in love with it and for the first time in my life, learned to listen.

Joe Gilchrist taught me how to listen, and from there, we became partners in the Flora-Bama, which holds the annual Frank Brown International Songwriter's Festival among others and has become world-famous over the last 50 years for hosting and being home to so many songwriters. We've been ranked the # 1 bar from Playboy to Maxim, CNN to Yahoo, and has the stamp from Jimmy Buffet, Kenny Chesney, etc. People think it's because of the parties and the fun that people have, and that's all great, but what made the Flora-Bama famous was all the musicians and songwriters – that's the secret sauce!

Catherine Powers: If you take Nashville or even Austin, who consider themselves big Music industry towns, the musicians and artists cannot make a living in these towns because they have to work for tips or they're getting a free meal. That's why when you mention the Flora-Bama to these folks, they refer to it as the "Songwriter's Paradise" because they can come down here and play and get paid a living wage and also get shown respect. On top of that, it doesn't make a difference whether it's a famous songwriter whose got 100 hits or an unknown, up and comer – they are all treated equally. So it's the music that brings people here, without the music, what would they do?

John McGinnis: That's the feeling you get, that the people on stage here love the Flora-Bama and love living here and playing their music and telling stories behind their songs, and the audience falls in love with that and feels like they're part of the show. And if the musicians and songwriters did not feel the way they do at the Flora-Bama, and weren't treated the way they are treated, the Flora-Bama would be another beach bar that maybe you'd heard of. But because the musicians and songwriters are the heart of it, that's why people come here, because they can't experience that anywhere else. Joe told me when we first partnered up together and I was excited to be diving into all this new expansion, he said, "Look, this is all important, but you got to understand one thing: The Flora-Bama is a shell with a bunch of great memories. That's all this building is, the people are the Flora-Bama."

People feel a sense of freedom when they come to the Flora-Bama, they can be themselves. They don't get to play what they want to play when they want to play it anywhere else in the business, vs. having to play hours of cover songs for tourists. Down here, Joe Gilchrist created the opposite, and so they are encouraged to play their own original songs or if they are covering somebody, it's one of their fellow songwriters most of the times.

Joe Gilchrist: So when Freddy was able to come over to the Flora-Bama, they would play some of his songs, and though we know he can't communicate, we know he's listening – anything that shows some respect to him given how many great songs he's written over the years.

John McGinnis: So with the musicians being in charge at the Flora-Bama, again, they pick their set-lists, how they want to play it, and they're in charge of entertaining the crowd and making everyone feel like they're hanging out together. We've expanded a little bit here because there's an extra four million people down here, and it's not as much about making money as it is providing people a good experience when they come here with all the expanding we're doing. So we have two restaurants now across the street, you don't have people waiting in the street anymore that drove here from Wisconsin because they heard about the personalized experience. We don't want to feel like we're moving cattle, and it's the same with the songwriters we employ. We've got 400 employees now, and of course, more buildings mean more stages for that many more songwriters to play on, and we want everyone to feel like we care about each and every one of them when they walk in the Flora-Bama: from the customer to the performing songwriter to veterans like Freddy, who were around as long as guys like Joe supporting the songwriting community.

We even have church services down here at the Flora-Bama on Sundays! Right about the time I got involved here, the Perdido Methodist Church down the street came to us and said they wanted to do an outreach and start a little church service in the tent out on the beach every Sunday. So I was thinking 10, 20 people every week, and the first weekend, we had 50 people, then the next week, 200, then it went to 500, and now it's up to 1400 attendees with two services every Sunday. It's totally transformed our community, you had all these people who were UN-churched and who were not treated right in church or church tried to get in between their direct relationship with God, and they just felt welcome down here and UN-judged – tattoos and all, whatever! And if you want a Blood Mary, Mimosa or Bushwhacker, you can have that too, but it's a no-judgment zone and we come and have a party for God and Jesus every Sunday, and everybody leaves high-diving each other. You'll find a lot of songwriters and audience members in the audience together, and this is now the largest attended church anywhere down here at the beach, and on Easter Sunday they had 3000!

Catherine Powers: The Flora-Bama really is a miracle, the way they saved me and saved Freddy, and given us a life, a good quality life. There's never any way I could ever repay them for all they've done for us.

John McGinnis: Catherine often jokes about the Lord blessing them with this place, and I feel like the Lord blessed us with them. She's a good, loving woman and Freddy was a wonderful man who used to come down here and support this place and treat us like we want to treat them now. Freddy and Catherine treated the Flora-Bama for years like it was their second home, and we're proud it's been their home the last 3 years! We were proud Freddy had that final chapter of his life at the beach in a songwriter's paradise.

"Outlaw Country Mainstay..."
– The Boot.com

"The jazz-country artist and songwriter whose compositions enriched the charts and repertoires of Willie Nelson, Merle Haggard and George Jones among others."
– Country Music Television

"Having already accomplished more than most in one lifetime, Powers was diagnosed with Parkinson's disease in 2004, which slowed down his productivity. But he continued to write and perform as long as he was able to sit in front of an audience and entertain."
– Austin City Limits

Rattlesnake Annie Performing for Freddy

CONCLUSION: GUITAR ON THE WALL

Catherine Powers: I have to tell you, I feel like the most honored and blessed wife ever. Freddy and I led such an amazingly interesting life together. Not just being married to a songwriter and performer, but actually being a center-focus and a part of it. Not only for the love and friendship Freddy and I have had, but to have been truly a part of all of this has been overwhelming for me. In the music industry, when we got together, Freddy already had that reputation and was pretty well known, but there's something I'll always remember that I kind of go by as my edict: it came when Floyd Tillman – one of Freddy's major heroes – and when Floyd died, there wasn't any mention of him, not even on our local radio station!

It was like he died and that was it, and Freddy looked at me and said "Mama, I don't want everything I've done to just disappear overnight and never be spoke of or played again," and I promised him, "That will never happen." I was fortunate while he was still able to perform that I was acting as his manager and doing all his bookings and dealing with the music publishers. Freddy and I first got together, I did work as his booking agent and his promoter out there on the road, and he trained me well with booking and promoting. So I was lucky to be able to draw from that real-music business experience in the more recent years as I continued running our business full-time.

> **Biff Adams**: I knew Catherine before she met Freddy, and over their years together in the business, he made her into what she is, and she worked her butt off for him managing his catalog once he was medically unable to any longer. They really deserve each other, and my wife – who got to be friends with Catherine when we were all up there on the lake together – used to say, "Now that's a devoted lady!" From the time they first got together and since, she's definitely dedicated herself to Freddy, and anybody who was ever around him can see that.

Catherine Powers: I have to say, when the internet came along, that connected us with the world. It became an huge tool and invaluable resource for me in utilizing social media and the digital music community to keep Freddy's name out there probably bigger than it's ever been before. Especially with the arrival of Facebook, etc., we've been able to not only keep his classic fan-base together, but also introduce his music to a whole new generation of Millennial fans. So I give the main credit for that not to myself but to world wide web, we've been able to keep in touch with so many old and new fans over the years, many of whom have become like family to us.

> **Tanya Tucker:** I see how Catherine works like a little bee, she's always buzzing around!

> **Sonny Throckmorton:** I'm amazed at what she does and has done. She's always been in Freddy's corner, she's always been there for him. She was his #1 promoter, and #1 everything for him, she's a jewel.

Catherine Powers: When I look back over the past 15 years at how honored Freddy was to receive inductions into the *Texas Country Music Hall of Fame, The Western Swing Society Hall of Fame and the Texas Heritage Songwriter's Association, recipient of Lifetime Achievement Awards by the Nashville Songwriter's Association International, the Texas Music Academy,* and *the Texas Guitar Association.* Ovation Guitar Company honored Freddy with his own signature guitar in acknowledgment of the unique Dixie-Jazz style he is largely credited for first introducing into country music. Freddy's legacy is distinguished and historic enough back home that Texas State University gave him his very own archives museum as part of their esteemed Whitliff Collections in conjunction with the Center for Texas Music History. There, Freddy's one and only Ovation guitar hangs proudly at the Country Music Hall of Fame. To top it all off, we're currently working on the film adaptation of his life story!

> **Austin American-Statesman**: "The first two inductees into the Hall of Fame were Sonny Throckmorton and Freddy Powers, not household names exactly, but between them they crafted hits for Merle Haggard, Kenny Rogers, Willie Nelson, George Jones and Big and Rich."

> **Texas Heritage Songwriters Association:** "With five solo albums under his belt in addition to his production and writing, Powers' career is unparalleled in country music...His award winning songs and production work are behind-the-scenes testaments to his talent and success."

Freddy Powers: I have always had great musicians working with me throughout the years. Guys like Paul Buskirk, Milton Quackenbush, Red Allred, Allen Barns, Stu Lanning, Joe Lynch, Tony Savage, Spanky Jones, Ben Wilhorn, B.B. Morse, Gary Xavier, Clint Strong, Tommy Roberts, Steve Joyce, Jay Thomas, Bob Minnetta, Bobby Black, Dan Steenbach, Tom Herzer, Perry Joe Shermer, Jimmy Day, Scotty Joss, Joe Manual, Abe Manual, Teri Cote, my nephew Troy Powers and my son Freddy II, Django Porter, Price Porter, Steve Carter, Gary Church, Moe Monsarrat, Pat McCann, Augie Savage, Floyd Domino, Mark Wilson, Ed Ferguson, Mike Pankratz, John Gerton, Ernie Hagar, Dale Bates, Mars Case, Tom Nehls, Diane Roan, Joy Simmons, Kirk Prebyl, Wild Van Crowell, Joe Craven, Bill Allred, and Bill Mahone, Spud Goodall and my beloved friend Deanie Bird' Reynolds, who passed away in 1996. There are many more that my mind will recall, I've always had lots of respect for good players that know how to swing

> **John Rich:** When a guy like me got to hang out with a guy like Freddy, it was always ratified air. Not many people can say they know a guy like Freddy, and really know him, and really have written with him, and really understand him. Freddy's songwriting and artistry is bigger than country music, it's truly American music. When you meet somebody like Freddy, you go out of your way to find times and find places to make sure you reconnect with him, because you know he's only going to be around for so long.

> Freddy's a really unique combination of things: he's a very low-key, behind-the-scenes kind of guy, but at the same time, I always called him a quiet rock star, it's what I called him. Because he played guitar like a rock

star or country star, and he was hilarious, really edgy and had hilarious jokes, and always has one joke after the next after the next. But then he had such substance with the stuff that he'd written and where he'd been and what all he accomplished in his life: he's been in the military, I mean, he did a lot of things in his life that have a lot of gravity. So he was always a real unassuming megastar in my mind.

Big Kenny Alphin: Going back and seeing him in his banjo/ragtime show, I think he was known as such an accomplished – almost vaudevillian – player during that era, and one of the first things I know of his musical history is that he was known as a very accomplished musician and entertainer. I think he's known as a songwriter, without a shadow of a doubt, the hits that he wrote with Haggard and many others are going to live on in the annals of time.

Marc Oswald, Music Manager/Promoter: I've never met anybody like Freddy, he's singular, and I think first off, as a rhythm guitar player, he was one of the greats. Everybody appreciated his skills, from his history of Vaudeville and his capability with all the stringed instruments: banjos, guitars, basses, anything with strings on it. And with his comedy capability, he'll be remembered as a comedian, a Vaudevillian, a jazz guitar, a multi-instrumentalist, a songwriter. When you add all that up, guys like Merle and Willie and the people Freddy has worked with, George Jones, Kris Kristofferson, it goes on and on, they all fell in love with him because he was always so humble.

He was always the most humble guy in the room, but he was always the star's star. I always thought of Freddy that way because our stars in Country Music in that period were Merle Haggard, Willie Nelson, Hank Jr., Waylon Jennings, they were the stars to us. Well, Freddy seemed to be the star to them. He was like at a different level in terms of being the guy that they followed and that they were fans of Freddy, all those mega-superstar country artists, and some other artists as well, were fans of Freddy, while we were all fans of them. It was just the strangest thing, and I think it was because he had a combination of all those skill sets, and his humility and his sense of humor. So I think it all started based on mutual admiration between those guys and stayed that way for the rest of their lives.

Freddy Powers: I have always had a great respect for really good players and those that knew how to swing. I will always be thankful to them for sharing part of their musical life with me. I can't imagine my life without music. Most of all, the people I love best are musicians or people who solely love music and have respect for it. As for my songwriting, I owe much of it to Merle and my sister Mary Lou.

Merle Haggard: Fred and I can drive 300 miles and never say a word, we don't have to talk.

Willie Nelson: I enjoy playing music with Freddy, he's a friend and a good musician.

Austin City Limits Executive Producer Terry Lickona: "Freddy might not have been a household name, but most of his musical buddies were. Willie & Merle were two of his closest friends, and they were kindred spirits, musically and personally. He had an infectious passion for what can best be called country jazz, and he had a direct hand in bringing Willie and Merle together for one of the most memorable songwriters shows we ever did, in Season 9. He was also a remarkable songwriter; my favorite was '*I Always Get Lucky With You*,' which became part of Merle's repertoire for many years. Freddy's spirit lives on!"

Tanya Tucker: Even near the end, I always knew he knew me when I seem him because his eyes just lit up and I could tell he knew exactly what I was saying to him and we'd have a conversation. It's such a great feeling to know that he knew who I was. He was like the Energizer Bunny, he just kept on ticking, and it was amazing.

Rattlesnake Annie: I know of all the women artists, I've recorded more of Freddy's songs than anybody. Over the years, I've recorded a whole album or more of his songs, and he's really one of my favorite songwriters in the whole wide world. I think he was without a doubt the best rhythm player I've ever met in my life. Freddy will be remembered for having his own kind of music.

Edith Royal: They have a music festival here every year at the start of Football season, and they always had a Pickin' Party the night before. Now, it lives on as a fundraiser for Alzheimer's Disease and the money goes up to Dallas to a medical hospital there where they study how to treat it, it's an Alzheimer's Fund. Freddy and Catherine always came to that party on the campus, all the way from when he played at them up through when Catherine was pushing him in a wheelchair. It was a little funny in spite of Freddy's condition, because they had him in a little roped-off area so people couldn't swarm him. They could come talk to him but not for a very long time because he had a lot of fans and only so much energy. Freddy is very recognizable in Texas.

Mary Sarah: Freddy's ability to touch you with his melodies and lyrics is a gift, something he practiced his entire life. If I was to describe what I know of Freddy: he was always sweet and sassy!

B.B. Morse: He had some of the most awesome focus and visionary accomplishments of any musician I had the pleasure to work with.

Moe Monsarrat: Freddy went through a lot of shit man, and I know it was rough on him, but I've never seen a braver person!

Wayne Ahart: Freddy was another one of the great ones!

Steve Carter: The word that really comes to mind is just trust, he trusted me, and never had to tell me do it this way or that way. He trusted me to do that, and it was from playing in the living room with him, asking "What's this chord? What's that chord? What are you doing there?" So he was like a father to me, really, I called him Papa, and made sure to be in touch with him on Father's Day, so it was that kind of a relationship for me. My Dad was gone at an early age, and Freddy was as dear a Dad as I could wish for. I think he'll be remembered as the Best Rhythm Guitar player in Western Swing in modern history.

John Rich: What you realize is that what Freddy is that he's a Great Grand Daddy of Country Music. He's an innovator that now, for generation after generation of country singers – including myself – has been impacted by his songwriting and playing, whether they realize it or not. Because what Freddy did with Merle back in those days, there's not one country singer out there that won't count Merle Haggard as an influence. And when you find out that one of the main men behind the curtain was Freddy Powers, well then you have to count Freddy Powers as an influence and just as important as Merle. And you have to wonder: would Merle have even written those songs had Freddy not been sitting there with him? So that makes a guy like me just blown away because it's like you're sitting there with somebody that should be on Mount Rushmore and had so much massive impact and success.

When I think about my favorite Freddy Powers' songs, I think right off the top of the list would have to be '*Natural High*', because first of all, it's just an absolute ridiculous melody, and in true country fashion, it gets right down to the heart of the matter, right off the top of the song. '*You stayed with me through thick and thin, you watch me lose, you watch me win,*' just real simple lines that cut really deep and ring really true. That's a really great example of Freddy Powers' incredible medley coupling up with a real simple country lyric and how impactful that can be. I think '*Always Get Lucky With You*', that's just unbelievable that song. '*When I'm down to a phone call, I'm minus a dime,*' that line just blows me away, every time it gets to that one, I have to say 'God, what a line!' You could talk about a lot of Freddy's songs that way, but those two probably hit me as hard as anything I've ever heard in country music. Matter of fact, some of his songs could have been recorded by Frank Sinatra or Dean Martin, they're on that level. He is a jewel, there's nothing like him anywhere out there. He's about musically is really ageless. The definition of a classic is something that was loved when it was brand new, and the older it gets, people love it even more, and I think that's Freddy to a T. He is the definition of a classic.

Big Kenny Alphin: He's a hall of fame hit songwriter, and with what he brought to country swing, there's no doubt he'll be known for that. Take that and add to it that he's just one of the funnier fellas you'll ever sit down and talk to, always had a joke for every occasion, and was an unforgettable sort of character. He was a friend to many.

Tanya Tucker: I had to call Catherine once to figure out where I met her because I told her I could always remember when I met an asshole, but I can never remember where I met my best friends. I put her in that category.

Rattlesnake Annie: I really admire how she took care of Freddy and kept him exposed in the community, because a lot of people hide away. That was a big job! Catherine was a great blessing to Freddy and enriched his life, and made his illness much more humane. I honor her for how good she was and how much she sacrificed for Freddy.

Pauline Reese: Before Freddy passed, I wrote a song for them called "*Wanderlust Fantasy*", and it's about Freddy and Catherine and their life and the way that they love each other.

"Wanderlust Fantasy"

Vs 1
I feel the sunlight on my face
The wind is blowing like a race
My feet are on the ground and I
Can't hear a sound, all I see is you

Chorus:
You haunt my days
You haunt my nights
Wanderlust fantasy

Give me your love and you'll be
Living a life of ecstasy
I would be your Queen
And you would be my king
Wanderlust fantasy

You haunt my days
You haunt my nights
Wanderlust fantasy
Come run away with me
Don't hide those feelings
We can't fight

I would be your Queen
And you would be my King
Wanderlust fantasy

Vs 2
Take my hand and you will find
There is no love like yours and mine
You will rule my world
And I would be the girl
To make you feel like home

You haunt my days
You haunt my nights
Wanderlust Fantasy

Vs 3
Take my heart and follow me
We'll build our kingdom you will see
Dancing on a cloud
Living life out loud
Wanderlust fantasy

You haunt my days
You haunt my nights
Wanderlust fantasy
I would be your Queen
And you would be my King
Wanderlust fantasy
I would be your Queen
And you would be my King
Wanderlust fantasy

Catherine Powers: If you look closely at Willie Nelson's beloved guitar Trigger, you can see Freddy's name etched into its hallowed body, just as permanently as his name is forever etched into Country Music, and we're truly grateful for the amazing journey this life in the music business has given us. It's given Freddy his legacy, but I know he was equally proud of being able to give back to his fans and friends, whether through the Special Olympics or his Parkinson's Foundation. Or with all the musicians he's helped get started in the business, keeping in the tradition of forefathers like Paul Buskirk who did the same for Freddy and Willie so many decades ago. Whenever Willie was still touring on the road, and whenever he'd come through town and Freddy was able to see his old friend still up there doing what he loves, I know it brought a big smile to his face. It was always nice to see how loyal those two old friends were to each other.

We lost our dear friend Merle Haggard in 2016, and the loss was devastating not only for Freddy and I, but for generations of Country Music fans who grew up on Merle's music, going all the way back to the early 60s. Freddy told me many times that his years writing and playing with Merle were the happiest of his life and career, and Merle would say the same thing. They truly were brothers in every sense of the word, and remained that way through Merle's passing. Freddy outlived so many of his siblings, countless medical expert projections, friends and musicians he played with throughout his life. Everybody who has crossed Freddy's path over his 84 years on this earth have all said they fell in love with him within moments of meeting him, and it was the same for me.

If I have one wish I hope has been fulfilled by the time someone finishes reading this last page of our story and closes the book, it's that they do so with a feeling of completion, of coming full circle, because that's exactly what we've done with it. I'll never forget, eight years ago when we really began working in earnest on this book, Freddy had just been baptized for the first time in his life. Ten days later, he wound up on life support at the V.A. Hospital in Nashville, TN. So here I am, crying and praying over him, "Please Lord, don't take him from me, I'm not ready…" All of a sudden, Freddy was able to open up his eyes and look up at me and say, "Mama, I just got baptized, I'm not going anywhere…", and in my heart or the hearts of his friends and fans, he never will…

"From a young age, Powers would become noteworthy for performances that blended traditional honky-tonk with Dixieland jazz…(A) lauded songwriter, producer and musician."
– ROLLING STONE COUNTRY

A book based on the life of late songwriter Freddy Powers, titled The Spree Of '83, will hit stores in July, and a movie about his life will be developed… The Spree of '83 will depict Freddy's start in the 1950s with Paul Buskirk and fellow unknown Willie Nelson before rising in the 1960s and 70s to the top draws on the West Coast Casino circuit, and kindling a 30-year friendship and songwriting collaboration with Merle Haggard." – MUSIC ROW MAGAZINE

"Freddy will be remembered for having his own kind of music."
– RATTLESNAKE ANNIE

EPILOGUE: JUNE 21ST, 2016

Catherine Powers: Freddy passed away on June 21st, 2016 with loved ones by his side. I was too distraught to remember much of the day, but felt fortunate to have family like our daughter Karen, dear friends Robin Harpster, Pastor Dan Stone and Freddy's nurse Joi with me that day…

Robin Harpster: I've never been through anything like that. It was a Tuesday morning and I was on my way to Bible Study at the Flora-Bama Light House, and I text Catherine to see if she wanted to join me, and she text back and said, "Robin, Oh My God, Freddy... It's an emergency, when you get done, please come over here." So I went over to the bus right after Bible Study, and it wasn't good at all: Freddy was having a hard time breathing, and she made a phone call to our Pastors Joe and Dan to come over and administer final rights, which was a very difficult call for her to make. Her strength was always amazing with Freddy, but especially that day, because when the Pastors both showed up, we all knew it wasn't looking good.

We were all talking to Freddy, telling him we loved him, and reassuring him Catherine wasn't alone. At that point, she asked us all to pray for Freddy because I think in her heart, she knew he wasn't going to last much longer. After we all said prayers for Freddy, their dog Olga all of a sudden jumped up on top of Freddy, and you could just feel something in the room at the time. So Olga was looking at him, kind of barking, and then we all looked at each other and you never know when something like that's going to happen, but it was time. There was a lot of tears and hugging and silence and sadness, just a lot of emotions, and she was shaking and beside herself, but at the same time, you felt this spiritual presence in the room. It's hard to explain, but after we'd said the prayer together, we saw something in Freddy where he seemed at peace, and suddenly had a different breathing mechanism, and we'd told him, "Its okay Freddy, if you go, we're going to take care of Catherine, you don't have to worry about her." That's what portions of our prayer was about, and you could just see he was relieved, and he passed shortly after that.

I was supposed to be at work that Tuesday but had just left that job the day before, and I feel like it was God working in our lives for sure, because had I gone to work, I wouldn't have been able to be there with Catherine. I know there was reason why everything happened the way it did, and being able to be with her at that moment meant the world to me, getting to experience that with someone so special in my life. She likes to joke now that Freddy and Merle were having a Pickin' Party for Jesus up in Heaven, and we all knew he'd gone on to a better place.

Joi Vinson Davis: I'm so grateful when Catherine called me and told me Papa wasn't doing good, I was debating on whether I needed to leave right then, and said, "No, I'll wait till tomorrow." When I called her the next morning, she told me it wasn't good, so I threw stuff in a bag and took off and was about two hours into my six-hour drive when they called and told me Freddy had passed. I lost it of course, and about 30 minutes later, Catherine called me, and she said, "How far are you?" I was still probably four hours out, and I got upset and said, "I'm not going to get to kiss him bye, I just want to kiss his face one more time," and she actually left Freddy there on the bus till I made it there, which wasn't till nine o'clock that night. But this beautiful, beautiful woman kept his body there so I could kiss my Papa bye one more time. That really meant a lot to me.

Catherine Powers: We celebrated Freddy's life on July 28th, 2016 in the place we'd both come to call home in our hearts, the Flora-Bama, with a full Military service by his fellow Marines, and comical stories and songs about and by Freddy from his friends and admirers.

Pastor Joe Brantley, Worship on the Water Campus Director: We're honoring Mr. Frederick Dale Powers, born October 10th, 1931, in Duncan, Oklahoma. He was raised in Seminole, Texas, and he died June 21st, 2016. He's survived by his wife, Catherine Allen Powers, his 5 children, 10 grandchildren, 2 great-grandchildren, and 1 sister, Ms. Norma Marlow, and many nieces and nephews. So he's surrounded by not only a large family, but also by a large community that stretched all over this country who dearly loved Freddy Powers.

Catherine wanted me to read a funny scripture, and the only one I could think of is, in Numbers 22:21-39, when *Balaam*'s Ass talks, he was riding on his Ass and it started talking to him. So I was thinking what better way to segway into Catherine talking, because she's been riding Freddy's ass for years, right? (Cheers from the crowd)

Catherine Powers: That's just a little taste of what you're in for today, because like Freddy said, "Mama," because he always called me Mama – so does half the people in the room – "I don't want no celebration of life where people are standing up crying and talking about how great I am – because I already know that!" (laughs) He said, "Mama, I want y'all to roast me like you did on my 70th Birthday and throw me under the bus, and make me and the Lord laugh so hard that we're falling off the clouds."

So today, we're actually going to be roasting Freddy, and I'm going to start with the story I'm going to roast my sweetheart with: I found out and I realized how crazy he was and what kind of ride I was going to be on when we hadn't even been dating a couple of weeks. I'm following him home from the Casino, about two or three in the morning, and we're driving down Main St. in south Lake Tahoe, and if you've ever been there, you know they only had one street when all of a sudden, he just stops in the middle of the street! He gets out of his car, and I'm rolling my window down thinking he had something he needed to tell me, when all of a sudden, he gets to the back of his truck, drops his pants, turns around and moons me, never takes a look back, gets back in his truck, and drove off... (crowd laughs) I knew right then I was in for one heck of a ride. I didn't know exactly where we were gonna go with this, but I knew I was going somewhere.

Then I found out another little thing about him, he was a liar, he could lie good. What he actually did was let me believe he was 49 years old. I was 31 at the time, so he just led me on and kept letting me assume that he was 49. Well, I went to the Doctor's office one time for his physical, and the nurse came in and was doing all his vitals and she says, "Freddy, how old are you?" And I saw this funny look on his face when he said, "It's in my file," (laughs). So the nurse persists, "Freddy, I'd have to go in there and dig it out! So just tell me how old you are?" This time, he's got a very stern, mean, ugly look on his face when he repeats it, "I said, it's in my file..." So she goes into the file, comes back out and says, "Hey Freddy, you've got a birthday coming up October 13th, 1931," and I looked at him, took a deep breath, and said "My daddy was born in '34!" (crowd cheers) Well, lucky for him, by this time, I already knew I was in love with him – from the first time I saw a picture of him, I hadn't even really met him yet, but saw a picture and was like, "That's the man I'm after!" So, 18 years, 23 years my senior, what did it matter, I was already there...

Then I found out he thought he was brave, and we were out on this camping trip and staying up in Bear country in the woods in Northern California, and we're walking on this trail as he's telling me what to do if a Mountain Lion or a Bear was to come up to us. So he tells me, if it's a Mountain Lion, make yourself really big and get loud and run them off, but if it's a Bear, whatever you do, do not turn away and start running. Just fall to the ground, roll up like a ball and they'll think they've already killed you and won't mess with you, and about the time he's telling me this story, I see the brush moving and I pointed us over there and said "I wonder what..." Well, about the same time I got the "what" out this big, old Brown Bear stands up, Freddy grabs me by the arm, picks up our dog Amelia and takes off running as I'm running alongside him going, "I thought we weren't supposed to run!" So to myself, I'm laughing thinking, "Okay, he's brave...

Then I found out, he's a wimp! He's a chicken. I go to the grocery store one day and I come back home, and walk in and have two guys – he and Sonny Throckmorton – setting in these red, lazy boy chairs, and I'm looking at them as they have this strange look on their faces, and Sonny's going, "I'm not gonna tell her, it's your house, you tell her..." So I'm like, "What??" So

Freddy goes, "Mama, I don't know what it is in here, but you need to go up in our bedroom, we've got this big old long, worm-looking thing crawling around the ceiling." So I go in the room, look up, and sure enough, there was this really big, huge red centipede about 6 inches long with a million legs, and guess who got it off the ceiling and got rid of it? Because neither one of those boys could to it!

So like I said, it didn't take me very long to find out what I was going to be marrying into, because Freddy Powers was someone who always wanted to keep people laughing, and I was his first audience always. For years, he was a stand-up comedian, and did what they call *slap-stick comedy*, with three banjos and a tuba, which got him on the Today Show, that's all he cared about! He got on the Today Show and followed by the Tonight Show, and before too long, had his own little T.V. show there in Ft. Worth, Texas on (WBAP?) T.V., but Freddy always loved to make people laugh. One of his favorite in recent times was the Freddy Powers Dirty Joke Night! (laughs)

I'm going to tell a funny one on Freddy and Gretchen Wilson, because most people know that if you were friends with Willie Nelson and Merle Haggard, it kind of just goes together that you do too, so when I explain this, you'll go "Oh!" So one time, Freddy was sitting in the back of the Limo with Gretchen, and somebody said "Freddy, you want a hit?", handed him a joint, and Gretchen laughed and said, "Freddy, you like that stuff?" So Freddy looks at her – and this is on film – and says to her, "If you see me, I'm high," then ducks down out of view of the camera and says, "If you don't see me, I'm high." Okay... Here's Mr. Bo Porter and Mr. Chris Newbury!

Bo Porter: Catherine and Freddy lived just a little bit down the road from me at La Hacienda R.V. Resort, and there were times that Catherine had to go out to the grocery store or Doctor's or something, and Freddy was still at the point where he could communicate, talk to you and he could walk with assistance. But he still needed someone there with him, so when Catherine called me one day and told me she had to go to the Doctor and asked if I'd please come sit with Freddy. So of course I said "Sure," headed down, and on the way there, I got to thinking of all the times I've spent with him and played music with him and talked, I'd never told him what he'd meant to me. Well, I just decided this was the day for me to tell him what he's meant to me, and when I got there, went on to tell him about how much he'd taught me about songwriting, he'd coached me a bit in that. And he taught me a lot about the music business, and about how to dress and how to respect an audience, and how to be a good bandleader, which was one of the big things he taught me.

So I'm just gushing on him, and I finally told him, "Freddy, you're just one of my heroes, and I want you to know that." So he told me thanks, then a few minutes later, looked at me with this sheepish little grin on his face, and says "I gotta shit." (laughs) I said, "Well by God, let's get it done!", and I got him up and helped him down the hallway, got him slipped into the bathroom, and I remember he's hanging onto my shoulder, and looks right at me and says, "Well, you gotta pull 'em down." So I said, "Oh, okay," and pulled his pants down for him and got him settled on the toilet, and Thank God, next he says, "Bo, I can do everything else."

We both laughed, I shut the door and went and sat up front waiting on him, and a few minutes later he knocked on the door and I went back and said, "You ready?", and he said, "Yeah", so I opened the door, and he's sitting there on the toilet. So I bent over, got him over my shoulder and off the toilet, and then he says, "Well, you gotta pull 'em up." Then I said, "Okay," and of course, about the time I bend down, I get into about the bathing suit region, if you will, and he says, "Hey Bo?", and I said, "Yes sir", looked up at him, and he said, "What do you think of your hero now?", and we both just busted up laughing! That was just Freddy humor, and he was good about that, setting up a punch line: his comedic timing was just the best. He probably sat there on the commode thinking about what he was going to say to get me. (laughs)

Chris Newbury: Thank You Mama Catherine! Okay, this is a roast, so I'm going to try and say something… but it's hard because this is a Hero of ours, all of ours, and I don't know if y'all know but Freddy started out on Banjo. He wasn't really a guitar player to start out with, but he really was one of the greatest guitar players in Country Music. So I have one story to tell, and fortunately, it looks like there are no kids in the audience, so I can use the real words because it's part of the punch line. But we were out partying one night over in the bus, and this is when Freddy had already been incapacitated for quite a while and couldn't get up and move around, but could still speak. So we were all laughing and having a good time, but apparently, he wasn't feeling so good because he'd already made a couple of comments about Jackals or Hyenas laughing, then after a couple hours, his nurse Joi says, "Papa, is there anything we can get you?", and Freddy says "Yeah, I'd like some fucking Crab Claws!" He'd been asking for hours, and we were like, "Papa, we're sorry, we've been partying and can't drive…" So I sobered up a little bit in the middle of the night, went down and picked him up a Shrimp Basket, came back, and said "Alright Papa, here are your fucking crab claws!" (cheers)

Catherine Powers: Alright, I'm ready for you Bo and Jo!

Bo Roberts: I think everybody knows that everybody in the world would probably love to have a Catherine Powers! (cheers) She's priceless... Okay, I'll tell a quick one, I met Freddy back in the '60s when he was playing the Showboat in Las Vegas and where I was working with an old Cowboy by the name of Eddie Dean. He was playing Banjo at the time, and he told me, "I got sick and damn tired of those banjo jokes, and I figured I'd be a guitar player." So he went down to the store, and said "I want a Stratocaster, I want a Marshall amp, stacks, effects, picks, strings, the works..." So the guy behind the counter looks at him and says, "You're a freakin' Banjo player!" (laughs) Freddy said, "How the hell'd you know that?", and the guy behind the counter says, "This is a Liquor store!"

Joe Gilchrist: I feel very privileged to have met a lot of United States Marines in my life, and Freddy carried that torch very well, and I'm very proud to see the Marines here. (cheers) One thing I was going to tell you is, I hang around a lot of the singer/songwriters, and most of them are pretty smart, but Freddy and Bo could stand some help! (laughs)

Bo Roberts: I got a mind like a steel trap.

Joe Gilchrist: Yeah, but the difference is, Bo can remember three or four songs, he writes one every year, but Freddy convinced me he was a lot smarter than he used to think he was when I got to know Catherine better. What a lucky guy, and what a lucky pair! I haven't had as much experience in marriage as Bo, I've only been married once...

Bo Roberts: Freddy had five kids, and I have five ex-wives. I was chasing the women and he... (laughs) He has five kids... (laughs)

Joe Gilchrist: I feel very fortunate that Fred and Catherine decided to come spend the last years of Freddy's life here, and I hope it was as enriching an experience for them as it's been for our little music community.

Bo Roberts: I got one more story... This is before Catherine settled him down, and Freddy loved women – hell, we all did. I remember standing at this bar one night and this gal had been waiting on us for a couple of days, and she walked by and said to Freddy and I, "You guys alright?" And I said, "Yep," and Freddy looked at her and said, "You know, I had two wet dreams 'bout you," and she went, "Oh Freddy," and he told her, "Would have had another but I went to sleep!" (laughs)

Catherine Powers: Freddy was always a comedian! There were times where I'd be looking outside, and seeing this guy standing there marching off in his own world, and I'd be sitting there looking at him going, "What are you doing?!!" But that was just Freddy – he didn't care if I knew for sure I was watching, but just on the chance I'd be watching, and he'd just get up and do something crazy, all the time. I can tell all these stories because I was married to the man, and I mean, you learn to say the "F" word real quick when you start hanging out with a bunch of musicians – because its every other word! Now, we'll hear a song from Christina Christian and Taylor Craven that they actually wrote about Freddy and I called "*The Book*."

Taylor Craven: I actually met Freddy Powers five or six years ago at the Frank Brown Songwriters Festival, and helped pick his wheelchair up with him in it to get him on the bus. Well, two years ago, we were up in the main room at the Flora-Bama and Chris Newbery was on stage, and he pointed to Freddy in his wheelchair with Catherine, and said, "That's the definition of love." I was staying at Mark Sherrill's condo by myself, so I went home that evening and started picking out this song on the guitar, and Christina Christian and I had a writing appointment the next day. Well, when she walked in, I hadn't been to sleep yet because I'd been up all night pickin' on this song and it was really about what Chris Newbery said, "Till death do us part," and Freddy and Catherine defined that. I had some situations in my family, Grandmothers and Aunts that had that same kind of commitment, and I always wanted to capture that.

Christina Christian: We finished the majority of the song in 2014, and we set it aside and let it marinate a little bit for about six months. Then finally, the next year after we'd written the song all together, we were pretty excited about it because we did have Catherine listen to it on the same stage we're performing it on today, and she loved it and asked me to start playing that song for different Freddy events. I feel like it's a fitting tribute and Freddy heard the song before he passed, and we felt it was relevant to the two of them because when you were out at the Flora-Bama and you would see Catherine and Freddy together, or I would go over to their bus to visit, and she was just with him 24-7. Once I started seeing more of that, I was more connected to the song and it was a bit more emotional for me too, because there are just so many different lyrics in the song where you can really tell what they mean individually to Catherine and Freddy. If you see how she took care of him while he was alive up through his passing, you just get every single line in this song about their love.

Catherine Powers: So this is what came out from hearing a story about Freddy and I...

"The Book"
(Written by Christina Christian, Taylor Craven,
and Megan McMillan)

Verse 1
They haven't given in or given out
'Cause giving up ain't what love's about
They've learned to lean on the vows they took
They keep turning pages
Till it's time to close the book

Verse 2
She recalls every promise made that day
He can too, but he can't say
Until death will they be one
They keep turning pages
Till the book is done

Chorus
There's laughter in the chapters of their past
With pages stained by tears that didn't last
There's no written rule how a happy ending looks
They keep turning pages, till it's time to close the book

Verse 3
From outside looking in no one can tell
How one look from him makes her heart swell
His hands are cool, but she melts at his touch
They keep turning pages, till it's time to close the book

Chorus
There's laughter in the chapters of their past
With pages stained by tears that didn't last
There's no written rule how a happy ending looks
They keep turning pages, till it's time to close the book

Turn Around
There's no written rule how a happy ending looks
They keep turning pages, till it's time to close the book

Tag
They haven't given in or given out
'Cause giving up ain't what loves about

Catherine Powers: Another touching tribute to Freddy came when our friend Ken Hart with Cary Stone wrote a salute to simply titled "THANK YOU FREDDY," that summed up perfectly why he'll be missed by so many.

"Thank You Freddy"

Once in a while someone comes along
Drives you wild with special little style of song
Makes you dance and makes you sing
Throws a little love in between
What a recipe he's famous for
He leaves his mark everywhere he goes
Plays his part but somehow steals the show
Puts a smile on your face
Boogies all your blues away
Guarantee, he'll always leave you wanting more
He gives you a taste but it's never enough
Takes you away and always lifts you up
A natural high, you can't come down
It's the hottest thing in town
He's your friend in California that's for sure

So don't be late, tickets are going fast
Show starts at eight and its gonna be a blast
Just hold on
All night long
He never runs out of songs
One more stop on his never-ending tour
Just hold on
All night long
We know you never run out of songs
Thank You Freddy
Could you sing us just one more?

(Copyright 2009
Ken Hart – Starlite 9 Music Sesac)

Catherine Powers: Finally, our dear friends Curly Corwin and Bo Roberts, who started out playing with Freddy back on the Casino circuit in the 1970s, and has known us as a couple for over 30 years, wrote this beautiful song about Freddy and my love story, and it was Freddy's wish that we close the show with it:

"The Powers In Love"
(Written by: Bo Roberts and Curly Corwin 2016)

Vs. 1
If someone should write a song about Freddy and Catherine
It would be so easy to write
Just picture all the love that they have for each other And write it down in every line
The powers in love
Is what keeps them together
Two hearts beating as one

If someone should write a song About Freddy and Catherine
It would be a sing-a-long love song
Oh they've tried to outlove one another
A competition they'll have for life
Everyday there's something new
Every night there is two
Lovers on a natural high
Oh it ain't no big surprise Catherine's had stars in her eyes
Since the night Freddy hung her the moon

And this song Ain't long enough to tell about all the love
Still going on between these two
Oh they've tried to outlove one another
It's a competition that they'll have for life
Everyday there's something new
Every night there is two

Lovers on a natural high
Yes the powers in love
Is what keeps them together
Two lovers on a natural high

Catherine Powers: Here's a final song Freddy wrote with our dear friend Gary Nicholson because it was the last song he wrote, it was one of Freddy's favorites...

"Guitar On the Wall"
(Written by Freddy Powers, Gary Nicholson)

Vs 1
My old friend quit the cigarettes
And cut way back on the booze
But there's some habits of a lifetime

Ain't that easy to lose
He'd been pickin' guitar
Since he was just a kid
Then one day the doctor told him
He'd never play again
And the saddest good-bye of all
Was when he had to hang his guitar on the wall

Vs 2
If that six strings could talk
Lord, the stories we would hear
It was there to bring the songs to life
Through the laughter and the tears
Now he knows his old guitar
Has made its final curtain call
And the saddest good-bye of all
Was when he had to hang his guitar on the wall

Vs 3
We've all lost things we love in this life
We've all said our share of good-byes
But the saddest good-bye of all
Was when he had to hang his guitar on the wall
Yeah, the saddest good-bye of all
Was when Freddy hung his guitar on the wall

Footnote: We had a star-studded remembrance in Nashville in the late fall of 2016 with the Musik Mafia in a beautiful wood-paneled lodge living room of country music legend Barbara Mandrell's house out at the famed Fontanel. The celebration featured an equal number of fellow superstars like John and Big Kenny of Big & Rich, Gretchen Wilson, and others in attendance to celebrate Freddy's life and times with their own memories, stories, toasts and roasts! Complete with Tanya Tucker taking a photo of myself and an unnamed co-conspirator smoking a joint in Freddy's honor! Freddy's first Rolling Stone Magazine story was also framed for later hanging in the Flora-Bama, and a beautiful night rounded out by performances from the aforementioned stars and other players from throughout Freddy's career celebrating his greatest and favorite hits!

In 2019, our team began work on the film adaptation of Freddy's life and times, a dream we'd talked about with him often in the final years before his passing, not because Freddy thought his life was a movie, but because everyone around him told him for years it was and we look forward to bringing that dream true on screen in the coming years. We've talked to some amazing musician/actors already about playing certain characters you've heard from already in this book and other stars in Freddy's orbit have already agreed to play themselves in cameos. Keeping Freddy's name and songs alive for his fans has always been my driving force, and remains so to this day as new generations of music listeners discover his songs on streaming services, YouTube, on TV, the radio, and maybe even still a few jukeboxes out there! Our friends and Freddy's fans have always called us Mama and Papa because they're all family to us, and will always be…

DISCOGRAPHY:

- Freddy Powers single – "*Be My Love*" / "*That's What I See In Your Eyes*" B-Side (Blue Bonnet Records, 1959)

- Freddy Powers single – "*Heartaches Of a Fool*" / "*He Gave Us A Heart*" B-Side (Longhorn Records, 1961, co-written by Willie Nelson)

- Freddy Powers & The Powerhouse IV – *THE GOOD LIFE* (Warner Bros, 1964)

- The Wilburn Brothers recorded "*Nothing At All*" (co-written by Freddy Powers and Harold Donny), *Carefree Moments* LP, 1962

- The Bear Family recorded "*Wasted Love*," "*Chapel In My Heart*," "*Loser*," "*Do You Remember*" and "*A Good Gal is Hard to Find*" on The Bear Family Album Collection (The Bear Family Records)

- Freddy Powers co-produced, sang and played guitar on Willie Neson's *Somewhere Over The Rainbow* (Columbia Records, 1981).

- Merle Haggard's recorded Freddy Powers' "*I Always Get Lucky With You*" (co-written with Merle Haggard and Gary Church) and included the track on *Big City* (Epic Records, 1981).

- Merle Haggard recorded Freddy Powers' "*Lonely Night*" and included the track on *Going Home For Christmas* (Epic Records, 1982).

- Merle Haggard and George Jones (Saturday 12 September 1931 - Friday 26 April 2013) recorded Freddy Powers' "*Silver Eagle*" and included the track on *A Taste Of Yesterday's Wine* (Epic Records, 1983); Freddy Powers also played guitar on the recording sessions for the album.

- George Jones (Saturday 12 September 1931 - Friday 26 April 2013) recorded Freddy Powers' "*I Always Get Lucky With You*" (co-written with Merle Haggard) and included the track on *Shine On* (Epic Records, 1983); the track was No.1 on the Billboard country music singles chart for one week in July/August 1983.

- Merle Haggard and Leona Williams recorded Freddy Powers' "*It's Cold In California Tonight*" and included the track on *Heart To Heart* (Mercury Records, 1983).

- Ray Charles (Tuesday 23 September 1930 - Thursday 10 June 2004) recorded Freddy Powers' "*Little Hotel Room*" and included the track on *Friendship* (Columbia Records, 1984); the track was a duet with Merle Haggard. Ray Charles' *Friendship* (Columbia Records, 1984) was re-issued by Columbia/Legacy Records in 2005.

- Merle Haggard recorded Freddy Powers' "*Let's Chase Each Other Around The Room*" (co-written with Merle Haggard and Sherrill Rodgers) and included the track on *It's All In The Game* (Epic Records, 1984); the track was No.1 on the Billboard country music singles chart for one week in September 1984. Freddy Powers also played rhythm guitar on the album.

- Merle Haggard recorded Freddy Powers' "*A Place To Fall Apart*" (co-written with Merle Haggard and Willie Nelson) and included the track on *It's All In The Game* (Epic Records, 1984); the track was No.1 on the Billboard country music singles chart for one week in February 1985. Janie Fricke provided harmony vocals on the track, while Freddy Powers played rhythm guitar on the album.

- Merle Haggard recorded Freddy Powers' "*Natural High*" and included the track on *It's All In The Game* (Epic Records, 1984); the track was No.1 on the Billboard country music singles chart for one week in June 1985. The track, which was also included on *Kern River* (Epic Records, 1984), featured Janie Fricke on harmony vocals on the track, while Freddy Powers played rhythm guitar on both albums.

- Merle Haggard recorded Freddy Powers' "*Little Hotel Room*" and included the track on *It's All In The Game* (Epic Records, 1984); Freddy Powers also played rhythm guitar on the album.

- Merle Haggard recorded Freddy Powers' "*All I Want To Do Is Sing My Songs*" and included the track on *It's All In The Game* (Epic Records, 1984); Freddy Powers also played rhythm guitar on the album.

- Merle Haggard recorded Freddy Powers' "*Ridin' High*" and included the track on *Kern River* (Epic Records, 1984); Janie Fricke provided harmony vocals on the track.

- Merle Haggard recorded Freddy Powers' "*You Don't Love Me Anymore*" and included the track on *Kern River* (Epic Records, 1984).

- Merle Haggard recorded Freddy Powers' "*Amber Waves Of Grain*" and included the track on *Amber Waves Of Grain* (Epic Records, 1985).

- Rose Maddox recorded "*Cold in California*," "*My Love is Too Hot For You,*" *Queen of the West* LP, 1983, Varrick Records

- Freddy Powers recorded the single "*Ridin' High*," Produced by Merle Haggard/ Jimmy Bowen (MCA Records, 1985)

- Freddy Powers recorded the single "*San Antonio Rose*" / B-Side "*Wouldn't That Be Something*" (MCA Records, 1985)

- Janie Fricke recorded the single "*Ridin' High*," The Very Best of Janie, (Columbia Records, 1985)

- Freddy Powers recorded *The Country Jazz Singer* LP (1986, In Orbit Records) – All Songs written by Freddy Powers, including "*Texas and Oklahoma,*" "*Two Timing Woman,*" "*A Friend in California,*" "*Little Hotel Room,*" "*Natural High,*" "*I'm Free At Last,*" "*I Don't Care Anymore,*" "*You Don't Love Me Anymore,*" and "*This Time I Really Do.*"

- Merle Haggard recorded Freddy Powers' "*Friend In California*" and included the track on *A Friend In California* (Epic Records, 1986).

- Merle Haggard recorded Freddy Powers' "*This Time I Really Do*" and included the track on *A Friend In California* (Epic Records, 1986).

- Merle Haggard recorded Freddy Powers' "*Texas*" and included the track on *A Friend In California* (Epic Records, 1986).

- Merle Haggard recorded Freddy Powers' "*Okie From Muskogee Is Comin' Home*" and included the track on *A Friend In California* (Epic Records, 1986).

- Merle Haggard recorded Freddy Powers' "*This Song Is For You*" and included the track on *A Friend In California* (Epic Records, 1986).

- Merle Haggard and Willie Nelson recorded Freddy Powers' "*Shotgun And A Pistol*" and included the track on *Seashores Of Old Mexico* (Columbia Records, 1987).

- Merle Haggard recorded Freddy Powers' "*1929*" and included the track on *Chill Factor* (Epic Records, 1987).

- Merle Haggard recorded Freddy Powers' "*More Than This Old Heart Can Take*" and included the track on *Chill Factor* (Epic Records, 1987).

- Merle Haggard recorded Freddy Powers' "*Man From Another Time*" and included the track on *Chill Factor* (Epic Records, 1987).

- Merle Haggard recorded Freddy Powers' "*Wouldn't That Be Something*" and included the track on *5:01 Blues* (Epic Records, 1988).

- Merle Haggard recorded Freddy Powers' "*Somewhere Down The Line*" and included the track on *5:01 Blues* (Epic Records, 1988)

- Merle Haggard recorded Freddy Powers' "Blue Jungle" and included the track on *Blue Jungle* (Curb Records, 1990).

- Merle Haggard recorded Freddy Powers' "Bar In Bakersfield" and included the track on *Blue Jungle* (Curb Records, 1990).

- "*Texas*" was written by Freddy Powers, Title Track to James Michener's 'Texas' film soundtrack, 1995

- Rose Maddox recorded *"Hard Time Letting Go"* and *"Back Playing Honky Tonks,"* 1996 LP.

- Willie Nelson, Merle Haggard, Johnny Rodriguez & 80 Special Olympic Athletes recorded The Nevada Special Olympics Theme Song *"Everybody Has A Chance To Win"*, written by Freddy Powers.

- Freddy Powers recorded *The Hottest Thing in Town* LP 1997 – *"Franklin D. Roosevelt Jones," "I Can't Give You Anything But Love," "Sweet Georgia Brown," "Out of Nowhere," "I'se Muggin'," "A Kiss to Build A Dream On," "Limehouse Blues," "Sheik of Araby," "On The Road to My Heart (Catherine's Song)," "Rosetta," "Back In Your Own Backyard," "Trashy Woman," "Caravan," "The Hottest Thing in Town"*

- Freddy Powers & Bill McDavid (Rogers & Hammerhead) co-wrote *"The Legend of Django," "I Don't Want to Say Goodbye," "The Truth About You," "Me and the Drummer," "Someone Should Have Told Him," "Texas All the Way," "So Little to Say"* and *"Springtime and the Fall"*

- Freddy Powers released the *Silver Eagle* LP, including *"Silver Eagle," "Beautiful Time," "If I Lay Down the Bottle," "You'll Never Know," "Shopping for Dresses," "I Love Women," "This Song Is For You," "You've Got Your Pride," "Women," "Star-Spangled Country Song,"* and *"Big Butter and Egg Man"*

- Freddy Powers co-produced and played on Merle Haggard's pop standards album *Unforgettable* (Capitol Records/Hag Records, 2004); Freddy also composed one of the featured tracks, *"Still Missing You."*

- Freddy Powers released *The Great Escape* LP in 2004 – All Songs written by Freddy Powers, including *"Like a Movie Star," "Old Country Singer," "On the Road to My Heart (Catherine's Song)," "Angel Of My Dreams," "Having A Good Time (With You)," "Tom Sawyer & Huckleberry Finn," "Daytime Nighttime Blues," "Wild Party Blues," "Romantic Waltz,"* and *"All I Want to Do Is Sing My Song"*, except *"My Great Escape"* (written by Big & Rich).

- John Cody Carter recorded *"You Don't Love Me Anymore"* off the *Don't You Think Its Time* LP, 2006; *"California Snow Storm," "My San Antonio Rose"*

- John Cody Carter/Willie Nelson recorded *"California Here I Come."*

- Merle Haggard recorded Freddy Powers' 'Wouldn't That Be Something' and included the track on *The Bluegrass Sessions* (McCoury Music/Hag Records, 2007).

- Merle Haggard recorded Freddy Powers' *"The Road To My Heart"* and included the track on *I Am What I Am* (Vanguard Records, 2010).

- Mary Sarah & Friends recorded *"All I Wanna Do Is Sing My Song"* Bridges LP (2014, Cleopatra Records)

- Kacey Jones recorded "*I'm Free Free At Last*" from Amen for Old Friends LP, 2014 iGo Records

- Johnny Bush recorded "*The Truth About You.*"

- Lynn Colvig recorded "*My Old Man.*"

- Suzy Bogguss recorded "*I Always Get Lucky With You*" and "*Chase Each Around the Room,*" Lucky LP, 2014

- Beans Sousa & Lacy J. Dalton recorded "*A Friend in California*"

- Scotty Joss recorded "*Back Playing Honky Tonk Again*" off *Invite Scott Joss into Your Living Room* LP, 1998; "*Free At Last*" off *A New Reason to Care* LP (Little Dog Records, 2000); "*Wouldn't That Be Something,*" and "*Road to My Heart (Catherine's Song).*"

- Pauline Reese recorded "*One Less Honky Tonk*" off *The Good, The Bad and The Ugly* LP (Paradora Records, 2004); "*No Dancing,*" "*I Always Get Lucky With You,*" "*The Truth About You*"

- The Texas Girls' Choir recorded "*Water,*" "*Happy Birthday To the Lord*" and "*Santa Why Can't Every Day Be Christmas?*"

- Kenny Chesney recorded "*I Always Get Lucky With You,*" When the Sun Goes Down LP

- Big & Rich recorded "*M-E-D-L-E-Y of the Hillbilly Jedi*" off *Hillbilly Jedi LP*

- Big & Rich recorded "*Filthy Rich*" off the *BIG & RICH LP*

- Rattlesnake Annie recoded "*World Full of Love*" & "*Little Hotel Room,*" World Full of Love LP, (Rattlesnake Records, 2012), "*Friend in California,*" "*My Old Man,*" "*Texas and Oklahoma,*" "*I Always Get Lucky With You,*" and "*If I Needed You*" on Crossroads LP among many more.

** All Songs Written or Co-Written by Freddy Powers unless indicated **

BIBLIOGRAPHY OF FREDDY POWERS INTERVIEW SOURCES:

Chapter 1

Heritage of Texas / Enchanted Rock Magazine, Jan 1997

Fretboard Journal, "On the Wagon: Following Paul Buskirk's Long, Dusty Trail," by Nathaniel RiverhorseNakadate

Chapter 2

Fretboard Journal, "On the Wagon: Following Paul Buskirk's Long, Dusty Trail," by Nathaniel RiverhorseNakadate

Texas Music Magazine by Jason Hardison, June, 2006

Heritage of Texas / Enchanted Rock Magazine, Jan 1997

Austin Songwriter Magazine, May, 1997, by Sharon Jones-LeFlore

Chapter 3

Texas Music Magazine by Jason Hardison, June, 2006

Radio Host Randi O'Connor, Oct. 1987

Chapter 6

"'Country Jazzman' Gets Lucky With 'New Country' Show", Robert K. Oermann

El Dorado Press Release

Reno Gazette-Journal, After Dark, by Guy Richardson, June, 1992

Stomp and Stammer Magazine, April, 2005, Dugan Trodglen

Chapter 8

Radio host Randi O'Connor, Oct. 1987

Chapter 9

Radio host Randi O'Connor, Oct. 1987

Chapter 10

Radio host Randi O'Connor, Oct. 1987

Chapter 13

Applause Magazine, December, 1996, by Kathleen Hudson

Heritage of Texas / Enchanted Rock Magazine, Jan 1997

Texas Music Magazine by Jason Hardison, June, 2006

Nevada Appeal, Star Talk, Thursday, Sept 21, 1989, by Pamela Bissell Crowell

Heritage of Texas / Enchanted Rock Magazine, Jan 1997

Conversation with radio host Johnny Johnson, KTRZ, Cortez, Colorado, Oct. 1987

Radio Host Randi O'Connor, Oct. 1987

Austin Songwriter Magazine, May, 1997, by Sharon Jones-LeFlore

Fun and Gaming, June, 1992

Chapter 18

Motorcycles Magazine, July, 2007, Amy Edgerly

Circus Circus Magazine, Inner View, by Kim Pryor

Austin Songwriter Magazine, May, 1997, by Sharon Jones-LeFlore

Chapter 19

"Django Texas Style" by Sharon Jones

San Antonio Express News, April, 2002, by John Goodspeed

Chapter 21

Austin Chronicle, August, 2008, by Doug Freeman

AllAboutJazz.com, 2006

Chapter 22

Stomp and Stammer Magazine, April, 2005, by Dugan Trodglen

Motorcycles Magazine, July, 2007, Amy Edgerly

Austin Chronicle, August, 2008, by Doug Freeman

Texas Music Magazine by Jason Hardison, June, 2006

Rolling Stone Magazine, Willie Nelson, Merle Haggard & Ray Price Play NYC, By Amanda Trimble, March 23, 2007

Chapter 23

Stomp and Stammer Magazine, April, 2005, by Dugan Trodglen

Austin Chronicle, August, 2008, by Doug Freeman

Motorcycles Magazine, July, 2007, Amy Edgerly

Chapter 25

Women in Texas Music: Stories and Songs," by Kathleen Hudson, University of Texas Press, November, 2007

CO-AUTHOR BIO:

Award-winning Music biographer Jake Brown has written 50 published books since 2001, featuring many authorized collaborations with some of rock's biggest artists, including 2013 Rock & Roll Hall of Fame inductees Heart (with Ann and Nancy Wilson), living guitar legend Joe Satriani, blues legend Willie Dixon (authorized w/the Estate), country music legends Merle Haggard/Freddy Powers, heavy metal pioneers Motorhead (with Lemmy Kilmister), country rap superstar Big Smo, late hip hop icon Tupac Shakur (with the estate), celebrated Rock drummer Kenny Aronoff, legendary R&B/Hip Hop Producer Teddy Riley, late Funk pioneer Rick James, and Mopreme Shakur. Brown is also author of a variety of anthology series including the superstar country music anthology 'Nashville Songwriter' Vol I and II & forthcoming III; the all-star rock producers anthology 'Behind the Boards' Vol. 1 and 2 and Behind the Boards: Nashville; all-star Rock & Roll drummers' anthology 'Beyond the Beats,' and the 'Hip Hop Hits' producers' series among many others. Brown recently released the audio books Beyond the Beats, Doctors of Rhythm, the Scientists of Sound Series, Prince in the Studio, and other titles to come under a long-term deal with Blackstone Audio, and has also appeared as the featured biographer of record on Fuse TV's Live Through This series and Bloomberg TV's Game Changers series, in all 6-parts of the BET "The Death Row Chronicles" doc-series and the forthcoming ABOUT THE AUTHORS TV streaming show. His books have received national press in CMT, CBS News, The Hollywood Reporter, Rolling Stone Magazine, USA Today, MTV.com, Guitar World Magazine, Billboard, Parade Magazine, Country Weekly, Fox News, Yahoo News, etc and writes for regularly for Tape Op Magazine (including the 2015 cover story feature with Smashing Pumpkins front man Billy Corgan). In 2012, Brown won the Association for Recorded Sound Collections Awards in the category of Excellence in Historical Recorded Sound Research.

NEW & AVAILABLE NOW FROM BLACKSTONE AUDIO

Available NOW from Jake Brown's Catalog of 50 Published Books Over 20 Years!!

Country Weekly -

"Nashville is a town built around songs, so it was only a matter of time before someone compiled a book based around the stories behind some of the greatest (songs)...coming out of Music Row's tunesmiths. In the new book, Nashville Songwriter: The Inside Stories Behind Country Music's Greatest Hits, author Jake Brown sits down... to talk about their successes as songwriters, as well as the stories behind their biggest hits."

Billboard Magazine -

"The book puts the songwriter in the spotlight!"

American Songwriter Magazine -

"This isn't an expose, but a real account of what songwriters go through in their struggles to get in, and stay in, the game. Nashville Songwriter is an outstanding read from cover to cover. If you have any interest at all in what goes on behind the scenes in the songwriting business, you need to read this book."

Nashville Songwriter Vol. 1 (ISBN 978-1940363172) features Exclusive Chapter-length interviews with Craig Wiseman, Dean Dillon, Bob DiPiero, Bill Anderson, Sonny Curtis, Tom Shapiro, Kelley Lovelace, Rivers Rutherford, Tom T. Hall, Wayne Carson, Chris DuBois, Dallas Davidson, David Lee Murphy, Freddy Powers, Jeff Silbar, Brett James, Ashley Gorley, Lee Thomas Miller, and Neil Thrasher, along with exclusive commentary from Willie Nelson, Merle Haggard, and John Rich.

NASHVILLE SONGWRITER VOL. II

THE INSIDE STORIES BEHIND
COUNTRY MUSIC'S GREATEST HITS

★★★ BY JAKE BROWN ★★★

FEATURING 300 #1'S AND EXCLUSIVE INTERVIEWS WITH 35 OF MUSIC ROW'S TOP HITMAKERS

Maverick Country Magazine -
"What I enjoy about Jake's writing is that he has a gift for humanizing the artists he covers and writes with."

American Songwriter Magazine -
"A prolific author and biographer, with this latest release, Brown has 45 books to his name."

Parade Magazine -
"Ever want to know the stories behind country's greatest hits? Nashville Songwriter Vol. II – The Inside Stories Behind Country Music's Greatest Hits by Jake Brown digs into the backstories of over 300 No. 1 hits by a collective roster of the biggest multi-platinum superstars."

Nashville Songwriter Vol. 2 (ISBN: 978-0983471684) Features Exclusive Chapter-length interviews with Shane McAnally, Hillary Lindsey, Tom Douglas, Rhett Akins, Lori McKenna, Josh Kear, Luke Laird, Liz Rose, Ashley Gorley, Rodney Clawson, Cole Swindell, Ross Copperman, Natalie Hemby, Josh Osborne, Nicolle Galyon, Zach Crowell, Matraca Berg, Scotty Emerick, Marla Cannon-Goodman, Chris Thompkins, Chris DeStefano, Tia Sillers, Ben Hayslip, Thom Schulyer, Whitey Shafer, Tim Nichols, Byron Hill, Chris Wallin, Nicolle Gaylon, JT Harding, James Otto, Jimmy Robbins, Jesse Frasure, Smo, and Charlie Bonnet III!!

NASHVILLE
SONGWRITER VOL. III

★ ★ ★ BY JAKE BROWN ★ ★ ★

Coming 2023: NASHVILLE SONGWRITER VOL. III – Featuring 30 songwriting legends including Bobby Braddock, Sonny Throckmorton, Dallas Frazier, Clint Black, Kinky Friedman, Earl Bud Lee, Jack Tempchin, Jim Owen, Willie Tea Taylor, Tim Dubois, Rock Killough, Larry Cordle, Wayne "The Train" Hancock, Jim Lauderdale, Mark Irwin, Wanda Mallette, Jim Rushing, Robert Earl Keen, Billy Kirsch, Steve Seskin, Jim Weatherly, Jim McBride, Kerry Chater, Victoria Banks, Sherrie Austin, Steve Dean, Larry Gattlin, Don Cook, Carl Jackson and Randy Brooks!

BEYOND THE BEATS: Rock & Roll's Greatest Drummers Speak! (ISBN: 978-0983471653) features Tommy Lee (Mötley Crüe), Lars Ulrich (Metallica), Joey Kramer of (Aerosmith), Jimmy Chamberlin (Smashing Pumpkins), Tico Torres of (Bon Jovi, Chad Smith (Red Hot Chili Peppers, Taylor Hawkins (Foo Fighters), Stephen Perkins (Jane's Addiction), Doug "Cosmo" Clifford of (Creedence Clearwater Revival), Steve Smith (Journey), Kenny Aronoff (John Mellencamp/John Fogerty), and Matt Sorum (Guns N' Roses/Velvet Revolver).

BEYOND THE BEATS II

BY JAKE BROWN

Featured: **Stewart Copeland** (The Police), **Topper Headon** (The Clash), **Bill Gibson** (Huey Lewis and the News), **Nicko McBrain** (Iron Maiden), **Chris 'Whipper' Layton** (Stevie Ray Vaughan and Double Trouble), **Greg Errico** (Sly and the Family Stone), **Simon Kirke** (Bad Company, Free), **Mike Portnoy** (Dream Theatre), **Carmine Appice** (Vanilla Fudge, Rod Stewart), **Manu Katché** (Peter Gabriel, Sting), **Steve Gadd** (Simon & Garfunkle, Paul Simon, Eric Clapton), **Dennis "Machine Gun" Thompson** (MC5), **Dino Danelli** (The Rascals), **Dave Lombardo** (Slayer, Suicidal Tendencies), **David Lovering** (The Pixies), **Danny Seraphine** (Chicago), **Matt Chamberlin** (Tori Amos), **Denny Carmasi** (Heart, Whitesnake, Montrose), **Atimus Pyle** (Lynyrd Skynyrd), **David Garibaldi** (Tower of Power), **Michael Shrieve** (Santana), **Tim Alexander** (Primus), **Phil Jones** (Tom Petty), **Alan White** (YES, John Lennon, George Harrison), **Lee Kerslake** (Ozzy Osbourne, Uriah Heep), **John 'JR' Robinson** (Michael Jackson, Steve Winwood), and **Arthur Googy** (The Misfits).

BEHIND THE BOARDS: Vol 1 & 2

Collectively, BEHIND THE BOARDS Vol. 1 (ISBN: 978-1458419729) and Vol. 2 (ISBN: 978-1480350601), published by Hal Leonard / Rowman & Littlefield, this first-of-its-kind series profiles in exclusive chapter-length interviews with Rock and Metal's most legendary soundmen, including

Jack Douglas, Mario Caldato Jr., Butch Vig, Linda Perry, Mike Fraser, Scott Humphrey and Tommy Lee, Hugh Padgham, Bones Howe, Bob Rock, Flemming Rasmussen, Don Was, Stephen Hague, Bob Ezrin, Don Gehman, Tom Werman, J. Mascus, Keith Olsen, Al Jourgensen, Ron Nevison, Michael Beinhorn, Dave Jerden, Tony Platt, Matt Wallace, Andy Johns, Tom Allom, Gil Norton, Ritchie Zito, Butch Walker, Kevin Elson, Eddie Kramer, Daniel Lanois, Bill Bottrell, Bill Szymcyk, Chris Kimsey, Chris Tsangerides, Danny Kortchmar, Frankie Sullivan, Howard Benson, Jim Gaines, Joe Blaney, Keith Forsey, Ken Scott, Mike Flicker, Mike Shipley, Narada Michael Walden, Nick Raskulinecz, and Nigel Grey!

MY LIFE IN A JAR: THE BOOK OF SMO

MY LIFE IN A JAR
THE BOOK OF SMO

BY **SMO** AND JAKE BROWN

(ISBN: 978-0692139998)

BE SURE TO CHECK OUT THE AWARD-WINNING,
TRADEMARKED "IN THE STUDIO" BOOK SERIES: